MW00718332

# Using
# HyperStudio®

## A Complete Tutorial
### for **Windows** and **Macintosh**

## Ana Weston Solomon
*University of California at Berkeley*

VISIT US ON THE INTERNET
# www.swep.com

## South-Western Educational Publishing
*an International Thomson Publishing company* I(T)P®
WWW: http://www.thomson.com

Cincinnati • Albany, NY • Belmont, CA • Bonn • Boston • Detroit • Johannesburg • London • Madrid
Melbourne • Mexico City • New York • Paris • Singapore • Tokyo • Toronto • Washington

You can request permission to use material from this text through the following phone and fax numbers:
Phone: 1-800-730-2214, Fax: 1-800-730-2215, or visit our web site at http://www.thomsonrights.com

ISBN: 0-538-72230-4
1 2 3 4 5 6 7 8 9 10 DR 08 07 06 05 04 03 02 01 00 99
Printed in the United States of America

I(T)P
International Thomson Publishing

South-Western Educational Publishing is a division of International Thomson Publishing Inc. The ITP logo is a registered trademark used herein under License by South-Western Educational Publishing.

HyperStudio is a registered trademark of Roger Wagner Publishing, Inc. All rights reserved worldwide. Windows is a registered trademark of Microsoft Corporation. Macintosh is a registered trademark of Apple Computer, Inc. The names of all products mentioned herein are used for identification purposes only and may be trademarks or registered trademarks of their respective owners.

| | |
|---|---|
| *Team Leader:* | Karen Schmohe |
| *Managing Editor:* | Carol Volz |
| *Project Manager:* | Anne Noschang |
| *Acquisitions Manager:* | John Wills |
| *Consulting Editor:* | Minta Berry |
| *Content Reviewers:* | Ella H. Fisher, Dr. Dolores Pusins |
| *Cover Design:* | Ann Small Wills |
| *Art/Design Coordinator:* | Mike Broussard |
| *Manufacturing Coordinator:* | Carol Chase |
| *Production Services:* | SETTINGPACE |

# Multimedia Made Easy!

Our exciting new *Using HyperStudio® for Windows® and Macintosh®: A Complete Tutorial* will provide everything needed to master HyperStudio in 75+ hours. In this book, users will learn how to combine text, sound, graphics, and video quickly and easily to create professional multimedia projects, Web displays, presentations, and more.

- *Using HyperStudio for Windows and Macintosh: A Complete Tutorial* (Solomon)
  Student Text (side spiral bound, hard cover)      0-538-72230-4
  Activities Workbook (soft cover with spine)       0-538-72231-2
  Electronic Instructor CD-ROM                      0-538-72233-9
  Testing Package                                   0-538-72232-0

## Other Complementary texts from South-Western:

- *Internet Concepts & Activities* (Barksdale and Rutter)
  Student Text (spiral bound, soft cover)           0-538-72088-3
  Student Text (soft cover with spine)              0-538-72166-9
  Electronic Instructor Package                     0-538-72131-6

- *Microsoft FrontPage 2000* (Ciampa)
  Student Text (soft cover with spine)              0-538-69092-5
  Electronic Instructor Package                     0-538-69093-3

The Electronic Instructor CD-ROMs contain
lesson plans, solutions, SCANS correlations, and much more.

South-Western
Educational Publishing

For more information about these
South-Western products and others:
Join Us On the Internet
**www.swep.com**

# How to Use this Book

What makes a good applications text? Sound pedagogy and the most current, complete materials. That is what you will find in the text, *Using HyperStudio for Windows and Macintosh: A Complete Tutorial*. Not only will you find a colorful, inviting layout, but also many features to enhance learning.

**SCANS** (Secretary's Commission on Achieving Necessary Skills) — The U.S. Department of Labor has identified the school-to-careers competencies. The five workplace competencies (resources, interpersonal skills, information, systems, and technology) and foundation skills (basic skills, thinking skills, and personal qualities) are identified in the exercises throughout the text. More information on SCANS can be found on the *Electronic Instructor*.

**Step-By-Step** — The step-by-step exercises guide you to mastery of the software.

**Challenge Activities** — Extra challenge activities in every lesson provide

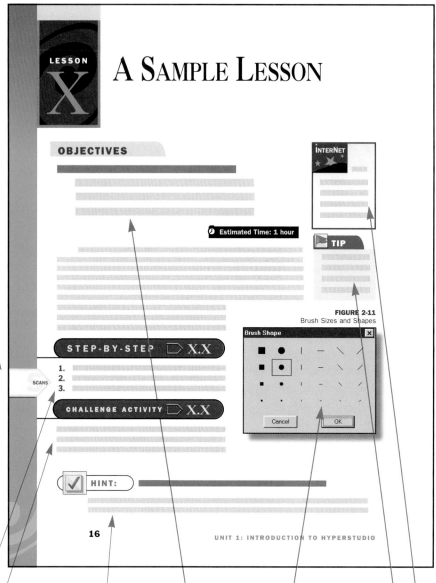

reinforcement opportunities.

**Hints** — These boxes provide helpful information to assist you in completing the exercises.

**Objectives** — Objectives are listed at the beginning of each lesson, along with a suggested

time for completion of the lesson. This allows you to look ahead to what you will be learning and to pace your work.

**Enhanced Screen Shots** — Screen shots now come to life on each page with color and depth.

**Tips** — These boxes provide enrichment information about features of the software.

**Internet** — Internet terminology and useful Internet information is provided in these boxes located throughout the text.

# How to Use this Book

**Summary** — At the end of each lesson you will find a summary to prepare you to complete the end-of-lesson activities.

**Vocabulary** — Vocabulary terms are listed at the end of each lesson.

**Review Questions** — Review material at the end of each lesson and each unit enables you to prepare for assessment of the content presented.

**Lesson Projects** — End-of-lesson hands-on application of what has been learned in the lesson allows you to actually apply the techniques covered.

**Critical Thinking Activity** — Each lesson and unit review gives you an opportunity to apply creative analysis to situations presented.

**Review of Procedures** — At the end of each unit, a review of procedures is provided for quick reference.

**End-of-Unit Applications** — End-of-unit hands-on application of concepts learned in the unit provides opportunity for a comprehensive review.

*Summary*

VOCABULARY

LESSON X REVIEW QUESTIONS

LESSON X PROJECT

CRITICAL THINKING ACTIVITY

*Review of Procedures*

UNIT X REVIEW QUESTIONS

UNIT X APPLICATIONS

Lesson (X) A Sample Lesson

3

# PREFACE

## To the Learner

Congratulations on choosing to learn HyperStudio. HyperStudio is a comprehensive software tool and this course is intended to teach you HyperStudio in a practical and fun environment. Learning to use the software should be an exciting challenge. By providing easy to follow steps and many screen captures, even novice computer users will enjoy learning and applying this software. By the end of this course, you will have learned how to use this valuable authoring tool to create dynamic presentations and multimedia projects.

## Organization of the Text

Before you begin the lessons, take a little time to look through this book. You will find that the book is organized into units. Each unit focuses on the HyperStudio tools and a specific area of multimedia. The lessons within each unit lead you through the procedures for creating the different effects and using the tools, menus, and features of HyperStudio.

The lessons guide you to create projects using a series of step-by-step exercises that clearly explain how to accomplish each task. Numerous illustrations and screen captures show you how your screen should look and help you keep on track with the project. You should proceed through the lessons in order. Each of the lessons will teach you new skills that you will continue to use in later lessons.

Each lesson begins with a list of objectives so that you can see what you will be learning in the lesson. Each lesson contains information about HyperStudio and about the multimedia elements you will be using for your projects. Most lessons include one or more Challenge Activities that allow you to test yourself by completing a part of a project using the procedures and tools you just learned.

Each lesson ends with a summary of the information and procedures presented in the lesson. A list of new terms introduced in the lesson are found in the Vocabulary section. These terms are defined in the Glossary at the end of the book. The lesson review questions help you review the information and procedures from the lesson. Take your time to read the material in the lesson carefully so that you will be able to answer the review questions. Each lesson includes one or more projects that allow you to practice the procedures you have learned by applying them to a new project that you will develop on your own. A critical thinking activity focuses your attention on the types of projects that may be created and the requirements for using various multimedia elements effectively.

Each lesson has a suggested time frame to let you know how much time it should take you to complete the lesson. The actual time needed to complete the lessons will vary for different people and different situations. The amount of time it takes for a learner to complete the lesson will depend upon many variables such as your previous computer experience and your previous exposure to working with multimedia elements. If you do not have time to complete a lesson, save the stack using the indicated file name and continue the lesson at the next opportunity. Don't worry if you take longer for the lesson than the suggested time.

At the end of the units are unit reviews. These reviews begin with a list of the steps needed to complete the various procedures introduced in the unit's lessons. The procedure review lists can be referenced in later units when you need a reminder of how to accomplish a specific task. The end-of-unit reviews also contain review questions, a unit project, and a critical thinking activity.

At the end of the book are a series of appendices that will provide you with more information about the Windows or Macintosh operating systems, Quick Reference Guides, a Mastery Checklist to track the skills you will developing, a list of keyboard shortcuts for HyperStudio commands, a list of HyperStudio tips, and a chart of the HyperStudio tools. The Mastery Checklist will help you and your instructor keep a list of the skills you will be learning and will help your instructor evaluate your progress.

# Other Resources

The Activity Workbook contains additional hands-on projects. The projects allow you to demonstrate the techniques and skills you are learning. The workbook also contains the planning and evaluation resources needed to plan and create polished projects.

Additional resource files are located on the HyperStudio CD-ROM from Roger Wagner Publishing. The resources on this CD-ROM should be available to all learners. Some lessons specifically require the use of files from the CD-ROM. Many of the projects can be made more complete by accessing these resources. Ask your instructor for these files.

# Before You Begin

If you are not familiar with using a computer, you should read the appropriate appendix at the end of the book that will familiarize you with the Windows or Macintosh operating system. If you are not sure which operating system you will be using, consult your instructor. Use these appendices to familiarize yourself with the environment you will be using during this course. When you are comfortable with the environment, you will be ready to begin the lessons. If you are willing to work consistently, you will find the Step-by-Steps exciting and fun. You will open the door to a whole new way of expressing yourself and creating dynamic projects and presentations.

# To the Instructor

An *Electronic Instructor*™ CD-ROM is available to accompany this book. It includes lesson plans, solution files, SCANS correlations, scheduling charts, screen illustrations, clip art files, and other resources. Valuable Internet sites that offer additional graphics, videos, and other multimedia elements are listed.

A testing package is also available to help instructors assess learners' progress.

# Acknowledgments

Many thanks to Minta Berry for her patience, good sense, and insightful suggestions as the consulting editor on this project. Thanks to John Wills for providing me the opportunity to develop this project, and to Anne Noschang for keeping it together and on track. I would also like to thank Joan Joosten and Morris and Anne Weston for their never-ending encouragement and support, especially when the going got tough, as well as my family and friends who believed in this book and in me.

# TABLE OF CONTENTS

## UNIT 1 — INTRODUCTION TO HYPERSTUDIO

## UNIT 2 — PLANNING PROJECTS AND STACKS

## UNIT 5 — WORKING WITH MULTIMEDIA

## UNIT 6 — ADVANCED TECHNIQUES

# START-UP CHECKLIST

## WINDOWS

### Hardware
- ✓ 486 processor or higher
- ✓ 4 MB RAM for Windows 3.1
- ✓ 8 MB RAM for Windows 95 or above
- ✓ Hard drive
- ✓ MPC-2 compliant CD-ROM drive
- ✓ Mouse
- ✓ Printer

### Recommended Components
- ✓ Windows sound system compatible card
- ✓ TWAIN-compatible scanner
- ✓ Digital camera
- ✓ Video digitizer

### Software
- ✓ Microsoft Windows 3.1 or above (Microsoft Windows 95 recommended)
- ✓ HyperStudio 3.1 or above
- ✓ QuickTime or Media Player

## MACINTOSH

### Hardware
- ✓ Macintosh 68030 or PowerMac
- ✓ 4 MB RAM
- ✓ Hard drive
- ✓ CD-ROM drive
- ✓ Mouse
- ✓ Printer

### Recommended Components
- ✓ Digital camera
- ✓ Video digitizer

### Software
- ✓ Mac OS 7.1 or higher
- ✓ HyperStudio 3.1 or above
- ✓ QuickTime 1.5 or higher

# INTRODUCTION TO HYPERSTUDIO

1

# LESSON 1

# INTRODUCTION

**Upon completion of this lesson, you will be able to:**

■ Explain the purpose of authoring tools.

■ Open HyperStudio.

■ Review samples of HyperStudio stacks.

■ Close HyperStudio.

**Estimated Time: 0.5 hour**

# *What Is Multimedia? What Are Authoring Tools?*

Welcome to the world of multimedia. HyperStudio is an exciting tool that will enable you to create a variety of reports, presentations, and projects. HyperStudio is a type of computer program called an "authoring tool." Authoring software allows you to integrate elements such as text, graphics, video, sound, and navigation without having to learn computer-programming languages. These elements are considered to be "multimedia" because they include a variety of different media resources that can be combined. Using these elements will give you an opportunity to "tell your story" through a computer. Everyone has their own story to tell whether it is a project, a report, or any material that you wish to save. Using multimedia elements will make your story more dynamic, innovative, and exciting. Although the written word can be very effective, imagine how a visual representation can add to the effect. This is especially true of ideas that are hard to visualize or explain, such as how a DNA cell looks or how the theory of aerodynamics works.

The world of technology is moving quickly. The Internet and the use of hypertext and object-oriented programs have created an environment that requires new and innovative ways to collect and present information. Hypertext allows you to click on a word to get more information or to move to another screen.

Multimedia authoring tools allow the programmer to use icons, text, or graphics to create the final product. The programmer can create products without having to learn complex and cryptic programming codes. These tools allow you to navigate and perform routine tasks, such as printing or saving a file, by simply clicking on an icon or choosing a command from the menu.

Another example of using object-oriented programs and hypertext is the Internet. In fact, the reason the Internet became so popular was because of the introduction of object-oriented programming that made it easy for users to access this resource. Prior to these programs, the Internet was used primarily for research and by the government because it required using a complicated ASCII language. The use of object-oriented programming and hypertext changed the way the Internet was accessed and opened the door to what would become the World Wide Web. This type of program was instrumental in coining the term "user-friendly."

No longer do you have to memorize a complicated language. Even inexperienced computer users can sit in front of a screen and can instinctively figure out what to do. With access to current information from all over the world and an authoring tool that can combine the dynamic aspects of the information, students and teachers can now create assignments that are much more interactive than the traditional use of paper and ink.

Authoring tools encourage dynamic learning. Whatever your personal interests are, you can find a way to express your vision of what you are exploring and learning. You can create and present your ideas and projects in a visual, customized, and dynamic way. HyperStudio can be used for such things as reports, presentations, projects, tutorials, and games.

# What Is HyperStudio?

HyperStudio is the tool you will use to create projects. HyperStudio projects are a series of screens or cards that are arranged in "stacks." Think of a stack as a stack of index cards that are linked together. Each screen represents a card. You can put anything you like on the card: text, graphics, photos, drawings, video, sounds, and even your own voice narrations. The first card in a stack is usually the Title card and may serve as the table of contents or main menu for the stack or group of stacks. See Figure 1-1.

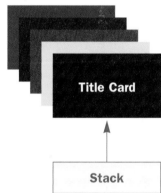

**FIGURE 1-1**
Sample Stack with Title Card

With HyperStudio, you can move from card to card in a linear manner (one right after the other), or you can jump around from card to card even if they are not next to each other. You can even move to a different stack or program. We'll talk more about that later.

Moving from point to point in the stacks is called "navigating" around the stacks. Navigation is the way you move from one place, or screen, to another. The means of navigation in HyperStudio includes buttons, hypertext, and icons.

- **Buttons** usually include an arrow or other directional symbol. For example, right and left buttons allow you to move forward and backward in a stack.

- **Hypertext** refers to highlighted words or phrases that allow you to move to another point in the stack. Hypertext usually appears in a different color and as underlined text. When you click on the word, you are automatically moved to another card in the stack or to another stack.

- **Icons** are pictures that visually describe the action. For example, you click on the open door icon in HyperStudio to open a new stack.

# Starting HyperStudio

Your instructor may have special instructions for starting HyperStudio on your school's computer. If not, use one of the following sets of instructions.

**Windows Users**

- Select the **HyperStudio** icon from the desktop, or

- Select **Programs** from the Start menu and choose **HyperStudio**.

**Macintosh Users**

- Locate the program on the hard drive or desktop.

- Double click on the application to open it.

When you have opened HyperStudio, your screen will appear as shown in Figure 1-2.

**FIGURE 1-2**
HyperStudio Opening Screen

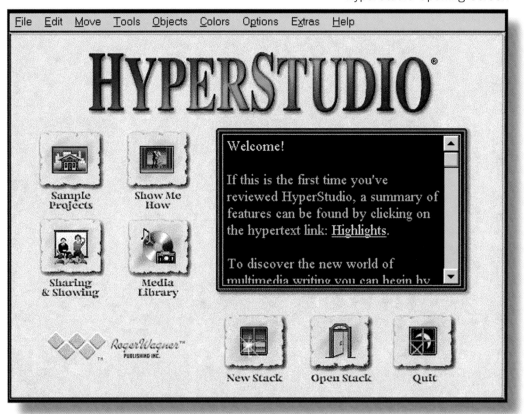

# *Reviewing Sample Projects*

HyperStudio has included some sample projects for you to see. Reviewing these projects will help you accomplish two things. First, you will have an opportunity to navigate some stacks. You can practice using the buttons and clicking on the icons to move around and make things happen.

Second, this is a good way to get ideas about the many ways you can use HyperStudio and to see what other users have created.

**STEP-BY-STEP** ⟹ **1.1**

1. Click the **Sample Projects** icon.

2. Now click on **At School**. You will see the Title card for the **At School** project, as shown in Figure 1-3.

**FIGURE 1-3**
At School Project

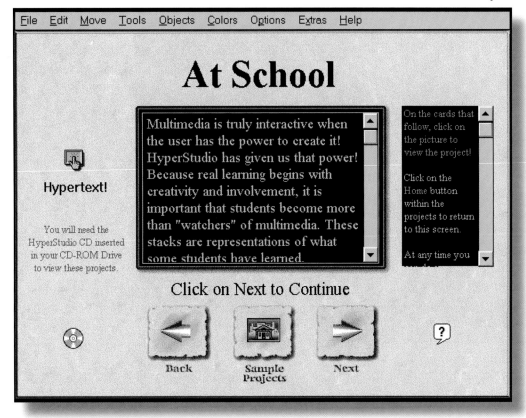

3. Click the **Next** button, as seen in Figure 1-3, until you see **The Apollo Program** in the center of the screen, as shown in Figure 1-4. Click on the picture of the astronaut.

4. Explore the project. Click on different buttons and icons to see what special effects they produce.

5. When you are finished, click the **Exit** icon.

(continued on next page)

**FIGURE 1-4**
The Apollo Program Project

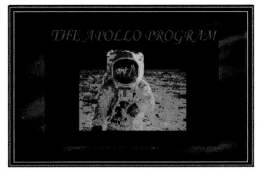

**6.** Click on the right arrow until you find Figure 1-5, **Ionic & Covalent Bonding.** Click on the **Ionic & Covalent Bonding** screen.

**7.** Use the buttons and icons to explore the project.

**FIGURE 1-5**
Ionic & Covalent Bonding Project

Now take some time to explore more of the projects on your own. Think about what you like and what doesn't work for you in the projects you are seeing.

# Closing HyperStudio

At the end of a work session, you will close the HyperStudio program, unless otherwise directed by your instructor.

**1.** When you are finished exploring these sample stacks, click the **Sample Projects** icon.

**2.** Click on the **Home** icon.

**3.** Click on the **Quit** icon.

**4.** When asked, "Are you sure you want to quit HyperStudio now?" choose **Yes**.

**INTERNET** The Internet is a telecommunications system that connects many different networks of computers. The Internet is often called a "network of networks."

**STEP-BY-STEP ⟹ 1.3**

Write a short review of three of the projects you have seen. Your review should include answers to the following questions.

1. What was the stack about? Please summarize or describe.

2. Did you learn anything new about the subject?

3. Did you like the graphics? Why?

4. Was the text easy to read?

5. Was it easy to navigate or move around the stack? Why?

6. What navigation tools did you use—icons, buttons, hypertext, or a combination of these?

# *Summary*

This lesson contained information to get you acquainted with HyperStudio and with how to navigate through HyperStudio stacks. In this lesson, you learned that:

■ Authoring software helps you create your own computer projects without learning complicated programming languages.

■ Multimedia contains various combinations of elements such as text, graphics, photos, video, and sounds.

■ Icons, hypertext, and buttons can be used to navigate through a stack or program.

■ HyperStudio is made up of stacks that are like stacks of index cards.

■ HyperStudio is easy to open and close.

■ Navigating through sample projects can give you good ideas about what HyperStudio can do.

**VOCABULARY**

Authoring tools

Buttons

Cards

Hypertext

Icons

Multimedia

Navigation

Object-oriented programming

Stacks

## TRUE/FALSE

**Circle the T if the statement is true or F if it is false.**

**T F** **1.** HyperStudio is an authoring tool.

**T F** **2.** HyperStudio requires that you learn an advanced programming language.

**T F** **3.** Multimedia authoring tools use icons, text, and graphics to create final products.

**T F** **4.** HyperStudio projects are a series of screens known as stacks.

**T F** **5.** HyperStudio can be used to create a tutorial.

**T F** **6.** In HyperStudio, clicking on a button will make something happen.

## WRITTEN QUESTIONS

**Write your answers to the following questions in the space provided.**

**1.** What are some of the ways you can move around the stacks? Please describe.

_____

_____

_____

**2.** What is hypertext and how does it work?

_____

_____

_____

**3.** What is a stack?

_____

_____

_____

4. What is a multimedia authoring program?

_____

_____

_____

5. What is meant by the term "user-friendly"?

_____

_____

_____

## LESSON 1 PROJECT 1.1

1. Open HyperStudio.

2. In the Sample Projects, find the stack, **Family & Community**.

3. Find the project, **A Tribute to Helen Burch**.

4. As you go through the project, make a list of the multimedia elements used by the authors.

5. Close the stack and close the program.

## CRITICAL THINKING ACTIVITY

SCANS

Through discussion in cooperative groups, create a list of activities and projects that you can create with HyperStudio. Discuss why using HyperStudio would be better than the way you might presently perform the activity. Write down the ideas you discover. Share your ideas with the entire class.

# LESSON 2

# USING HYPERSTUDIO TOOLS

**Upon completion of this lesson, you will be able to:**

- Identify and use the tools on the tool palette.
- Open a stack.
- Create a stack.
- Name a stack
- Save a stack.

**Estimated Time: 0.75 hour**

## *Creating a Stack*

Before you can create a project, you must learn how to use the tools. When you learn how to drive a car, you have to learn the rules of the road and how to operate the brakes, accelerator, and clutch. The same type of learning occurs with any computer program. In this lesson, you will begin to learn how to operate HyperStudio by exploring the tool palette. Before you use the tools, you must create a practice stack.

### STEP-BY-STEP ▷ 2.1

1. Open HyperStudio.

2. Click the **Home** icon. You should see the opening screen for HyperStudio, as shown in Figure 2-1.

3. Click the **New Stack** icon.

4. You will be asked if you are sure you want to leave the Home Stack now. (See Figure 2-2.) Click **Yes**.

5. If you are asked if you want to keep the same card size, as shown in Figure 2-3, click **Yes**.

6. You should now see a blank card with the name Untitled at the top, in the title bar.

7. Keep your stack open for the next Step-by-Step.

**FIGURE 2-1**
HyperStudio Home Card

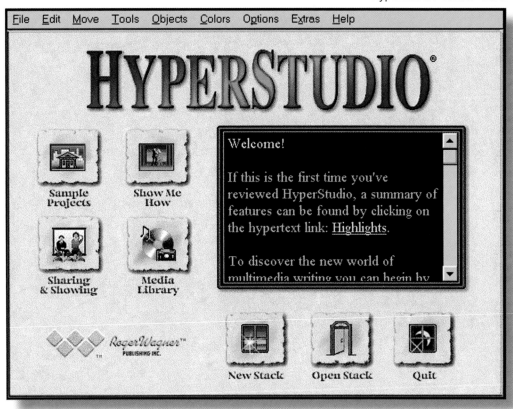

**TIP**

Macintosh users will be asked if they want to change the number of colors in the stack. For now, you will not change the number of colors.

**FIGURE 2-2**
Leave Home Stack Dialog Box

**FIGURE 2-3**
Change Card Size Dialog Box

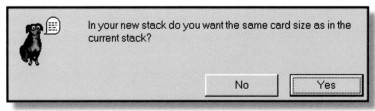

# Using the Tool Palette

The tool palette is used to customize your HyperStudio stacks. You may notice that the tools available for HyperStudio are similar to many other computer programs you may have used. The tool palette has two sections containing the edit and paint tools.

# Edit Tools

The edit tools allow you to change, move and manipulate existing objects such as text fields, buttons, and graphics.

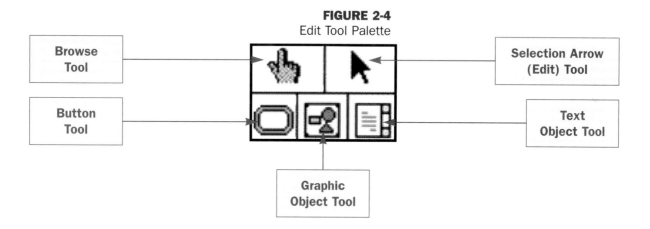

**FIGURE 2-4**
Edit Tool Palette

Browse Tool

Selection Arrow (Edit) Tool

Button Tool

Text Object Tool

Graphic Object Tool

The Browse tool allows you to navigate through your stack and activate buttons and links on your screen. When you choose this icon, you are in Browse mode. You will need to be in the Browse mode in order for your buttons to work.

The Selection Arrow (Edit) tool allows you to edit, select, move, resize, or delete objects that include buttons, text objects, and graphic objects. When you activate this icon, you are in Edit mode.

## STEP-BY-STEP ▷ 2.2

1. On the menubar, select **Tools**. Hold down the mouse and drag the tool palette alongside your screen. The entire palette should now be next to your screen, as shown in Figure 2-5.

2. Click the **Browse** tool. (See Figure 2-4.) As you move the mouse around the screen, you should see a hand icon that matches the Browse tool icon on the tool palette.

3. Click the **Selection Arrow (Edit)** tool. (See Figure 2-4.) As you move your mouse across your screen, you should see an arrow that matches the Selection Arrow (Edit) tool icon on the tool palette. This tool allows you to make changes in objects, text fields, and buttons.

4. Click the **Button** tool. This tool allows you to edit or change an existing button.

**5.** Click the **Graphic Object** tool. This tool allows you to edit or move graphic objects.

**6.** Click the **Text Object** tool. This tool allows you to edit text objects, change the size of the text in a text object, or move a text object.

**7.** Keep your stack open for the next Step-by-Step.

**FIGURE 2-5**
Tool Palette

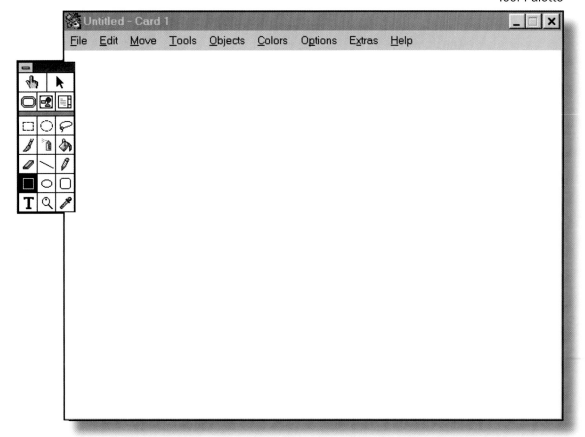

INTERNET
An Internet address is a group of characters that uniquely identifies the user or computer. Every user and computer on the Internet must have a unique address so that the system knows where to send electronic mail and other data. When contacting someone on the Internet, you must enter their address correctly. One wrong character will cause the system to return the item to you undelivered or to send the item to the wrong user.

# Paint, Selection, and Object Tools

The paint tools allow you to create and manipulate many elements in HyperStudio. Figure 2-6 describes the various tools. You will begin your exploration of these tools with the Text tool.

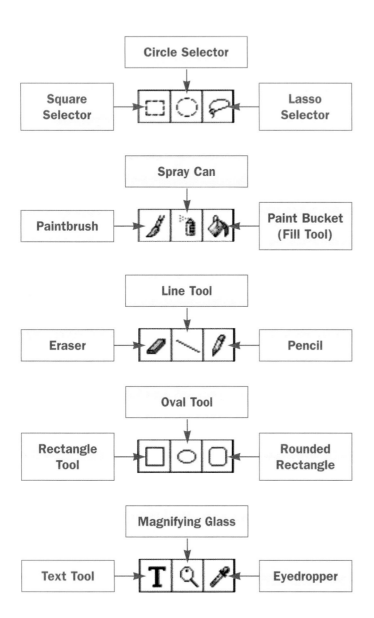

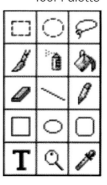

**FIGURE 2-6**
Paint, Selection, and Object Tools on the Tool Palette

## Text Tool

HyperStudio allows you to put text in your stacks in two different ways. One way is by creating a text object or text field. That feature is similar to a word processing program. When you use a text field, you can easily change what you have typed. You will practice entering text in text fields in a later lesson.

The other way to place text in your stack is to use the Text tool. You can change the font, size, and color of the text using this tool. However, once you have placed text on your card with the Text tool, it is not easy to change. You will practice using this tool in the next Step-by-Step.

# STEP-BY-STEP ⟩ 2.3

1. Click the **Text** tool. (See Figure 2-6.) It is located in the left bottom corner of the palette. This tool is used to "paint" text onto your screen.

2. When you move your mouse, you should see a text cursor on the screen. Click once anywhere on the screen. The point you selected is where the text will be inserted.

3. Key **Welcome to the world of multimedia**. If you come to the edge of the screen, press **Enter** and continue the phrase on a new line.

4. Click on another point on the screen. Double click on the **T** in the tool palette. This brings up a window that allows you to format the text size, font, color, and style. Choose the **Arial** font, make the size **36**, and choose a color, as shown in Figure 2-7.

5. Key your name. Notice that the size, font, color, and style choices you made are applied to your name.

6. Keep your stack open for the next Step-by-Step.

**FIGURE 2-7**
Text Style Window

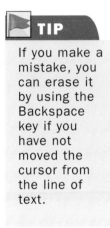

**TIP**

If you make a mistake, you can erase it by using the Backspace key if you have not moved the cursor from the line of text.

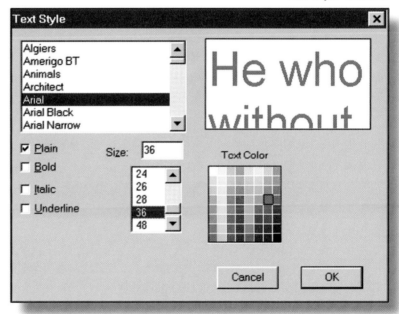

**HINT:**

Once you have moved your cursor from a line of painted text, you will not be able to change the words as you would in a word processing program. Try to change the words you first typed. What happens?

## Drawing Tools

Above the Text tool is a row of tools for drawing shapes. (See Figure 2-8.) Use these tools to draw different-size rectangles, ovals, and rounded rectangles. Once you have selected one of these tools, your cursor becomes a crossbar (+).

**FIGURE 2-8**
Drawing Tools

---

### STEP-BY-STEP ▷ 2.4

**1.** Click the **Rectangle** tool.

**2.** Position your cursor at any point on the screen. Click and drag your mouse to create a rectangle. Notice how the shape changes as you move your mouse. Release the mouse button to complete the rectangle. It is easy to make boxes of any size using the Rectangle tool.

**3.** Now use the Oval and Rounded Rectangle tools to create two additional shapes on the screen.

**4.** Your screen will now display text and three shapes.

**5.** Keep your stack open for the next Step-by-Step.

---

## Eraser Tool

Directly above the Rectangle tool is an eraser. (See Figure 2-9.) It does just what the name implies. When this tool is selected, your cursor becomes the shape of an eraser. The Eraser tool may also be used to fill the background of the card with a color. This action will cover everything on the card.

**FIGURE 2-9**
Eraser

---

### STEP-BY-STEP ▷ 2.5

**1.** Click on the **Eraser** tool.

**2.** Click and drag the eraser to practice erasing a portion of one of your shapes. (Don't worry if some of the text is erased in the process.)

**3.** Double click on the **Eraser** tool. A window will appear that asks you to select a background color.

**4.** Choose a **red** and click **OK**. The entire card will fill with the color you selected. It will cover any objects you have drawn.

**5.** Now let's undo the last action. Pull down the Edit menu on the menubar and choose **Undo**. You should see the screen the way it was before you choose the erase color.

**6.** Keep your stack open for the next Step-by-Step.

**TIP**

You can undo from the keyboard by pressing **Ctrl + Z** (for Windows) or  **+ Z** (for Macintosh). Undo will only undo your *last* action.

**HINT:**

Whenever your practice screen is too full, just double click on the Eraser tool and select white as the background color. This will give you a blank card.

## Paint Tools

The row above the eraser consists of three paint tool icons: the Paintbrush, the Spray Can, and the Paint Bucket. (See Figure 2-10.) The Paintbrush and Spray Can tools allow you to draw and paint on the screen.

The Paint Bucket tool is a bit trickier. The paint bucket fills any object or screen with whatever color or pattern you choose. When you are using the Paint Bucket tool, it is important to remember that the object must be closed if you want to fill only that object. If it has any holes or the lines do not completely meet, the paint will leak out and fill the entire card. If this happens, use the Undo command immediately. You will learn to use the Paint Bucket tool in a later lesson.

**FIGURE 2-10**
Paint Tools

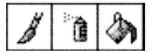

**STEP-BY-STEP ⟩ 2.6**

1. Select the **Paintbrush** tool. Click and drag the **Paintbrush** tool to create some shapes on your screen. (Remember that you begin a new shape by releasing the mouse button, moving to another location on the screen, and clicking and dragging the mouse to create a new shape.)

2. Double click on the **Paintbrush** tool. This brings up a window that allows you to select the size and shape of your paintbrush, as shown in Figure 2-11. Click on the second largest dot.

3. Paint on your screen using this tool.

4. Double click on the **Paintbrush** tool again. Choose the large square. Using this shape for the tool, paint on your screen.

5. Click on the **Spray Can** tool. See what happens when you click and drag the mouse across your screen.

6. Write your name using the **Spray Can** tool.

7. Keep your stack open for the next Step-by-Step.

**FIGURE 2-11**
Brush Sizes and Shapes

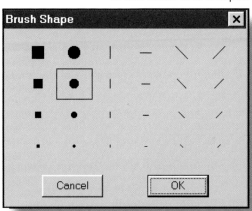

**HINT:**

In a later lesson, you will learn to change the color and pattern of the spray paint.

## Selector Tools

The top row of the paint tools contains the selector tools, as shown in Figure 2-12. These tools appear as dotted lines. The Square Selector tool allows you to surround a square area so that you can move, edit, copy, cut, delete, resize, flip, or rotate the area within the square.

It is also possible to select objects that are not square. The Circle Selector and Lasso Selector tools allow you to easily select oval, round, and irregular shapes. When you select an object, the background is included as part of the selection.

**FIGURE 2-12**
Selector Tools

## STEP-BY-STEP ▷ 2.7

1. Click on the **Square Selector** tool. When you move your mouse over the screen, the cursor becomes a crossbar (+).

2. Click and drag the mouse to surround an area of your screen that has text or a drawing in it. The area you selected should now have "moving ants" surrounding it. (See Figure 2-13.) Remember that the background within the red "ants" is also part of the object you have captured.

3. Place your cursor in the middle of the area. The shape should change to a four-headed arrow ┼. This allows you to move, copy, or delete the area.

4. With the mouse in the middle of the selected area, drag the selection to a different place on the card. Release the mouse button.

5. With the area still selected, go to the menubar and choose **Edit**. Then choose **Copy**. Now choose **Paste**. This process creates a copy of your selection.

6. Click and drag from the center of the selected area to move the copy to another location on the card. See Figure 2-14 for an example of the result.

(continued on next page)

**FIGURE 2-13**
Shape Selected with the Square Selector Tool

**FIGURE 2-14**
Copied Shape

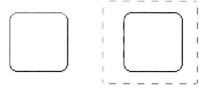

**7.** Click outside the selected area. The "moving ants" are gone. The selection has now been copied and moved to a new location.

Now you will use the other two selector tools.

**8.** Click the **Circle Selector** tool.

**9.** Select an area on the screen. Click inside the selection and drag it to a different location. Notice that the tool selects the background area as well.

**10.** Click on the **Lasso Selector** tool.

**11.** Click and drag the mouse to select an area on the screen. Move your selection to a new location. Notice that the Lasso Selector tool is more difficult to control.

**12.** Keep your stack open for the next Step-by-Step.

**TIP**

When you copy and paste an object or an area, the copied item will be on top of the original. You must move it from the location on top of the original to its new location.

# *Saving a Stack*

It is a good idea to save your stack often, especially when you are busy adding new ideas. Saving a stack is a two-part action. First, you have to decide where it will be saved. Ask your instructor if there is a place on your computer's hard drive where you can store your work. You can also save your work on a diskette or ZIP disk. Second, you must name the stack so that you can find it again. The name of a stack is the file name used to save your stack. You will be able to locate your stack by its file name on your computer.

The first time you save a stack, you choose Save As from the File menu. This allows you to name the stack and designate where the stack should be saved. After the stack has been named, you can work on the stack to make additions and changes. When you are ready to save again, you choose Save from the File menu. Save lets you keep the changes you have made to the stack without changing the name of the stack.

## Save As

■ Use this command the first time you save a stack. It allows you to name the stack and to decide where it will be saved.

■ Use this command to save a file with a new name. This creates a new file and maintains the original file as well.

## Save

■ Use this command to save changes or additions to an existing file.

To avoid having to redo many hours of work, save often, even if you are not finished working on your stack. Before you begin Step-by-Step 2.8, ask your instructor to inform you where you will be saving your files.

## STEP-BY-STEP ▷ 2.8

**1.** To save and name a stack for the first time, select **File** from the menubar. The options available on the File menu are shown in Figure 2-15.

**2.** Select **Save Stack As. . .**. A window similar to the one in Figure 2-16 will appear.

**3.** Locate the area on your computer where you will be saving your work. You may have to ask your instructor for a specific location.

**4.** In the File name field, key **Prac1**, as shown in Figure 2-16. Click **Save**. Your stack is now saved.

**5.** Keep your stack open for the next Step-by-Step.

**FIGURE 2-15**
File Menu

| | |
|---|---|
| New Stack | |
| Open Stack... | Ctrl+O |
| Save Stack | Ctrl+S |
| Save Stack As... | |
| Import Background... | Ctrl+I |
| Export Screen... | Ctrl+E |
| Add Clip Art... | Ctrl+A |
| Print... | Ctrl+P |
| Page Setup... | |
| Print to Video... | |
| Exit | |

**FIGURE 2-16**
Save As Screen

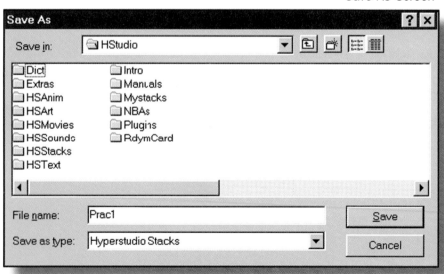

## Line and Pencil Tools

There are a few more tools to be explored. The two other tools in the row with the Eraser tool are the Pencil and Line tools. (See Figure 2-17.) The Line tool can be used to draw lines from one point to another. The Pencil tool can be used as a drawing tool just as you would use a regular pencil on paper. The Pencil tool requires practice to use effectively.

**FIGURE 2-17**
Line and Pencil Tools

Holding down the Shift key while drawing or erasing a line will keep a straight line.

 **2.9**

1. Use the **Eraser** tool to change the card to a white background.

We practiced this technique in Step-by-Step 2-5.

2. Click on the **Line** tool.

3. Draw a box on the card.

4. Draw a stick figure of yourself.

5. Double-click on the **Line** tool. The window displays different sizes of lines. From this window, you can choose the thickness of your lines. See Figure 2-18.

6. Choose the line thickness by clicking on one of the lines. Click **OK**.

7. Use the **Line** tool to draw a house on your screen. Change the thickness of the line as you draw the house. Use at least two different thicknesses.

8. Keep the stack open for the next Step-by-Step.

**FIGURE 2-18**
Line Size Screen

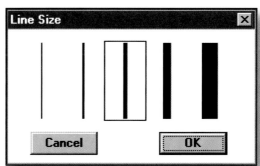

1. Click on the **Pencil** tool.

2. Draw a stick figure of yourself again. Notice the difference in the tools.

3. Pull down the File menu and choose **Exit**. (See Figure 2-15.)

4. You have already named your stack. Click on **Save** to save the changes and exit HyperStudio. (See Figure 2-19.)

**FIGURE 2-19**
Save Changed Stack Screen

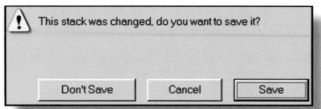

This stack was changed, do you want to save it?

Don't Save      Cancel      Save

# Summary

This lesson introduced the basic tools used in HyperStudio. You learned:

■ How to create a new stack.

■ How to name and save a stack.

■ How to use the variety of tools for editing, selecting, and drawing in HyperStudio.

■ How to exit from HyperStudio.

## VOCABULARY

Arrow (Edit) tool

Browse tool

Button tool

Circle Selector tool

Drawing tools

Edit tools

Eraser tool

Eyedropper tool

Graphic Object tool

Lasso Selector tool

Magnifying Glass tool

Oval tool

Paintbrush tool

Paint Bucket tool

Pencil tool

Rectangle tool

Rounded Rectangle tool

Save

Save as

Selector tools

Spray Can tool

Square Selector tool

Text tool

Text Object tool

Tool palette

## LESSON 2 REVIEW QUESTIONS

SCANS

### SHORT ANSWER QUESTIONS

1.  Describe the step-by-step process of naming and saving a stack.

    _____

    _____

    _____

    _____

2.  Name three of the button options on the HyperStudio opening card and describe what they do.

    a. _____

    _____

    _____

    b. _____

    _____

    _____

    c. _____

    _____

    _____

SCANS

### WRITTEN QUESTIONS

**Without using your notes, draw a picture of the tool that is named and describe what it does.**

1.  Paintbrush tool:


2.  Lasso Selector tool:

3. Text tool:


4. Pencil tool:


5. Square Selector tool:

## LESSON 2 PROJECT 2.1

1. Create a new stack. Using the tools in the tool palette, draw the picture you see in Figure 2-20.

**FIGURE 2-20**
Lesson 2 Project Picture

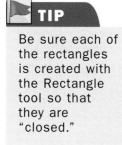

**TIP**

Be sure each of the rectangles is created with the Rectangle tool so that they are "closed."

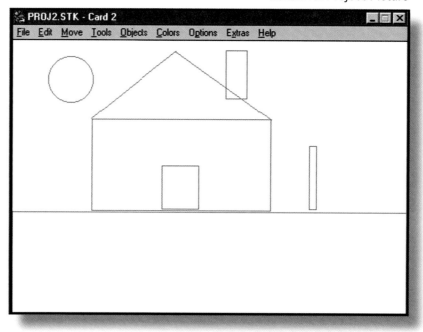

2. Use the Rectangle tool to draw the following objects:

- main part of the house

- the chimney

- the tree

- the door in the front of the house

3. Use the Oval tool to draw the sun.

4. Use the Line tool to draw the roof of the house

5. Save the stack and name it **Proj2**.

6. Close HyperStudio.

## LESSON 2 PROJECT 2.2

**SCANS**

Using paper and pencil, draw a screen for each tool and a sample of what that tool does. You should have a series of pages.

## CRITICAL THINKING ACTIVITY

**SCANS**

Think about the tools you have explored in the exercises. List several ways you might apply each of the tools to a specific project or purpose. For instance, with the drawing tools, you could design any setting that you might want for a project.

# OBJECTS, BACKGROUNDS, LAYERS, AND COLORS

## OBJECTIVES

**Upon completion of this lesson, you will be able to:**

- Create backgrounds.
- Create new cards.
- Print your stacks.
- Use the paint tools.
- Use the color palette.
- Create patterns and borders.
- Create objects.

**⏱ Estimated Time: 1.5 hours**

Since HyperStudio is such a visual tool, it is time to introduce colors and patterns to liven up your cards. In HyperStudio, there is a hierarchy, or system, of how different elements lay on your card.

## *Creating Backgrounds*

The very bottom layer is the background. Each card in your stack can have a different background, or groups of cards in your stack can share a background. When you plan a stack, it is useful to organize the cards so that cards with similar topics or purposes share the same background. If you think of your stack as a book, then each set of cards might be separated like the chapters in that book. Similarly, cards with similar purposes may share the same background. If your stack has several sections, the Title cards of each section may share the same background. By planning a strategy for the use of backgrounds, you provide visual clues that your viewer can use to understand the message you are hoping to convey.

Other objects can be placed on top of the background. For instance, text, buttons, graphics, and the objects created with your drawing tools are placed on the background. The background is the bottom layer. Clip art and paint objects become part of this layer. In Figure 3-1, the background and the word "Background" are on the bottom layer. The second layer is the text object, the third layer is the button, and the fourth layer is the graphic object. The background must be placed first. In most cases, objects can be placed on the background in any order.

**FIGURE 3-1**
Layered Card

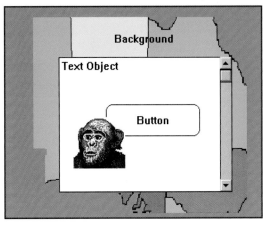

## STEP-BY-STEP ⟹ 3.1

1. Open HyperStudio.

2. Click on **New Stack** icon from the Home card. Choose the appropriate answers until you have a new blank card. (See Lesson 2 if you need help with this process.) (Windows users may be asked: **"Do you want to use the same card size as in your current stack?"** Choose **Yes**.)

3. Pull down the File menu and choose **Import Background**. See Figure 3-2.

4. You will be asked to select a source for the background, as shown in Figure 3-3. Choose **Disk file** and click **OK**.

(continued on next page)

**FIGURE 3-2**
Import Background

**FIGURE 3-3**
Where do you want to get your graphic? Window

TIP

Macintosh users may move directly to the window to select the folder and picture file.

**2 7**

**5** Locate the **HSArt** folder. For many users, the HSArt folder will appear in the Look in box shown in Figure 3-4. If the folder does not appear, navigate through the folders to locate it.

**6.** Scroll through the list of files in the HSArt folder until you locate **Usa**. Highlight it and click the **Open** button. (See Figure 3-4.)

The HSArt folder is located in the HyperStudio folder. First find and open the HyperStudio folder on your network or hard drive. Then locate and open the HSArt folder.

You may select any file from a list by double clicking on the file's icon.

If you are using a large monitor, you may get a message to resize your graphic. If you do, select Yes.

**FIGURE 3-4**
Select USA Folder

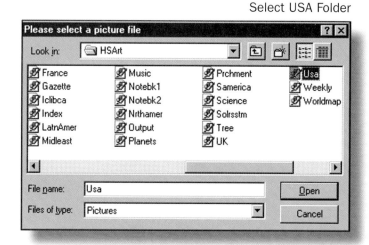

The screens to locate files will be different for Macintosh and Windows users. In all cases, choose **Usa** or **Usa.bmp** in the **HSArt** folder.

**7.** Your card should look like Figure 3-5. Save your stack as **USA**.

**8.** Keep your stack open for the next Step-by-Step.

See Lesson 2 if you need help remembering how to save a stack. Remember to save your stack frequently.

**FIGURE 3-5**
USA Background

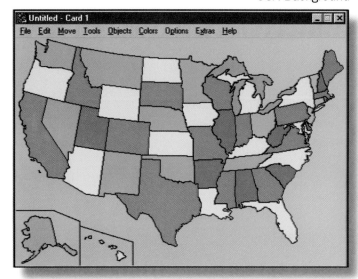

# *Using the Text Tools*

In Lesson 2, you learned how to access the tool palette and use the various tools. When you first open HyperStudio, the tool palette does not appear, although it is available. Since it is convenient to have the tools in view, you can pull the palette off the menu and place it alongside your Hyper-Studio card. (See Figure 3-6.) You may position the palette on either side of the card. The figures in this textbook vary the position of the tool palette to remind you that you can place the palette wherever is most comfortable for you. You can also move the palette while you are working by clicking on the bar at the top of the palette and dragging it to a new position.

**FIGURE 3-6**
USA Card with Tool Palette

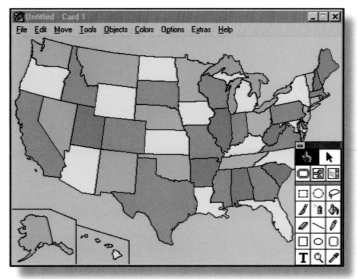

1. Click on the **Tools** menu. Drag the tool palette to the side of the card, as shown in Figure 3-6.

2. Double click on the Text tool. You will see the Text Style window as shown in Figure 3-7.

3. Choose **Arial** for the font.

4. Choose **Bold** for the style.

5. Choose **36** for the font size.

6. Leave the color **Black**.

7. Click **OK**.

**HINT:**

The Macintosh and Windows text color palettes are slightly different. However, the basic color choices are the same.

**TIP**

If the Arial font does not appear on your list of fonts, select a different font from the list. Use the scroll bar to move up and down the list. Notice that the font you select displays in the box.

**FIGURE 3-7**
Text Style Window

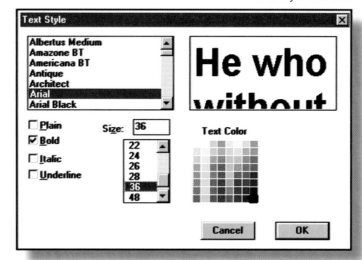

8. You will add a title that prints over the background, as shown in Figure 3-8. Refer to the figure before you click your cursor on the starting point for the first word. Key **ABOUT MY** on one line. If the words don't appear as you would like them to, backspace and start over by placing your cursor in a different place on the screen.

9. When you are satisfied with the position of your first line of text, press **Enter**. Key **STATE** on the next line and press **Enter**. Key the name of your state on the third line and press **Enter**.

10. Save your stack, and leave it open for the next Step-by-Step.

**TIP**

Notice that your text position is not fixed until you press Enter. However, once you press Enter or move your cursor to another line, you cannot move the text.

**HINT:**

Remember that once you have painted on the text, you cannot go back later and change it. However, you can use the space bar to move the position of the first letter of a line to the right. Once you press Enter or move the cursor with your mouse, the text and its position are fixed and cannot be changed. The only way to remove the text is to use the selector tools or use the Eraser tool. However, the Eraser tool will also erase the background. To see the effect of the Eraser tool, complete the next Step-by-Step.

**FIGURE 3-8**
About My State Painted Text

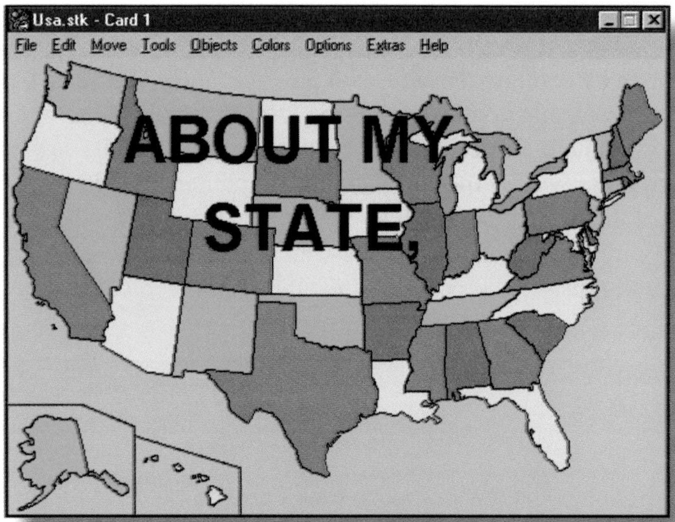

**STEP-BY-STEP ⟩ 3.3**

1. You should have ABOUT MY as the first line of text on the card.

2. Choose the **Eraser** tool and drag it to erase these words.

3. You will see that the background has been erased along with the text.

4. Pull down the Edit menu and select **Undo**. This will undo the erasure.

**HINT:**

HINT: The keyboard shortcut for undo is **Ctrl + Z** for Windows or ⌘ **+ Z** for Macintosh. Anytime you need to undo a step, use the menu or the shortcut key, whichever works better for you.

5. Select the **Text** tool again. Try to position the cursor at the end of the line and use the backspace to erase the words. It doesn't work, does it?

6. Keep your stack open for the next Step-by-Step.

**▶ TIP**

If you cannot correct the mistakes, import the background again and repeat the steps to enter the text.

# Adding New Cards

What if you made an error you did not catch before you pressed Enter? You can correct the problem by deleting the card with the error and creating a new one. This method gives you a fresh start, but it means that you lose all of the work you have done.

Although a stack can be one card, a stack usually has more than one card. New cards are always added directly after the current card. If you need to add a card between two existing cards, move to the first of the two cards. When you insert a new card, it will be added after the first card. New cards do not overwrite existing cards, but are simply added to the existing stack of cards. In the next Step-by-Step, you will repeat the process of creating a new Title card.

## STEP-BY-STEP ▷ 3.4

1. From the Edit menu, choose **New Card**, as shown in Figure 3-9.

2. Pull down the File menu and choose **Import Background**.

3. Choose **Disk file** as the source and click OK.

4. From the HSArt folder, select **Usa**.

5. Double click on the **Text** tool.

6. Choose **Arial** for the font.

7. Choose **Bold** for the style.

8. Choose **36** for the font size.

9. Leave the color **black**.

10. Click **OK**.

11. Key **ABOUT MY** on one line and press **Enter**. Key **STATE,** on the next line and press **Enter**. Finally, key the name of your state on the third line and press **Enter**. Make sure that the text for each line is properly positioned before pressing Enter.

12. Your completed card should look similar to Figure 3-10, with the name of the state you live in on the card.

**TIP**

The keyboard shortcut for adding a new card is to press **Ctrl + N** for Windows or  + N for Macintosh.

**FIGURE 3-9**
Edit Menu

**13.** Save your stack. Once the stack has been named, as you already did in Step-by-Step 3.1, you should use Save rather than Save As from the File menu.

**14.** Keep the stack open for the next Step-by-Step.

**FIGURE 3-5**
USA Background

> ### TIP
>
> HyperStudio gives you several ways to perform the same task. Once you have named your stack, you can save it by:
>
> ■ Choosing Save from the File menu on the menubar.
>
> ■ Pressing **Ctrl + S** (for Windows) or  **+ S** (for Macintosh) from the keyboard.

# Working With Stacks

Since you added a new card, your stack actually contains two cards. The cards can only be viewed one at a time. In the next Step-by-Step, you will make one addition to your new Title card, then you will delete the first card.

The addition you will make to your card is to include the name of your state within the borders of your state or in a nearby location. Before you complete Step-by-Step 3.5, identify your state on a United States map. Decide where you will place the name of your state. Look ahead to Figure 3-15 for an example.

Before anyone views your stack, you should always view each card in the stack to make sure it is correct. You move among the cards using the Move menu. The number of the card currently displayed appears in the title bar next to the file name as shown in Figure 3-11. You will learn shortcuts to moving among the

**FIGURE 3-11**
Card Name and Number

cards in a later lesson when you have several cards in your stack. You delete cards using the Edit menu. When you tell HyperStudio to delete a card, it deletes the card that is currently displayed. You need to visually identify the card for deletion before you use the Delete Card command.

1. Double click on the **Text** tool. Use the same font, but make it plain and much smaller (probably 9, 10, 11, or 12 points, depending on the geographic area available).

2. Key the name of your state within the borders of your state or in a nearby location.

3. Save your stack.

4. Now that your new Title card has been completed, you can delete the original Title card. From the Move menu, choose **First Card**. (See Figure 3-12.)

5. From the Edit menu, choose **Delete Card**.

6. A dialog box will appear asking you if you want to delete the entire card, as shown in Figure 3-13. Choose **Yes**. You should have one card in your stack now, the Title card, ABOUT MY STATE.

7. Save your stack and keep your stack open for the next Step-by-Step.

**HINT:**

If the font size is either too large or too small, you can backspace to remove the text and double click on the Text tool again. You can then choose a different size font.

**FIGURE 3-12**
Move Menu

**FIGURE 3-13**
Delete Card Dialog Box

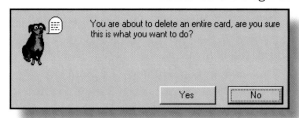

# *Printing in HyperStudio*

HyperStudio provides several printing options for you. If you have a color printer, HyperStudio projects will automatically print in color. If you are using a black and white printer, the cards will print in black and white.

You will be given the option of printing one card, the current card on your screen, or all of the cards in the stack. You also can choose to print one card per page, two cards per page, or four cards per page. This last option is useful because it reduces the amount of paper needed to print a large stack. Unless your instructor directs otherwise, use the one card per page option to print your assignments.

**STEP-BY-STEP ⟹ 3.6**

1. With the **USA** stack open, go to the File menu and choose **Print**. (See Figure 3-14.)

2. Choose **Current card** and **One card per page** from the Print Stack window, as shown in Figure 3-15. Click **OK**.

**FIGURE 3-15**
Print Stack Window

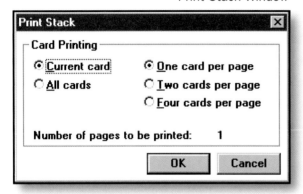

**FIGURE 3-14**
Print Option Selected from the File Menu

# *Using the Color Palette*

HyperStudio's color palette contains a wide variety of colors that you can use for text, objects, and drawings. For now, you will simply learn how to select and use colors. In later lessons, you will be asked to plan color palettes that are visually pleasing. The wise choice of colors, used in consistent ways throughout your stacks, is an important part of creating presentations that other people will enjoy viewing.

Colors are selected from a color palette. This palette, like the tool palette, can be placed beside your card for easy reference. When you have two palettes open, place them so that the palettes do not overlap. This allows you quick access to either palette. As you can see in Figure 3-16, the tool palette is placed on one side of the card and the color palette on the other side. As you work with HyperStudio, you should identify a placement system that works for you, and then use that system consistently.

**FIGURE 3-16**
Color Palette Displayed Alongside Card

**3 5**

In addition to color swatches, the color palette shows three color selections. These indicate the current choices for lines, for erasures, and for text. You will learn to how to change these colors in Step-by-Step 3.7.

**HINT:**

Sometimes the pattern and color palette will not appear until you have selected a paint tool.

**STEP-BY-STEP 3.7**

1. Pull off the color palette from the Colors menu the same way you pulled off the tool palette. Place the color palette alongside your stack. (See Figure 3-16.)

2. Double click on the **Paintbrush** tool in the tool palette and select a small, round brush size.

3. Click on a color swatch of a dark color that does not currently appear in the United States map. You will use this color to encircle your state.

4. Use the **Paintbrush** tool to draw a circle around the state in which you live. The completed Title card appears as shown in Figure 3-17. Notice that the selected color is the color the paintbrush uses.

5. When you are finished, save and close the stack.

**HINT:**

If you make a mistake or don't like the way it looks, choose **Undo** and repeat the process until you like it. Don't forget: You can only undo your last action.

**FIGURE 3-17**
Finished Title Card

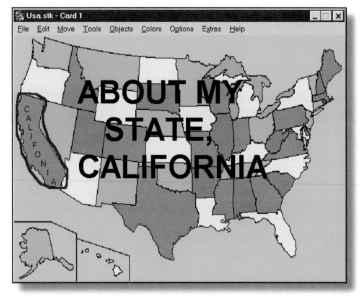

# *Creating Borders and Patterns*

Another way to decorate or separate groups of cards in a stack is with borders. Borders are used to frame the card or a portion of the card. Colors or patterns from the color palette can be used to fill the space within the border, creating interesting visuals for cards and objects. The same border can be used throughout the stack, or different borders can be used to identify different types of cards or sections of the project, like chapters in a book. Patterns can be used just like colors to add distinctive graphics, emphasize objects or text, or create backgrounds or borders.

Borders can be created:

■ Using the tools from the tool palette,

■ Using the graphics included in HyperStudio, or

■ Using borders imported from other software.

Patterns can be created:

■ by drawing or painting a shape and using the Paint Bucket to fill the area with a pattern from the color palette.

■ by copying a pattern from a graphic object and pasting it where you want the pattern to appear.

## STEP-BY-STEP ⟩ 3.8

1. Open HyperStudio and create a new stack.

2. Choose the **Rectangle** tool from the tool palette. Starting in the upper right corner, click and drag the crossbar cursor (+) across the screen until you have created an equal border that looks like a box within the screen, as shown in Figure 3-18. Be sure to leave a small space between the border and the edges of the card.

(continued on next page)

**FIGURE 3-18**
Border Area Created

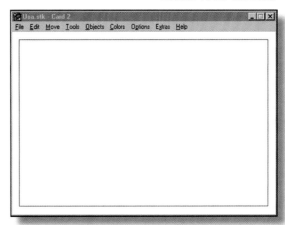

**INTERNET**

The Internet reaches schools in more than 140 countries. Through e-mail and other connections, you can learn about students in other countries and foreign students can learn about you. The Internet allows you to correspond almost instantaneously with people all over the world.

3. Select the **Paint Bucket** tool from the tool palette, as shown in Figure 3-19.

4. Select a pattern from the color palette.

5. Very carefully, place the paint bucket so that the "paint" flow will fall between the lines of the outside and inside borders. Be sure that the paint can does not go into the center square of the screen.

6. Click the **Paint Bucket** tool. You should see the pattern you selected forming a border around the inner square, as shown in Figure 3-20.

7. Save your stack as **Prac2**.

8. Print your stack and leave it open for the next activity.

**FIGURE 3-19**
Paint Bucket Tool Selected

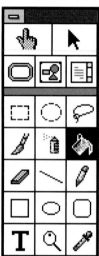

**HINT:**

If your pattern fills the screen or you want to choose a different pattern, choose the Undo command immediately after your last action.

**FIGURE 3-20**
Border with Pattern

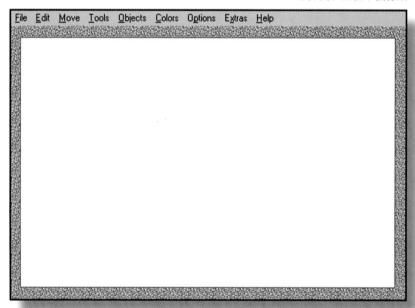

## CHALLENGE ACTIVITY ▭▷ 3.1

Challenge activities will be included in many lessons. To complete them, use your knowledge of HyperStudio and your creativity. The challenge activities will give you the opportunity to use the skills you practiced in previous Step-by-Steps.

1. Using the variety of tools from the tool palette, draw several different objects. Include at least one oval, one rectangle, and a figure eight.

2. Fill each object with a color or pattern. Be careful not to let the pattern bleed into the rest of the card or other objects.

3. Using the selector tools, move the objects to different places.

4. Use the Spray Can tool and different colors to write or draw on the remaining part of the screen. If you use up the available space, erase the center and begin over.

5. Add a new card.

6. Choose a light color for your background such as yellow and fill the entire card with the color.

7. Print your stack.

8. Save your stack as **Prac3**. Close HyperStudio.

You can create a figure eight by drawing two equal ovals and then using the Selection Arrow (Edit) tool to connect them. Be careful not to include a white border at the edge of the figure you are connecting.

If you double click the Eraser tool, you will delete your border also.

# Summary

In this lesson, you learned that:

- HyperStudio stacks are layered with backgrounds, objects, pictures, and text.

- The Text tool can be used to add text on top of a background.

- Files from the HSArt folder can be used for backgrounds.

- New cards can be added to your stacks.

- Stacks can be printed with one, two, or four cards per page.

- You can use the paint tools to create borders.

- Patterns and colors can be used to fill areas of the card.

- Mistakes can be undone by using the backspace key, by undoing the last action taken, or by starting over.

## VOCABULARY

Backgrounds                       Import background

Borders                           New card

Color palette                     Patterns

Delete card                       Printing

Fonts

## LESSON 3 REVIEW QUESTIONS

### TRUE/FALSE

**Circle the T if the statement is true or F if it is false.**

**T    F    1.** The first time you save a stack, you use the command Save.

**T    F    2.** When you use the Undo command, it will only change the last action.

**T    F    3.** The Text tool makes it easy to go back and change text.

**T    F    4.** The color palette gives you access to different colors and patterns.

**T    F    5.** You can create your own borders.

**T    F    6.** The Paint Bucket tool can be used like an eraser.

### SHORT ANSWER QUESTIONS

**Answer the questions below in the space provided.**

**1.** What is the bottom layer in a stack called?

2. What is the name of the first card in a stack?

3. How can you eliminate a mistake?

4. How can you eliminate a card in a stack?

5. How can you change the font and font size for painting text?

6. Name two ways to access the Save command.

   a.

   b.

7. How do you create a new card?

8. Name two ways to identify cards of the same topic in a stack.

   a.

   b.

9. What do you have to watch out for when using the Paint Bucket tool?

# LESSON 3 PROJECT 3.1

1. Open your stack, **Proj2**.

2. Using the tools from the tool palette, fill in the objects you created, as shown in Figure 3-21.

3. Add an additional object of your own design to the card.

4. Print your stack.

5. Save your stack as **Prj3-1**.

6. Close the stack.

**FIGURE 3-21**
Sample Using Paint Tools and Colors and Patterns

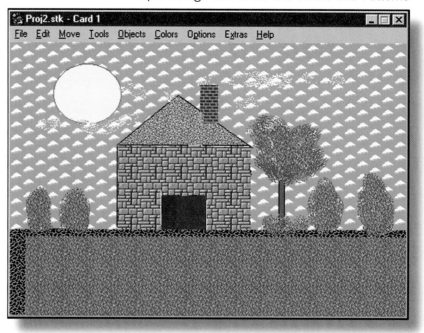

## LESSON 3 PROJECT 3.2

1. Create a new stack.

2. Create a Title card by importing a background from the HSArt folder.

3. Include a title on your card that connects to the background you have chosen.

4. Create a second card.

5. Create a border for your second card.

6. Save the stack as **Prj3-2**.

7. Print your stack.

8. Close the stack.

## CRITICAL THINKING ACTIVITY

You are planning a project with HyperStudio. List several ways that the introduction of colors and patterns change the way you can use the tools from the tool palette. Compare your list with several other learners.

# *Review of Procedures*

| | |
|---|---|
| **Starting HyperStudio** | **Windows:**<br>From the desktop, double click on the HyperStudio icon or from the Start menu select Programs and double click the HyperStudio icon.<br>**Macintosh:**<br>Open the hard drive and double click on the HyperStudio folder. Double click on the HyperStudio 3.1 icon. Or, from the  menu, double click the HyperStudio icon alias. |
| **Closing HyperStudio** | From the File menu, select Quit. |
| **Naming a stack** | From the File menu, select Save As to name a stack. |
| **Saving a stack** | From the File menu, select Save. |
| **Printing a stack** | From the File menu, select Print. Choose the number of cards per page (1, 2, or 4). Choose to print the current card or the entire stack. |

## UNIT 1 REVIEW QUESTIONS ▽

### FILL IN THE BLANKS

Complete the following statements by keying or writing the correct answers on a page to be submitted to your instructor. Center *Unit 1 Review Questions* at the top of the page. Number your answers to match the numbers listed here.

1. Multimedia authoring software allows you to integrate a variety of elements such as

   _____ , _____ , and _____ .

2. HyperStudio cards are saved together as a _____ .

3. Moving from one card to another in HyperStudio is called _____ .

4. You can create objects and draw shapes in HyperStudio using these three tools: the

   _____ , the _____ , and the _____ .

5. You can use these tools to paint in HyperStudio: the _____ tool, the

   _____ tool, and the _____ tool.

6.  If you make a mistake in HyperStudio, to correct it you can choose the _____ feature from the Edit menu or you can choose _____ from the keyboard.

7.  You can create a new card by selecting _____ from the _____ menu.

8.  The bottom layer in a stack is the _____ .

9.  If you double click on the _____ you can change the font size of the painted text.

10. The _____ _____ gives you access to colors and patterns for your paint and drawing tools.

## WRITTEN QUESTIONS

**Key or write your answers to the following questions. Number your answers. Use complete sentences and good grammar.**

11. Why is HyperStudio considered to be an authoring tool?

12. Name four of the HyperStudio tools on the toolbar and explain what they do.

    a.

    b.

    c.

    d.

13. How do you save a stack in HyperStudio?

14. What does layering mean in HyperStudio stacks?

15. What is the difference between Save and Save As?

## UNIT 1 APPLICATIONS

### UNIT 1 PROJECT

1. Create a two-card stack using a topic of your choice.

2. For Card 1:

   a. Import a background for the Title card.

   b. Key a title for the stack.

3. On Card 2:

   a. Create a border for the card.

   b. Use the paint tools to draw a picture for your topic.

   c. Key text describing the picture.

4. Save the stack as **EP1**.

## UNIT 1 CRITICAL THINKING ACTIVITY

Write a brief description of some of the uses for a multimedia-authoring program like HyperStudio.

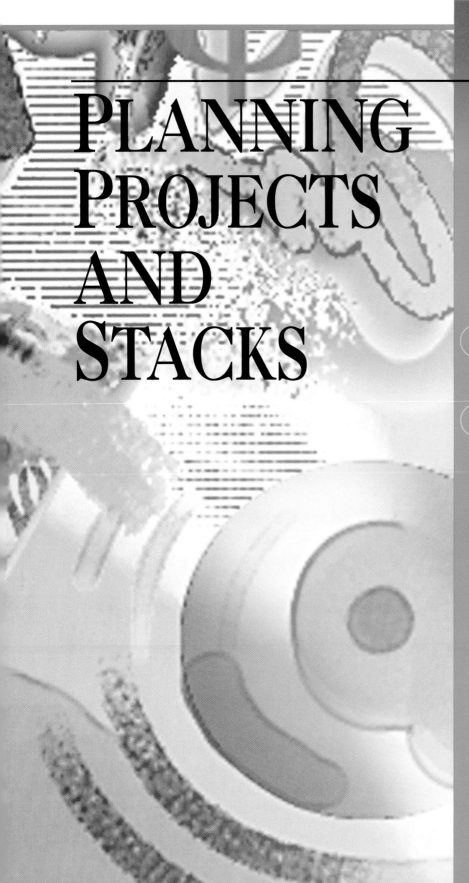

# PLANNING PROJECTS AND STACKS

## UNIT 2

**LESSON**

**4**

# SCREEN DESIGN

## OBJECTIVES

**Upon completion of this lesson, you will be able to:**

- Organize your HyperStudio project.

- Create a storyboard.

- Create the primary cards for a stack.

- Recognize the elements of a good stack.

- Design your stack.

🕐 **Estimated Time: 1 hour**

Now that you have learned to use the fundamental tools in HyperStudio, it is time to plan your first project. The planning is important, whether you are working in a group or on your own endeavor. It is hard to reach your goal if you don't know where you are going. Also, good planning at the start can save you a lot of time later. An informative, well-planned project is not hard to create. Applying some simple guidelines will help you set realistic goals and accomplish them.

Let's go through the process of planning and implementing your first HyperStudio project. First, you need to decide on the topic, estimate the time needed to complete the project, and define the project's requirements.

# *Planning a Project*

## The Topic

Sometimes this part is easy—your teacher will give you an assignment. If you are not assigned a topic, you will have to develop some techniques for selecting and researching a topic. When selecting a topic, think about your interests. Or perhaps you can brainstorm with other people you respect and like. This could include friends, family, and other class members. Additional sources of topics may be found on the Internet, at the library, or in a newspaper or magazine.

## The Theme

You may notice as you explore and evaluate HyperStudio stacks that authors often create a theme for their stacks based on their topic. It is called a "metaphor." A metaphor is a term for a symbol that represents one thing being used to represent another. For instance, you could use a book as a metaphor for your stack and have each topic in the stack be represented by a chapter.

## Research

Once you have decided on a topic, you can begin to research it. You need to ask yourself:

- Is my topic broad enough? Is there enough information to meet the requirements of the project?

- Is my topic too broad? Is it necessary to tighten it up a little in order to meet the requirements and deadline? For instance, *sports* might be too broad of a topic. It might help to narrow it down to one particular sport, for instance, *skiing*. Even then, you might have to narrow it down more, depending on the requirements for the project.

- Do I have access to reliable sources? Most projects are based on researched information with some reliable way of measuring the accuracy of the sources. Projects generally should not be based on someone's opinion unless that is the nature of the assignment.

- Are pictures, graphics, maps, videos, etc. accessible? Some or all of these elements may be needed to make the project interesting.

# Organizing a Project

## Storyboards

Two tools that are useful for organizing your project are storyboards and organizational charts. A storyboard is useful for organizing thoughts and ideas. It was originally developed for movie and video production, and is a way for the production team, the writer, director, cinematographer, artists, and so on to coordinate the process of assimilating all of the parts, camera angles, scripting, sound tracks, and images to appear in a shot. For our purposes, the storyboard will help to keep track of the cards, the order of the cards, and the elements that will appear on each card.

A storyboard is a group of pictures or descriptions of elements that can be arranged in any order. Imagine a stack of index cards. Each card contains a picture or description, and any text needed to convey the idea of that card. The same is true when you are planning a HyperStudio stack. Using paper or index cards, start out with your Title card. Next will be the Main Menu card. On this card you will have a list of subtopics, then a card for each of the subtopic cards in the stack. See Figure 4-1.

**FIGURE 4-1**
Storyboard

## Organizational Charts

An organizational chart can also be used to organize a project. Figure 4-2 shows an example of an organizational chart. These are also called flowcharts. The pertinent information appears in each box. The chart shows how cards are connected and how they will interact with each other.

For each project you create, you should organize it using a storyboard or an organizational chart before you create anything in HyperStudio.

**FIGURE 4-2**
Organizational Chart

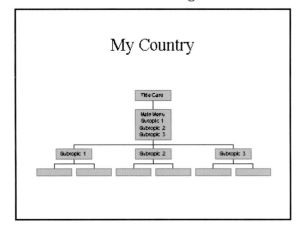

# *Project Description*

In this lesson, you will create a unique project. The Step-by-Steps will give you general directions. You will use these directions to help you create the project. The assignment is to create a five-card stack about a country. You will:

■   Choose the country.

■   Create a storyboard for your stack.

■   Create a Title card.

■   Create a Main Menu card that leads to the three subtopic cards.

■   Create three subtopic cards that relate to the main topic.

Some ideas for subtopic cards about a country might be: geography, government, history, wildlife, vegetation, cultures, artistic influences, or sports.

Later you will create the component cards to go with each subtopic. You will also create the navigation to move around the stack.

## STEP-BY-STEP ⟹ 4.1

1.  The theme is the country. Decide on the country you would like to research.

2.  Decide on the subtopics you plan to research for your stack.

3.  Create an organizational chart of your stack using the criteria in Step 4.

 **TIP**

For experience, you are creating both a storyboard and an organizational chart. As you plan and organize projects, use whichever method works better for you.

**STEP-BY-STEP ⟹ 4.1 CONTINUED**

**4.** Create the storyboard using pen and paper or index cards. This will be a detailed storyboard. Create a simple drawing for each of the cards in your preliminary stack. The stack will contain the following cards:

**Title card**, which should include:

■ The name of the stack and the name(s) of the creator(s) of the stack. For this project, the name of the country should be used as the name of the stack.

■ A background or picture(s) that sets the tone or theme of the stack. (See Figure 4-3.)

■ Navigation button to take you to the Main Menu card.

**FIGURE 4-3**
Sample Title Card

**Main Menu card** (see Figure 4-4), which should include:

■ The name of the card or other identifier.

■ The subtopics of the stack.

■ Navigation buttons to take you to the subtopic cards.

■ An exit button.

**Three subtopic cards**, which should include:

■ Graphics or backgrounds to convey the idea or theme of the subtopic.

■ Navigation buttons.

■ Video, sounds, pictures, and text.

**FIGURE 4-4**
Sample Main Menu Card

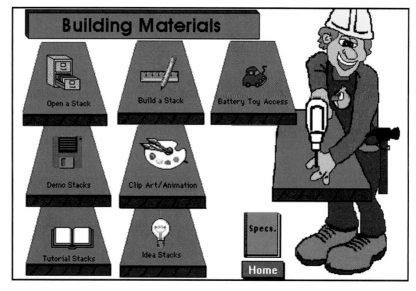

# *Elements to Include on the Cards*

Now that you have the general structure of the stack, you must decide on the features to include on each card.

Most cards will include text and graphic elements to convey information. Have you ever heard the phrase, "A picture is worth a thousand words"? Remember that multimedia is usually a visual medium. Whenever possible, let the pictures convey the meaning, instead of the words. In other words, let the pictures tell the story.

Another feature that must be included in your stack is some way to navigate from card to card. Generally, this will be done with buttons, icons, or text that acts like a button. Consistent and easy-to-use navigation is an important element of good project design. You do not want the user of your project to have a difficult time moving from card to card.

Two elements that may be included are video and sound. Both elements enhance the project, but they are not generally used on every card in the stack. The other elements to mention are **transitions**, how the screen looks when you go from card to card, and **animations**. Animations are ways to make objects or text move across the screen independently. You will learn to add all these dimensions to your stack in later lessons.

## STEP-BY-STEP 4.2

1. Using the cards you created in Step-by-Step 4.1, look at the graphics, or placeholders for pictures and the text you plan to include. Decide if the pictures add to the general theme and intention of the stack. Change or delete any that do not fit or that clutter the card.

**HINT:**

Less is more. Don't distract from your main point by using up too much of the space.

2. Which one would you rather read, Figure 4-5 or 4-6?

**HINT:**

3. Browse through the HSArt folder on your HyperStudio CD and try to find a few pictures that would go well with your plan for the stack.

It is hard to read a lot of text on a computer screen. When using hypermedia, it is a good idea to use small amounts of text on each card and to use more cards.

4. Either draw a rough sketch of the images you plan to use, or write the file names and a brief description of the image on your cards.

**FIGURE 4-5**
Text on a Page

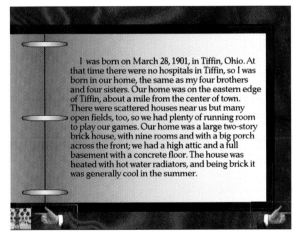

**FIGURE 4-6**
Text on a Page

**HINT:**

Don't worry about being an artist. It is only necessary to create a placeholder so that you can go back later and remember the image you want to place on your card.

# Planning Navigation

Like other elements in your stack, the navigation should be thoroughly planned. One rule of screen design is to never leave your user stuck on a card. Generally, you want users to be able to move forward or backward and to quit whenever they want. Your forward and backward buttons may contain direction arrows (symbols) or explanatory text such as Next Page and Previous Page. Whichever system you decide to use, use it consistently throughout the presentation.

You will also need to keep in mind that you must be able to go from the Main Menu card to the various subtopic cards, as shown in Figure 4-7. This nonlinear movement is easy to create in HyperStudio.

To allow users to quit at any point during the presentation, include a Quit or Exit button on each card or have a way to return to the Main Menu on each card. (See Figure 4-8.)

You should be able to Quit or return Home from the Main Menu card. See Figure 4-9.

Home usually takes you to the HyperStudio Home Card. This is the opening card when you begin the HyperStudio application, as shown in Figure 4-10.

**INTERNET** The Internet can be found on all seven continents, including Antarctica. A host at the South Pole sends out scientific information.

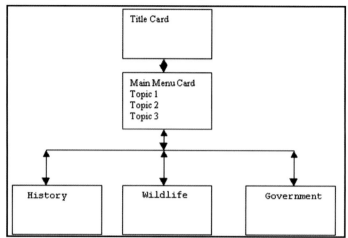

**FIGURE 4-7**
Organizational Chart Showing Navigation to Subtopic

**FIGURE 4-8**
Return to Main Menu Button

**FIGURE 4-9**
Main Menu Card with Access to Home

FIGURE 4-10
HyperStudio Home Card

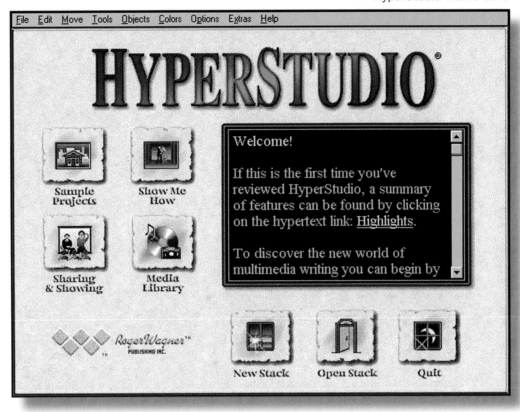

Another important point to remember is that the buttons for each action should be placed in the same place from card to card. This will keep your user from searching all over the card for the means of navigation.

Notice in Figures 4-11 and 4-12 that the buttons that go from page to page and the Done button are in the same place on each card.

FIGURE 4-11
Previous Page

FIGURE 4-12
Next Page

1. Using the storyboard cards from the previous Step-by-Steps, include a marker for where you plan to place your navigation buttons.

2. The Main Menu card should have buttons that will connect to each of the subtopic cards.

3. Write in where each of the buttons will take you. Don't forget to provide a way back.

**HINT:**

If you are using index cards, you can move them around to represent the navigation you are planning for your stack. On the organizational charts, you can draw the navigation paths with arrows.

# Stack Design Guidelines

One of the best ways to learn how to build good stacks is to explore existing stacks. By evaluating what does and does not work well, you can begin to get a feel for the kinds of design and navigation techniques that you will use in your own projects. In the next Step-by-Step, you will evaluate one of the stacks included on the HyperStudio CD-ROM. Careful evaluation of stacks will help you learn how to build good stacks.

**STEP·BY·STEP** $\Rightarrow$ 4.4

Complete the following review for a stack of your choice on the HyperStudio CD-ROM. Ask your instructor if he or she has a preference of which stack you will evaluate. If not, you may choose any stack you would like to review. Use the following questions to evaluate the stack.

1. What is the name of the stack?

_____

_____

2. Is there a Title card? Does it set the tone for the stack?

_____

_____

**STEP-BY-STEP 4.4 CONTINUED**

**3.** Is the Main Menu attractive? Does it set the tone for the stack?

_____

_____

**4.** Notice the pictures. Do they help to convey the message of the project?

_____

_____

**5.** How is the text used? Is there enough or too much? Is it easy to read?

_____

_____

**6.** Which colors or sizes of text work the best?

_____

_____

**7.** Describe the navigation. Does it allow you to make choices about what you want to explore? Does it allow you to stop or return to the Main Menu when you are ready?

_____

_____

**8.** Are the buttons easy to understand and read?

_____

_____

**9.** Are the buttons in the same place on each card?

_____

_____

(continued on next page)

**10.** Does the stack use sound or video? Is it used in a way that helps to convey the message of the stack? Is it easy to access?

_____

_____

**11.** Is the stack interactive? How much does it require the user to participate?

_____

## Creating a Review Checklist

Now that you have reviewed stacks created by others, you are ready to create a checklist that you can use to evaluate each stack you build. The checklist can be used throughout the remaining lessons to complete a self-evaluation of your stacks.

**STEP·BY·STEP ⟹ 4.5**

**1.** Using the questions from the previous Step-by-Step, create a Stack Guidelines Checklist for designing your stacks.

**2.** Take the checklist and review the cards you created in your storyboard.

**3.** Make any changes or corrections that would improve your stack.

**4.** Save your storyboard and organizational chart to use in the next lesson.

# *Summary*

In this lesson, you learned that:

■ The preparation and planning of a stack are critical to producing a good, informative project.

■ Two tools to use in planning a stack are a storyboard and an organizational chart.

■ There are a variety of ways to decide on a topic.

■ Once you have decided on a topic, it is important to do the research to support your choice.

■ Most stacks have a Title card, a Main Menu card, and subtopic cards.

■ The elements included on a card can be a variety of text, graphics, buttons, icons, video, and sound.

- Well-designed multimedia projects let the graphics do the work of the text whenever possible.

- It is not good to crowd too much text on a card.

- The navigation should be user-friendly and provide the user with choices about where to go in the stack.

- Evaluating other stacks helps you learn how to improve your own stacks.

## VOCABULARY

Component cards                 Navigation

Flow chart                      Organizational chart

Hypermedia                      Storyboard

Main Menu card                  Subtopic cards

Metaphor                        Title card

## LESSON 4 REVIEW QUESTIONS

### TRUE/FALSE

**Circle the T if the statement is true or F if it is false.**

T  F  **1.** The first phase of stack design is organization.

T  F  **2.** When researching a topic, it is important to verify source information.

T  F  **3.** The Title card should have buttons to access the subtopic cards.

T  F  **4.** The Main Menu card should have a Home button.

T  F  **5.** Navigation is a key element in stack design.

T  F  **6.** When designing a storyboard, it is best to include the actual graphics that will be on the card.

## SHORT ANSWER QUESTIONS

**Answer the questions below in the space provided.**

1. Name five elements of a HyperStudio card.

   a.

   b.

   c.

   d.

   e.

2. What is a storyboard and how is it used for stack design?

3. Compare a storyboard to an organizational chart. What are the similarities? What are the differences?

4. Define a metaphor and give some examples of possible metaphors you might use in designing a stack.

5. What is the metaphor used in Figure 4-4?

## MULTIPLE CHOICE

**Circle the letter of the item that best completes the following statements.**

1. The Title card should include:
   **A.** stack name
   **B.** the author's name
   **C.** relevant graphics
   **D.** all of the above

2. The Main Menu card
   **A.** should set the tone for the stack
   **B.** is usually the first card in the stack
   **C.** generally lists the subtopics
   **D.** A and C but not B

3.  When researching a topic, you
    **A.** should consider the requirements for the project
    **B.** may brainstorm with friends
    **C.** may use the Internet
    **D.** all of the above

4.  Navigation in a hypermedia program
    **A.** depends on the topic
    **B.** is always with buttons
    **C.** is sometimes with text
    **D.** is always with graphics

5.  Text on a page
    **A.** is not a good idea
    **B.** should not fill the entire page
    **C.** should not be combined with graphics
    **D.** should fill the entire page

6.  From the Main Menu card, you should be able to:
    **A.** return Home
    **B.** quit
    **C.** access subtopic cards
    **D.** all of the above

7.  When creating buttons,
    **A.** placement on the card is not important
    **B.** they do not need to be consistent
    **C.** you should design them after you have designed the rest of the stack
    **D.** all of the above

8.  When reviewing a hypermedia stack, you should evaluate
    **A.** the navigation
    **B.** the way the text is used
    **C.** the general tone of the stack
    **D.** all of the above

## LESSON 4 PROJECT 4.1

### STACK DESIGN—INTERNET SAFETY

**The Lesson 4 projects are exercises that use paper or index cards. You will not use HyperStudio to complete these projects.**

You have been asked to create a stack for a local school. The topic is Internet Safety. You will have to research the topic. Then you will use either paper or index cards to create the storyboard and organizational structure for the stack.

1. Decide on a theme or metaphor for the stack. Write a description of the metaphor.

2. Research the available resources for this topic, and identify graphics, video, and sounds that you may want to use. List potential resources.

3. Create the storyboard and organizational chart.

4. Design your Title card. Include relevant information and navigation.

5. Design your Main Menu card. Include relevant information and navigation.

6. Design the subtopic cards. Include relevant information and navigation.

7. Fill in the appropriate graphics, navigation and text on your storyboard.

8. Review your storyboard using the Stack Guidelines Checklist that you created in Step-by-Step 4.5.

9. Have someone else review your storyboard and organizational chart.

10. Make appropriate changes.

## LESSON 4 PROJECT 4.2

### STACK DESIGN

1. Decide on a topic for a HyperStudio stack.

2. Research the topic and write some of the areas you would like to cover in this project.

3. Decide on the theme or metaphor for the stack. Include it in your notes.

4. Create the storyboard and organizational chart for the stack.

5. Design the Title card including relevant information and navigation.

6. Design the Main Menu card including relevant information and navigation.

7. Design the subtopic cards including relevant information and navigation.

8. Draw in the appropriate graphics, navigation, and text in a detailed storyboard.

9. Review your storyboard using the Stack Guidelines Checklist that you created in Step-by-Step 4.5.

**10.** Have someone else review your storyboard and organizational chart.

**11.** Make appropriate changes.

## CRITICAL THINKING ACTIVITY

Using an outline or list, describe the steps for a systematic plan for researching a topic. Write a list of criteria that would help you decide how to determine if this topic were feasible for you. Write a list of research sources that would provide good sources of information.

# DESIGNING A FIVE-CARD PROJECT

## OBJECTIVES

**Upon completion of this lesson, you will be able to:**

- Access and utilize the Objects menu.

- Execute copy, paste, and cut commands.

- Insert text fields.

- Format text in a text field.

- Create buttons.

- Create icons as buttons.

- Develop a five-card HyperStudio stack from design to execution.

**⏱ Estimated Time: 1.5 hours**

## *Developing a Five-Card Project*

The previous lesson gave you some experience with planning a stack. Your storyboard and organizational chart have defined the plan. By the end of this lesson, you will have the skills you need to execute your design. However, before you can complete the stacks you designed, you will need to learn how to create and integrate objects such as buttons and text fields.

In this lesson, you will learn new techniques and how to use some new tools. One of the tools you will need is the ability to create buttons. As we discussed in earlier lessons, buttons enable your user to navigate through the stack.

You will also learn some techniques that will save you time and help your button placement to be consistent. These techniques are copy, paste, and cut. This is the time when all of the planing will really pay off as you begin your stack.

## *The Objects Menu*

In your storyboard, you included buttons for navigation. To add buttons, you will use the Objects menu from the menubar. The Objects menu allows you to add objects to the stack. It also gives you access to information about a card in the stack or about the stack in general. (See Figure 5-1.)

For instance, if you want to know the number of the card you are on, you can choose About this Card from the menu. You will see the window that appears in Figure 5-2.

From this window, you can see where the card is in the stack (About Card - 1), assign the card a name, and see how much memory the card takes. (This entire card uses 144K.) You can make things happen just by arriving at, clicking on, or leaving the card. You can also change card settings and define how the cursor will look. You will learn about these options in a later lesson.

By choosing About this Stack, you can access information about the stack, as shown in Figure 5-3. For instance, you can find out the number of cards in the stack, the number of colors available for the stack, and the size of the cards. You can also make some of the same choices about arriving at, clicking on, or leaving the stack as you can about a single card. The shape of the cursor can also be chosen. See Figure 5-3. You will be working with the stack you created in Lesson 3 as you learn to use the Objects menu.

**FIGURE 5-1**
Objects Menu

**FIGURE 5-2**
About Card Window

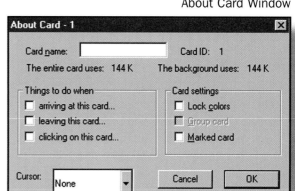

**FIGURE 5-3**
About Stack Window

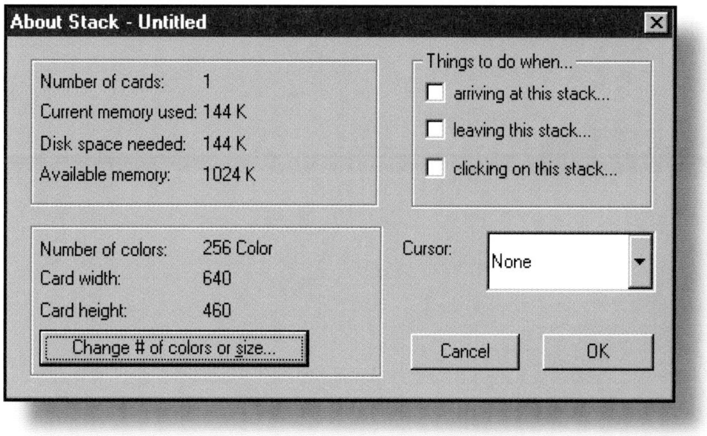

1. Open HyperStudio.

2. Open your **USA** stack.

3. Pull the tool palette to the side of your card.

4. From the Edit menu, choose **New Card**. You will see a blank card.

5. Pull down the Objects menu and choose **About this Stack**. Notice that there are two cards in the stack.

6. Click **OK**.

7. From the Objects menu, choose **About this Card**. Notice the information on the card.

8. Click **OK**.

9. Leave your stack open.

There are several ways to move from card to card in your stack. You can add buttons to move from card to card. You can choose from the Move menu on the menubar. (See Figure 5-4.) You can also use a keyboard shortcut to override the buttons or to move about the stack before you add buttons.

**FIGURE 5-4**
Move Menu

**HINT:**

Macintosh users will have a similar menu substituting ⌘ for Ctrl.

🚩 **TIP**

- To move one card left: Macintosh users press ⌘ + <; Windows users press **Ctrl + <**.

- To move one card right: Macintosh users press ⌘ + >; Windows users press **Ctrl + >**.

- To move to the first card of the stack: Macintosh users press ⌘ + **1**; Windows users press **Ctrl + 1**.

- To move to the last card of the stack: Macintosh users press ⌘ + **9**; Windows users press **Ctrl + 9**.

## STEP-BY-STEP ⟹ 5.2

1. Pull down the Move menu.

2. Choose **Previous Card**.

3. Pull down the Move menu again.

4. Choose **Next Card**. You should be back on Card 2, the blank card you just inserted.

5. From the keyboard, choose the keys to move to the next card and back again.

6. With your stack on Card 2, leave your stack open for the next Step-by-Step.

# *Adding Buttons*

In your storyboard, some buttons were designed to move the user to the next card, while other buttons moved the user to other places. The appearance of the buttons should indicate the action they are supposed to perform. For instance, if you want your button to go to the next card, you could put an arrow pointing to the right to indicate to move forward, or to the next card. Or you could also place text on the button indicating the action it will perform.

Buttons are not only used for navigation. You can use buttons to show hidden objects on your card. If you include a button that accesses a QuickTime movie, the button could include an icon, such as a picture of a movie projector and the name "Play Movie." Buttons with icons may also be used to access hidden text or a hidden picture when the user clicks on the button.

Buttons that have the same jobs on each card should be in the same places from card to card. This will ensure that your interface is user-friendly and easy to navigate.

## STEP-BY-STEP ⟹ 5.3

1. From the Objects menu, choose **Add a Button**. You will see the Button Appearance window, as shown in Figure 5-5.

2. Be sure that Show Name and Highlight are selected. Key **Previous** in the Name box.

3. Click on **Icons**.

4. You will see a window of icons. Select the icon with the hand pointing left, as shown in Figure 5-6.

5. Click **OK**.

6. The Button Appearance window is displayed again. Click **OK**.

(continued on next page)

**7.** The button **Previous** is displayed in the middle of the screen on the blank card surrounded by red "marching ants." With your cursor in the middle of the button, move the button to the bottom left corner.

**TIP**

Be sure to keep the cursor in the middle of the "marching ants." If you click outside of the "ants," you will not have a chance to move your button. If you make this mistake, click **Cancel** and start over. In a later lesson, you will learn how to modify button placement and actions.

**8.** Click on the card outside of the "marching ants." You will see the Actions window, as shown in Figure 5-7.

**9.** Choose **Previous card** in the Places to Go column.

**FIGURE 5-5**
Button Appearance Window, Previous

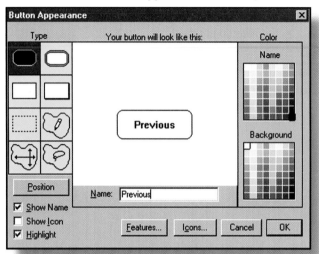

**FIGURE 5-6**
Button Icons Window

**FIGURE 5-7**
Actions Window

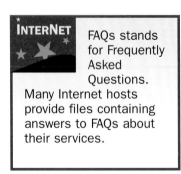

**INTERNET**
FAQs stands for Frequently Asked Questions. Many Internet hosts provide files containing answers to FAQs about their services.

10. You will the see the Transitions window, Figure 5-8. Choose **Diagonal right**. Leave the default speed **Fast**.

11. Click **Try it** to see the effect.

12. Click **OK**.

13. From the Actions window (Figure 5-7), click **Done**.

14. Your card should look like Figure 5-9. From the tool palette, click on the Browse tool, to return to the Browse mode.

15. Leave your stack open.

**FIGURE 5-8**
Transitions Window

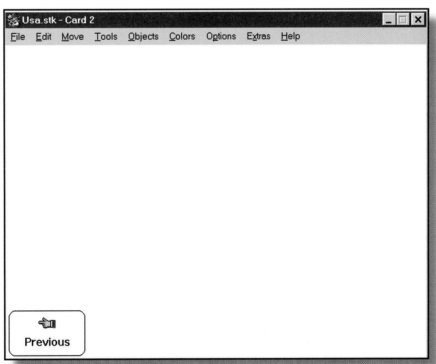

**FIGURE 5-9**
Previous Button on Card 2

**TIP**

It is important to return to the Browse mode after working with tools on the tool palette. If you do not return to the Browse mode, you will not be able to use your buttons or key text. Some of your actions will not work unless you are in this mode. You can tell when you are in Browse mode because your cursor will look like the hand icon on the tool palette.

# *Maintaining Button Consistency*

In most situations, when you have a Previous button, you will also have a Next button. This allows the user to move back and forth between the cards. In addition to consistent button placement, it is important that the appearance of the buttons match. For example, if you are using an arrow to go to the previous card, you generally will use a matching arrow, pointing in the opposite direction, to go to the next card. Keep this in mind as you complete the projects for this lesson when you implement your storyboard.

## STEP-BY-STEP ⟹ 5.4

**FIGURE 5-10**
Creating Next Button

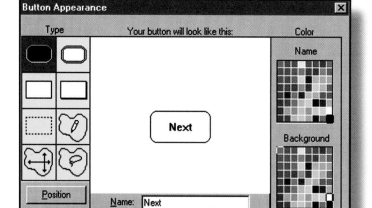

1. With your USA stack open to the second card, click the **Previous** button. This should bring you to the first card in your stack, the Title card.

2. Choose **Add a Button** from the Objects menu.

3. Name this button **Next**, as shown in Figure 5-10.

4. Click the Icons button.

5. Select the hand pointing to the right and click **OK**.

6. When you return to the Button Appearance window, click **OK**. (The boxes, Show Name, Show Icon, and Highlight should all be checked.)

7. Move your button to the bottom right corner.

8. Click outside of the "marching ants."

9. Choose **Next card** from the Actions window.

10. Choose **Diagonal right** and **Fast**.

11. Click **OK**.

 **TIP**

Another way to accomplish the positioning of the button is to choose Position in the Button Appearance window (Figure 5-10) and move the button where you want it placed on the card. After it is positioned, click outside the button and proceed with the steps.

**12.** Choose **Done**.

**13.** Your card should look like Figure 5-11.

**14.** Save your stack as **USA1**.

**15.** Leave your stack open.

**FIGURE 5-11**
Title Card with Next Button

# *The Button Tool*

In order to work with buttons once they have been created, you will need to use a new tool from the tool palette. This is the Button tool. (See Figure 5-12.) Located in the top section of the tool palette, the Button tool is located on the left side, just below the Browse tool. When you select this tool and click on a button with your cursor, red "marching ants" surround the button. This lets you know that the button is selected. Once it is selected, you can work with the button to change, copy, or move it. You can also use the Selection Arrow tool for editing buttons.

**FIGURE 5-12**
Tool Palette, Button Tool

Good layout design requires that buttons appear in the same place from card to card. A button that is even slightly off will look like it moves as you navigate to the next card. It gives a sloppy look to your interface design. A simple way to ensure that button placement is correct and the proper programming remains the same is to copy and paste buttons. When you copy a button, all of the characteristics (icons, name, and actions) are duplicated. When you paste a button on another card, it appears in the same place on the new card as the original button you copied. This helps your interface look attractive and clean.

# Copy, Paste, and Cut

These three commands are elementary techniques for working with most computer programs. Like many of the HyperStudio tools, they are common to many computer programs. If you have not used these commands before, you will certainly appreciate and use them again, not just in HyperStudio but in many other computer applications.

In the days when people relied on typewriters for word processing, you had to retype the entire page if you wanted to move a word or paragraph to another place. Now with the click of a few keys or a command from the menubar, you can duplicate and move whole passages of text. You can also copy pictures and objects and paste them in different locations.

The **Copy** command allows you to duplicate selected text, objects, pictures, or graphics. This command can save you time, for instance, if you are putting buttons on cards that will have exactly the same characteristics from card to card, the Copy command saves you the steps needed to create a new button.

**Paste** is the command that allows you to place the item you have copied or cut. To paste text, you place the cursor where you would like your duplicate to go and choose Paste. To paste other objects, you move to the card where the object will be placed and execute the command. You may paste an object on the same card, for example, if you need several circles on the card, you can create one circle, then copy and paste the circle. In this case, the pasted object will appear directly on top of the copied object. When you select the pasted object and move it, you will see the original object in its original location.

The **Cut** command removes the original object. It is different from the Copy command in that copying gives you an additional item along with the original. Cut removes the original object and allows you to either place it somewhere else or eliminate it. You use the Paste command with the Cut command to place the object or text in another location after you cut it. Cut does not duplicate the item. Once an object is cut, it remains in the computer's memory until it is pasted, another object is cut or copied, or the computer is shut down.

There are two ways to copy, paste, and cut. You can use the Edit menu or you can use the keyboard.

From the Edit menu (Figure 5-13), you can choose Cut button, Copy button, or Paste button. From the keyboard, you can choose:

- **Copy:** ⬛ + **C** (Macintosh); **Ctrl** + **C** (Windows)

- **Paste:** ⬛ + **V** (Macintosh); **Ctrl** + **V** (Windows)

- **Cut:** ⬛ + **X** (Macintosh); **Ctrl** + **X** (Windows)

**TIP**

Only the most recent object that was cut or copied is available to be pasted.

**FIGURE 5-13**
Edit Menu

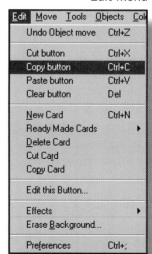

**S T E P - B Y - S T E P ⟹ 5.5**

1. With the **USA1** stack open to the Title card (Card 1) and your tool palette positioned along the side, choose the **Button** tool from the tool palette.

2. Click on the **Next** button to select it.

3. From the Edit menu, choose **Copy button**.

4. Using one of the techniques above, move to Card 2 in the stack.

5. From the Edit menu, choose **Paste button**. The Next button appears in the bottom right corner of Card 2 in the same place as the Next button on the Title card. Figure 5-14 shows the result.

6. Return to the Browse mode and click on the buttons, going back and forth between the two cards. Notice that the Next buttons are in exactly the same position on both cards.

7. Save your stack.

8. Leave your stack open.

**TIP**

If you continue to press Next, you will loop through your stack and begin over.

**FIGURE 5-14**
Card 2 with Next Button Added

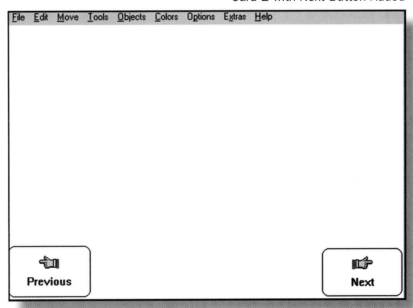

# Text Fields

In your storyboards you included areas for text. Now you will learn how to provide places for text on your cards. As you learned in Lesson 2, one way to add text to a card is by using the Text tool from the tool palette. The other way to add text to your HyperStudio stack is to create text fields and place them on your cards. Text fields can be any size and placed anywhere on the card. In addition, you can have more than one text field on a card. You can select the font's color, type, size, style, and alignment. You can also choose a background color for the text.

When you have sentences or passages of text, it is advisable to use text fields. Like a word processing program, you can easily edit the text in text fields. This is unlike the Text tool, which is "painted" and permanent. Text fields can be copied and pasted to other cards. HyperStudio allows you to include text you have previously written in a word processing program or other writing application. You are also able to include text from other resources such as the Internet or reference CD-ROMs. This can be done by copying the text in the original program and pasting it in a text field. You may lose some of the formatting, such as tabs, font size or style, or bullets, but you can replace the formatting after the selection has been pasted.

As you work with text field objects in the next Step-by-Step, keep in mind the possibilities of the text appearance so that you will have a good idea how you want the text to look when you implement your storyboards.

## STEP-BY-STEP ⟹ 5.6

1. Go to Card 2 in your USA1 stack.

2. From the Objects menu, choose **Add a Text Object**. You will see a square in the center of your card with red "marching ants" around it. With your cursor in the middle of the square, move the square across to the right side of the card, midway between the top and bottom.

3. Click outside the square when you have placed your text field in the position you want.

4. You will now see the Text Appearance window. Remove the check marks in the Draw scroll bar box and the Scrollable box so that only Draw frame is checked. (See Figure 5-15.)

**FIGURE 5-15**
Text Appearance Window

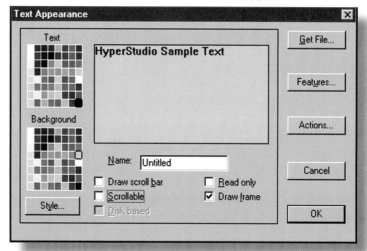

**5.** Click the **Style** button. The Text Style window appears, as shown in Figure 5-16.

**6.** Choose the font **Arial**, size **18**, and align **Center**. (Figure 5-16 shows the Windows version. The Macintosh window varies slightly.)

**7.** Select **black** as the text color, and select a **light blue** as the background.

**8.** Click **OK**.

**9.** This returns you to the Text Appearance window. Click **OK**.

**10.** Your screen should look like Figure 5-17.

**11.** With the cursor in the blue text field, key **Sports** and then press **Enter** twice. On the next line key, **In (your state), you can enjoy many sports from (name a sport) to (name another sport)**. See the example in Figure 5-18.

**12.** Save your stack as **Personal**.

**13.** Keep your stack open.

**NOTE:**

To select or deselect any checkbox item, simply click on the appropriate checkbox. An item is selected when the check appears and deselected when the box is empty.

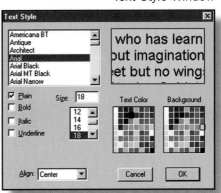

**FIGURE 5-16**
Text Style Window

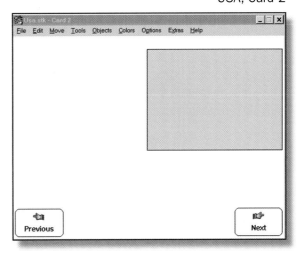

**FIGURE 5-17**
USA, Card 2

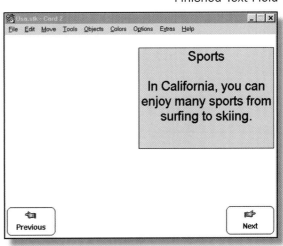

**FIGURE 5-18**
Finished Text Field

# Copying Cards

Just as you are able to copy buttons and maintain their characteristics, you can copy cards that have the same attributes. When you copy a card, you copy all of the buttons, fields, and graphics that are on the card. This is a great way to keep your interface user-friendly and consistent. Once a card is copied, you can change the text in the fields but maintain the same text color, font, background color, and text field position.

## STEP-BY-STEP ⟹ 5.7

1. With your **Personal** stack open, choose **Copy Card** from the Edit menu.

2. From the Edit menu, choose **Paste card**. You should now have three cards in your stack. The new card will look just like Card 2 but will have Personal-Card 3 at the top.

3. With your cursor, highlight all of the text in the text field on Card 3. (You may need to select the Browse tool before you can highlight the text.)

4. From the keyboard, press **Delete**.

5. Key **History**. Then press **Enter** twice.

6. On the next few lines key **(Your state) is famous for (name an historical event)**. See Figure 5-19 for an example.

7. Save your stack.

8. Keep your stack open for the Challenge Activity.

**TIP**

When you paste a card, it is placed immediately after the card that appears on the screen.

**FIGURE 5-19**
Card 3, History

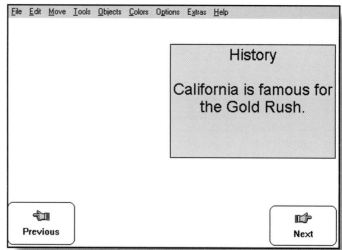

SCANS

## CHALLENGE ACTIVITY ⟫ 5.1

1. Using the tools you learned in the previous Step-by-Steps, add one more new card to the Personal stack. Use the title, "My Favorite Thing About (Your State)." Include a short phrase about one thing that you like about living in your state.

2. Save as **Person1** and close your stack.

# *Summary*

In this lesson, you learned that:

■ You can use the Objects menu to create buttons.

■ You can use the Objects menu to create text fields.

■ The Copy, Paste and Cut commands can be used in interface design to save time and ensure consistency.

■ You can format text fields.

■ You can create buttons that display names and icons.

■ You can select button actions.

■ You can create icons as buttons.

■ You can develop a five-card HyperStudio stack from design to execution.

■ You can navigate through a stack using the keyboard.

■ You can navigate through a stack using the Move menu.

## VOCABULARY

Alignment

Font

Interface

QuickTime movie

User-friendly

Word processing

### TRUE/FALSE

**Circle the T if the statement is true or F if it is false.**

**T   F**   **1.** A button can have a name with no icon.

**T   F**   **2.** A button can have an icon with no name.

**T   F**   **3.** The Transitions window decides the button's actions.

**T   F**   **4.** The Transitions window decides the style and font in a text field.

**T   F**   **5.** Choosing New Card from the Edit menu places the new card at the end of the stack.

**T   F**   **6.** The appearance of a button should match its action.

**T   F**   **7.** When you copy a button, the position of the button is up to you.

### SHORT ANSWER QUESTIONS

SCANS

**Answer the questions below in the space provided.**

**1.**   What are three ways to navigate through a stack?

    **a.**

    **b.**

    **c.**

**2.**   Why is it important for buttons to be consistent?

**3.**   Name two ways to copy text or buttons.

    **a.**

    **b.**

4. Choosing About this Card from the Objects menu will tell you:

5. Why use About this Stack from the Objects menu?

6. Why do you need to return to Browse mode after working with tools on the tool palette?

7. Name three things you can customize in a text field:

   a.

   b.

   c.

8. Describe how you copy a card in a stack.

9. Describe how you copy and paste buttons.

## LESSON 5 PROJECT 5.1

Now that you have learned how to add buttons and text fields and create consistent interface design, you are ready to apply the storyboards from Lesson 4 to actual stacks.

1. Using the storyboard and organizational chart you created in Lesson 4, Project 4-1, execute the stack for Internet Safety. Don't forget to leave space for graphics.

2. Include the following:

   ■ At least three text fields.

   ■ At least three graphic placeholders.

   ■ Navigation buttons from the Title card to the Main Menu card.

   ■ Navigation buttons from the Main Menu card to the subtopic cards.

   ■ Navigation buttons from the subtopic cards back to the Main Menu card.

3. Save the stack as **Safety1**.

4. Compare it to your Stack Guidelines Checklist. Make any changes.

5. Print the stack.


## LESSON 5 PROJECT 5.2

1. Using the storyboard and organizational chart you created in Lesson 4, Project 4-2, create a new stack. Include appropriate buttons and text fields. Don't forget to leave space for graphics.

2. Include the following:

   ■ At least three text fields.

   ■ At least three graphic placeholders.

   ■ Navigation buttons from the Title card to the Main Menu card.

   ■ Navigation buttons from the Main Menu card to the subtopic cards

   ■ Navigation buttons from the subtopic cards back to the Main Menu card.

3. Name the stack **MyTopic1**.

4.  Compare it to your Stack Guidelines Checklist. Make any changes.

5.  Print your stack.

### CRITICAL THINKING ACTIVITY

You are assigned a project to create a HyperStudio stack that interprets a very long poem. You wish to include the entire poem, which takes up three pages of text in a printed book. How would you use text and graphics to present the poem? Draw some examples of the ideas that you have in storyboard format.

# Review of Procedures

**⏱ Estimated Time: 3 hours**

**Planning a stack**
1. Decide on a topic.
2. Draw a storyboard.
3. Draw a flowchart or organizational chart.

Common items recommended for a stack are:
Title card
Main Menu card
Topic cards
Subtopic cards, if applicable
Navigation for the stack

**Adding a button**
1. From the Objects menu, select Add a Button.
2. Name the button.
3. Select icon, if desired.
4. Place the button on the card.
5. Select the button action.
6. Select the transition and speed.
7. Test the transition.

**About this card**
From the Objects menu, select About this Card.

**Adding a new card**
From the Edit menu, select New Card.

**Copy**
From the Edit menu, select Copy.
**Windows:**
From the keyboard, press **Ctrl + C**.
**Macintosh:**
From the keyboard, press **⌘ + C**.

**Paste**
From the Edit menu, select Paste.
**Windows:**
From the keyboard, press **Ctrl + V**.
**Macintosh:**
From the keyboard, press **⌘ + V**.

**Cut**
From the Edit menu, select Cut.
**Windows:**
From the keyboard, press **Ctrl + X**.
**Macintosh:**
From the keyboard, press **⌘ + X**.

**Add a text object**
1. From the Objects menu, select Add a Text Object.
2. Place the text object on the card.
3. Click outside the object.
4. Select the appropriate Text Appearance information.
5. Select the font type, size, colors, and alignment.
6. Return to Browse mode and key the text.

## FILL IN THE BLANKS

**Complete the following statements by keying or writing the correct answers on a page to be submitted to your instructor. Center *Unit 2 Review Questions* at the top of the page. Number your answers to match the numbers listed here.**

1. A stack should have these two cards: a _____ card and a _____ card.

2. _____ is a key element in stack design.

3. Two organizational tools used to design stacks are _____ and _____ .

4. To add a button to a card, you would choose Add a Button from the _____ menu.

5. To get information about a card, you would choose _____ from the Objects menu.

6. To copy, you can choose Copy from the _____ menu or you can press

   _____ from the keyboard.

7. When creating a text object, you can choose the font _____ , the font

   _____ and the font _____ .

8. A button's appearance can have a name and an _____ , if you choose.

9. The Transitions window is used when creating _____ actions.

10. When you add a new card to a stack, it will go directly _____ the card you are on.

## WRITTEN QUESTIONS

**Key or write your answers to the following questions. Number your answers. Use complete sentences and good grammar.**

11. What is a storyboard and why is it a useful tool?

12. What are the general rules of navigation for the Main Menu card and the Title card?

13. Name two button actions.

    a.

    b.

14. What should be included on a Title card?

15. What method would you use to have the same button on more than one card?

## UNIT 2 APPLICATIONS

### UNIT 2 PROJECT

1. Choose a topic that interests you.

2. Create a storyboard for a five-card stack on your topic. Draw appropriate graphics for your cards.

3. Create a flowchart for your stack.

4. Create the stack. (You will not insert the graphics at this time.) Include the following:

- Title card

- Main Menu card

- Three topic cards

- Text objects for the topic cards with key information about the topic.

- Buttons to navigate through the stack. (Copy and paste the buttons that have the same functions.)

5. Save the stack as **EP2**.

## UNIT 2 CRITICAL THINKING ACTIVITY

List some of the problems in creating a stack that can be avoided by using a storyboard.

# CUSTOMIZING YOUR STACKS

## UNIT 3

# DESIGN FUNCTIONS AND TECHNIQUES

## OBJECTIVES

**Upon completion of this lesson, you will be able to:**

■ Use the Text Object and Button tools on the tool palette.

■ Edit buttons.

■ Create transitions.

■ Edit text fields.

🕐 **Estimated Time: 1 hour**

## *Design Functions*

Customizing a stack is the way you place your particular imprint on a stack. If everyone in the class were given the same topic, the same tools, and the same amount of time, all of the projects would look different, have variations in the information provided, and have a different style. The process is similar to writing a book report. All learners would have read the same book, but each report would differ because each author creates a unique product.

You have learned how to create text fields and buttons, but sometimes you may change your mind while working on a project, or you may get a new idea and want to modify your stack to accommodate it. The ability to edit text, buttons, objects, and even graphics allows you to work creatively.

## STEP-BY-STEP ▷ 6.1

1. Using the storyboard you created in Step-by-Step 4.1 as your planning tool, create a new stack.

2. Import the **worldmap.bmp** background for your Title card. (See Figure 6-1.) The file is located in the HSArt folder.

3. Double click on the **Text** tool and select the font **Arial**, size **26**. Click **OK**.

4. Enter the following text. Use Figure 6-1 as a sample.

**My Country**
**Created by**
**(Key your name here)**

**5.** Create a new card. This will be your Main Menu card.

**6.** Save your stack as **Country**.

**7.** Leave the stack open for the next Step-by-Step.

**FIGURE 6-1**
Country Title Card

STEP-BY-STEP ⇒ 6.2

**1.** With the Country stack open, go to the Title card.

**2.** From the Objects menu, choose **Add a Button**.

**3.** Name the button **Next**.

**4.** Click the **Icons** button.

**5.** Select the green button icon, as shown in Figure 6-2.

**FIGURE 6-2**
Green Button Icon

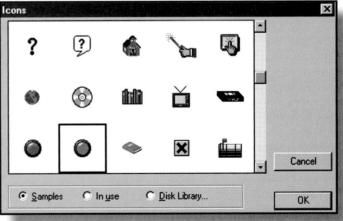

 **HINT:**

You may need to use the scroll bar to locate the green button from the list of icons shown.

(continued on next page)

**6.** Click **OK**.

**7.** Choose **blue** for the background color and **white** for the name color.

**8.** Click **OK**. You may need to click **OK** again if an information window appears.

**9.** Move the button to the bottom right corner.

**10.** Move your cursor to the top left corner of the button. When the cursor changes to a double-headed arrow, click and drag to reduce the size of the button.

**11.** Click outside the button.

**12.** Choose **Next card** from the Actions window.

**13.** Choose **Dissolve** from the Transitions window.

**14.** Choose **Try It**.

**15.** Click **OK**.

**16.** Choose **Done**. Your completed card should be similar to Figure 6-3.

**17.** Save the **Country1** stack and leave it open.

**FIGURE 6-3**
Card with Button

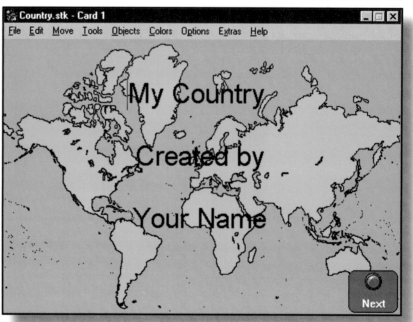

# *Using the Editing Tools from the Tool Palette*

The edit tools are located on the top portion of the tool palette, as shown in Figure 6-4.

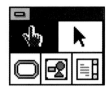

**FIGURE 6-4**
Edit Tools Palette

The top row contains the Browse and Selection Arrow (Edit) tools. You use the Browse tool, shown as the hand icon, to navigate through a stack. The Selection Arrow (Edit) tool, shown as the arrow icon, is used when you need to move or edit buttons, graphics, and text fields. When the Browse tool is selected, you are in Browse mode. You will need to be in this mode for the button actions to work.

The second row contains the Button tool, the Graphic Object tool, and the Text Object tool. As you learned in the last lesson, when you choose the Button tool, you can select buttons and work with them. The Graphic Object and Text Object tools have similar functions. The Text Object tool allows you to select and edit text fields. When the Button, Text Object, Graphics Object or Selection Arrow tools are selected, you are in Edit mode. This means you can change, delete, or move objects.

 **TIP**

A text field must exist before you can use the Text Object tool. **You must be in the Browse mode to key text into a text field.** The cursor changes from a hand icon to an I-beam when you are in a text field and can enter text.

 **STEP-BY-STEP 6.3**

**1.** With your Country1 stack open, use the **Next** button to move to the next card, which will become the Main Menu card.

**2.** Insert a text object, accepting the default settings. Choose **light blue** for the letters and **dark blue** for the background.

**3.** Click on the **Style** button. Set your field for **Arial**, size **24**, and **Bold**.

**4.** Key **MAIN MENU** into the text field. Your text object should resemble Figure 6-5.

(continued on next page)

**TIP**

You can return to the Browse tool with a keyboard shortcut: **Shift + Tab** for Windows users and ⌘ **+ Tab** for Macintosh users.

**5.** You will edit the text field to make it more attractive. From the tool palette, select the **Text Object** tool.

**6.** Click anywhere inside the Main Menu text field. You will see the red "ants" surrounding the field, as shown in Figure 6-6.

**7.** Double-click in the text field. Remove the checks from Draw scroll bar, Scrollable, and Draw frame.

**8.** Click the **Style** button. Change the size of the font to **36**, choose **Center** for alignment, and click **OK** twice.

**9.** Choose the **Text Object** tool.

**10.** Select the text field by clicking one time inside the field.

**11.** Move your pointer to the bottom right corner. Move your pointer until the cursor changes into a double-headed arrow.

**12.** Place the cursor in the corner and drag upwards, making the box shorter and wide enough so that the words Main Menu fit on one line.

**FIGURE 6-5**
First Main Menu Field

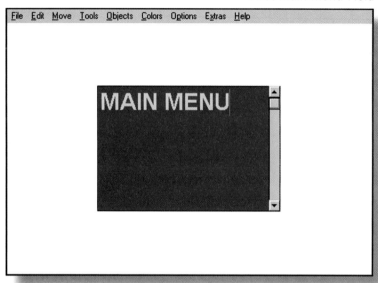

Text Object tool

**FIGURE 6-6**
Selected Text Field

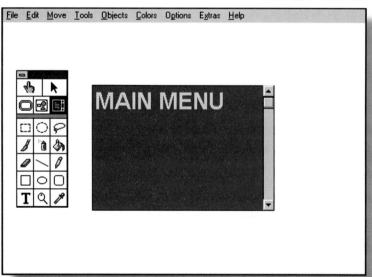

**13.** Now place the cursor in the center of the text field. Click and drag the field to the top center of the card. After completing this process, your Main Menu card should resemble Figure 6-7.

**14.** Save your stack.

**15.** Create a new text object. Click outside the text object. Deselect the default boxes for the type of text field (no scrolling, no frame). Select a **red** background and **black** text color.

**16.** Click the **Style** button. Arial should still be selected as the font. Choose a size of **24**, **Bold**, and **Left** alignment. Click **OK** twice.

**17.** Key in the title of the first subtopic card, **Government**.

**18.** Resize the field to fit the topic. Move the field under the heading, as shown in Figure 6-8.

**19.** Select the **Text Object** tool, if necessary.

**20.** Select the Government text field by clicking once on it.

**21.** From the Edit menu, choose **Copy text field**. (For Macintosh, the command is **Copy text object**.)

(continued on next page)

**FIGURE 6-7**
Resized Text Field

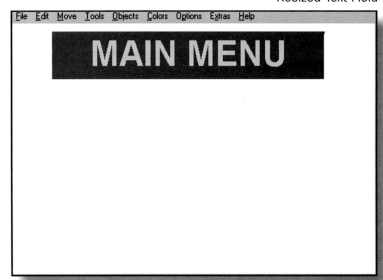

**FIGURE 6-8**
Government Text Field

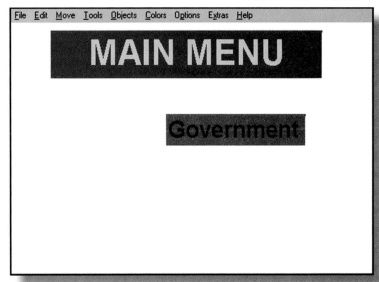

**22.** From the Edit menu, choose **Paste text field**. (For Macintosh, the command is **Paste text object**.)

**23.** The copy will be on top of the original. Drag the copied Government text field below the original.

**24.** From the Edit menu, choose **Paste text field** again.

**25.** Drag the copy below the second text field. All three should be lined up in a column, as shown in Figure 6-9.

**26.** With your cursor in Browse mode, highlight and key the second subtopic card name, **History**. Do the same for the third subtopic card, **Wildlife**.

**27.** Click on the **Text Object** tool and double click the **History** text field.

**28.** Change the background color to **green** and leave the text color black. Change the alignment to **Center**. Do not make any other changes.

**29.** Change the Wildlife field to a **pink** background with **black**, **centered** text. Your results should be similar to those shown in Figure 6-10.

**30.** Save your stack as **Country2**.

**31.** Leave your stack open.

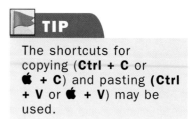

**TIP**

The shortcuts for copying (**Ctrl + C** or ⌘ **+ C**) and pasting (**Ctrl + V** or ⌘ **+ V**) may be used.

**FIGURE 6-9**
Pasted Text Fields

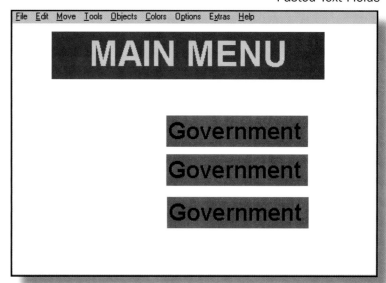

**HINT:**

Click on the Style button to change the alignment.

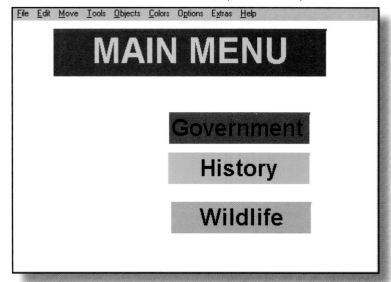

**FIGURE 6-10**
Main Menu with Completed Subtopic Text Fields

# *Transitions*

Y ou already have some experience using transitions to go from card to card in the Country stack. Transitions are special animation effects that appear when you leave a card. HyperStudio includes a list of transitions. As you may have noticed, some transitions move from right to left and some move from left to right. When selecting a transition, think about the direction you are moving the user. For example, a common transition for a Next button is the left to right transition. Likewise, a common transition for a Previous button is the right to left transition.

There are variable speeds for transitions: fast, medium, and slow. You can experiment with different transitions at different speeds to see the effects. As with most of the design aspects of creating a multimedia project, consistency is an important factor. The same buttons should have the same transitions; for example, all of the Next buttons should have the same transitions.

# *Creating Nonlinear Buttons*

N ext you will create the subtopic cards and the buttons to move to each of them. So far, the buttons you have created have been linear, going in order from one card to the next. The buttons you will work with in this section will not be linear. They will allow you to move to a card that is not the next or the previous card. This is one of the innovative aspects of HyperStudio. It gives the stack's author a wide range of opportunities in creating a stack. Imagine some of the projects or games you can create with this capability. The nonlinear buttons on this card will move the user from the Main Menu card to each of the subtopic cards and return them to the Main Menu card.

# STEP-BY-STEP ⟹ 6.4

1. With your Country2 stack open to the Main Menu card, add three new cards to your stack.

2. Create a text field on the first new card (Card 3 in your stack).

3. Double click in the text field. Remove the checks from **Scrollable**, **Draw scroll bar**, and **Draw frame**. Match the **red** background and **black** text color to the text field for Government on the Main Menu card.

4. Click the **Style** button. Make the text **Arial**, size **36**, **Plain**.

5. Key **GOVERNMENT**.

6. Using the Text Object tool, size the field to fit the topic letters and place the text field at the top center of the card, as shown in Figure 6-11.

7. From the Edit menu, choose **Copy text field**.

8. Move to the next blank card using the keyboard shortcut or **Move** menu.

9. From the Edit menu, choose **Paste text field**.

10. Repeat Steps 7 through 9 for the last subtopic card.

11. Replace Government with the appropriate subtopic name for each card. Change the background color and text color to match the text fields on the Main Menu card.

**FIGURE 6-11**
Economics Subtopic Card

12. Save your stack.

13. Return to the Main Menu card. (This should be Card 2 in your stack.)

 **TIP**

If Card 2 is not the Main Menu card, move to the unwanted card, select Delete Card from the Edit menu, and repeat steps 1 through 13 of Step-by-Step 6.4.

14. From the Objects menu, choose **Add a Button**.

15. Highlight and delete the **New Button** from the Name field.

16. Uncheck the **Show Name** box.

17. Choose the **red** background color to match the text field.

(continued on next page)

**18.** Click **OK**. You may need to click **OK** again in response to a dialog box.

**19.** Move the button to the left of the Government field on the Main Menu.

**20.** Use the double-headed arrow cursor to make the button smaller. Your results should look like Figure 6-12.

**21.** Click outside the button. From the Actions window, choose **Another card**.

**22.** When you see the Move to card window, as shown in Figure 6-13, click the **right arrow** until you reach the Government card. (NOTE: You should have to press the right arrow key only once.)

**23.** Click **OK** when you reach the correct card.

**24.** Choose **Iris open** from the Transitions window and **Medium** for speed. Choose **Try it** to see the effect.

**25.** Click **OK**.

**26.** Click **Done**.

**27.** Test your button.

**28.** Save your stack as **Country3**.

**29.** Leave your stack open.

**FIGURE 6-12**
Red Button

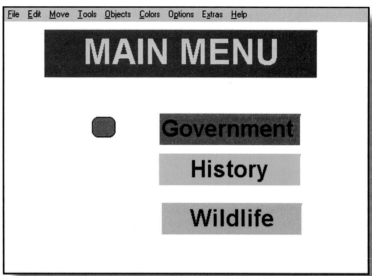

**FIGURE 6-13**
Move to Card Window

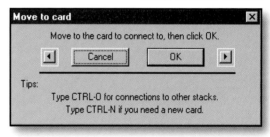

# Return Buttons

In any well-developed layout design, a consistent protocol allows users to choose how long they wish to participate in a stack, to make choices about where they want to go, and to quit in a reasonable way. Whenever you send users to a place with a button, you should always provide a way back to a central place or the place that they just left.

## STEP-BY-STEP 6.5

**1.** With the Country3 stack open, you should be on the subtopic card Government. Choose **Add a Button** from the Objects menu.

**2.** Name this button **Main Menu**. Select **Show Name**.

**3.** Click on the **Icons** button. Find the finger pressing a button icon as shown in Figure 6-14, and select it. If you do not have this icon as a default icon choice, then choose another one as your button icon.

**FIGURE 6-14**
Finger Pressing a Button Icon

**4.** Click **OK**.

**5.** Choose a **pale yellow** background and **black** for the button's name.

**6.** Place the button in the center bottom of the card and reduce the size. Be sure you can still see the name and the icon.

**7.** Choose **Another card** from the Actions window.

**8.** Press the left arrow until you return to the Main Menu card.

**9.** Click **OK**.

**10.** Choose **Iris close**, and speed **Medium** from the Transitions window.

**11.** Choose **Try it** to see the effect.

**12.** Click **OK**.

**13.** Click **Done**. Your card should look like Figure 6-15.

**14.** Save the stack.

**15.** Leave the stack open.

**FIGURE 6-15**
Main Menu Button

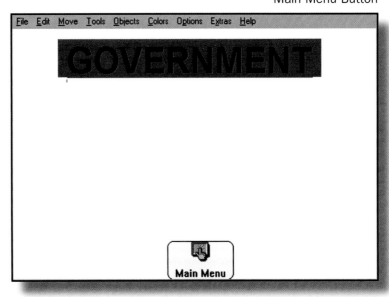

File  Edit  Move  Tools  Objects  Colors  Options  Extras  Help

GOVERNMENT

Main Menu

## CHALLENGE ACTIVITY ⟹ 6.1

SCANS

1. Select the **Button** tool. Use the Copy and Paste commands to copy the Main Menu button and then paste it on the two other subtopic cards.

2. Test your buttons. Make any corrections necessary.

3. When you are finished, return to the Main Menu card and save the stack as **Country4**.

4. Leave the stack open.

## STEP-BY-STEP ⟹ 6.6

SCANS

1. With the Country4 stack open to the Main Menu card, select the **Button** tool.

2. Select the red Government button.

3. From the Edit menu, choose **Copy button.**

4. From the Edit menu, choose **Paste button**.

5. Move the copied button to a space below the red button and adjacent to History.

6. Choose **Paste button** again and move the third button to the space next to Wildlife.

(continued on next page)

**7.** Using the **Button** tool, double-click the button next to History. Change the background to match the green History text field background.

**8.** Click on **Actions** from the Button Appearance window.

**9.** Click the selection box next to **Another card** even though it is already selected.

**10.** Use the arrows in the Move to Card window to find the History card. Click **OK** when you find it.

**11.** Do not change the transitions. Click **OK**.

**12.** Choose **Done**.

**13.** Test the button. Use the Main Menu button to return to the Main Menu.

**14.** Repeat steps 7 through 13 for the button to go to the Wildlife card. The Main Menu card should look like Figure 6-16.

**15.** Test all of your buttons.

**16.** Save the stack as **Country5**.

**17.** Leave the stack open.

Click Another card even though it already has a mark in the selection box. You must reselect it to change the card's action.

When editing buttons, you can bypass the Button Appearance window and go directly to the button actions by: holding down **Ctrl** while double-clicking on the button for Windows users or holding down  while double-clicking on the button for Macintosh users.

**FIGURE 6-16**
Completed Country Main Menu Card

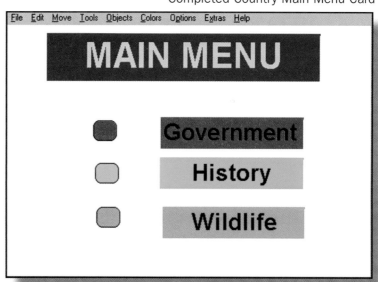

# Text Field Types

When you are using text fields, there are three types of fields from which you can choose. When you create a text field, you are given some choices about how that field will look. Figure 6-17 shows the choices you are given in the Text Appearance window.

Scrollable text fields are used when you need to provide more information than will fit on one card. When possible, it is best to break up the text into small segments that appear on several cards. However, there are times when you need to complete a thought or provide information that cannot be easily broken into small segments. Scrollable fields, such as the one shown in Figure 6-18, allow you to insert more text than can be viewed at one time. The person viewing the presentation uses the scroll bar to navigate through the text.

To create a scrollable text field, you must select the Scrollable option from the Text Appearance window. If this option is selected without selecting the Draw scroll bar option, users will only be able to view text using the keyboard to navigate through the text field. Also, no visual clue will be given to the user that more text is stored in the field. When the Draw scroll bar option is also selected, users can navigate through the text field using their mouse or keyboard, and they have a visual clue—the scroll bar—to let them know that not all of the text in the field appears on the screen.

The Draw frame option adds a border around the text field, as shown in Figure 6-19. You used this option in Lesson 5 to create frames around the text field on each card. Frames help define the boundaries of a text field. They are especially useful when the background of the card and the text field are the same or similar colors, and you want the text field to stand out as a separate element. Generally, you would choose to use a frame around the field for a specific look or design effect.

Removing the checks in all of the boxes will give you a text field with no frame that appears as if it is floating on the screen, as shown in Figure 6-20.

The Read only option is used when you do not want your user to be able to change the text on a card. It is best not to use this option until you are finished with your project. Otherwise, you may have to unlock each text field before being able to make changes or corrections.

**FIGURE 6-17**
Text Field Types

**FIGURE 6-18**
Scrollable Text Field

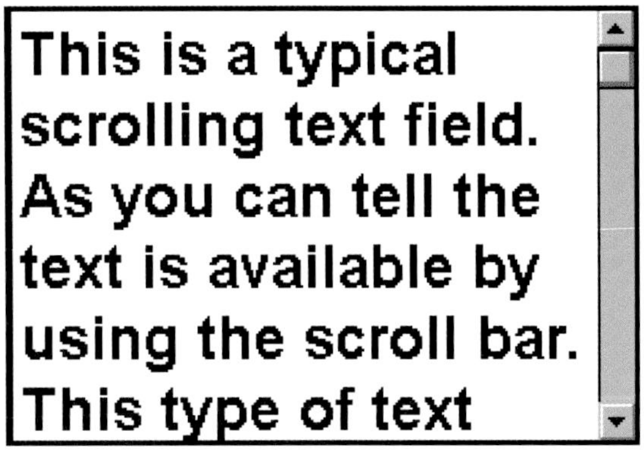

This is a typical scrolling text field. As you can tell the text is available by using the scroll bar. This type of text

**FIGURE 6-19**
Text Field with a Frame

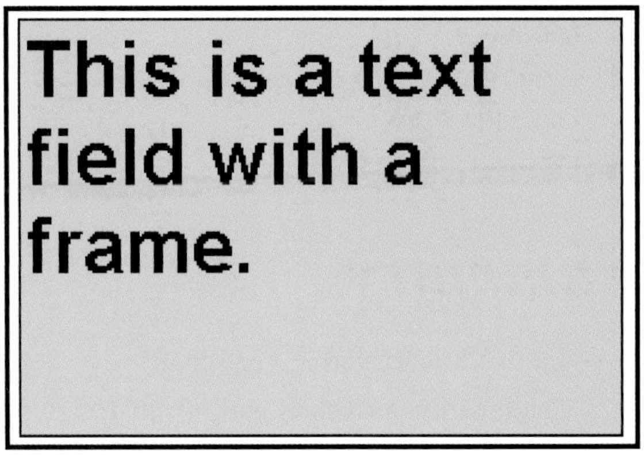

This is a text field with a frame.

**FIGURE 6-20**
Text Field with No Frame

**TIP**

You can tell that there is a text field on a card when your Browse tool turns from a hand icon into an I-beam for keying in text. This cursor change will not occur if you select Read only.

This text field has no frame, if the background were white, you would not even know there was a text object here.

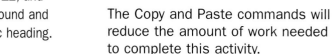

**CHALLENGE ACTIVITY ⟹ 6.2**

**SCANS**

1. On each subtopic card in the Country5 stack, create text fields that have a frame but are not scrollable. Use **Arial**, **Plain**, size **12**, and aligned **Left** for the text. The background and text color should match the subtopic heading. For now, use the title of the card as placeholder copy for your text field.

2. Save your stack as **Country6** when you are finished.

3. Close the stack.

✓ **HINT:**

The Copy and Paste commands will reduce the amount of work needed to complete this activity.

# *Summary*

In this lesson, you learned that:

- Customizing a stack is part of the design process.

- You can create transitions for buttons.

- You can use the edit tools from the tool palette to alter existing text fields.

- You can customize a text field using the Text Object tool.

- You can alter a text field by changing the size, position, font attributes, and background and text colors.

- Copying and pasting text fields creates a uniform look from card to card.

■ You can create nonlinear buttons.

■ You can edit buttons to change their appearance, size, position, and action.

■ You can copy and paste buttons to maintain a uniform appearance.

■ There are a variety of text field types: scrollable, nonscrollable, with frame, and without frame.

## VOCABULARY

Browse

Default settings

Nonlinear buttons

Protocol

Text fields

Transitions

## LESSON 6 REVIEW QUESTIONS

### TRUE/FALSE

**Circle the T if the statement is true or the F if it is false.**

T  F  **1.** A scrollable text field allows you to place large amounts of text on a card.

T  F  **2.** The Text Object tool is located on the tool palette.

T  F  **3.** You can change a button by using the Objects menu.

T  F  **4.** Only the Edit menu can be used for editing text and buttons.

T  F  **5.** Once you have created a text field, it cannot be changed.

T  F  **6.** You can use the cursor to resize a text field.

T  F  **7.** Nonlinear buttons go from card to card in sequential order.

T  F  **8.** Transitions are special effects.

T  F  **9.** All text fields are scrollable.

## COMPLETION

**Answer the questions below in the space provided.**

1.  How can you alter a button's appearance?

2.  Name and describe three types of text fields:

    **a.**

    **b.**

    **c.**

3.  Name three transition effects:

    **a.**

    **b.**

    **c.**

4.  Why would you use transitions?

5.  Why would you copy and paste a text field from one card to another?

6.  Name three ways you can modify a text field icon:

    **a.**

    **b.**

    **c.**

7. What is the process to copy and paste a button from one card to another?

8. What are nonlinear buttons? What is their purpose?

## LESSON 6 PROJECT 6.1

1. Open the stack **MyTopic1**. Insert or edit text fields and buttons to conform to the following guidelines :

   a. Create at least three nonlinear buttons.

   b. Provide a way back to the Main Menu from each subtopic card.

   c. Be sure all of your buttons work and are consistent.

   d. Use at least two button transitions you have not used before.

    **NOTE:**

   > Keep consistency in mind and decide what will best illustrate the theme of your cards.

   e. Use at least two types of text fields in your stack.

   f. Choose a consistent color palette for the text fields.

2. Save your stack as **MyTopic2**.

## LESSON 6 PROJECT 6.2

1. Open the stack **Safety1**. Insert or edit text fields and buttons to conform to the following guidelines:

   a. Create at least three nonlinear buttons.

   b. Provide a way back to the Main Menu from each subtopic card.

   c. Be sure all of your buttons work and are consistent.

   d. Use at least two button transitions you have not used before.

   e. Use at least two types of text fields in your stack.

   f. Choose a consistent color palette for the text fields.

2. Save your stack as **Safety2**.

## CRITICAL THINKING ACTIVITY

**Either form small groups or work independently on the following activity:**

1. List several types of HyperStudio projects that would require nonlinear buttons.

2. List the types of buttons that could be applied to two of the projects listed in Step 1.

# WORKING WITH GRAPHICS

## OBJECTIVES

**Upon completion of this lesson, you will be able to:**

- Insert graphics and clip art.
- Size graphics.
- Edit graphics.
- Change card sizes.
- Use the Graphic Object tool from the tool palette.
- Create icon actions.

⏱ **Estimated Time: 2 hours**

## *Working with Graphics and Clip Art*

Now that you have some experience with stacks this lesson will give you a dynamic tool to add to your creative projects. That tool is graphics. Graphics add a dimension to your work that will make your projects more exciting and innovative. Graphics allow you to not only tell your story better, but also give the user a better understanding and perhaps a better sense of your presentation.

Most things that you can explain or write about have a greater impact when a visual component is included. Certainly, the written word can be dynamic and important to spark imagination. However, with multimedia, it is a good game plan to use less text, make the text really count, and use visual means to express as much as you can. Let the pictures do the talking. Try to create a different language with the use of pictures and visual effects.

Graphics set the mood or tone for the piece. You can use graphics to get the user's attention, demonstrate what you have written, and involve the user in your piece. Another way to use graphics is to create backgrounds and borders for your stacks that not only keep your theme, but help organize the way you present your information.

In HyperStudio, there are several ways to use graphics. You can use the clip art and graphic objects that are included with the program in the HSArt folder. You can import graphics from other applications. You can scan in graphics on a scanner, and then import the file into HyperStudio. You can also create your own graphics using the tools in the tool palette and the range of paint colors and patterns included in the HyperStudio tools. In another lesson, you will learn to import graphics from other sources.

Since graphic objects and clip art function differently in HyperStudio, the following table lists the differences between these two items.

| CLIP ART | GRAPHIC OBJECTS |
|---|---|
| ■ Can only be edited when it first appears on the card. | ■ Can be edited at any time using the Selection Arrow tool or the Graphic Object tool. |
| ■ Becomes a permanent part of the background. | ■ Floats over the background. |
| ■ Can be animated. | ■ Can be assigned actions. |
| ■ Can be scaled and rotated. | ■ Can be used with the Hide/Show NBA. |
| ■ Can be used with Filter effects. | ■ Can be used in layered animations. |
| ■ Can be selected with selector tools but will alter the background if moved or changed. | ■ Can be deleted. |
| ■ Can be erased. | |

STEP-BY-STEP 7.1

1. Open the stack **Country6**.

2. Go to the first subtopic card, Government. Move and resize your text field so that it is on the right half of the card. See Figure 7-1.

3. From the **Objects** menu, choose **Add a Graphic Object**.

4. Choose **Disk file** from the "Where do you want to get your graphic?" window, as shown in Figure 7-2. Click **OK**.

5. Open the **HSArt** folder.

6. Double click on **Flags** from the HSArt folder.

7. You will see a page of flag icons, as shown in Figure 7-3. Scroll down the page and with your cursor in the + mode, select a flag using the **Square Selector** tool.

(continued on page 112)

 **HINT:**

You can choose any country of interest to you for this project.

**TIP**

Macintosh users may not be prompted with the "Where do you want to get your graphic" window. You should simply continue with Step 5.

 **HINT:**

If you don't get the entire flag selected on the first try, simply click outside the selected area and begin the selection process again.

**FIGURE 7-1**
Government Subtopic Card

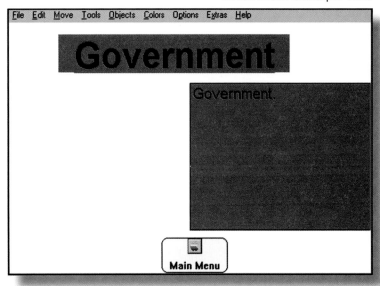

**FIGURE 7-2**
"Where do you want to get your graphic?" Window

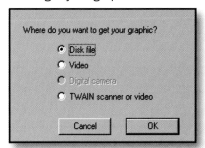

**FIGURE 7-3**
Flag Icons

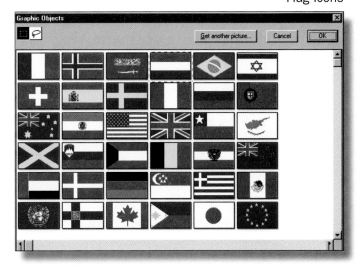

**8.** Click **OK**. If a dialog box appears, click **OK** again.

**9.** You will see the flag in the middle of your card surrounded by "red ants." Place your cursor in the center of the ants and move the icon to the middle of the left column.

**10.** With you cursor in the corner of the "ants," drag the icon and make it larger, as shown in Figure 7-4.

**11.** Click outside the graphic when you are satisfied with your placement, and click **OK** in the Graphic Appearance window. (See Figure 7-5.)

**12.** Using the **Line** tool from the tool palette, draw a flagpole along the left side of the flag, as shown in Figure 7-6.

**13.** Save your stack as **Country7**.

**14.** Leave your stack open.

**15.** Go to the next subtopic card, History.

**16.** Move and resize your text field so that it is on the right half of the card.

**17.** From the Objects menu, choose **Add a Graphic Object**.

**18.** Click **OK** to select a disk file.

**19.** In the HSArt folder, find and select **educatn1**.

**FIGURE 7-4**
Enlarged Flag

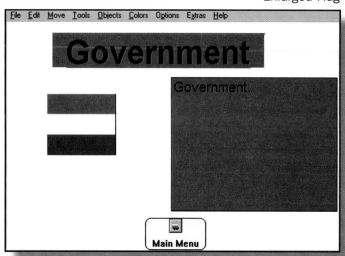

**FIGURE 7-5**
Graphic Appearance Window

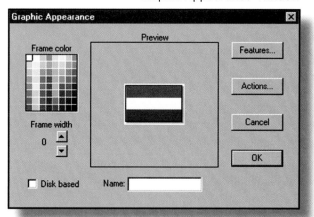

**TIP**

Macintosh users should select the **Education1** file. The file names in these steps are limited to eight characters for Windows 3.1 users. Since Macintosh does not have the file name limitation, the Macintosh HyperStudio file names are more complete. You should select the file name that most closely matches the name shown in the steps.

**112**

**20.** Select the picture of the open book. Click **OK**.

**21.** Move the picture of the book to the center of the left column as you did on the previous card.

**22.** Click outside of the graphic and click **OK**.

**23.** Save your stack.

**24.** From the tool palette, select the **Graphic Object** tool or the **Arrow (Edit)** tool. The **Graphic Object** tool is selected in Figure 7-7, and the **Arrow (Edit)** tool is shown in Figure 7-8.

**25.** Click on the picture of the book. You will see the "red ants," which show that the book is selected. Move the book to the upper left side of the column so that your screen resembles Figure 7-9. Click outside of the graphic.

**26.** Save your stack as **Country8**.

**27.** Leave your stack open.

**FIGURE 7-6**
Flag with Flagpole

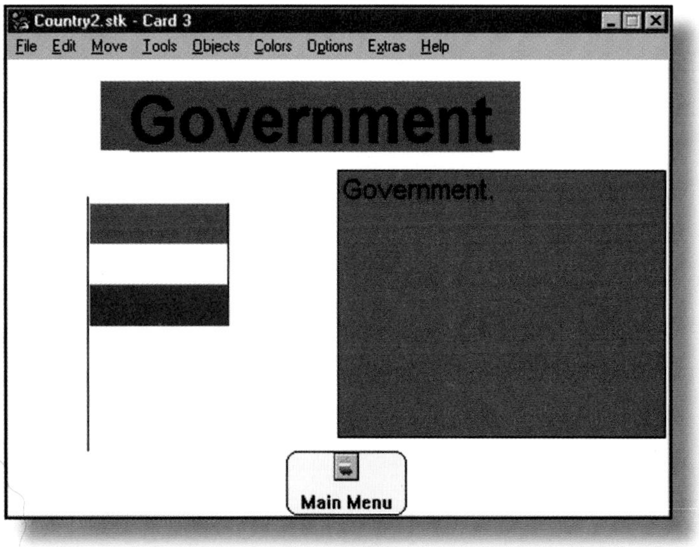

Country2.stk - Card 3

File Edit Move Tools Objects Colors Options Extras Help

# Government

Government.

Main Menu

**FIGURE 7-7**
Graphic Object Tool

**FIGURE 7-8**
Arrow (Edit) Tool

**FIGURE 7-9**
Moved Book

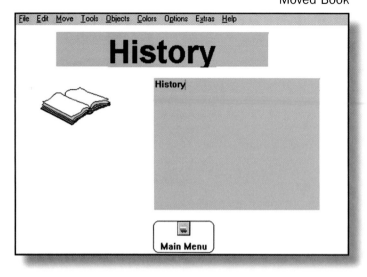

## CHALLENGE ACTIVITY ➡ 7.1

**FIGURE 7-10**
Wildlife Card

Complete the stack by moving, resizing the text field, and adding a graphic to the final subtopic card, Wildlife. From the HSArt folder, find the graphics with a picture of an elephant and place it on your card. Your final card should look like Figure 7-10. When you are finished save the stack as **Country9** and close the stack.

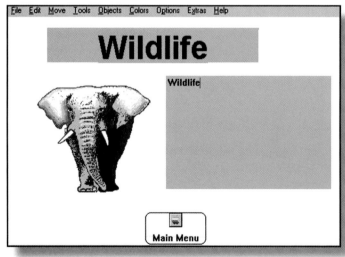

# *Changing Card Size and Setting Preferences*

HyperStudio provides a variety of sizes for your cards. The size defines how much of the screen space the cards will take. The default HyperStudio size uses part of the screen. A variety of other sizes can be specified depending on your monitor's screen size. The screen size is stated in pixels. A 14-inch monitor generally displays 640 x 480 pixels. For presentations, a full-screen card is aesthetically pleasing and easier to see when viewed by a group. However, it is important to remember that the larger the card size, the more memory you will need, especially if you are using a lot of color graphics or video clips. The card size window offers a variety of sizes as in Figure 7-11. The choices include:

**FIGURE 7-11**
Card Size Window

- Current card size, whatever the size is when you create the new stack.

- Full screen, which will fill the screen but will vary in size depending on your screen size.

- Standard which is 512 x 342 pixels.

Depending on the version of HyperStudio, the type of computer you are using, and the size of your screen, you may be offered other size choices as well as color choices. For the color choices, it is acceptable to access the largest number of colors available to you.

Preferences are choices you make about how HyperStudio will appear and act. One choice is to tell HyperStudio that you are an experienced user. Experienced users see fewer reminder windows. They are also automatically presented with different choices in certain places. For example, each time an experienced user opens a new stack, the user is directed to choose a card size for the new stack. If you have not told HyperStudio that you are an experienced user, you will not see this window, and HyperStudio will automatically use its default card size.

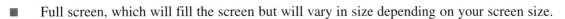

**STEP-BY-STEP 7.2**

1. Create a new stack.

2. When you see the window, "In your new stack do you want the same card size as in the current stack?" choose **No**. (See Figure 7-12.)

3. Next, HyperStudio will ask you to pick the size of the cards, as shown in Figure 7-13. Choose **Full screen size**.

4. Click **OK**. HyperStudio will make the necessary adjustments for your screen size so that you will see a full, blank screen-size card.

(continued on next page)

**5.** From the Edit menu, select **Preferences**.

**6.** If it is not selected, select "I'm an experienced HyperStudio user" from the Program Preferences. By having this option selected, you will be prompted to select a card size each time you create a new stack.

**7.** From the File menu, choose **Add Clip Art**. Click **OK**.

**8.** From the HSArt folder, double click on **Dingbat2**.

**9.** Choose **Get another picture**. (See Figure 7-14.)

**10.** Click **OK**. Then double click on **Dingbat1**.

**11.** Select the entire page and click **OK**.

**12.** The copied file should be in the middle of your card. Click outside of the selected area.

**13.** Using the **Square Selector** tool from the tool palette, select all of the items on the card except the border, as shown in Figure 7-15.

**14.** With the interior objects selected, press the **Delete** key from your keyboard. Everything in the area that is selected is deleted, and only the border remains.

**15.** Using the **Square Selector** tool, select the entire border. Move the border to the upper left corner of the card, as shown in Figure 7-16. If needed, drag the tool palette to the right side of the screen.

**FIGURE 7-12**
New Card Size

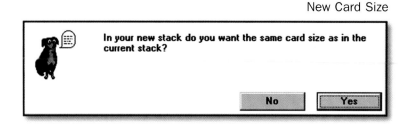

**FIGURE 7-13**
Card Size

**FIGURE 7-14**
Get Another Picture

**TIP**

Be careful not to select any white area outside the border. If your selection is not accurate, click outside the "ants" and reselect. Or, you can choose **Undo** from the Edit menu.

**116**

**16.** Save your stack as **Border**.

**17.** Leave the stack open.

**FIGURE 7-15**
Objects that are Not the Border

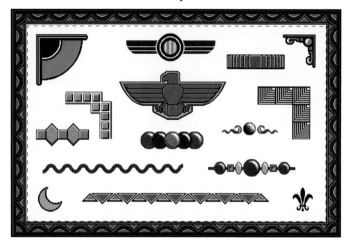

**FIGURE 7-16**
Border in Upper Left Corner of Card

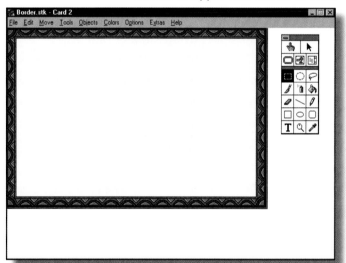

 **HINT:**

You can move your tool palette at any time by dragging it to a new location. It is best to keep it away from the area in which you are working.

# Modifying Borders

In Lesson 3, you created a border for decorative effect. Borders may also be used to set the tone or theme of the stack. They can be a way to organize the material or to separate different aspects of your presentation, like book chapters. You can use some of the borders provided in HyperStudio, or you can create your own.

The borders you import as clip art may not fit the size of the cards in your stack. You may increase or decrease the size using the double-headed arrow cursor. However, this changes the size of the design elements in the border. In the next Step-by-Step, you will learn a technique to cut and paste segments of the border to maintain the size of the design elements. This process is somewhat arduous and requires practice. Refer to the figures frequently as you complete the steps.

 **TIP**

You can continue cutting and pasting segments until you are satisfied with the results.

---

**STEP-BY-STEP ➡ 7.3**

 **NOTE:**

If your monitor is 17 inches or larger, you will have to repeat the copy and paste process described in these steps until you have created a border around your entire card.

**1.** With the Border stack open, use the **Square Selector** tool to select the left side border from the point where it meets the top of the border to the bottom of it. (HINT: Do not include the segment where the top border meets the side border.) Refer to Figure 7-17 to verify that you have selected the correct segment.

**2.** From the Edit menu, choose **Copy** and then **Paste**.

**3.** Drag the segment down to the bottom of the card so that there is a full border along the left side, as shown in Figure 7-18.

**FIGURE 7-17**
Selected Left Border

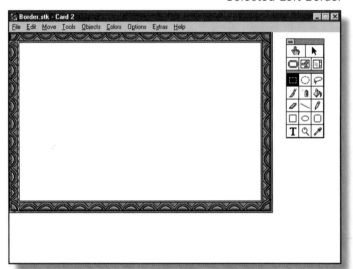

**4.** Select the bottom border from the point that it meets the left panel to the end.

**5.** Then drag the bottom border to the bottom of the screen, as shown in Figure 7-19.

**TIP**

Be careful to include all of the border but not the white background. Whatever you include in your selection will be moved. If your selection is not correct, either click outside the ants and reselect it or use the Undo command.

**6.** Save your stack.

**7.** Select the right border from the point that it meets the top of the border to the bottom of the border.

**8.** Copy, paste, and drag it to meet the bottom border.

**9.** Select the entire right border and drag it to the right side of your card.

**10.** Don't worry if a black or colored bar is left where the original border was. You will correct that later.

**11.** Select an area of the top border. Copy, paste, and drag it over to meet the right border section.

(continued on next page)

**FIGURE 7-18**
Full Left Border

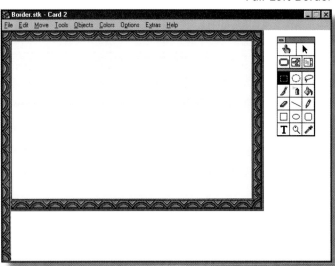

**FIGURE 7-19**
Selected Bottom Border

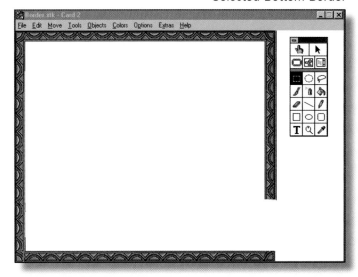

**12.** Repeat the process for the bottom border.

**13.** If there is a discolored area on the card, use the eraser, in white, to cover it. Your card should have a full border surrounding it, similar to Figure 7-20.

**14.** Save your stack as **Border1** and leave it open.

**FIGURE 7-20**
Full Border

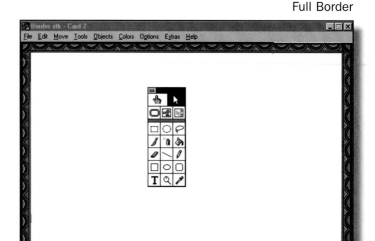

 **TIP**

You can copy and paste over any small areas that do not line up well. You can also use the eraser to clean some mistakes. Remember, you can erase in any color or pattern that you choose.

# Clip Art and Graphic Objects

You may have noticed that to insert graphic objects you use the Objects menu and to insert clip art, such as your border, you used the File menu command Add clip art. However, there are differences between clip art and graphic objects. Clip art becomes part of the background. That is why we had to use the eraser to cover the area left by the border clip art in the previous Step-by-Step.

Graphic objects "float" over, or on top of, the background. They do not become part of the background. What is more, they can have actions attached to them the same way buttons do.

## File Formats

There are many types of file formats for graphics. Graphic formats are a way of storing and saving graphics. Some have more detail and take up more space or memory. Others have less detail, and use less memory. The choice of graphic format will often depend on the amount of memory that is feasible for your project and the importance of the detail in your graphic. HyperStudio stores all of the graphics it supplies as bitmaps, often shown with a .BMP file extension. A few of the standard graphic formats supported by HyperStudio are:

 **NOTE:**

Extension does not always appear, especially with Macintosh.

- PICT
- TIFF
- JPEG
- PCX
- BMP
- GIF
- MacPaint
- Photo-CD

# *Changing Colors in Graphics*

HyperStudio allows you to change and replace colors in clip art and graphic objects. Using the Replace colors option, you can replace all of one color in an object. If, for example, you have a patterned background and would like to change a color in it, you can specify the original color and a replacement color. Everything in the original color will automatically change to the new color you have selected. This feature allows you to modify the standard graphic files supplied by HyperStudio to create a unique look for your stacks.

By double clicking on any of the colors in the color palette, you will see a larger variety of colors from which to choose, as shown in Figure 7-21.

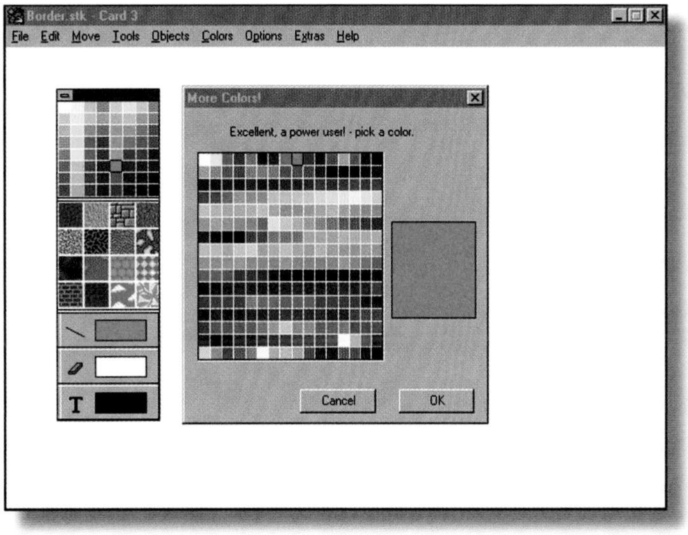

The Eraser tool is a very handy tool not only for erasing graphics or painted text, but because you can erase in any color you choose so that you can maintain your background. Don't forget that if you erase clip art, you will also erase whatever is under it. This means that the Eraser tool does not only erase but it can be used, like paint to cover an area. You cannot erase a graphic object, but you can select and delete it.

**FIGURE 7-21**
Expanded Color Palette

**TIP**

To delete a colored area from your card, select the area and choose **Clear** or **Cut** from the Edit menu. You can also press the **Delete** key or use the eraser.

1. With the **Border1** stack open, choose **Effects** from the Edit menu.

2. Choose **Replace Colors**. The Replace/Exchange Colors window shown in Figure 7-22 appears.

3. Select the **red** color on the Replace side.

4. Click on the **purple** on the "with" side.

5. Click **OK**.

6. Notice the change in the border. Undo the color replacement.

7. Save the stack.

8. From the Edit menu, choose **New Card**.

9. From the File menu, choose **Add Clip Art**.

10. Click **OK** to choose Disk file, if necessary.

11. Open the **music** file from HSArt folder.

12. Select the **treble clef sign**, as shown in Figure 7-23. Do not select the red border around the symbol.

**FIGURE 7-22**
Replace/Exchange Colors Window

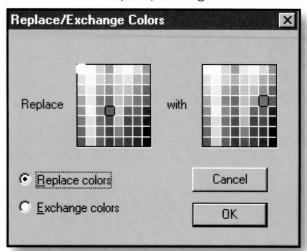

**FIGURE 7-23**
Treble Clef

 **HINT:**

The Undo shortcut is **Ctrl + Z** (for Windows) or **⌘ + Z** (for Macintosh).

**13.** Click **OK**.

**14.** With your cursor in the center of the clip art, move it to the top left corner, as shown in Figure 7-24.

**15.** From the Edit menu, choose **Effects**. From the Effects submenu, choose **Replace colors**.

**16.** Replace **black** with **purple**.

**17.** From the File menu, choose **Add clip art**.

**18.** Select the **music** file again.

**19.** Select a musical note and click **OK**.

**20.** Move it under the treble clef symbol, as shown in Figure 7-25. (NOTE: You may have selected a different musical note, but the placement should be the same.)

**21.** Replace the **black** note with **dark blue**.

**22.** Choose another musical note from the **music** file.

**23.** Change the color of the note from **black** to **red**.

**24.** Place this note on the top border to the right of the treble clef.

(continued on next page)

**FIGURE 7-24**
Treble Clef in Top Left Corner

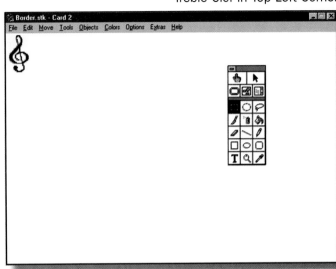

**FIGURE 7-25**
Musical Note

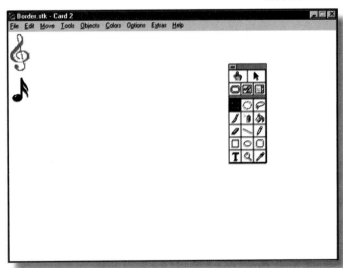

 **TIP**

You can resize a clip art piece when it first appears on the screen and is selected by the marching "red ants" by dragging the corner of the clip art either to enlarge or diminish it. If you resize using the corner, it will resize proportionally. If you resize along the sides, it will not change proportionally.

**123**

**25.** Copy and paste the blue musical note. Drag it alongside the red note on the top border and change it from blue to black.

**26.** Copy and paste the red note. Drag it below the red note on the left border. Change the color from **red** to **black**. Your results should be similar to Figure 7-26.

**27.** Select the three notes along the left border.

**28.** Copy, paste, and drag the copied selection below the three notes to finish the left border.

**29.** Select the three graphics along the top of the screen.

**30.** Copy, paste, and drag the copied selection to the right of the three selected notes. Repeat the process as needed to fill the top border, as shown in Figure 7-27.

**HINT:**

If you select the wrong blue when you are replacing the colors, you will notice that the note does not change colors. Simply repeat the process, selecting another blue until the note changes to black.

**FIGURE 7-26**
Start of a Musical Border

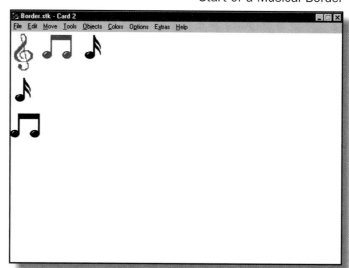

**FIGURE 7-27**
Left and Top Musical Border

**TIP**

Depending on the notes selected and their placement, you may need to use the Eraser tool to remove a portion of the note from the top border. Also, if you have a larger monitor, you may need to copy, paste, and drag the notes more than once.

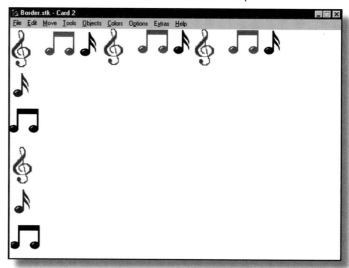

**31.** Select, copy, and paste the entire left border. Drag it to the right side of the screen to create a right border.

**32.** Select the middle section of the top border leaving out the treble clef signs in the top right and left corners. Copy, paste, and drag the selected area to the bottom of the screen to create the bottom border. Your completed border should be similar to Figure 7-28.

**33.** Save your stack as **Border2**. Leave it open.

**FIGURE 7-28**
Completed Musical Border

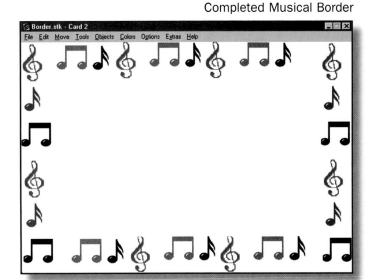

**CHALLENGE ACTIVITY ⟹ 7.2**

Create a new card in the stack Border. Using some of the clip art in the HSArt folder, customize your own border for the new card. Use the techniques you learned in the previous Step-by-Step to create your own pattern for the border. Save the stack as **Border3**. Keep the stack open.

**STEP-BY-STEP ⟹ 7.5**

**1.** Open the **Border3** stack, if necessary. Move to the first card.

**2.** Select **Add a Graphic Object** from the Objects menu.

**3.** From the HSArt folder, open the **iclibca** file.

 **TIP**

The Macintosh file name for the iclibca file is **Icon Library-Clip Art**.

(continued on next page)

**4.** Select the wave icon, as shown in Figure 7-29.

**5.** Click **OK**.

**6.** Drag the corner of the graphic to make it about twice as large.

**7.** Move the graphic to the upper left side, as shown in Figure 7-30.

**8.** Click outside the graphic. When the Graphic Appearance window appears, click on the **Actions** button.

**9.** Choose **Next card**, as shown in Figure 7-31. Leave the transition as Left to right and the speed as Fast. Click **OK** and then **Done**. The icon will now behave like a button.

**10.** Save the stack as **Border4**.

**11.** Leave it open.

**FIGURE 7-29**
Wave Icon Selected

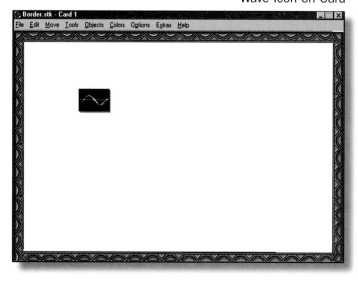

**FIGURE 7-30**
Wave Icon on Card

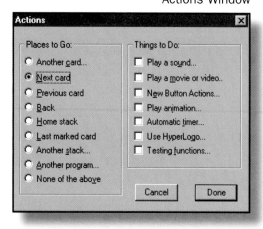

**FIGURE 7-31**
Actions Window

# *Attaching Sounds to Icons*

Y̲ou have created actions for icons that move you from card to card in a stack. Other kinds of actions can be attached to icons. One type of action connects a sound, movie, or video file to an icon. When the user selects the icon, the file attached to it is played. In the next Step-by-Step, you will attach a sound file to an icon. In a later lesson, you will learn to attach video clips to an icon.

Sound files are saved with the extension .WAV. You can use the sound files supplied with HyperStudio, or you can use sound files from other sources. If you have the correct equipment, you can even create sound files.

You must have a sound card and speakers for your computer in order to hear the sound you will attach to the icon. Make sure the speakers are turned on. If you are working with this Step-by-Step in a classroom or computer lab, the volume on the speakers should be set low. You want to be able to hear the sound without disturbing others in the class or lab.

## S T E P - B Y - S T E P ⟹ 7.6

1. Make sure the Border4 stack is open and you are on the first card.

2. Select **Add a Graphic Object** from the Objects menu.

3. From the HSArt folder, open the **iclibca** file.

4. Select the **microphone** icon and click **OK**.

5. Enlarge the icon to about twice the size of the original and move it to the lower right corner of the screen.

6. Click outside the icon. From the Graphic Appearance window, click the **Actions** button.

7. From the Actions window, check **Play a sound**.

8. Select **BEAMDOWN.WAV** from the list of sounds on the right side of the Tape deck window, as shown in Figure 7-32. The file name appears in the Selection field of the tape deck. Click the **Play** button. You should hear a sound.

**TIP**

Macintosh users cannot resize a graphic object. Simply move the graphic to the lower right corner of the screen.

**TIP**

Macintosh users may need to select another sound if BEAMDOWN is not available. Also, the extension .WAV is not included with any of the HyperStudio sound files.

(continued on next page)

**9.** Select **HARPTAG.WAV** and click **Play** to hear this sound.

**10.** Choose **OK**.

**11.** Click **Done**.

**12.** Click **OK**.

**13.** To see how the icon functions, select the Browse tool and click on the icon. It should play the sound you selected.

**14.** Save the stack as **Border5**. Leave it open.

**FIGURE 7-32**
Tape Deck

## CHALLENGE ACTIVITY ⟹ 7.3

Start a new stack. Include three cards in the stack. Create a different border for each card. You can use borders from the HyperStudio graphics or you can create your own. Be sure to include at least one border you have created yourself. Save the stack as **Chaleng7**.

## CHALLENGE ACTIVITY ⟹ 7.4

Print the USA stack, using each of the following options:

- Print one card per page.
- Print two cards per page.
- Print four cards per page.

# *Summary*

In this lesson, you learned that:

- Graphics add an important dimension to a multimedia project.
- There is a difference between graphic objects and clip art.
- Graphic objects float over the background layer of the card.
- Clip art becomes part of the background.
- You can insert and edit graphics.
- You can change the size of graphics using the Graphic Object tool or the Arrow (Edit) tool.
- You can create customized borders with clip art.
- HyperStudio recognizes a variety of graphic formats.
- You can assign actions to graphics.
- Graphics can play sounds.
- You can manipulate graphics by copying and pasting.
- You can replace colors on a card.

## VOCABULARY

| | |
|---|---|
| Bitmaps | Interface |
| Clip art | Pixels |
| File formats | Preferences |
| Graphic objects | Sound files |

## LESSON 7 REVIEW QUESTIONS

### TRUE/FALSE

**Circle the T if the statement is true or F if it is false.**

T  F  1. Graphics are not considered to be multimedia elements.

T  F  2. HyperStudio supplies graphics in a BMP file format.

T  F  3. Graphics can only be sized with the cursor in a corner of the selected item.

**T  F    4.** You can replace all of the same color on a card.

**T  F    5.** There is more than one color palette in HyperStudio.

## COMPLETION

**Answer the questions below in the space provided.**

1.    You can access clip art from the _____ menu.

2.    You can access graphic objects from the _____ menu.

3.    Graphic formats are the way _____ are stored.

4.    Different file formats require _____ amounts of memory.

5.    There is/are _____ card size(s) for HyperStudio.

## SHORT ANSWER QUESTIONS

**Answer the questions below in the space provided.**

1.    What is meant by "graphic objects float on the background"?

2.    Which tools are used to edit graphics?

3.    Name two graphic formats.

      **a.**

      **b.**

4.    What is the difference between clip art and graphic objects?

**5.** How do you size a graphic proportionally?

**6.** What are the steps used to copy a graphic?

**7.** Name three possible sources for graphics or clip art.

**a.**

**b.**

**c.**

**8.** Describe how you set the card size of your stack.

## LESSON 7 PROJECT 7.1

This project will complete the Safety stack that you modified in Lesson 6. To finish the project you will have to expand the project by adding information cards for each subtopic. Use the Safety2 stack. Be sure to include:

■ a different border for each subtopic and the same border for the information cards that go with the subtopic.

■ at least eight graphics.

■ graphic actions for at least four of the graphics, including at least one sound.

■ text fields where appropriate.

■ appropriate navigation.

Review your stack using the Stack Guidelines Checklist. Make any changes indicated by your evaluation. Print your completed stack, unless your instructor directs otherwise. Save your stack as **Safety3**.

## LESSON 7 PROJECT 7.2

In this project, you will create a five-card stack. The topic of the stack should be an area of interest to you. It can be a topic from the news, sports, or a hobby.

Plan the stack to include:

- a storyboard

- a Title card, Main Menu card, and three subtopic cards.

- a border for the Title and Main Menu cards.

- a different border for each subtopic card.

- at least one graphic on each subtopic card.

Create the stack you have planned, using the following guidelines:

- Copy one of the graphics from each subtopic card to the Main Menu, reduce the size and attach the appropriate action for the graphic to take the user to the matching subtopic card.

- Attach other actions to at least two of the graphics on subtopic cards.

- Save the stack as **Graphic1**.

- Print the stack, unless your instructor directs otherwise.

- Ask someone to review your stack using your Stack Guidelines Checklist.

## CRITICAL THINKING ACTIVITY

By using examples, list the ways that graphics and color can change the dynamics of a black-and-white print project.

# TEMPLATES AND READY MADE CARDS

## OBJECTIVES

**Upon completion of this lesson, you will be able to:**

- Use ready made cards as templates for your stack.
- Copy backgrounds to other cards.
- Share backgrounds among cards.
- Use the Extras menu.
- Create special effects with graphics.

 **Estimated Time: 2.5 hours**

## *Templates*

A template is a type of pattern or mold used for duplicating something. HyperStudio supplies a variety of templates for you to use as cards for your stacks called Ready Made Cards. Usually a template will provide the structure for a card with the background, areas for graphics, text fields, and button positions already placed. You can also create your own templates and save them to use over again.

> **TIP**
>
> Macintosh users will find some differences in the names of the Ready Made cards.

The six Ready Made Card templates available with HyperStudio are shown in Figure 8-1.

## *Working with Backgrounds*

The backgrounds are the base or bottom layer of your card. All cards have backgrounds, even if it is a solid color such as white. When you start a new stack, the first card, before you make any changes, has a white background. You can customize a background just as you did in earlier lessons when you imported a background. You used the HSArt library to load the USA map as your background. You can use any graphic, color, or pattern as a background, but you will want to be sure that your background allows any text or graphics that you put on it to show up clearly. This will take some practice and trial and error.

FIGURE 8-1
Ready Made Card Templates

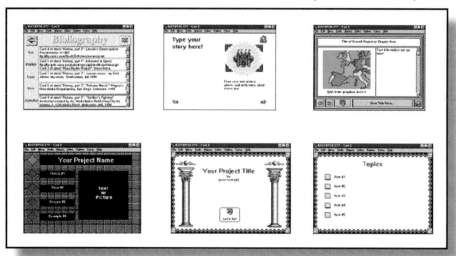

Once you have chosen a background, you can copy it to a new card or share the background among other cards. Copying a background and sharing a background will cause two different results. If you copy a background to a new card, any changes you make to the background of either card will not affect the other card or cards. If cards share a background, changes on one card will affect the other cards. In Step-by-Step 8.1, you will explore copying backgrounds.

**STEP-BY-STEP 8.1**

1. Open HyperStudio and begin a new stack. Use the same size as the current stack.

2. From the Edit menu, choose **Ready Made Cards**, as shown in Figure 8-2.

3. Select **INFODISP.STK**. Your screen should look like Figure 8-3.

4. Key **EUROPE** in the title area.

5. From the Edit menu, select **Ready Made Cards** again.

**FIGURE 8-2**
Ready Made Cards Menu

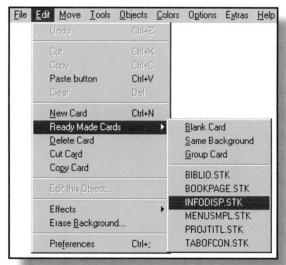

**6.** Select **Same Background**. Your screen should look like Figure 8-4.

**7.** Try to key some text in the title area. You will not be able to because it is not a text field. When you select the same background, only the background is copied, not any text fields or other objects that may appear.

**8.** Select **New Stack** from the File menu and do not save the current stack.

**9.** Leave HyperStudio open.

**FIGURE 8-3**
INFODISP Ready Made Card

**FIGURE 8-4**
Same Background

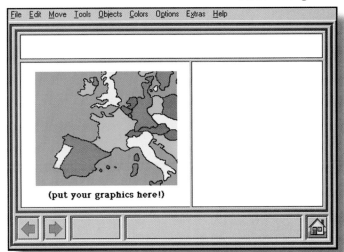

INTERNET A browser is a software program that gives access to most Internet services. A browser is required to connect to the multimedia documents on the World Wide Web.

# Sharing Backgrounds

Sharing backgrounds is a little different than copying backgrounds. Sharing can save time and conserve memory. Sharing backgrounds reduces the overall size of a stack because the cards actually "share" the same background. In other words, one background is used on two or more cards in a stack. Any changes you make to the background on any of the cards will result in the same changes on all the shared cards. Group cards are different from cards that share the same background. Group cards share background and objects such as buttons and text field objects. You will practice sharing backgrounds and working with group cards in Step-by-Step 8.2.

## STEP-BY-STEP ⟹ 8.2

1. Start a new stack. Use the same card size as the current stack.

2. From the Edit menu, choose **Ready Made Cards**.

3. Select **BOOKPAGE.STK**. Your screen should look like Figure 8-5.

4. Select **Ready Made Cards** from the Edit menu and choose **Group Card**. A second card is added with the same components as the first card.

**FIGURE 8-5**
Book Page

 **HINT:**

Notice that the Ready Made Card file names include the .stk extension at the end of the file names. The extension is required for naming stacks for Windows 95 and earlier formats. If you are planning to use stacks on a Windows system, use the following guidelines when naming stacks:

- Limit file names to eight characters if the stack will be used on a Windows 3.1 system.

- Include a three-character extension after the file name that identifies the type of file. HyperStudio automatically adds .stk to all stack file names.

**5.** Pull the tool palette to the side of your card. Select the **Button** tool and see the buttons highlighted.

**6.** Move to the first card and verify that the same buttons are highlighted. Notice that the same buttons appear on both cards.

**7.** Select the **Text Object** tool. Locate the text fields on each card. Notice that the text fields have been created on both cards.

**8.** Move to Card 2, if necessary.

**9.** Select **Ready Made Cards** from the Edit menu and choose **Group Card** to add a third card to your stack. Notice that the third card has the same elements as the first two cards.

**10.** Select Ready Made Cards and choose **Same Background**. You will notice that the buttons and the text fields are not included on this card.

**11.** Save the stack as **Bckgrnd**. Leave HyperStudio open.

# Extras Menu

The Extras menu is located on the HyperStudio menubar. The Extras menu has some practical features that allow you to make your stack look more creative and polished. The list of options in Figure 8-6 should be accessible to you.

**FIGURE 8-6**
Extras Menu

Extra Manager
Check Spelling...
Box Maker
Export WebPage
Menu Tamer
StoryBoard
Title Card

**HINT:**

If you cannot access the extra features on the Extras menu, select Preferences from the Edit menu. Uncheck the box in Program preferences that says: "I'm an experienced HyperStudio user."

The first item, Extra Manager, lets you add or delete extra options from the menu. You will not use this option in this text. The Spell Checker, (see Figure 8-7), is a feature you would find in most word processing programs. It has the capacity to search for correct spelling of the text on one card, a stack, or paint text, depending on the choices you select. It also offers access to a variety of dictionaries including a legal and medical dictionary. Before you finalize any project that contains text, you should use the spell checker. However, do not assume that the spell checker will find all "spelling" mistakes. It will not identify a correctly spelled word that is used incorrectly, for example, if you key "you" when it should be "your," the spell checker will not identify your error. In addition to using the spell checker, you should proofread each card in your stack.

**TIP**

Sometimes it is difficult to find your own mistakes. Before you finalize a project, have someone else proofread your stack.

**FIGURE 8-7**
Check Spelling Window

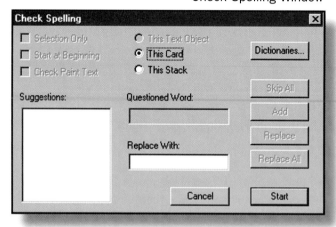

The spell checker gives you the following choices:

## SPELL CHECKER

| BUTTON | ACTION |
|--------|--------|
| **Replace** | Replaces the word with the correct spelling. |
| **Replace All** | Replaces all of the same words that are spelled incorrectly. |
| **Add** | Adds a new word to the dictionary and leaves the spelling on the card unchanged. Generally, you should only add words to the dictionary that you commonly use. |
| **Skip All** | Makes no change to the spelling and skips all future occurrences of the same spelling. The word is spelled the way you want it spelled and, although the dictionary does not recognize it, it is not a mistake. This is common with names, technical jargon, and foreign words. |

The other options on the Extras menu are:

■ **Box Maker** feature, which lets you draw three-dimensional boxes.

■ **Export Web Page** feature, which lets you put your stacks on the Internet. This tool creates an HTML file that lets your browser display your stack within the browser's window.

■ **Menu Tamer** feature, which gives you the choice of whether or not you want the menubar to show on your cards. When you are creating the stack, you will, of course, need to use the menubar. However, in presentation mode, it makes the stack look more dynamic to have the menubar hidden.

 **HINT:**

You can also hide or show the menubar from the keyboard: **Ctrl + M** (for Windows) and  + M (for Macintosh).

■   **Storyboard** feature, which puts all of the cards in a stack in miniature version so that you can see them all at once. You can rearrange the cards, or delete a card or cards. You can also move more than one card at a time by holding the Shift key and selecting all of the cards you would like to move. Figure 8-8 shows a stack using the Storyboard feature.

**FIGURE 8-8**
Storyboard

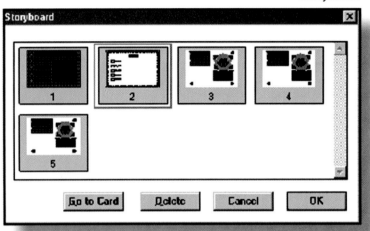

■   Title Card feature, which lets you make any card the first card in the stack no matter where it was originally located. Figure 8-9 shows the Title Card window.

**FIGURE 8-9**
Title Card Window

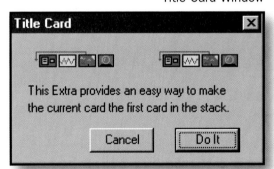

## STEP-BY-STEP ⟩ 8.3

1.   With the **Bckgrnd** stack open, move to Card 3.

2.   From the Edit menu, choose **Ready Made Cards** and **TABOFCON.STK**.

3.   From the Edit menu, choose **Ready Made Cards** and **MENUSMPL.STK**.

4.   You should have six cards in your stack with the fifth card showing. From the Extras menu, choose **Title Card**.

5.   Click **Do It**. Card 5 should now be Card 1.

(continued on next page)

**6.** Go to the Extras menu and choose **Storyboard**. You should see the same configuration.

**7.** Drag Card 5 up to make it Card 2. As you are dragging the card, the area above the storyboard will indicate which card is being moved and where it will be positioned.

**8.** Click **OK**.

**9.** Save the stack as **Family** and keep it open.

**10.** Go to Card 1. This will be the Title card for the project. In the top text field, key **My Family**.

**11.** In the text fields, replace Choice #1 with **Created by:**

**12.** Replace Point #2 with your first name.

**13.** Replace Reason #3 with your last name.

**14.** Delete Example #4.

**15.** You will add a picture in the **Text or Picture** box. From the Objects menu, choose **Add a Graphic Object**.

**16.** Choose **Disk file**, if necessary and click **OK**.

**17.** From the HSArt folder, double click on **Photos** folder.

**18.** Double click on **Fampicts** folder.

**19.** Double click on **Stefanie** for a girl's picture or **Aaron** for a boy's picture.

**TIP**

You will learn how to scan images in Lesson 19. If you have a scanner, you will be able to replace this picture with another of your choice.

**20.** Using the **Arrow (Edit)** tool, select the picture cropping about 1/2" from the top and left sides and about 1" from the right side. Your selection should resemble the approximate size of the placeholder on the Title card.

**NOTE:**

When you crop a picture, you can eliminate the parts that you do not want or that will not fit into the space you have.

**21.** Click **OK**. You will see the screen, as shown in Figure 8-10. Click **OK**.

**22.** Drag and size the photo until it fits neatly into the placeholder **"Text or Picture."** Your card should resemble Figure 8-11.

**TIP**

If you don't like the way the photo looks after you have sized it, repeat the process and crop the photo differently.

**23.** Save your stack as **Family1**.

**24.** Select the
**Storyboard** feature
on the Extras menu.

**25.** Select Card 2 and
click **Delete**. When
the window appears
that asks "Are you
sure you want to
delete this card?"
choose **Yes**. Then
click **OK**.

**26.** From the Edit menu,
choose **Copy Card** to
copy the Title card
for the stack.

**27.** From the Edit menu,
choose **Paste card**.
This card will
function as the Main
Menu card for your
stack.

**28.** Select and delete
the picture.

(continued on next page)

**FIGURE 8-10**
Graphic Object Window

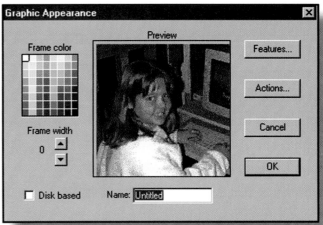

**FIGURE 8-11**
Title Card with Photo

**141**

**29.** Replace the text in the three text fields on the left side of the screen with the names of three family members. (You can include your pets, your cousins, friends, or whoever feels like a part of your family.) Your completed card should resemble Figure 8-12.

**30.** Save the stack as **Family2**. Leave the stack open.

**FIGURE 8-12**
My Family Main Menu Card

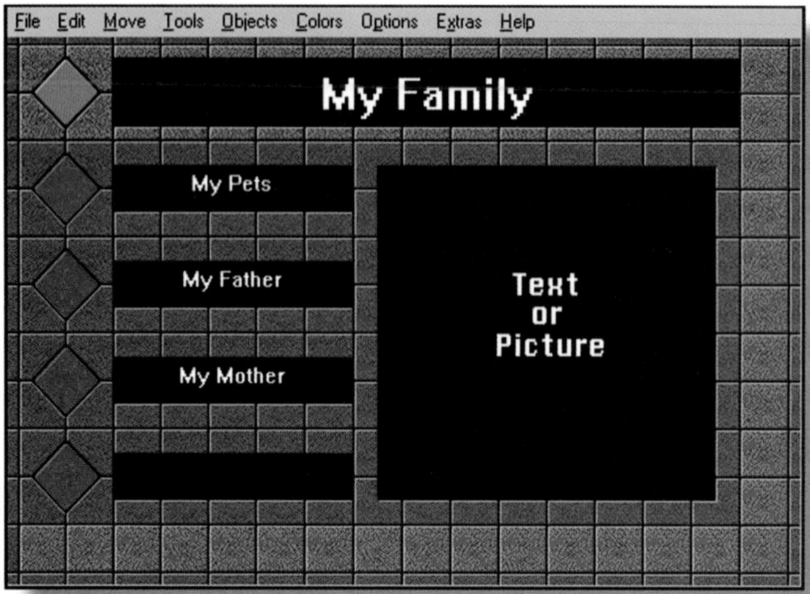

# Customizing a Stack Using Shared Backgrounds

You will now have the opportunity to customize the stack using the ready made cards and to observe how to manipulate cards that share backgrounds. To accomplish this you will add on two new sections to the stack and create buttons and graphics for the stack. This will give you a good chance to see how easy it is to work with cards with shared backgrounds. However, you will also have a chance to practice copying and pasting the objects because, even though the placeholders will remain constant for text fields and buttons, you will have to copy and paste them from card to card to keep them consistent.

## STEP-BY-STEP ⟩ 8.4

**1.** With the Family2 stack open, move to the last card in the stack and delete it. Delete another card. You should now be on the last card in the stack, Card 4.

**2.** From the Edit menu, select the **INFODISP.STK** ready-made card. Then create another card as a group card. These cards will represent your second family member: one is an information card and the other is a subtopic card. You should now have six cards in your stack.

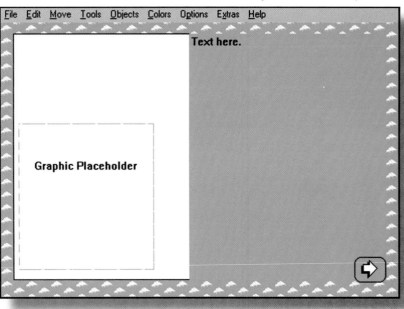

**FIGURE 8-13**
Third Family Member Subtopic Card

**3.** For the third family member, you will create a template of your own. Select **New Card** from the Edit menu.

**4.** Create a border for the card.

**5.** Create a text object that is on the right half of the card.

**6.** Draw a box to serve as a placeholder for a graphic object. Your card should resemble Figure 8-13.

**7.** From the Edit menu, choose **Ready Made Cards** and **Group Card**. You should now have a card with the duplicate background as the previous card you customized. There should be eight cards in your stack.

**8.** Save the stack.

**9.** Go to the first subtopic card, Card 3. Using the **Arrow (Edit)** tool or the **Button** tool, double click on the hand button that is pointing right. Click the **Actions** button. Make sure the button action is **Next card**. Click **Done**.

**10.** Save the stack as **Family3**, and leave it open.

You have the stack with a topic, "My Family," and a Main Menu card. You have three subtopic cards, one for each family member. And you have a matching information card to go with each subtopic card. An example of a subtopic card is shown in Figure 8-14.

**FIGURE 8-14**
Sample Subtopic Card

To complete the stack, you need to do the following:

■ Place a graphic or photo in the Main Menu placeholder.

■ Attach actions to the buttons on the Main Menu card to move to each subtopic card. Note that the red diamonds already have buttons in place, but you need to define the actions.

■ Check the buttons' actions to verify that the buttons lead from each subtopic card to its information card and from the information card to the Main Menu card. Make adjustments where necessary.

■ Make sure you can return to the Main Menu from each subtopic card.

■ Add navigation from the Title card to the Main Menu card.

■ Insert appropriate graphics on the subtopic and informational cards.

■ Insert appropriate text on the subtopic and information cards.

■ When you are finished, save the stack as **Family4**.

■ Close the stack.

 **HINT:**

You can use the buttons that are included on the ready-made cards, and customize the actions.

# *Creating Special Effects with Painted Objects*

The special effects in this next section will only work with clip art or paint objects. You can manipulate the images you create in HyperStudio using special effects. The special effects shown in Figure 8-15 are:

**FIGURE 8-15**
Effects Menu

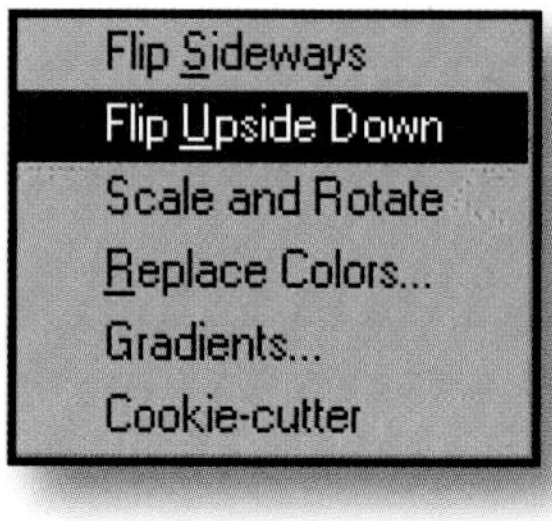

| Flip Sideways |
| Flip Upside Down |
| Scale and Rotate |
| Replace Colors... |
| Gradients... |
| Cookie-cutter |

## SPECIAL EFFECTS

| EFFECT | RESULT |
|---|---|
| Flip Sideways | Creates a mirror image of the object. |
| Flip Upside Down | Turns the image upside down by rotating the image 180 degrees. |
| Scale and Rotate | Allows you to proportionally scale the image or rotate the image to any angle. |
| Replace Colors | Changes one color to another color. You used this effect in Lesson 7. |
| Gradients | Allows you to create a blend from one color to another. |
| Cookie-cutter | Allows you to create a pattern to be used on your selected object. |

## Cookie-Cutter Effect

The first effect that you will work with is the Cookie-cutter effect. This special effect allows you to select an area of a card and cut a pattern, just as you would with a cookie cutter if you were making cookies in different shapes. For instance, you can have a background become the fill for text letters.

**STEP-BY-STEP** $\Longrightarrow$ **8.5**

1. With HyperStudio open, create a new stack with two cards. Make the card size full screen.

2. On the first card, double click on the **Text** tool. Choose the font **Arriba** and size **72**. (NOTE: If you do not have the Arriba font, choose another font.) Do not change the text color or alignment. Try to center the text and key **Title Card**, as shown in Figure 8-16.

3. Move to Card 2. From the File menu, select **Add clip art** and click **OK**.

4. From the HSArt folder, open **africa**. Select the entire image and click **OK**.

5. Center the image horizontally and place it along the bottom margin, leaving room for text above it, as shown in Figure 8-17.

6. Go back to Card 1. Use the **Lasso Selector** tool to select the letters of the paint text.

7. Copy the selected text.

8. Go to Card 2 and paste the selected text.

 **NOTE:**

From this point on, only change the card size if you are directed to do so.

**HINT:**

If you do not like the placement of your text, you can double click on the Eraser tool and choose white for the background. With the text erased, repeat Step 2.

**FIGURE 8-16**
Title Card Text

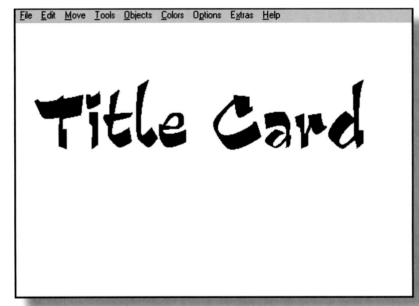

**STEP-BY-STEP 8.5 CONTINUED**

**9.** Position the text over the map area but *do not click outside the selected area.*

**10.** From the Edit menu, choose **Effects**. Choose **Cookie-cutter**.

**11.** Now move the selected text to the top of the card over the image of Africa, as shown in Figure 8-18.

**12.** Save the stack as **Effects**. Leave the stack open.

**FIGURE 8-17**
Africa on Card 2

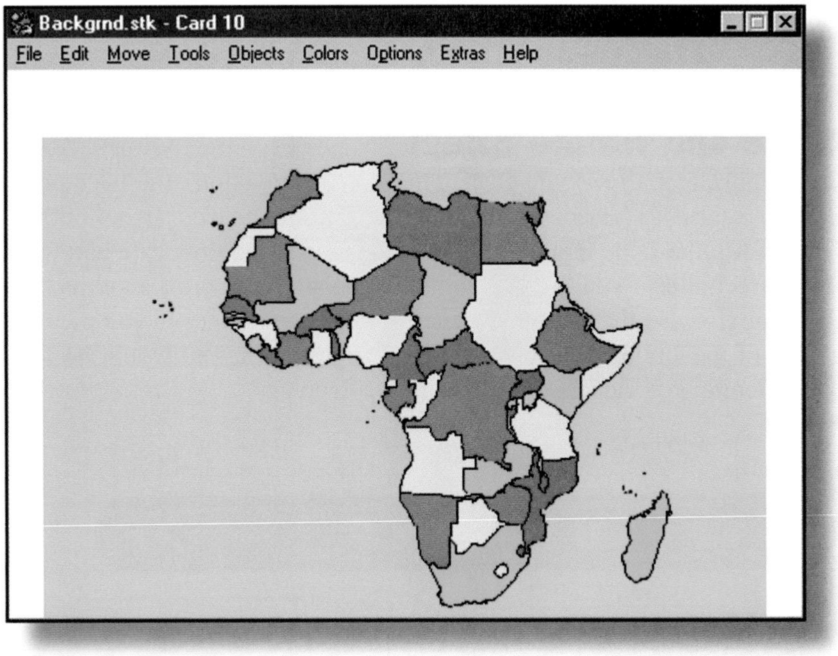

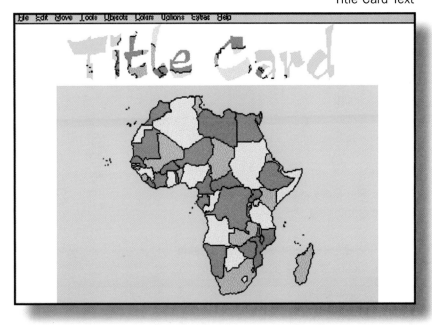

**FIGURE 8-18**
Title Card Text

Create a new card in the Effects stack using the Cookie-cutter effect. Choose your own text and background or clip art image. Save the stack as **Effects1** and leave it open.

## Scale and Rotate Effect

This effect allows you change the size and position of a piece of clip art or paint object. You have already scaled an object by dragging the double-headed arrow cursor to resize the object. You can accomplish the same thing with more precision using the Scale and Rotate option on the Effects menu. This effect allows you to proportionally change the size of an object. In addition to scaling an object, you can also use the effect to rotate or angle the image. If you picture a circle, 45 degrees would be eighth of the circle, 90 degrees would be one-fourth, 180 would be one-half, etc. If you want to angle your picture, you can choose the angle by degrees.

# STEP-BY-STEP ⟹ 8.6

1. With the Effects1 stack open, create a new card.

2. From the File menu, select **Add Clip Art** and click **OK**.

3. From the HSArt folder, select **animals**.

4. Select the ape using the **Rectangle Selector**, and click **OK**.

5. With the ape selected, choose **Effects** from the Edit menu.

6. Select **Flip Sideways**. Notice that the ape image is mirrored.

7. From the Effects menu, select **Flip Upside Down**. Notice that the ape is now standing on its head.

8. From the Effects menu, select **Flip Upside Down** again. The ape should be right side up.

9. With the image still selected, choose **Scale and Rotate** from the Effects menu.

 **HINT:**

You must use the Square Selector tool to select the image. You cannot access the effects if you use the Lasso tool to select the image.

**10.** In the Scale factor box, key **75**. In the Rotation angle box, key **45** as shown in Figure 8-19. Click **OK**.

**11.** Your image should resemble Figure 8-20. Save the stack and leave it open.

**FIGURE 8-19**
Scale and Rotate Window

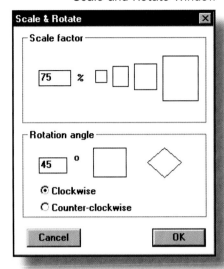

**FIGURE 8-20**
Scaled and Rotated Image

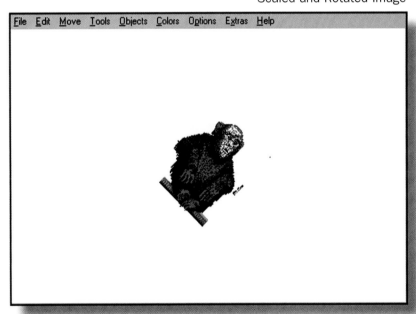

# Gradients

The Gradient effect refers to color blending. This effect makes it possible to alter the color of an object so that the color varies and blends in shading either from side to side, top to bottom, or inner to outer edge.

1. With the Effects1 stack open, add a card.

2. Using the **Circle Selector** tool, draw a circle.

3. From the Edit menu, choose **Effects**, then **Gradients**. You will see the color palette in Figure 8-21.

**HINT:**

The Circle Selector tool is the dashed-line circle. This effect does not work with the Oval tool.

 **TIP**

You can draw a circle by holding the Shift key while you draw the circle with the Circle Selector tool.

**FIGURE 8-21**
Gradient Window

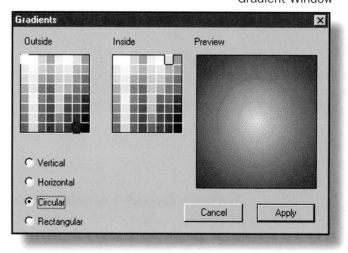

**STEP-BY-STEP 8.7 CONTINUED**

4. Choose **Circular**, and click in the **darkest purple** on the Outside palette and the **lightest purple** on the Inside palette. Then click **Apply**.

5. Repeat the process using the **Square Selector** tool with different color settings, as in Figure 8-22.

6. When you are finished, you should have a screen similar to Figure 8-23. Save your stack as **Effects2**.

7. Open a new stack. Do not change the card size.

8. Add a second card to the stack.

(continued on next page)

**FIGURE 8-22**
Rectangular Settings

**FIGURE 8-23**
Gradient Colored Shapes

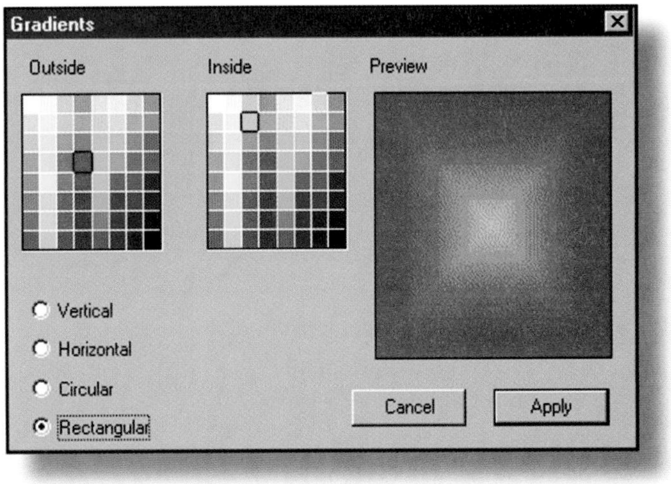

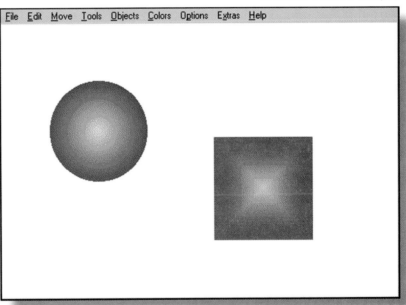

**9.** On the first card, draw a line across the bottom third of the card. Be sure the line goes completely across from edge to edge so that a closed area is formed. This bottom section of the card will represent grass.

**10.** Use the **Square Selector** tool to surround the area that will be the grass. With the area selected, use the gradients tool to make the bottom of the card look like a lawn. Choose **Vertical**, make the top **light green** and the bottom **dark green**. Choose Apply. (See Figure 8-24.)

**11.** Use the **Square Selector** tool to select the remaining top area of the card that will be the sky. From the Edit menu, choose **Effects**, then choose **Gradients**. Select **Vertical** and set the top for a **light blue** and the bottom for a **dark blue**, as shown in Figure 8-25.

**12.** Using the **Circle Selector** tool, create a sun in the sky. Add a circular gradient to the selection that moves from **dark yellow** on the outside to **dark tan** on the inside, as shown in Figure 8-26.

**13.** Save the stack as **Animat**.

**14.** Close HyperStudio.

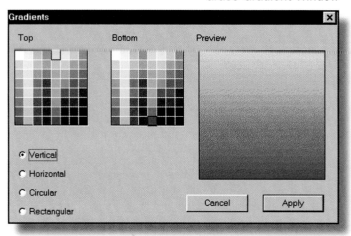

**FIGURE 8-24**
Grass Gradient Window

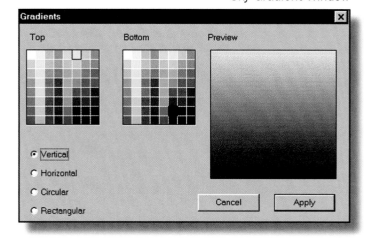

**FIGURE 8-25**
Sky Gradient Window

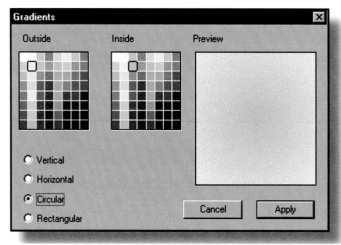

**FIGURE 8-26**
Sun Gradient Window

**152**

# Summary

In this lesson, you learned that:

- You can use templates to create stacks.

- HyperStudio supplies ready made card templates for you to use.

- You can copy backgrounds from card to card.

- You can share backgrounds between cards.

- When you share backgrounds, any changes to the background of one card will affect all of the cards sharing the same background.

- You can group cards to share buttons and text fields.

- The Extras menu offers a variety of useful options.

- The Spell Checker will check and correct spelling in your stacks.

- The Storyboard feature gives you an overview of all of the cards in a stack and allows you to rearrange or delete cards in the stack.

- The Title Card feature lets you make any card in the stack the Title card.

- There are special effects features for paint objects and clip art on the Edit menu.

- You can use the Cookie-cutter effect to show backgrounds through text.

- You can use the Gradients effect to blend and shade colors in painted objects.

- You can use the Scale and Rotate effects to change the size of images proportionally and to change the angles of the images on the cards.

## VOCABULARY

Copied background

Gradients

Ready Made cards

Rotate

Scale

Shared background

Templates

## TRUE/FALSE

**Circle the T if the statement is true or the F if it is false.**

**T   F   1.** You can load backgrounds or use Ready Made backgrounds, but you cannot create your own template backgrounds.

**T   F   2.** When you use a shared background, all of the buttons and text fields from one card will be copied to the other cards.

**T   F   3.** When you copy a background, all of the buttons, text fields, and graphics from one card will be copied to the other cards.

**T   F   4.** You cannot delete cards using the Storyboard feature.

**T   F   5.** To utilize the Effects features from the Edit menu, you can only use clip art.

**T   F   6.** Scale refers to the number of degrees that an image is turned.

## COMPLETION

**Complete each sentence below in the space provided.**

**1.** The white color on a new card is the _____ .

**2.** To utilize the effects filters from the Edit menu, you must select this type of object

_____ .

**3.** Rotating an image 180 degrees will turn it _____ .

**4.** Gradients change the _____ of an image.

**5.** The Title card feature lets you make _____ a title card.

## SHORT ANSWER QUESTIONS

**Answer the questions below in the space provided.**

**1.** What is the difference between sharing and copying backgrounds?

SCANS

2. What is a template?

3. Name three features of the Extras menu and describe what they do:

   a.

   b.

   c.

4. Name two ways you can make any card in the stack the first card:

   a.

   b.

5. Name three effects from the Effects menu and describe what they do:

   a.

   b.

   c.

6. If you are using the Gradients feature and the color bleeds over the entire card, what can you do to correct this?

7. Which tool do you use to select the image in order to utilize the Cookie-cutter effect and why?

8. Describe the steps to use the Cookie-cutter effect.

9. What are ready made cards?

10. What is the procedure for creating shared backgrounds?

## LESSON 8 PROJECT 8.1

- Use the Spell Checker to check and correct the spelling in all of the previous projects you have created so far with this book.

- Unless instructed otherwise, print out the cards from the projects that you have changed using the Spell Checker tool.

## LESSON 8 PROJECT 8.2

1. Create a stack to represent the effects that you learned to use in this lesson. Include:

- Title card

- Main Menu card

- Topic card for each effect

- A sample graphic object to demonstrate each effect.

- A Ready Made Card on at least one of the cards.

- A template of your own for at least two of the cards and share the background.

2. Save the stack as **Effects2**.

## LESSON 8 PROJECT 8.3

SCANS

1.  Open the **Animat** stack.

2.  On Card 2, create a card with three areas: a beach area, an ocean area, and a sky area. Use gradients to create these areas. Your completed card should look like Figure 8-27.

3.  Save the stack as **Animat1**.

**FIGURE 8-27**
Three Gradient Areas

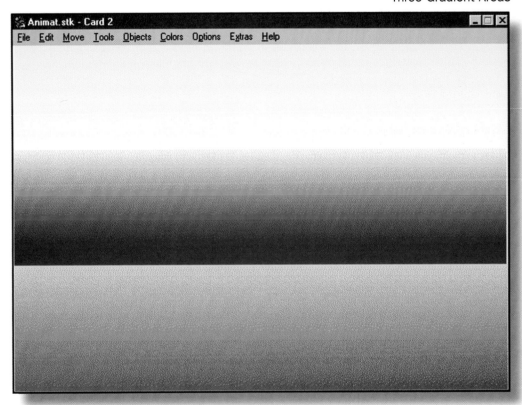

## CRITICAL THINKING ACTIVITY

SCANS

List the advantages and disadvantages of using shared backgrounds. If you were working on a large project with a group of people, would there be any advantage to using shared backgrounds? Why or why not?

**Adding graphics**
1. From the Objects menu, select Add a Graphic Object.
2. Select the source for the graphic. (Windows users only.)
3. Select the file for the graphic.
4. Select the graphic with the Selector tool.
5. Position the graphic on the card.
6. Click outside the graphic.
7. Click OK.

**Editing a graphic**
1. Using the Arrow (Edit) tool or the Graphic Object tool, select the graphic.
2. Double click on the graphic.
3. Move, copy, or edit the graphic as needed.

**Adding clip art**
1. From the File menu, select Add Clip Art.
2. Select the source for the clip art. (Windows users only.)
3. Select the file for the clip art.
4. Select the clip art with a selector tool.
5. Position the clip art on the card.
6. Click outside the clip art.
7. Click OK.

**Print**
1. From the File menu, select Print.
2. Select current card or stack.
3. Select the number of cards you would like on a page.

**Special effects with painted objects**
1. Using a selector tool, select the object.
2. From the Edit menu, select Effects.
3. Choose the effect you wish to use.

**Cookie-cutter effect for text**
1. Key the text you want to use with the Text tool.
2. Add clip art.
3. Use the lasso selector tool to select the painted text.
4. Copy the selected text.
5. Paste the selected text over the clip art.
6. While text is selected, choose Effects from the Edit menu.
7. Choose Cookie-cutter.
8. Move the text to its desired location.

**Scale and Rotate**
1. Select a paint object or clip art.
2. From the Edit menu, choose Effects.
3. Choose Scale and Rotate.
4. Key the number (percent) to scale or rotate.

**Gradients effect**
1. Select the area to add gradients.
2. From the Edit menu, choose Effects.
3. Choose Gradients.
4. Select the colors and the style.

## UNIT 3 REVIEW QUESTIONS

### FILL IN THE BLANKS

Complete the following statements by keying or writing the correct answers on a page to be submitted to your instructor. Center *Unit 3 Review Questions* at the top of the page. Number your answers to match the numbers listed here.

1. A button that moves to the next card in a stack is a _____ button.

2. You can edit a button by selecting the _____ tool or by selecting the

   _____ .

3. The editing tool that can be used to edit buttons, text objects, and graphics is the

   _____ .

4. A _____ is an object that floats over the background.

5. An "Iris close" is a _____ .

6. You can add clip art from the _____ menu.

7. You can add a graphic object from the _____ menu

8. Three file formats for graphics are _____ , _____ and

   _____ .

9. Graphic formats are a way of _____ graphics.

10. Changing the size of clip art or paint objects proportionally is called _____ .

## WRITTEN QUESTIONS

**Key or write your answers to the following questions. Number your answers. Use complete sentences and good grammar.**

11. What are the three types of text fields and what are their attributes?

    a.

    b.

    c.

12. How can you change the card size of a stack?

13. How can you access a larger color palette than the one on the Colors menu?

14. What is the function of the Effects options on the Edit menu?

15. What effect does sharing a background have on the cards in a stack?

## UNIT 3 APPLICATIONS

### UNIT 3 PROJECT

1. Choose a topic for a stack.

2. Create a storyboard and organizational chart for the stack using the elements listed in Step 4.

3. Create at least a five-card stack based on the storyboard.

4. Include at least one each of the following in your stack:
   - Title card
   - Main Menu card
   - Three topic cards
   - Subtopic cards, if needed
   - Text fields
   - Navigation
   - Graphics
   - Clip art
   - Cookie-cutter effect for text
   - Scaled and rotated clip art
   - Gradient effect

5. Save the stack as **EP3**.

### UNIT 3 CRITICAL THINKING ACTIVITY

Explain the ways that sharing backgrounds will affect the size of the stack in terms of good use of memory.

# WORKING WITH ANIMATIONS

# LESSON 9

# PATH ANIMATIONS

## *Animations*

HyperStudio has a variety of animations that are available to complement and expand your stacks. You have already worked with simple animations when you created transitions using the special effects to move from card to card in your stack. In HyperStudio, many of the animations are called NBA or New Button Animations because the buttons control the animation sequences. In other words, you press a button and something happens.

You can use animations to illustrate an action, for example, to show how the solar system turns. You can include animations to provide directions to the user, for instance, how to use a mouse. And you can use animations for special effects. Some other types of animations that you will explore are path animations, cell animations, multi-image animations, preanimated images, frame animations, and animating your own images.

## *Hide/Show NBA*

There are a variety of NBAs. The Hide/Show NBA allows you to create a button that will make an object appear, disappear, or move. In the following part of the lesson, you will see how to create an object and then, using a button, make it appear through a dissolve transition effect. You can use this effect on graphics, text, or even buttons.

# STEP-BY-STEP ⟹ 9.1

1. Open the stack **Animat1**.

2. Go to the second card in the stack, the beach scene you created in Lesson 8.

3. Use the Title Card feature from the Extras menu to make the beach card the first card in the stack.

4. Copy and paste this card. You should now have three cards in your stack.

5. Return to the first beach card.

6. Add a graphic object from the HSArt folder. Select the **iclibca** file.

7. Select the **mouse** using the **Lasso Selector** tool, as shown in Figure 9-1.

8. Place the graphic on the sand of your beach, as shown in Figure 9-2.

(continued on next page)

**TIP**

HyperStudio's file names for Macintosh users are different from the Windows' file names, since the names are not limited to eight characters. The file name that correlates with iclibca is Icon Library-Clip Art. Throughout this lesson, Macintosh users will need to identify and use the corresponding file names.

**HINT:**

It is a good idea to create a backup of a card that you will be trying new work on. If you make a mistake, you can delete the spoiled card, create another backup card, and attempt the process again. This way you do not have to create the entire card over again if you make a mistake.

**HINT:**

You must use a graphic object for this NBA. Clip art will not work.

**FIGURE 9-1**
Iclibca File with Mouse Selected

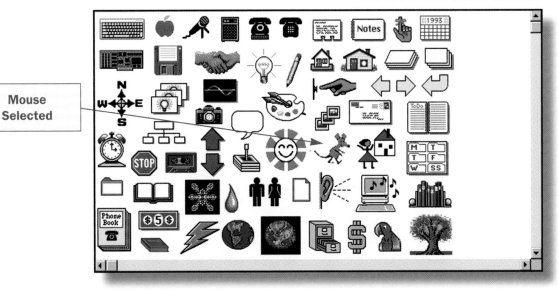

Mouse
Selected

**9.** Click outside the graphic. When you see the Graphic Appearance window, key the name of the graphic, **Mouse**, as shown in Figure 9-3. Click **OK** to place the graphic as a separate layer on the card.

**10.** Add a button to the card.

**FIGURE 9-2**
Mouse on Card

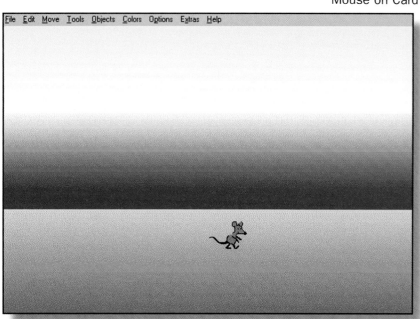

**FIGURE 9-3**
Graphic Appearance Window

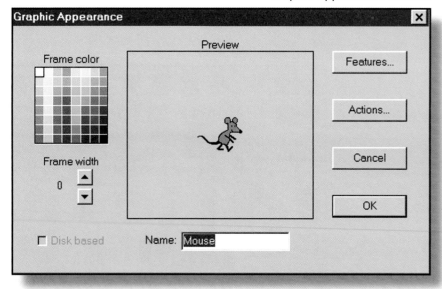

**11.** Choose the shadow box button, name the button **Mouse**, and choose a background color that matches the beach, as shown in Figure 9-4. Click **OK**.

**12.** Drag the button to the bottom of the screen and click outside the button.

**13.** Choose **New Button Actions** from the Actions window.

**14.** Choose **HideShw2 NBA** from the New Button Actions window, as shown in Figure 9-5.

**FIGURE 9-4**
Mouse Button Appearance Window

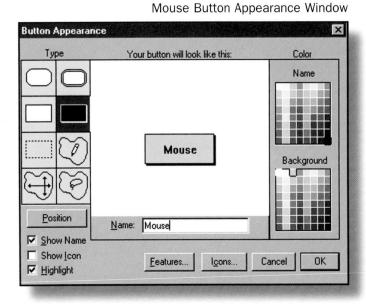

**TIP**

For Macintosh users, choose the HideShow NBA.

**15.** The information in the Info field describes the action as follows:

**This NBA allows you to hide, show or flip the appearance of one of HyperStudio's screen objects. This NBA only works with objects that are on the current card.**

**16.** Click **Use this NBA**.

(continued on next page)

**FIGURE 9-5**
HideShw2 NBA Window

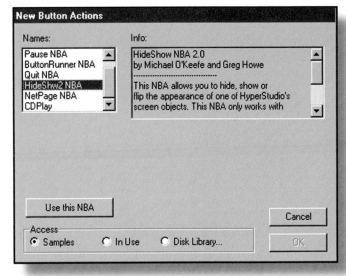

**17.** In the Hide/Show window, key **Mouse** in the Enter name of object field. Select **Graphic** in the "What kind of object is it?" field. Select **Flip (hide/show)** in the "What Should I do?" field. The choices are shown in Figure 9-6.

**18.** Click **Show Effect**. Select **Dissolve** for effect and **Medium** for speed, as shown in Figure 9-7. Click **Try it**.

**19.** Click **OK** from the Show Item Transitions window, click **OK** from NBA window, click **OK** from New Button Actions window, and click **Done** from the Actions window.

**20.** Return to Browse mode and double click the button to view the effect.

**21.** Save the stack as **Animat2**. Keep your stack open.

**FIGURE 9-6**
Hide/Show Window

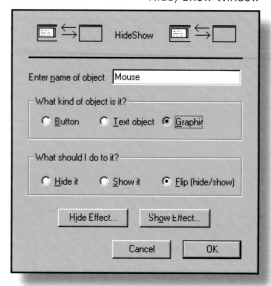

**FIGURE 9-7**
Show Item Transitions

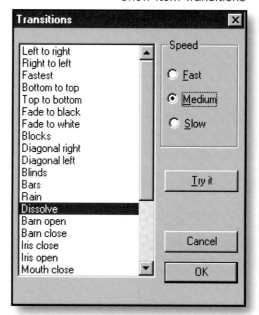

# *Preanimated Images and Path Animations*

In the previous Step-by-Step, you used a stationary graphic and created a Hide/Show button animation. In the next portion of the lesson, you will work with a preanimated graphic that is provided in HyperStudio. Preanimated graphics are different from stationary ones in that they have some motion built into the graphic. Stationary graphics provided by HyperStudio are saved as **bmp** files. You have used many of these images in earlier lessons. HyperStudio also includes a library of animated images that you can insert into your animations. These animated images are saved as **gif** files. Examples of preanimated graphics are a bird that moves its wings as if in flight or a frog that jumps.

Path animations allow you to design a path for an object to follow across a card. You can combine preanimated images and path animations. For instance, the jumping frog may be made to move across the screen using a path animation. Creating path animations in HyperStudio is as easy as creating a new button. The animator is an NBA that allows you to move the objects along a path you have chosen. You will create a path animation using a preanimated image in Step-by-Step 9.2.

## STEP-BY-STEP ⟹ 9.2

1. With the Animat2 stack open, go to the beach card with the mouse NBA button. (This should be Card 1 in your stack.)

2. From the Objects menu, choose **Add a Button**.

3. Name the button **Fish**. Choose the double oval button. Choose **white** for the Name color and a **dark blue** for the Background color. These options are shown in Figure 9-8. Click **OK**.

4. Move the button to the bottom left corner of the ocean, as shown in Figure 9-9.

5. Click outside the button. Select **Play animation** from the Actions window.

**FIGURE 9-8**
Button Appearance Window

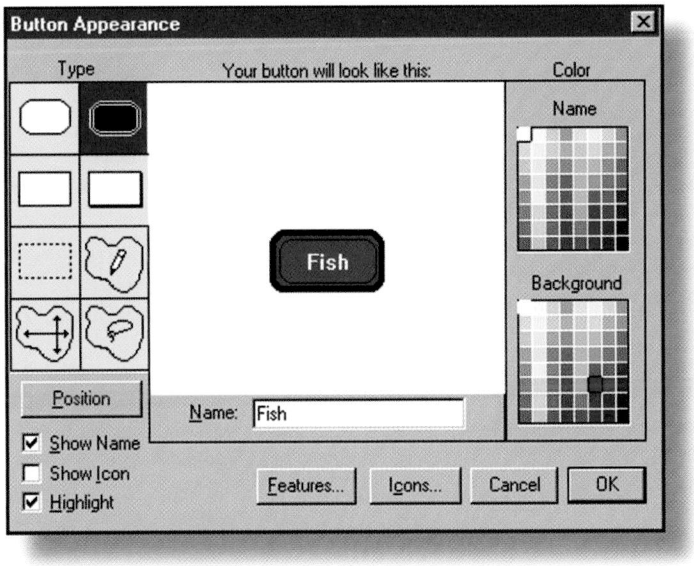

6. Click on **Disk Library** from the "Where would you like to get your image from?" window as shown in Figure 9-10.

7. Double click on **Fish.gif** from the Please select a picture file window, as shown in Figure 9-11.

8. Follow the instructions in the Path Edit window to create a path. Be creative with your path; it does not need to be a straight line. Press **Enter** when you have finished making the fish move across the screen.

**FIGURE 9-9**
Fish Button on Card

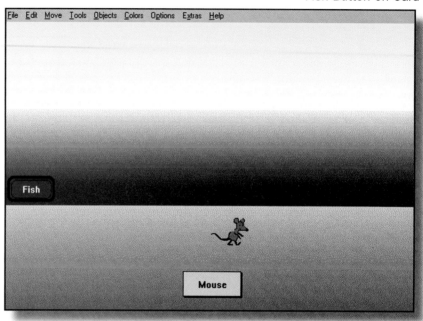

**FIGURE 9-10**
"Where would you like to get your image from?" Window

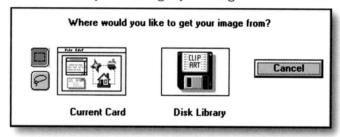

**FIGURE 9-11**
Fish.gif File

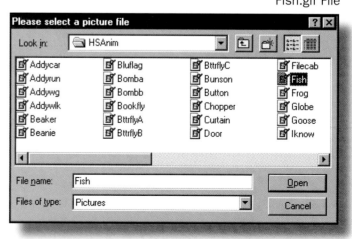

UNIT 4: WORKING WITH ANIMATIONS

**STEP-BY-STEP** ⟹ **9.2 CONTINUED**

9. Click **Try It** from the Animation window, as shown in Figure 9-12.

10. Pull down the Path menu by clicking on the down arrow beside the Path field. Click on **New Path**. Click **OK** if you see a dialog box asking if you want to create a new path.

11. Create a new path for your fish. Then click **Try It**. Click **OK**. Click **Done** from the Actions window.

12. With your cursor in Browse mode, click on your **fish** button. The card should resemble Figure 9-13.

13. Delete the extra backup card for the beach.

14. Save your stack as **Animat3**. Keep your stack open.

**FIGURE 9-12**
Animation Window

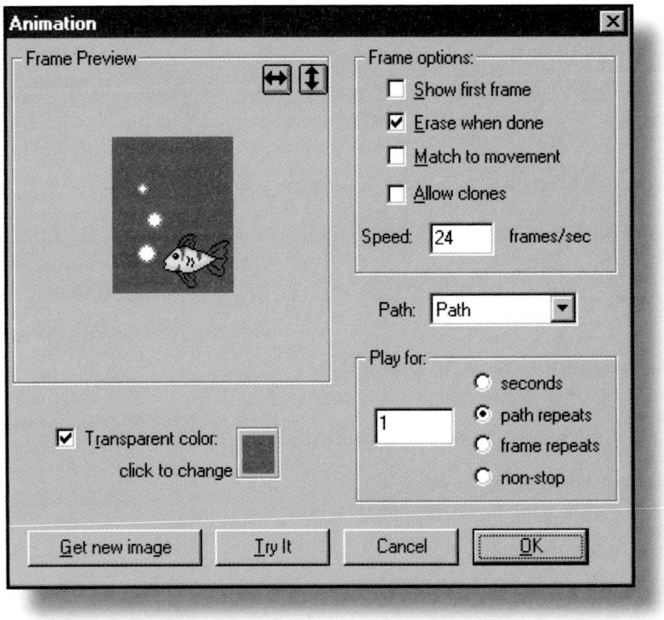

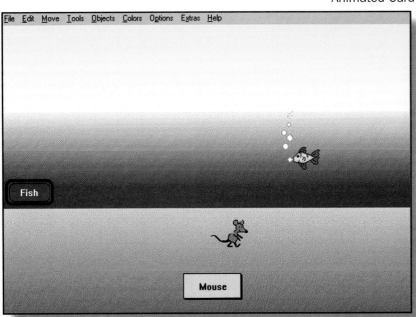

**FIGURE 9-13**
Animated Card

# Animating Static Objects

In HyperStudio, you can also create animations using stationary graphics. You can animate the images that are stored in the HyperStudio HSArt folder, images imported from other sources, or images you draw. As you have learned, you can hide/show the images or you can move them across a path that you design.

One of the button types that are available for you in HyperStudio is the invisible button. In this lesson, you will use an invisible button to create a path for a static object.

## STEP-BY-STEP 9.3

1. Open **Animat3**, if necessary.

2. Go to Card 1, the card with the grass, sky, and sun. Copy and paste this card to create a backup card.

3. Return to Card 2.

4. From the File menu, choose **Add Clip Art**.

5. From the HSArt folder, choose the **Dingbat2** file, as shown in Figure 9-14.

**FIGURE 9-14**
Dingbat2 File

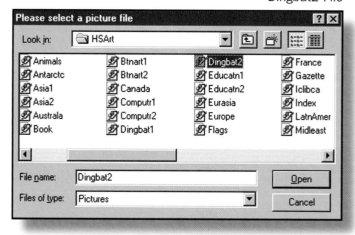

6. Use the **Lasso Selector** tool to select the rocket, as shown in Figure 9-15. Click **OK**.

**FIGURE 9-15**
Rocket Selected

**7.** With the rocket still selected, move it to the bottom right corner of the card, as shown in Figure 9-16. Do not cut off the tail of the rocket.

**8.** Add a new button. Name the button **ROCKET**. Select the invisible button, which is the dotted line rectangle. Note that when you select the invisible button, the Show Name box is automatically deselected. Your Button Appearance window should match Figure 9-17.

**9.** Move the button to the lower left corner of the card.

**10.** Click outside the button.

**11.** Choose **Play animation** from the Actions window.

(continued on next page)

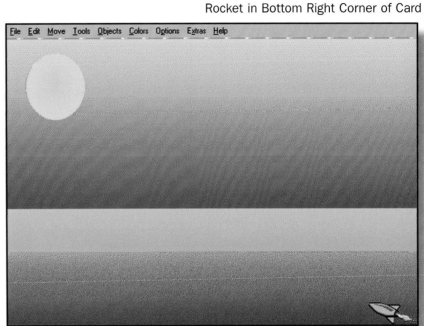

**FIGURE 9-16**
Rocket in Bottom Right Corner of Card

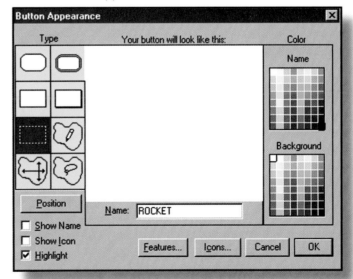

**FIGURE 9-17**
Button Appearance Window for the ROCKET Button

**12.** Select the **Lasso Selector** tool, as shown in Figure 9-18, and choose **Current Card**.

**13.** Use the **Lasso Selector** tool to select the rocket, taking care to keep the path as close to the outline as possible. Line up the selected rocket so that it perfectly aligns with the original rocket. When you have it lined up, hold down the mouse button and drag the rocket diagonally across the screen from the bottom right to the top left corner.

**14.** Release the mouse button and press **Enter**.

**15.** Choose **Try It** from the Animation window, as shown in Figure 9-19.

**16.** Choose **New Path** from the Path pull-down menu.

**17.** Create a new path for the rocket.

**18.** When you are satisfied with the rocket and its path, click **OK** and **Done**.

**19.** Return to Browse mode. Test the button. (Remember, it is in the lower left corner of the screen.)

**20.** Delete the backup card.

**21.** Save the stack as **Animat4**, and keep it open.

**HINT:**

You can always locate an invisible button by clicking on the Button tool. It will show all of the buttons on the card.

**FIGURE 9-18**
Current Card and Lasso Selector Tool Selected

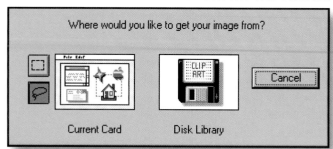

**TIP**

If you are not satisfied with the rocket outline you have chosen, select Get new image from the Animation window and redraw the outline. You can repeat this process as needed until you are satisfied with your selection.

**FIGURE 9-19**
Animation Window with Rocket

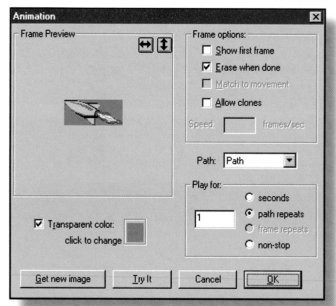

# *Multiple Animations*

Hyperstudio allows you to have a number of animations on the same card. You are only limited by the memory in your computer and the question of whether or not the animations support the ideas you are presenting. Animations are fun to use, but don't let them override the initial concept of your stack or card. In the following Step-by-Step, you will create two more animations on the card with the rocket. Both of these animations are preanimated. This will give you an idea of how to create separate paths for objects that will be observed on the same card at the same time. Later you will create one button to run all of the animations on a card at the same time.

## STEP-BY-STEP ⟹ 9.4

1. The Animat4 stack should be open. Go to Card 1, the grass, sky, and sun card.

2. Copy this card to create a backup. Then return to Card 1.

3. From the Objects menu, choose **Add a Button**.

4. In the Button Appearance window, key **BFLY** as the Name. Choose the invisible button (the dotted line rectangle). The check in the Show Name box will be automatically removed, as shown in Figure 9-20. Click **OK**.

5. Move the button to the left of the screen above the invisible button for the rocket.

6. Click outside the button. Select **Play animation** from the Actions window.

7. Choose **Disk Library** from the "Where would you like to get your image from?" window.

8. Double click on **BttrflyB.gif**.

(continued on next page)

**FIGURE 9-20**
Button Appearance Window

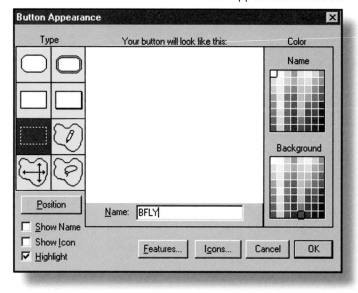

**INTERNET** The future of the Internet includes the ability to send and receive voice and video mail. If the person you are contacting is not available, you will be able to leave a message for video playback later.

9. Create a curly path that winds across the screen like a butterfly might fly. It might resemble the white line in Figure 9-21.

**FIGURE 9-21**
Sample Animation Path

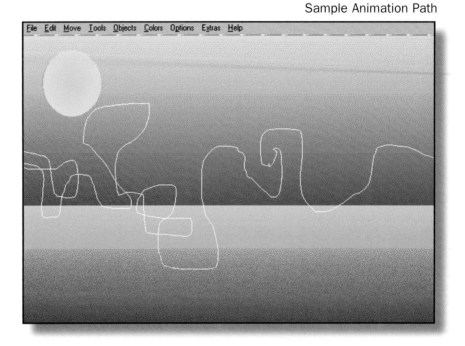

10. Choose **Try It** from the Animation window.

11. Select **New Path** from the Path pull-down menu.

12. Create a new path for your butterfly. Click **Try It**. Then click **OK**. Finally, click **Done** in the Actions window.

13. Make sure you are in Browse mode and try your button.

14. Save your stack as **Animat5** and keep it open.

## CHALLENGE ACTIVITY ➞ 9.1

Create an additional invisible button that will be placed directly above the invisible button for the butterfly. Use this button to fly a goose **(Goose.gif)** across the sky. The invisible buttons should end up being stacked, similar to what is shown Figure 9-22. Delete the backup card, Card 3. Save the completed stack as **Animat6**. Keep the stack open.

**FIGURE 9-22**
Invisible Buttons for the Three Animations

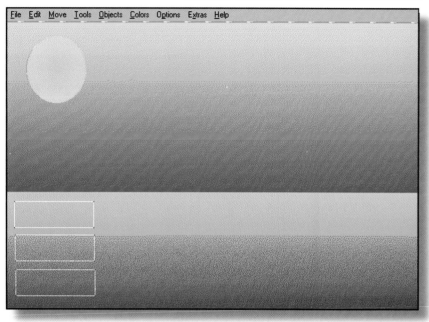

# *ButtonRunner NBA*

A useful NBA is the ButtonRunner NBA. This button enables you to use a single button to control multiple button actions on a card. Instead of having to click on each button separately for several animations, you can control all animations at the same time by using a ButtonRunner button. In the next Step-by-Step, you will create a ButtonRunner button to control all of the path animations on the card.

### STEP-BY-STEP ⟩ 9.5

1. With stack Animat6 open, add a new button.

2. In the Name box, key **Things that Move**. Select the double oval button. You will keep the default Show Name box selected. Select

a **dark green** for the Background color and **white** for the Name color. Figure 9-23 shows these selections.

(continued on next page)

**177**

3. Click **OK**. Position the button in the center on the bottom of the card, as shown in Figure 9-24.

4. Click outside the button and choose **New Button Actions** from the Actions window.

**FIGURE 9-23**
Things That Move Button Appearance Window

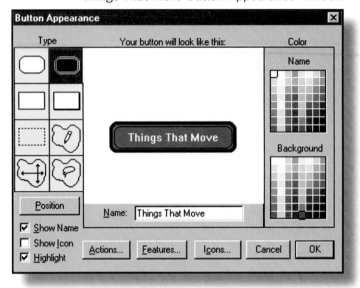

**FIGURE 9-24**
Button on Bottom of Card

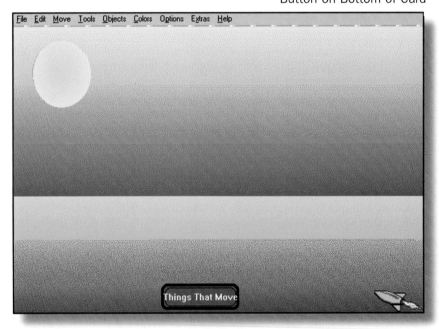

**5.** Select **ButtonRunner NBA**, as shown in Figure 9-25.

**6.** Click **Use this NBA**.

**7.** Key the names of the invisible buttons on the card. Press **Enter** after each button name so that each one is on a separate line. As shown in Figure 9-26, key:

**GOOSE**
**ROCKET**
**BFLY**

 **HINT:**

The names of the buttons must exactly match what you key.

**8.** Click **OK**, then click **Done**. Test your button. All three animations should move across the card at the same time.

**9.** Save the stack as **Animat7**. Close HyperStudio.

**FIGURE 9-25**
ButtonRunner NBA Selected

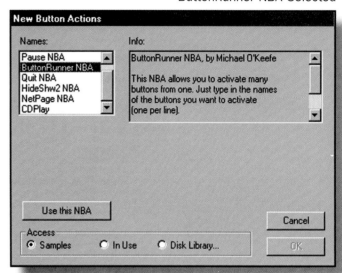

**FIGURE 9-26**
New Button Actions Window

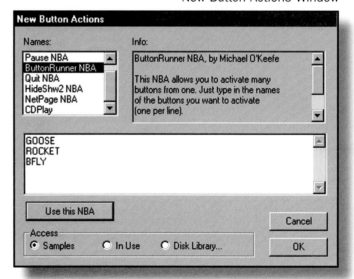

# Summary

In this lesson, you learned that:

- HyperStudio offers a variety of animations for you to use.

- NBAs are New Button Actions.

- NBAs are used in HyperStudio to control many animations.

- Animations have a variety of uses in HyperStudio.

- Hide/Show NBAs will hide or reveal a graphic, text, or button.

- Only graphic objects, not clip art, can be used for Hide/Show animations.

- Preanimated images can be used for complex animations.

- Preanimated images have motions built into the graphic.

- Path animations are animations that allow you to move an object across a screen.

- Variable paths can be created for path animations.

- Static objects can be animated.

- Multiple animations can exist on the same card.

- The ButtonRunner NBA is a button that controls one or more buttons on a card.

## VOCABULARY

Animations

ButtonRunner NBA

Hide/Show animations

New Button Action (NBA)

Path animations

Preanimated images

Static images

Stationary graphics

## LESSON 9 REVIEW QUESTIONS

### TRUE/FALSE

**Circle the T if the statement is true or F if it is false.**

T  F  **1.** The ButtonRunner NBA is used to move an object along a path.

T  F  **2.** Most preanimated graphics are saved as bmp files.

T  F  **3.** To create a path animation, you must choose Play animation from the Actions window.

**T  F**   **4.** Once you have created a path for your object, you cannot change it.

**T  F**   **5.** You cannot animate static objects.

**T  F**   **6.** You can animate text.

**T  F**   **7.** You can't animate objects that you draw on the screen.

**T  F**   **8.** You can have multiple animations on one card.

**T  F**   **9.** The ButtonRunner NBA can control all of the animations in a stack.

**T  F**   **10.** When you create a path animation, you can only move in one direction across the screen.

## COMPLETION

**Answer the questions below in the space provided.**

**1.**   What is the name of the NBA that allows you to move an object across a screen?

**2.**   What is the name of the controlling device that controls many of the different types of animations in HyperStudio?

**3.**   Name two types of animations you can use in HyperStudio:

**a.**

**b.**

**4.**   Why is it suggested that you create a backup card for your stack when you are creating animations?

5. What is one way to locate an invisible button?

6. Why do you use the Lasso Selector tool to select a stationary graphic that you wish to animate?

7. What is the sequence for creating a ButtonRunner NBA?

8. What are some of the choices you have regarding where you can find graphics to animate?

## LESSON 9 PROJECT 9.1

In your Safety3 stack, create a new card. Place the card in an appropriate place in the stack. Use animations that will be useful in your stack.

1. Design a background that fits with the appearance of your stack.

2. Explore the animated graphics that are available and include one of them on your card, with a path animation.

3. Choose a stationary graphic and create an animated path for it.

4. Create a Hide/Show NBA with another graphic.

5. Create a ButtonRunner NBA to control all of the animations on the card.

6. Save the stack as **proj91**.

## LESSON 9 PROJECT 9.2

1. Create a two-card stack.

2. On one card, use text and graphics to explain what a computer mouse is and how it works.

3. On the other card, include a drawing of a computer monitor and mouse. Create a path animation to show how a mouse moves the cursor on the monitor.

4. Save the stack as **Mouse**.

HINTS:

■ Draw the computer monitor screen using the tools in the tool palette so that you will be able to animate the cursor.

■ You will have to create two separate animations (one for the mouse and one for the cursor on the screen. Try to have the mouse and cursor use the same motions.

■ Create a ButtonRunner NBA to control them both.

## CRITICAL THINKING ACTIVITY

In groups, describe how you would animate a card of the solar system. What would you animate, how, and why? Prepare a storyboard showing the animations.

# LESSON 10

# FRAME ANIMATIONS

**Upon completion of this lesson, you will be able to:**

■ Create frame animations.

■ Edit and save screen captures.

■ Work with shadowed text.

■ Roll credits.

🕐 **Estimated Time: 2.5 hours**

## *Frame Animations*

In Lesson 9, you were introduced to animations. In this lesson, you will work with frame animations. This type of animation is based on the movement from one card to another to create an effect like cell animation, which is the process used for animating cartoons. You create almost identical cards with a slight variation from card to card. As you move through the cards, it appears that the object is moving and changing.

This technique will work for text, as in animating a title page. It could also work for presentations in which you are presenting text with bullets, for instance, you may want to introduce one item at a time but still show several items on a card. You can also use this technique for graphics, for instance, you could illustrate how a house is built, beginning with a picture of the foundation and adding pieces in a sequential progression.

### STEP-BY-STEP ➯ 10.1

1. Open the **Mouse** stack.

2. Create a new card. Use the Title Card feature from the Extra menu to move the new card to the first, or Title card, position.

3. Add clip art of the two figures using the computer from **computr1** as the background for your card. The figures are shown in Figure 10-1.

**4.** Move the clip art to the left and center it vertically on the card. (Look ahead to Figure 10-4 if you need help placing the clip art.)

**FIGURE 10-1**
Clip Art Window Showing Computr File

**5.** Create a text object. Move it to the right side of the screen. Extend its length to fill most of the screen, and center it vertically.

**6.** Click outside the object. In the Text Appearance window, deselect **Draw scroll bar** and **Scrollable**. Leave **Draw frame** selected. Choose **black** for the Text color and a **medium blue** for the background color, as shown in Figure 10-2.

(continued on next page)

**FIGURE 10-2**
Text Appearance Window

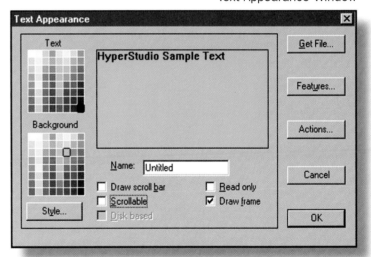

**7.** Click the **Style** button. Make the following choices in the Text Style window, as shown in Figure 10-3:

| | |
|---|---|
| Font | **Arial Black** |
| Size | **24** |
| Align | **Center** |

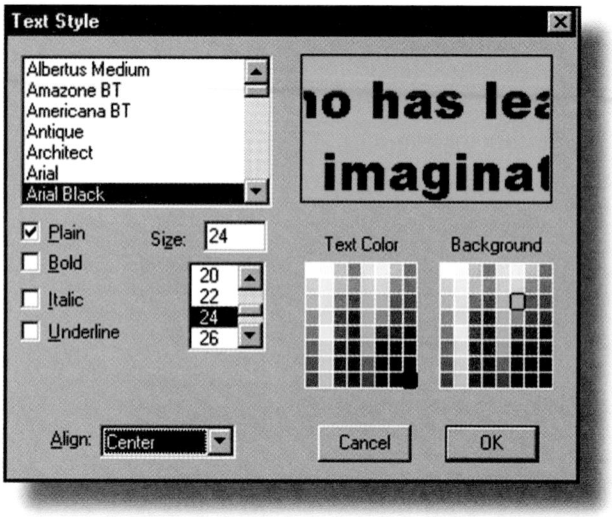

**8.** Click **OK** twice.

**9.** In the text field, key:

**How**
**To**
**Use**
**A**
**Mouse**

Your card should look like Figure 10-4.

**10.** Copy the card and paste it until you have a total of six of the same cards.

**11.** Save the stack as **Mouse1**.

**FIGURE 10-3**
Text Style Window

**FIGURE 10-4**
Title Card

 **HINT:**

You only need to copy one time. Each time you paste, the last image you copied will be pasted.

STEP-BY-STEP ⟹ 10.1 CONTINUED

**12.** Move to the first card and, in Browse mode, select and delete all of the text on the card, as shown in Figure 10-5.

**TIP**

The current card number is displayed in HyperStudio's title bar.

**13.** Move to the second card. Select and delete all text except **How**, as shown in Figure 10-6.

(continued on next page)

**FIGURE 10-5**
First Card in Mouse1 Stack

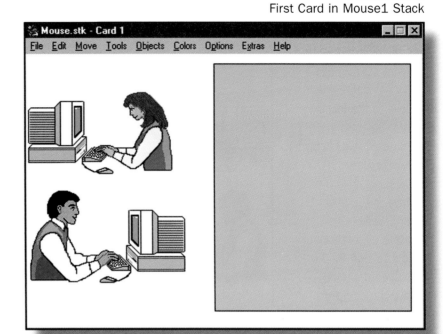

**FIGURE 10-6**
Card 2 in Mouse1 Stack

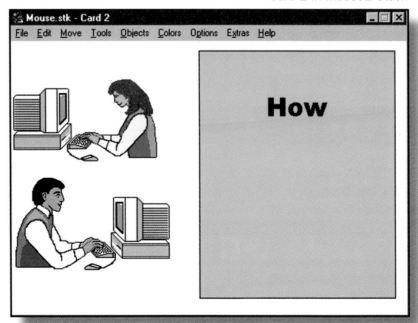

**14.** Move to the third card. Select and delete all text but **How To**, as shown in Figure 10-7.

**15.** Move to the fourth card. Select and delete all text except **How To Use**.

**16.** Move to the fifth card. Select and delete all text except **How To Use A**. The sixth card should have the complete title.

**17.** Save the stack as **Mouse2** and keep it open.

**18.** Using your keyboard, move through the six cards you just created. Watch the animation effect as you move from card to card.

**FIGURE 10-7**
Card 3 in Mouse1 Stack

**TIP**

The keyboard shortcut to move to the next card is **Ctrl + >** (for Windows) and  + > (for Macintosh).

## CHALLENGE ACTIVITY ⟹ 10.1

Using the technique you practiced in the previous Step-by-Step, create an animation for a presentation in which you will animate the card shown in Figure 10-8.

**1.** Create a new stack, using the default card size.

**2.** Create the background using the one of the techniques you practiced in earlier lessons such as:

➥ Select areas of the card and apply gradients.

■ Draw borders around the card and apply colors or patterns using the Paint Bucket tool.

■ Import a background from the HSArt folder.

**3.** Add a text object including the text on the card.

**4.** Copy and paste the card to create four additional cards. The Title card should include the **Uses for Animation:** title. Cards 2 through 5 should add the numbered items, one by one.

**5.** Save the stack as **Present**.

**6.** Test the stack to make sure the numbered items appear one at a time.

**7.** Close the stack.

**FIGURE 10-8**
Present Stack

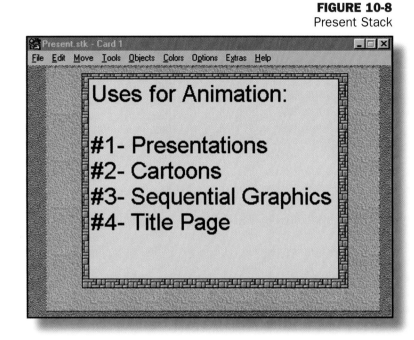

# *Editing and Saving Images as Screen Captures*

As you scrolled through the Mouse2 stack, you were able to see the animation effect of the cards even though you moved through the stack manually. The effect can also be made to work without using the manual controls. To create an automatic animation, each screen must be saved separately as a screen capture. HyperStudio will automatically number each of the screen captures in the order they are created.

**STEP-BY-STEP ⊃ 10.2**

**1.** Open the **Mouse2** stack. Using the **Arrow (Edit)** tool, click outside the text object.

**2.** From the File menu, select **Export Screen**. From the Save As window, double click on the name of the folder where you save your work. Click **Save** to save the screen capture as **Pict01**. (See Figure 10-9.)

 **TIP**

Do not change the name or number of the screen name. It should be Pict01.

(continued on next page)

**189**

**3.** Move to Card 2 and repeat the process from Step 2. This time the file name will be Pict02.

**FIGURE 10-9**
Saving Pict01

**TIP**

The keyboard shortcut to export a screen is **Ctrl + E** (for Windows) and  + E (for Macintosh).

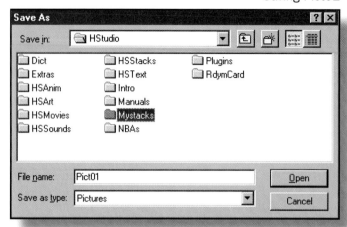

**4.** Repeat this exporting process for each of the remaining four cards in the title sequence. You should have six screen captures: **Pict01** through **Pict06**, as in Figure 10-10.

**FIGURE 10-10**
Pict01 through Pict06

**5.** Move to the first card in your stack.

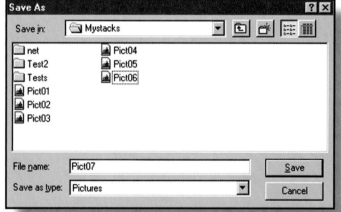

**INTERNET** In the 1960s, the first version of the Internet was called the Advanced Research Projects Agency Network (ARPANET). ARPANET was designed so that scientists and military experts could keep communicating even if part of the network was damaged by a natural disaster or nuclear attack. Today's Internet is just as durable and flexible.

**6.** Create a new button. Select the double oval button and name the button **Start**, as shown in Figure 10-11.

**7.** Select **Icons**, choose the hand with the wand, and click **OK**.

**8.** Click **OK** and move the button to the bottom of the card under the computer image. You may have to resize the button to make it fit under your image. Do not put it in the text field. Your card should resemble Figure 10-12.

**9.** Click outside the button. From the Actions window, choose **Play animation**.

**10.** When asked where you want to get your image from, choose **Disk Library**. Then locate the folder containing **Pict01** through **Pict06**.

**11.** Double click on the **Pict01** file.

**12.** Use the **Square Selector** tool to select the entire text field. Click **OK**.

(continued on next page)

**FIGURE 10-11**
Button Appearance Window

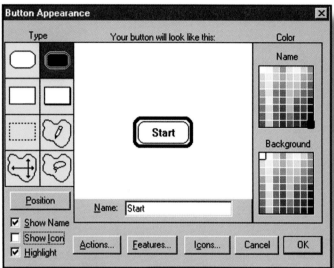

**FIGURE 10-12**
Button Placement on Card 1 of the Mouse1 Stack

**191**

**13.** Do not click the mouse button. Use the mouse to drag the object and carefully position the selected field over the text object on the card. When it is positioned, click the mouse button. Then press **Enter** from the keyboard. You will see the screen in Figure 10-13.

**HINT:**

When you click the mouse, one or more of the words may appear. Ignore the words for now.

**14.** From the Animation window, change the Speed to 6 frames/sec and change the Play for option to 4 path repeats. Your choices should match Figure 10-14. Click **OK**. Then **Done**.

**TIP**

The higher the speed, the faster the animation moves.

**15.** In the Browse mode, click the button to view the animation.

**TIP**

To edit the button, select the **Button** tool or the **Arrow (Edit)** tool and double click on the button. Click **Actions** from the Button Appearance window. Deselect and reselect **Play animation**. Then make the changes.

**FIGURE 10-13**
Frame Animation Window

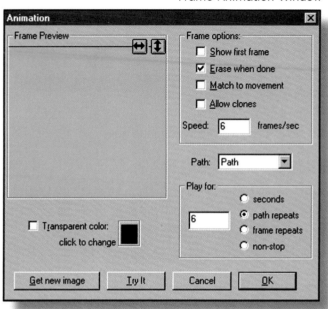

**FIGURE 10-14**
Animation Window

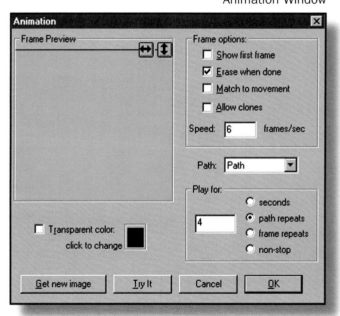

## STEP-BY-STEP 10.2 CONTINUED

**16.** Using the **Storyboard** feature, move Card 6 to the first place in the stack, the Title card spot, as shown in Figure 10-15.

**17.** Cut the button from what is now Card 2 and paste it on the Title card, Card 1. Your Title card should look like Figure 10-16.

**18.** Save your stack as **Mouse3**. Keep the stack open.

**FIGURE 10-15**
Storyboard Window

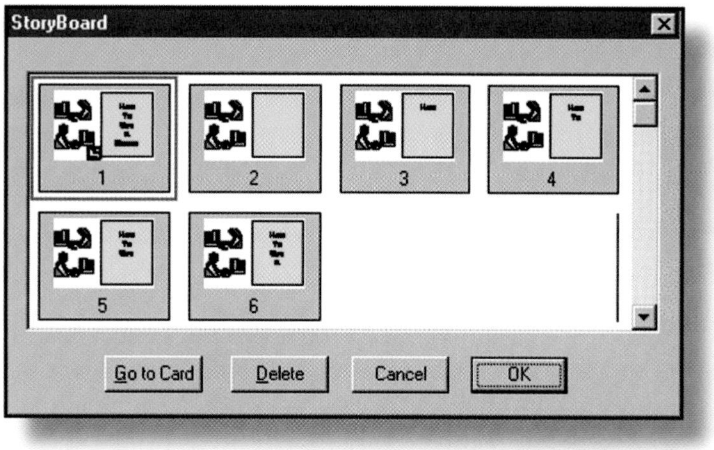

**FIGURE 10-16**
New Title Card

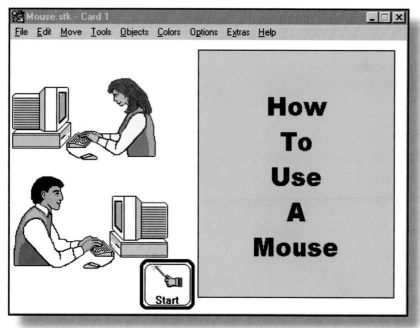

The last TIP explained how to edit the button actions. Use this process to experiment with different speeds and counts for your animation. Do not save any of the experiments.

# Shadowed Text

Shadowed text is a special effect for text. Using this effect, the text appears to be three-dimensional. It is a good technique for highlighting important text. However, it can be a distraction if overused.

To create shadowed text, you use two transparent text objects. Both text objects contain the same text: one is colored text, and the other is a different color of text, usually to black or gray. Then one is placed behind the other, but slightly off from the original frame, creating a shadow effect for the text.

## STEP-BY-STEP ⟹ 10.3

1. With the **Mouse3** stack open, create a new card. Use the Storyboard feature to move this card to the seventh card position as shown in Figure 10-17.

2. Create a text object on the blank card. The text field should be centered across the top of the card. Click outside the text field.

3. Click the **Style** button. Use a font of your choice. Make the font size **36**. Make the text **dark blue** and **center** aligned. Make the background **white**. Click **OK** twice.

4. Key **Main Menu** in the text field.

**FIGURE 10-17**
Seventh Card in Storyboard

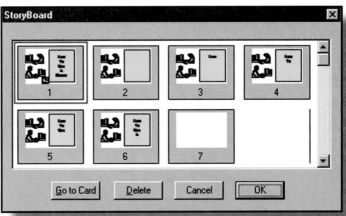

**5.** Using the **Text Object** or **Arrow (Edit)** tools, double click on the text field. Make the field **Read only**. Deselect: **Draw scroll bar**, **Scrollable**, and **Draw frame**, as shown in Figure 10-18.

**HINT:**

Read only text fields cannot be changed by the cursor on the card.

**FIGURE 10-18**
Read Only Text Field Object

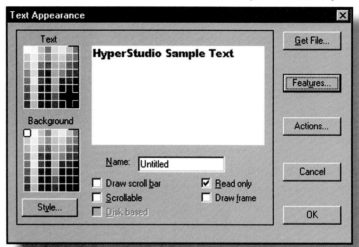

**6.** Click the **Features** button on the right side of the Text Appearance window.

**FIGURE 10-19**
Transparent Feature

**7.** From the Features menu, select **Transparent**, as shown in Figure 10-19. Click **OK** twice.

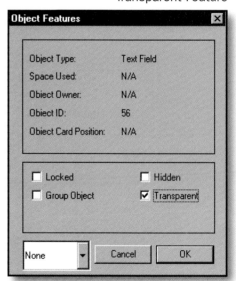

(continued on next page)

**8.** Copy and paste the text object. Drag the copied text below the first field. Double click on it and change the Text color to **dark gray**. Click **OK**. The result will look like Figure 10-20.

**FIGURE 10-20**
Copied Text Field

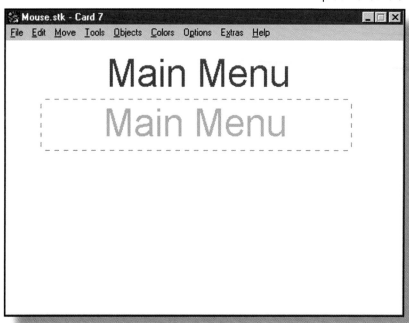

**9.** Select the second field. Drag the dark gray text slightly above and to the left of the dark blue text, as shown in Figure 10-21.

**10.** Save the stack as **Mouse4**. Keep the stack open.

You can use the arrow keys on your keyboard to make small directional movements on a selected object.

**FIGURE 10-21**
Shadowed Text

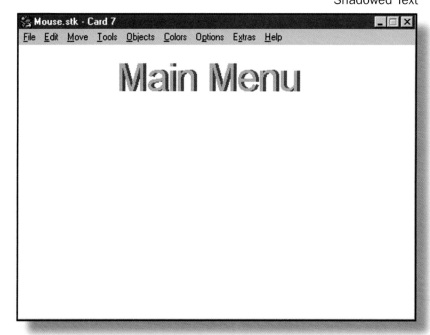

# *RollCredits NBA*

One of the NBA (new button actions) features offered by HyperStudio is RollCredits. This NBA gives your stack a look like the one you see when the credits roll at the end of a movie. It is a very nice effect that automatically scrolls the text that you type. You can use this feature for long passages of text that would need a scroll box. However, it is not particularly effective for complex text passages because the user may need to think about your statement before reading additional text. Therefore, you may scroll a list of items, but would not likely scroll something such as a poem. RollCredits is often used to list those who contributed to the stack, to list resources included in the stack, or to provide information about the creation of a stack.

You can control the rate and look of the scroll in the following ways:

- **Scroll lines:** This option makes the field scroll one line at a time.

- **Scroll pixels:** This option makes the field scroll by the number of pixels you specify. (Remember, pixels are the dots that make up the pictures on your computer.)

## STEP-BY-STEP 10.4

1. With the stack **Mouse4** open, create a new card. Use the Storyboard feature to move it to the end of the stack. (See Figure 10-22.)

2. Create a new text object. Stretch the field to fill the screen vertically.

3. In the Text Appearance window, select only the **Scrollable** field. The Text color should be **dark blue** and the Background color should be **light blue**. These choices are shown in Figure 10-23.

(continued on next page)

**FIGURE 10-22**
New Card at End of Stack

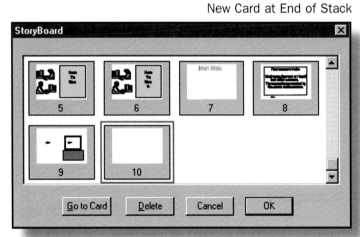

**4.** From the Styles window, choose the font of your choice. Make the font size **24** and **Center** aligned.

**5.** In that text object, press **Enter** four or five times and then key in the following:

> **This**
> **Stack**
> **Was**
> **Created**
> **By**
> **Your**
> **Name***
> **For**
> **My**
> **HyperStudio**
> **Project.**

\* Key your name in place of the **Your Name** placeholder in the copy above.

**6.** Press **Enter** four or five times at the end of your text to create the effect of the text moving off the screen.

**7.** Using the **Text Object** tool or **Arrow (Edit)** tool, double click on the text object.

**8.** Click the **Actions** button in the Text Appearance window.

**9.** Select **New Button Actions**, as shown in Figure 10-24.

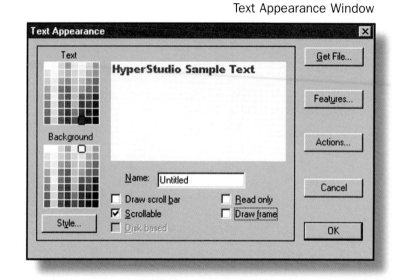

**FIGURE 10-23**
Text Appearance Window

**FIGURE 10-24**
New Button Actions Selected

**10.** Select **RollCredits** from the New Button Actions window, as shown in Figure 10-25. Click the **Use this NBA** button.

**11.** In the RollCredits window, change the Speed (steps/sec) to **30** and # of pixels to **5**. Click **Test Speed**. Then change the Speed (steps/sec) to **10** and # of pixels to **2**, as shown in Figure 10-26. Click **Test Speed**. Read the information in the scrolling text box. Click **OK** or **Done** as needed to complete the process.

**12.** Move to the previous card, then return to the card on which you just created the credits. Click inside the text field to see it scroll. In the Browse mode, click outside the text field to stop it.

**13.** Save the stack as **Mouse5**. Keep the stack open.

**TIP**

If you have more than one text field on a card, you must name the text field to be used to roll the credits. You must give it the same name in the Text Appearance window and the RollCredits window. The names must be *exactly* the same.

**FIGURE 10-25**
RollCredits NBA

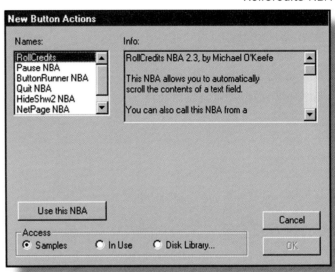

**FIGURE 10-26**
RollCredits Window

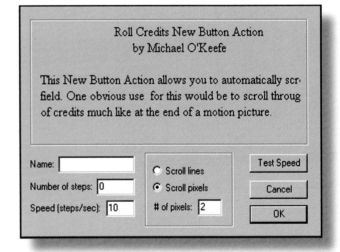

**NOTE:**

When a card first appears, the RollCredits feature will always start at the beginning of the text field.

Create the following navigation in the **Mouse5** stack:

■ Insert a button to go from the Title card to the Main Menu card.

■ Use the mouse graphic as the navigation tool to go to the text page about the mouse.

■ Use the mouse graphic as the navigation tool to go to the animated page about how to use the mouse.

■ Use the mouse graphic as the navigation tool to go to the scrolling text page.

■ Include a button to return to the Main Menu card. (This button should appear in a consistent position on all appropriate cards.)

Save the stack as **Mouse6**.

# Summary

In this lesson, you learned that:

■ There are a variety of uses for frame animations.

■ You can create frame animations for title pages and presentations.

■ You can copy screens and save them as screen captures.

■ You can create shadowed text.

■ You can use the RollCredits NBA to create movie-type scrolling text.

## VOCABULARY

Frame animations

Pixel

RollCredits NBA

Screen captures

Scroll lines

Shadowed text

## LESSON 10 REVIEW QUESTIONS

### TRUE/FALSE

**Circle the T if the statement is true or F if it is false.**

**T   F**    **1.** Frame animations can be used to animate text.

**T   F**    **2.** Frame animations can be used for presentations.

**T   F**    **3.** When using screen captures, they do not need to be in any specific order.

**T   F**    **4.** The higher the speed of a path in an animation, the slower the movement of the animation.

**T   F**    **5.** There is no difference between the speed of the animation and the frame repeats.

**T   F**    **6.** The shadowed text effect requires that you use two different text colors in the process.

**T   F**    **7.** To use shadowed text, you must have transparent text fields.

**T   F**    **8.** You can't use the RollCredits NBA if you have more than one text field on a card.

**T   F**    **9.** You can use the RollCredits NBA if you have more than one text field on a card, but you must name the text field objects.

**T   F**    **10.** In a RollCredits NBA, speed refers to the number of pixels.

### COMPLETION

**Answer the questions below in the space provided.**

**1.**    Explain what a frame animation is.

**2.**    List three uses for a frame animation:

   **a.**

   **b.**

   **c.**

**201**

3. What is a screen capture and how is it used in a frame animation?

4. How can you change the speed of an animation?

5. Name two ways to move cards around your stack:

   a.

   b.

6. What is shadowed text?

7. Why would you use the shadowed text effect?

8. Describe a RollCredits NBA.

9. Why would you use a RollCredits NBA?

10. What are the two ways to control the speed of a Roll Credits NBA?

   a.

   b.

## LESSON 10 PROJECT 10.1

Open **Proj91** and create the following:

■ A RollCredits text field listing your name as the creator of the stack.

■ A button to go to the roll credits card.

■ Shadowed text for the subtopic cards.

Save the revised stack as **Safety4**.

## LESSON 10 PROJECT 10.2

You will work with the stack you created in Project 5-1, MyTopic. Open the **MyTopic2** stack. Consider how you will use animations, icon actions, graphics, path animations, and frame animations. Include the following:

■ At least three graphics.

■ At least one shared background.

■ At least one icon with an action.

■ One path animation or a frame animation.

■ Navigation to move around the stack.

NOTE: If the project you created in Project 5-1 does not lend itself to these additions, redo Project 5-1 with the new goals in mind.

Save as **MyTopic3**.

## CRITICAL THINKING ACTIVITY

You are asked to prepare some topics for short presentations. With this in mind, list some appropriate uses for frame animation other than text. List five or more specific topics that would be more easily understood using a frame animation. Discuss your list with three other learners. Create a combined list containing your group's five best ideas.

# WORD ANIMATIONS— HYPERTEXT

**Upon completion of this lesson, you will be able to:**

■ Create hypertext links.

■ Create a time line.

■ Use Box Maker.

■ Create a slide show animation.

🕐 **Estimated Time: 2 hours**

## *Hypertext Links*

Hypertext links are words that, when clicked on, create some kind of action, similar to button features. When you click on hypertext words or phrases, they generally take you to another place. A common use of a hypertext link is to take you to another card that gives you more information about the phrase or hypertext word. For instance, if you click on the word *lion*, you might be taken to a picture of a lion or a page with more information about the lion. You can have more than one link on the card, and each link can take the user to a different location. If you have used the Internet, you have seen a common use of hypertext links. Hypertext is a way to make a stack more interactive since the user controls the movement to the link. Hypertext links also allow you to present any amount of information in small, manageable portions.

### STEP-BY-STEP ⟹ 11.1

1. Create a four-card stack. Use the default card size.

2. Leave Card 1 blank. On Card 2, use **Add Clip Art** to insert a picture of a personal computer, as shown in Figure 11-1.

3. On Card 3, create a text object with a frame, as shown in Figure 11-2. Use the **Arial** font, size **14**. Key the following in the text field:

**The modem allows your computer to connect to another computer through a process known as a handshake.**

**It is the use of the modem that has made the Internet so accessible.**

(continued on next page)

**FIGURE 11-1**
Personal Computer

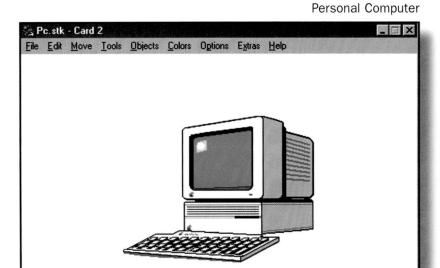

**FIGURE 11-2**
Card 3

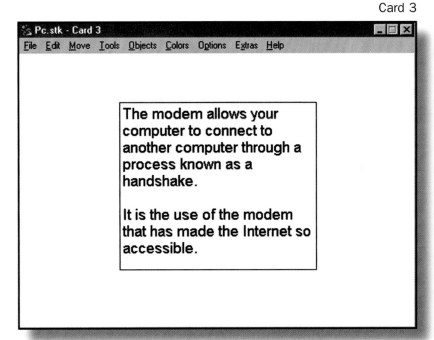

4. On Card 4, create a text object with a frame. Use the same font and size as you did with Card 3. Key the following:

**The Internet, also called the information highway, is the largest computer network in the world. It was originally created for worldwide communication among researchers, scientists, and the military.**

5. Return to Card 1. Add a text object with a frame. Continue using the same font and size as you used with Cards 3 and 4. Key the following and size the text field to fit the text:

**Computing has advanced dramatically in the last decade. With the introduction of PCs or personal computers, a wide variety of information has become accessible to many people in their homes. Computer use is no longer limited to business and research.**

**When a modem is part of your computer, it has the added advantage of making the Internet and all of its resources readily available.**

6. Add a blue background around the text object on Card 1. Highlight the text **PCs**. With the text highlighted, change the text's color to a **medium blue**. Use the same color to change the following words: **modem, Internet**. Your screen should look like Figure 11-3.

**HINT:**

You can change the text color by selecting Set Text Color from the Options menu.

7. With **PCs** highlighted, choose **Hypertext Links** from the Object menu, as shown in Figure 11-4.

**FIGURE 11-3**
Highlighted Text

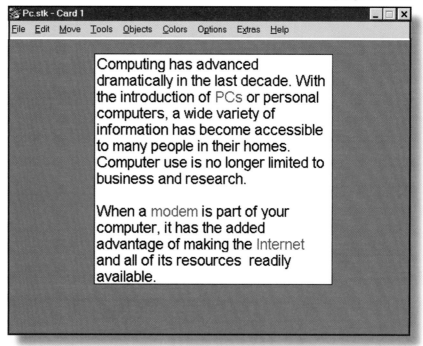

**FIGURE 11-4**
Hypertext Links

8. Choose **Add Link**.

9. Click on **Actions**. Choose **Another card**.

10. Use the right arrow to find the card with the picture of the PC on it. Then click **OK** twice and **Done** twice.

11. While in the Browse mode, test the link by placing your cursor on the word and clicking. If the link has been correctly connected, you will move to Card 2, the card with the picture of the computer.

12. Return to Card 1.

13. Highlight the word **modem**. From the Objects menu, choose **Hypertext Links**. Choose **Add Link**. Choose **Actions**. Choose **Another card**. Use the right arrow to find the card with the information about the modem, Card 3. Click **OK** twice and **Done** twice.

14. To change a hypertext link, choose **Hypertext Links** from the Objects menu. Select the word **modem** from the list and choose **Delete**.

15. When the warning shown in Figure 11-5 asks if you want to delete this link, click on **Yes, delete it**. Then click **Done**.

16. Repeat step 14 to put the hypertext link for the word **modem** back on the list.

17. Use the same procedure to create a link for the word **Internet**. Link the word to the card with the information about the Internet, Card 4.

18. Test all three links.

19. Create a **Back** button for Cards 2, 3, and 4 that returns to the first card. A sample Back button is shown in Figure 11-6.

20. Test all your buttons and links. Save the stack as **PC**. Keep the stack open.

**FIGURE 11-5**
"Are you sure you want to delete this link?" Window

**FIGURE 11-6**
Back Button

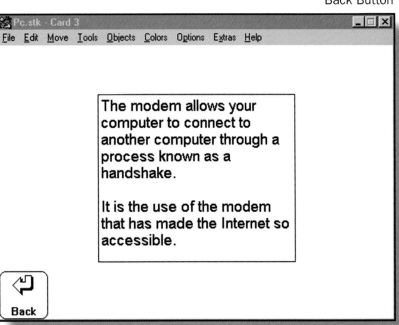

1. With the PC stack open, move to the card with the PC graphic on it, Card 2.

**FIGURE 11-7**
Three Text Fields on Card 2

2. Create a text object with a frame. Use the **Arial** font, size **10**. Specify the Background color as **white** and the Text color the same **blue** as the hypertext on the first card. In the text field, key **Keyboard**. Size the text object to frame the word. Move the object near the keyboard.

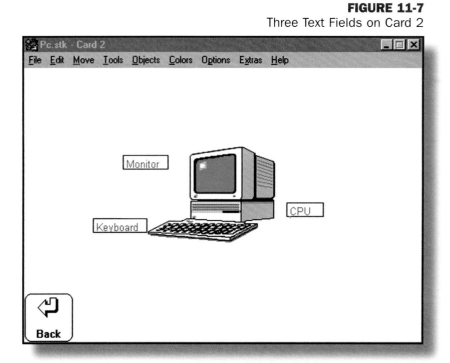

3. Copy and paste the text field two times to create two more fields. Move the fields to the appropriate positions around the graphic. Key **Monitor** in one field and **CPU** in the third field. Your card should resemble Figure 11-7.

4. Add a card to the stack.

5. Create a text object without a frame. Use the **Arial** font, size **14**. Key the following:

**Input, Output, and Processing**

**The keyboard is used for the input of data.**

**The monitor is used for the output of data.**

**The CPU or Central Processing Unit is used to process data.**

6. Size the text object as needed.

7. Return to the card with the picture of the PC, Card 2. Create hypertext links from each of the text fields to the Input, Output, and Processing card.

8. Create a button on the card that will take you back to the picture of the computer. Use a PC icon for the button and name it **Back to PC**, as shown in Figure 11-8.

9. Save your stack as **PC1**. Keep your stack open.

# *Adding Actions to a Hypertext Link*

O**ne of the advantages of using hypertext links is that you can create several layers of links to expand any of the information you wish to present. Hypertext links can only be created for text within text objects. You cannot add hypertext links to paint text.

In the last two Step-by-Steps, the action for the hypertext links took the user to other cards. A hypertext link can feature more than one action. For example, you can have a link go to another card and also play a sound or use one of the NBAs.

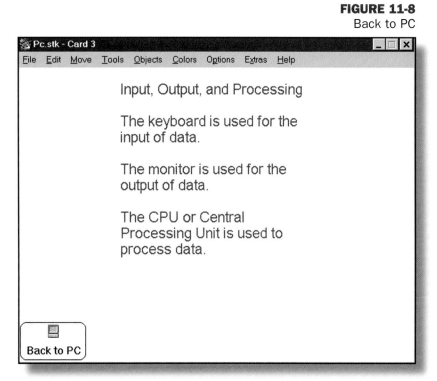

**FIGURE 11-8**
Back to PC

---

**STEP-BY-STEP** ▷ **11.3**

1. With the PC1 stack open, move to Card 1. From the Objects menu, choose Hypertext Links.

2. Select the **modem** link, as shown in Figure 11-9, and choose **Actions**.

3. Select **Play a sound** from the Things to Do section of the Actions window.

**NOTE:**

Another card should still be selected in the Places to Go section of the Actions window.

**FIGURE 11-9**
Modem Link

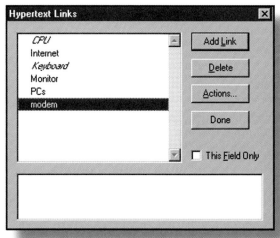

**4.** Choose **OPENNOTE.WAV** from the list of sounds, as shown in Figure 11-10. Click the **Play** button to hear the sound. Click **OK**.

**5.** Click **Done** twice.

**6.** Try the link. You should hear the sound and the program should move to the correct card.

**7.** Save your stack as **PC2**. Close the stack.

**FIGURE 11-10**
OPENNOTE.WAV

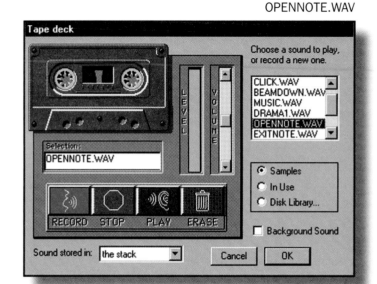

# Time Lines

A time line is a unique way of looking at historical information. Generally, a time line gives an overview of a particular period of time and shows the events that occurred. A time line can focus on a particular country or sequence of events, or it can be much broader in scope. It could show all of the significant events that occurred all over the world in the last decade, which would be a very broad time line. Time lines are useful in putting a lot of information in perspective.

Time lines and hypertext elements are often combined in HyperStudio stacks. This combination has the advantage of presenting an overview on one card in a stack and allowing more detailed information to be easily available to the user.

You have learned how to use all the tools you need to create a time line as well as how to use hypertext links to provide more detailed information. The next activity challenges you to use your skills to create a time line of recent presidents similar to the one shown in Figure 11-11.

**FIGURE 11-11**
Presidents Time Line

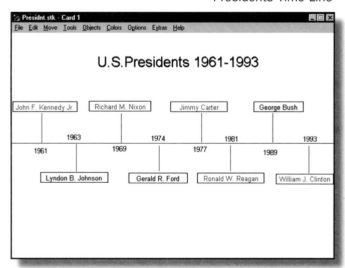

# CHALLENGE ACTIVITY 11.1

**1.** Create a new stack. Change the card size to full screen.

**2.** On the first card, create a time line for the presidents of the United States from 1961 through 1993. Use Figure 11-11 as an example.

**3.** Include the following:

- Hypertext links for five of the presidents.

- A different text color for the hypertext links.

- A card for each link with a brief biography, graphic, and/or anecdote about that president. An example is shown in Figure 11-12.

- A Back button from each card to return to the time line card.

- A shadow text title on the time line card.

**4.** Save the stack as **Presidnt**. Close the stack.

## HINT:

For information about the presidents of the United States, either use a reference book or go online to the White House's Internet site at www.whitehouse.gov. If you use the Internet site, go to **White House History** and choose **Presidents**. Do not copy the material since it is copyrighted. You may, however, use the information as a basis to write your own comments.

**FIGURE 11-12**
JFK Information Card

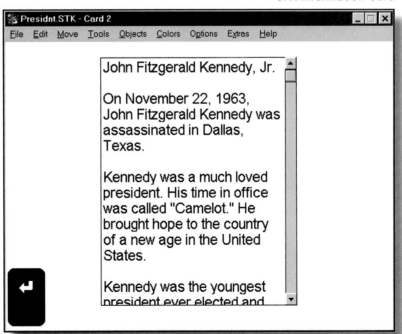

# Box Maker

The Box Maker feature is found on the Extras menu. Using the Rectangle tool from the tools palette, you were able to draw two-dimensional boxes. This tool enables you to create three-dimensional boxes in two easy steps. Three-dimensional objects create a sense of depth on the card.

Once you use the Box Maker feature to create a three-dimensional box, you will be able to manipulate it like other objects. You can rotate and flip it, copy and paste it, and use various colors and patterns to fill in the box.

## STEP-BY-STEP ▷ 11.4

1. Create a new stack. Use the default card size.

2. From the Extras menu, select **Box Maker**, as shown in Figure 11-13.

3. Click and drag to draw a rectangle in the middle of the card. Once the rectangle is drawn, release the mouse button. The cursor changes to a four-headed arrow. Without clicking the mouse button, drag the end of the rectangle so that it is long. It should look like Figure 11-14. Then click the mouse button to set the shape of the box.

**FIGURE 11-13**
Box Maker from Extras Menu

**FIGURE 11-14**
Long Box

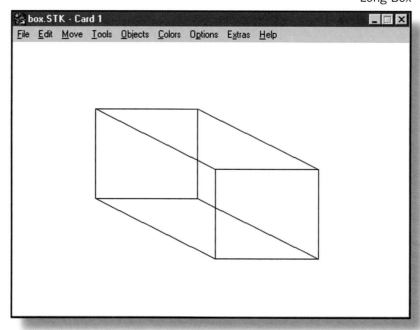

4. Copy and paste the card. Using the **Square Selector** tool, select the object on Card 2 and choose **Effects** from the Edit menu. Select **Flip Upside Down**. Your result should resemble Figure 11-15.

5. Return to Card 1. Copy Card 1 and paste it into the Card 3 position.

6. Save the stack as **Box**. Keep the stack open.

7. Using the **Paint Bucket** tool, fill the sides of the box on Card 3 with the brick pattern to make it look as though you were looking down on the outside of it. See Figure 11-16.

(continued on next page)

HINT:

When you paste a card, it is placed directly after the current card. If you do not have the card in the correct position, use the Storyboard feature to correct the card order.

FIGURE 11-15
Three-Dimensional Box Flipped Upside Down

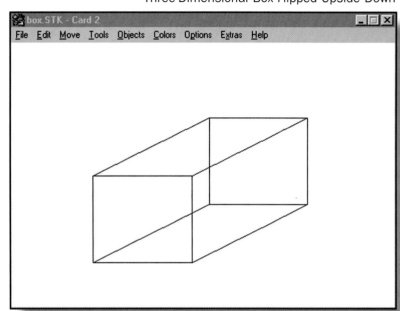

FIGURE 11-16
Brick Fill on the Sides of the Box

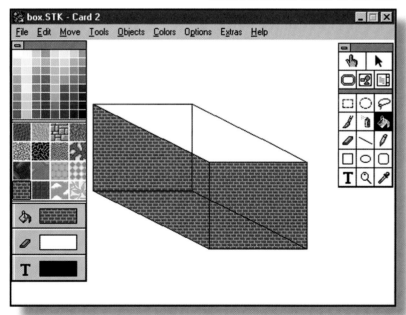

**213**

**8.** Use the **Paint Bucket** tool to fill the remaining surfaces with **dark red**, so that it appears to be the inside of the box, as shown in Figure 11-17.

**9.** Save the stack. Keep the stack open.

**FIGURE 11-17**
Dark Red Fill

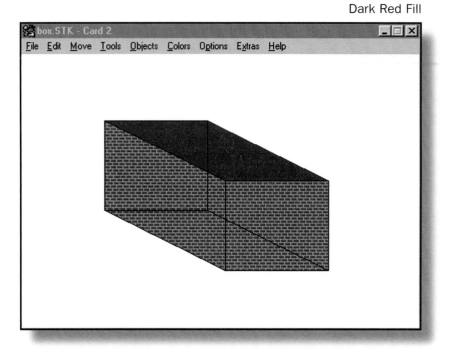

# *Slide Show Animation*

A slide show animation allows you to set up an automatic action that moves from card to card in your stack, which provides an automated display of your stack. Slide shows work best with stacks that have a linear flow.

When creating a slide show animation, you must decide the card transition types, speed of the transition from card to card, and length of time the user will view the card before the animation moves to the next card. When an animation has reached the end of the stack, you can choose to loop through the stack, return to the first card, or exit the stack. If you choose to loop through the stack, the slide show animation will repeat the stack once it has reached the last card. You can manually create a slide show or use the SlideShow NBA. First, you will create the effect manually.

## Adding the Quit NBA

In the next Step-by-Step, you will learn how to access and use the Quit NBA. This NBA is usually attached to a button labeled Quit. It provides the user with a way to exit HyperStudio from your stack.

**STEP-BY-STEP 11.5**

1. With the Box stack open, create a new card. Place this card in the title position. Design an attractive Title card. Use Box Maker as the title for the stack.

2. On the Title card, add a new button. Make this an invisible button. The Button Appearance window will appear, as shown in Figure 11-18.

   From the Places to Go section of the Actions window, choose **Next card**. Select the **Mouth open** transition at **Medium** speed from the Transitions window. Click **OK**.

3. When the program returns to the Actions window, choose **Automatic timer**, as shown in Figure 11-19.

   (continued on next page)

**FIGURE 11-18**
Invisible Button

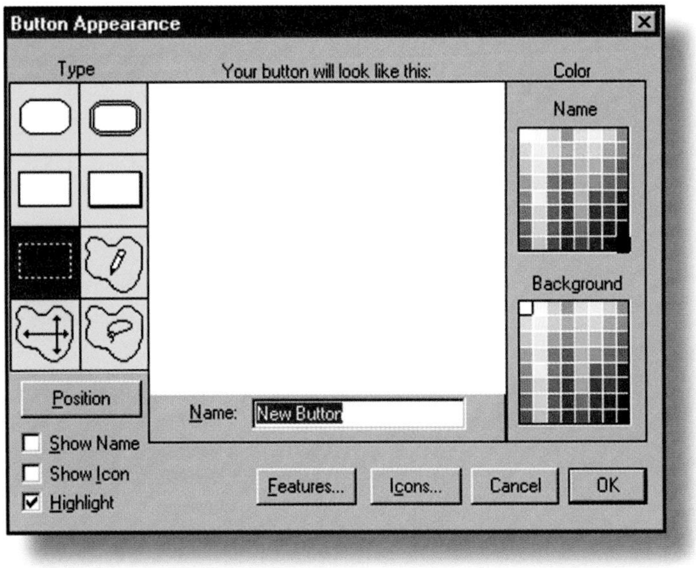

**FIGURE 11-19**
Automatic Timer Button Action

INTERNET

In certain browsers and other Internet programs, a bookmark or hotlist is a special file used to save addresses and locations. By saving and recalling addresses, it is easy for you to visit your favorite sites over and over.

**4.** Use the default setting of **Activate button after card is shown**. Key **2** for the seconds, as shown in Figure 11-20. Click **OK**, then **Done**.

**5.** Move the button out of the way of the title on the card. Copy this button and paste the button on Cards 2, 3, and 4.

**6.** On Card 4, create two new buttons. Use a square shape for these buttons. The first button name is **Begin**. Choose an appropriate icon. Move the button to the bottom left of the card. The button action is **Another card**. Use the arrow until you reach Card 1. Keep the default transition.

**7.** Name the second button **Quit**. Add the **EXIT** icon shown in Figure 11-21. Move it to the bottom right of the card.

**8.** From the Actions window, choose **New Button Actions**.

**9.** Select **QuitNBA**, as shown in Figure 11-22.

**10.** Click **Use this NBA**. Click **OK** and **Done**.

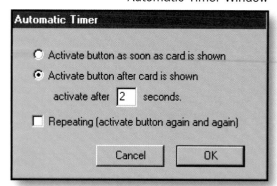

**FIGURE 11-20**
Automatic Timer Window

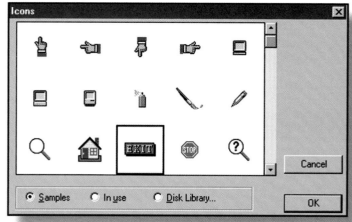

**FIGURE 11-21**
Exit Icon

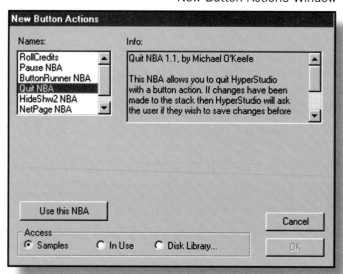

**FIGURE 11-22**
New Button Actions Window

**11.** Save the stack as
**Box1**.

**12.** The buttons should
resemble Figure
11-23. In the Browse
mode, test the
buttons in your
stack. Leave the Quit
button for last. Your
stack should
automatically move
from card to card
until you reach the
last card. When you
select the **Quit**
button, a window will
appear that asks if
you want to save
your stack. Select
**Yes**. The Quit button will automatically close
HyperStudio.

**13.** Reopen HyperStudio and the **Box1** stack after
you have tested the Quit button.

**FIGURE 11-23**
Last Card After Buttons Have Been Added

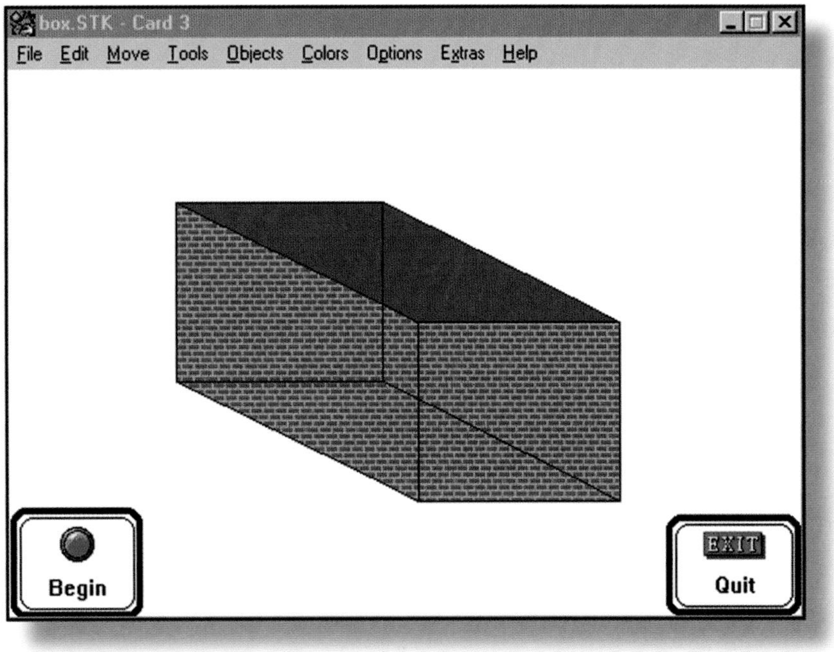

✓ **HINT:**

If you want your stack to stop the
automatic animation of the slide show,
select one of the tools from the tools
palette. That will suspend the action
until you return to Browse mode.

# *SlideShow NBA*

Now that you have learned how to create a slide show using the automatic timer and creating
your own transitions, you will learn how to use the built-in slide show feature of HyperStudio, called
the SlideShow NBA. This NBA is located on the HyperStudio CD-ROM or on your network. In the next
Step-by-Step, you will animate the same stack using the SlideShow NBA.

1. Open the Box stack.

2. With the Box stack open, create a new card. Place this card in the title position. Design an attractive Title card. The title of the stack is Box Maker.

3. Add a new button. Name the button **Begin**.

4. From the Actions window, select **New Button Actions**.

5. With the HyperStudio CD-ROM in the drive, select **Disk Library** at the bottom of the New Button Actions window, as shown in Figure 11-24.

6. Select **Sldshow.nba**, as shown in Figure 11-25.

**FIGURE 11-24**
Disk Library Selected

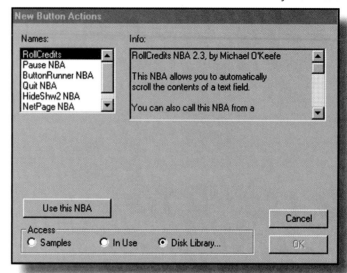

**FIGURE 11-25**
Sldshow.nba

**TIP**

If you are using HyperStudio through a network, ask your instructor for the location of the files located on the HyperStudio CD-ROM.

7. Click **Open**. Click **Use this NBA**, as shown in Figure 11-26.

8. You will see the Slide Show NBA window. Select **Return to original card on exit**, as shown in Figure 11-27. Click **OK**.

9. Click **OK**.

10. Test the button.

11. Add a Quit button on the Title card, using the Quit NBA.

12. Save the stack as **Box2**.

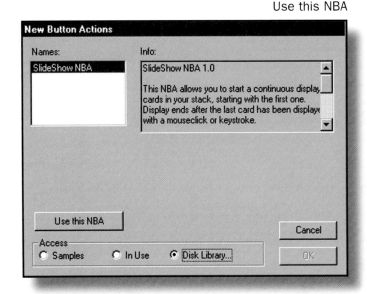

**FIGURE 11-26**
Use this NBA

**FIGURE 11-27**
SlideShow NBA Window

## CHALLENGE ACTIVITY 11.2

1. Open the **Graphic1** stack from Lesson 7, Project 7.2, and animate it as a slide show using the automatic timer and creating your own slide show.

2. Save the stack as **Graphic2**.

3. Open the **Graphic1** stack and animate it using the SlideShow NBA.

4. Save the stack as **Graphic3**.

# *Summary*

In this lesson, you learned that:

- HyperStudio allows you to create hypertext links within your stacks.

- Hypertext links use the same actions as buttons.

- You can have several layers of links in a stack.

- You can combine more than one hypertext action in a link.

- A time line is a valuable tool for presenting historic events.

- You can combine hypertext links in a time line to present in-depth information.

- You can use the Box Maker feature to create three-dimensional boxes.

- You can create slide show animations using automatic timer actions to present your stacks.

- You can create slide show animations using the SlideShow NBA.

- Slide show animations can have variable transitions and actions.

- HyperStudio offers additional NBAs for you to incorporate into a stack.

- The Quit NBA allows you to exit HyperStudio from a stack.

## VOCABULARY

Box Maker

Hypertext links

Slide show animation

Time line

## LESSON 11 REVIEW QUESTIONS

### TRUE/FALSE

**Circle the T if the statement is true or F if it is false.**

T  F  **1.** A hypertext link is generally used to connect a word to another place, text, or graphic.

T  F  **2.** A hypertext link cannot be used on the Internet.

T  F  **3.** You need to use the Edit menu to create a hypertext link.

T  F  **4.** Any word or phrase can become a hypertext link.

T  F  **5.** A hypertext link can have more than one action connected with it.

**T  F**   **6.** A hypertext link can have only a sound action.

**T  F**   **7.** Time lines are one of the Extras features in HyperStudio.

**T  F**   **8.** Box Maker is an NBA.

**T  F**   **9.** You cannot use colors or patterns with the Box Maker feature.

**T  F**   **10.** Slide show animation is one of the New Button Actions that is located on the HyperStudio CD-ROM.

## COMPLETION

**Answer the questions below in the space provided.**

**1.** Describe the advantages of using a time line.

**2.** How can hypertext make a program more interactive?

**3.** Describe the process for creating a hypertext link.

**4.** What are some of the subjects that would be more easily presented using the Box Maker feature?

**5.** What is a slide show animation?

6. What are some of the variables that you can choose to use with a slide show animation?

7. What is the process for setting up a slide show animation?

8. Where is the SlideShow NBA located and how do you access it?

9. What does the Quit NBA do in a stack?

## LESSON 11 PROJECT 11.1

1. Create a stack that is based on a time line.

2. Choose a period in history and select five events to place on the time line.

3. Create an information card for each of the five events.

4. Create hypertext links from the five events.

5. Include five text fields and at least two graphics in the stack.

6. Include navigation buttons to return to the time line card.

7. Use the time line as the Title card for the stack.

8. Save the stack as **Timeline**.

## LESSON 11 PROJECT 11.2

1. Create a storyboard for a slide show animation on a topic of your choice.

2. Include at least five cards.

3. Include a Title card.

4. Include two buttons on the last card: a Quit NBA and a Return to Beginning button.

5. Save as **Show**.

## CRITICAL THINKING ACTIVITY

Make a list of subjects and projects, other than history, for which a time line could be used to present information.

**Hide/Show NBA**
1. Add or select an object on a card.
2. Name the object.
3. Choose New Button Actions.
4. Choose Hide/Show NBA.
5. Choose Use this NBA.
6. Enter the name of the object.
7. Select the type of object.
8. Select Flip (hide/show).
9. Select Show Effect.
10. Choose transition.
11. Click OK, OK, and Done.

**Path Animation**
1. From Objects menu, select Add a Button.
2. Name the button.
3. Select Play animation from the Actions window.
4. Choose the location of your animated object file.
5. Select the file.
6. Create a path by dragging the mouse across card and press Enter when finished.
7. Select Try it.
8. Click OK, Done.

**ButtonRunner NBA**
1. From the Objects menu, Add a Button.
2. Name the button.
3. Select New Button Actions from the window.
4. Select ButtonRunner NBA from the New Button Actions window.
5. Select Use this NBA.
6. Key the names of the buttons you wish to control on separate lines.
7. Click OK, OK, and Done.

**Frame Animations**
1. Create a series of cards with a small difference on each card.
2. Save each card as a screen capture.
3. From the File menu, select Export Screen.
4. Locate the folder where you will save the screens.
5. Click OK.
6. Repeat this process for each card.
7. Add a new button.
8. Select Play animation from the Actions window.
9. Locate the folder with the screen captures.
10. Select the first file.
11. Select and match the area you are animating to the area on the card.
12. Press any key on the keyboard.
13. Choose the appropriate selections from the Frame Preview window.
14. Click OK.

| **Shadow Text** | 1. Create a text field on a blank card. |
| | 2. Key the text you wish to shadow. |
| | 3. Select the text object. |
| | 4. Make the field Read Only. |
| | 5. Deselect all other choices. |
| | 6. Click Features, select Transparent, and OK. |
| | 7. Copy the text object. |
| | 8. Drag it below the first object. |
| | 9. Select the field and change the text color to a dark color. |
| | 10. Select the second field and drag it up and to the left of the first field. |

| **RollCredits NBA** | 1. Create a text object. |
| | 2. Press Enter four or five times. |
| | 3. Key the text line by line. |
| | 4. Press Enter four or five times. |
| | 5. Select the text object. |
| | 6. Click Actions in Text Appearance window. |
| | 7. Select New Button Actions. |
| | 8. Select RollCredits. |
| | 9. Select Use this NBA. |
| | 10. Test the speed; click OK. |
| | 11. Click inside text field to roll the credits. |

| **Hypertext links** | 1. Highlight a word or phrase in a text object. |
| | 2. From the Objects menu, select Hypertext Links. |
| | 3. Click Add Link. |
| | 4. Select the link. |
| | 5. Click Actions. |
| | 6. Select the action. |
| | 7. Click OK, OK, Done, and Done. |

| **BoxMaker** | 1. From the Extras menu, select BoxMaker. |
| | 2. Draw the box object. |

| **SlideShow animation** | 1. Create the cards you wish to animate. |
| | 2. Add a button to the first card. |
| | 3. Select Automatic timer from the Actions window. |
| | 4. Key in the amount of time to wait. |
| | 5. Click OK. |

| **Quit NBA** | 1. Add a button. |
| | 2. From the Actions window, select New Button Actions. |
| | 3. Select Quit NBA. |
| | 4. Select Use this NBA. |
| | 5. Click OK and Done. |

| **SlideShow NBA** | 1. Create the cards you wish to animate. |
| | 2. Add a button on the first card. |
| | 3. Select New Button Actions from the Actions window. |
| | 4. Select the folder containing the slide show animations. |
| | 5. Choose the speed. |
| | 6. Click OK and Done as needed. |

### FILL IN THE BLANKS

Complete the following statements by keying or writing the correct answers on a page to be submitted to your instructor. Center *Unit 4 Review Questions* at the top of the page. Number your answers to match the numbers listed here.

1. You would use the _____ to control several button actions on a card.

2. Two possible types of animation in HyperStudio are _____ animations and

   _____ animations.

3. You can locate invisible buttons on a card by selecting the _____ .

4. The button action that allows you to move a graphic across a screen is the _____ action.

5. Animated scrolling text is created with a _____ NBA.

6. To create shadow text, the text object must be _____ .

7. The higher the speed of a path animation, the _____ the movement of the animation.

8. A word that has an action attached to it is called _____ .

9. You can draw a three-dimensional box using the _____ extra.

10. The name of the NBA that allows you to exit HyperStudio is the _____ .

### WRITTEN QUESTIONS

Key or write your answers to the following questions. Number your answers. Use complete sentences and good grammar.

11. Describe two types of animations:

    a.

    b.

12. How would you animate a stationary graphic on a card?

**13.** What is a timeline? Describe some ways that a timeline would be a useful presentation tool.

**14.** What is a slide show animation?

**15.** Describe how hypertext links are used in stacks.

## UNIT 4 APPLICATIONS

### UNIT 4 PROJECT

**1.** Choose a topic for a stack that lends itself to animation.

**2.** Create a storyboard for the stack that includes a Title card, Main Menu card, and several topic cards.

**3.** Create a stack, including appropriate text objects and graphic objects.

**4.** Include at least two of the following in your stack:
- Hide/show NBA
- Path animation, slide show animation, or frame animation
- ButtonRunner NBA
- Shadow text
- RollCredits NBA
- Hypertext link
- Quit NBA
- SlideShow NBA

**5.** Save the stack as **EP4**.

### UNIT 4 CRITICAL THINKING ACTIVITY

You have been asked to present reasons supporting using animations in HyperStudio presentations. List topics for which animations can add creativity and aid the presentation of information. Explain ways that animations can be used for two or more of the topics you list.

# WORKING WITH MULTIMEDIA

# UNIT 5

# LESSON 12

# SOUND

## OBJECTIVES

**Upon completion of this lesson, you will be able to:**

■ Insert existing sounds.

■ Insert narrations.

■ Insert sounds from the HyperStudio Samples Library.

■ Create buttons to control an audio CD.

■ Access graphics and sounds from the HyperStudio Media Library.

■ Use the Menu Tamer feature.

🕘 **Estimated Time: 1 hour**

# *Sound*

HyperStudio is a multimedia-authoring program. Sound can be a dynamic addition to a presentation or project. It can enhance stacks and create a more interactive and creative project. Sound can get a user's attention and can also be used to convey information, provide feedback, reproduce common sounds, and set a mood or feeling in a stack.

When you use sound as feedback, it is a good idea to follow some guidelines. Feedback should always be positive. If the user makes a correct choice, you want to reward them with a happy sound such as applause. However, if the user makes an incorrect choice, you do not want to embarrass them or make them feel bad. You would want to find a sound that would let them know that they have made a mistake, such as a "boing" sound, without discouraging them. You will probably want to preview some of the different sounds to identify ones that give positive feedback and ones that let users know that they have made mistakes.

In Lesson 7, you were introduced to sounds by adding a sound to an icon. In this lesson, you will explore different kinds of sounds. You will also learn how to attach sounds to buttons and graphics.

## Working with Existing Sounds

HyperStudio provides a variety of sounds in the samples.stk. The samples.stk was loaded on the hard drive or network server when HyperStudio was installed. The sound bites in the samples.stk range from animal sounds to musical scales.

# STEP-BY-STEP ⟹ 12.1

**1.** Open a new stack. Use the default stack size.

**2.** Create a text object across the top of the card. The object should not be scrollable or have a frame. Select suitable background and text colors. Also choose an appropriate font and size. The text in the object should read, **Which animal makes this sound?** (See Figure 12-1.)

**FIGURE 12-1**
Text Object

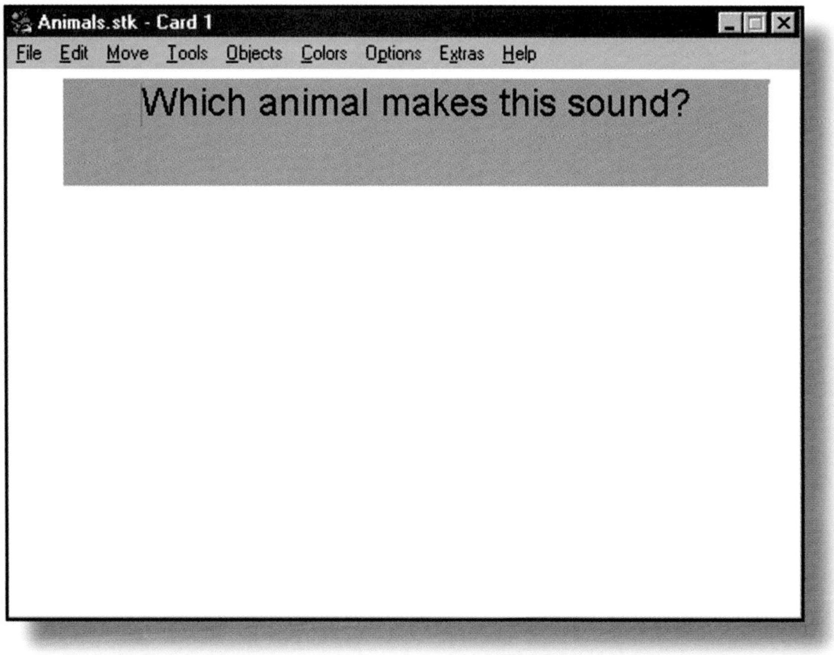

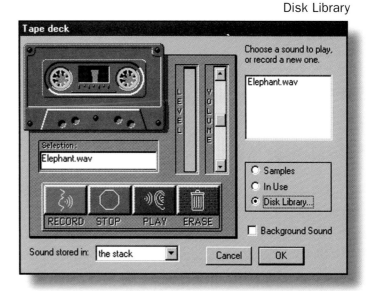

**3.** Add a new button. Name the button **Click Here**. Move the button up and under the text field.

**FIGURE 12-2**
Disk Library

**4.** From the Actions window, choose **Play a sound**.

**5.** From the Tape deck window, choose **Disk Library**, as shown in Figure 12-2.

(continued on next page)

**6.** Double click the **elephant.wav** file, which is highlighted in Figure 12-3.

**7.** Click the **Play** button on the Tape deck window to hear the sound. Click **OK** and **Done**. Test the button. You should hear the elephant roar.

**8.** Save your stack as **Animals**.

**9.** From the Objects menu, select **Add a Graphic Object**.

**10.** Select **Disk file**, if necessary.

**11.** Double click on the **Animals** file, which is highlighted in Figure 12-4.

**FIGURE 12-3**
Elephant.wav

**FIGURE 12-4**
Animals

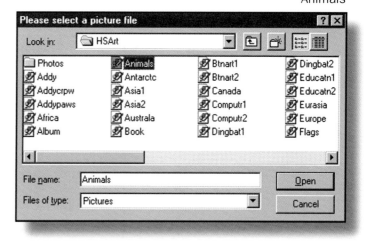

 **HINT:**

Depending on how HyperStudio was installed, you may need the HyperStudio CD-ROM to access the sound.

**12.** Use the Lasso tool to select the picture of the **elephant** from the animals file, as shown in Figure 12-5. Click **OK**.

**13.** Click outside the elephant. In the Graphic Appearance window, name the graphic **elephant**, as shown in Figure 12-6.

**14.** Select **Actions** and **Play a sound**.

(continued on next page)

**FIGURE 12-5**
Elephant Graphic Selected

**FIGURE 12-6**
Name the Graphic Elephant

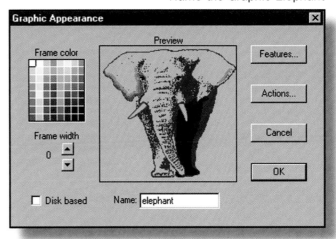

**INTERNET**

The Internet is a telecommunications system that connects many different networks of computers. The Internet is often called a "network of networks."

**15.** Choose the **Disk Library** as your source, if necessary. Double click **applause.wav**, which is highlighted in Figure 12-7.

**16.** Click **Play** in the Tape deck window to preview the sound. Click **OK**, **Done**, and **OK**.

**17.** Select the elephant and move it to the bottom left of the card.

**18.** Make sure you are in Browse mode. When you click on the elephant, you should hear applause. Your card should resemble Figure 12-8.

**19.** Save the stack. Keep the stack open.

**FIGURE 12-7**
Applause.wav

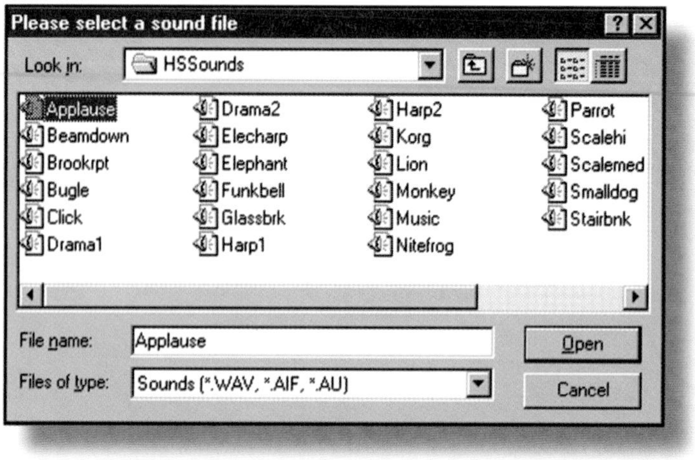

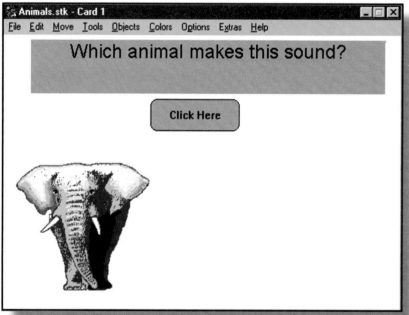

**FIGURE 12-8**
Elephant Graphic with Sound Attached

**20.** Add another graphic object. Use the Lasso tool to select the **parrot** from the animals file. Move the parrot to the center of the card. Name the graphic **parrot**. Select **Actions**, and **Play a sound**. Select the **BOING.WAV** file from the samples listed, as shown in Figure 12-9. Click **OK**, **Done**, and **OK**.

**21.** Save the stack as **Animal1**.

**22.** Add another graphic object, repeating the process for adding a sound to the graphic. Use the **monkey** graphic from the animals file. Move the monkey to the right side of the screen. Use the sound file **BOING.WAV**. When you have completed the addition, your card should resemble Figure 12-10.

**23.** Test your completed card as follows: Click on the **Click Here** button to hear the sound. Then select one of the animals by clicking on it. Since elephant is the correct sound, you will hear applause when you click on the elephant. When you click on the parrot or monkey, you will hear the "Boing" sound, since these are incorrect responses.

**24.** Save your stack. Keep the stack open.

**FIGURE 12-9**
BOING.WAV

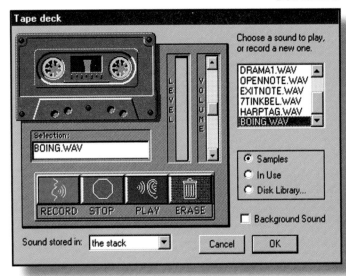

**FIGURE 12-10**
Finished Card

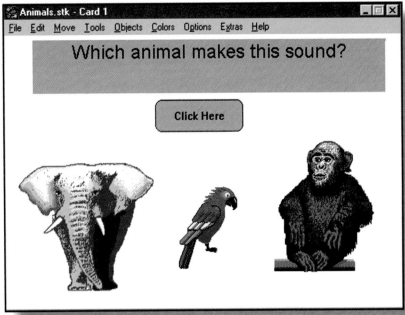

 **TIP**

You must be in Browse mode to hear the sounds that accompany the buttons and objects.

# Narrations

If your computer has a microphone attached to it, you can record and use your own sound files. The use of narrative is a good way to give directions, reinforce the reading of text, and add additional impact and special effects to any stack. Adding your own narration means that you are not dependent on prerecorded sounds.

You can create and save your own sound files to fit the needs of your stack or project. For instance, if your project is designed to teach a foreign language, you might create a stack that contained pictures of objects with sound files attached to them. When the user clicks on the object in the Browse mode, the user hears the name of the object in the foreign language. This type of stack helps reinforce proper pronunciation and inflection of foreign words and phrases.

## STEP-BY-STEP ▷ 12.2

1. With the Animal1 stack open, add a new card.

2. Copy the text field object and the Click Here button from Card 1 to Card 2.

3. On Card 2, use the **Button** tool and double click on the **Click Here** button.

4. Click the **Actions** button.

5. Deselect and reselect **Play a sound**.

**If you can record on your computer, complete Steps 6 and 7. If you cannot record, skip to Step 8.**

6. You will record the word **Parrot** on the tape deck. When you are ready to say the word, click the **Record** button. Watch the sound level move as you speak. Click the **Stop** button when you have completed the word. Your selection will be saved as **NewSnd##** in the Selection field. The ## represents a number, and the number will vary depending on how many times the tape deck has been used to record sounds.

7. Click the **Play** button on the tape deck to listen to your recording. If you are satisfied with your recording, continue with the next step. If you would like to change your recording, repeat Step 6. Click **OK** and **Done** when you have completed your recording.

8. If you cannot record your own narration, use the parrot.wav sound for the button action sound. The parrot.wav file is located in the Disk Library.

9. Save the stack as **Animal2**. Keep the stack open.

### FIGURE 12-11
Record a Sound File

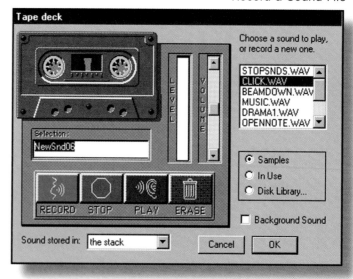

**CHALLENGE ACTIVITY ⟹ 12.1**

With the Animal2 stack open:

- Add a parrot graphic and two other animal graphics to the card.

- Add an applause sound file for the parrot graphic action.

- To the graphics of the other two animals, add a "Boing" or other sound to signify the wrong choice.

- Save as **Animal3**.

# Playing Sounds from an Audio CD

You have now used sounds from two different sources. First, you used sounds that were prerecorded and stored in the HyperStudio Library. Second, you recorded your own sound file using the microphone attached to your computer. By using the CDPlay NBA, you can attach sound files from outside sources such as audio CDs and CD-ROMs to buttons and other objects.

Your audio selections from CDs are controlled using the CD-Audio Controller. The controller allows you to select specific tracks and specific starting and stopping points for the track. You can also adjust the volume of the audio. If you are completing this lesson in a classroom or computer lab, please keep the volume to a minimum to avoid disturbing others.

The CD-Audio Controller has the following options:

**CD-AUDIO CONTROLLER**

| BUTTON | ACTION |
|---|---|
| Pause/Play | Pauses or continues play of the CD. When Pause is the available option, the CD is playing. When Play is the available option, the CD is paused. |
| Eject | Ejects the CD from the drive. |
| Left/Right | Allows you to control which audio channel is playing the sounds. |
| Set Start | When the CD is playing, clicking Set Start will mark the starting point for an audio clip. |
| Set End | When the CD is playing, clicking Set End will mark the ending point for an audio clip. (NOTE: The CD continues to play when Set End is clicked.) |
| Try It! | Allows you to listen to the clip you have chosen. Try It! works only after a Set Start and Set End have been chosen and the Pause button has been clicked. |
| Keep | Keeps the audio clip and returns you to the New Button Actions window. |
| Options | Allows you to set additional controls over the audio device. |
| Cancel | Exits the controller without saving the audio clip. |

1. Open a new stack. Use the default card size.

2. Insert an audio CD into the CD player that accompanies your computer.

3. Add a new button. Name the button **Play Music**. Choose the type of button (not invisible) and the color of the button background and text. Click **OK** when you have completed your selections.

4. Click outside the button. Choose **New Button Actions** from the Actions window.

5. Choose **CDPlay** from the Names list, as shown in Figure 12-12.

6. Select **Use this NBA**.

7. You will see the CD-Audio Controller window, as shown in Figure 12-13.

8. Press the **Play** button on the controller. You should hear the first track of your CD. If Audio Channels are available, click several times on the **Left** and **Right** Audio Channels to raise and lower the volume.

**FIGURE 12-12**
CDPlay

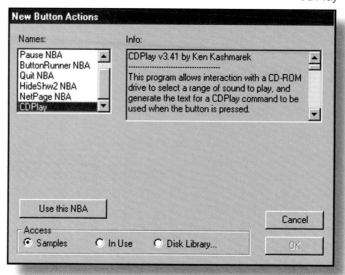

**FIGURE 12-13**
CD-Audio Controller

9. Click **Pause**. Use the arrows above the Track slot to change the track. Click **Play** to listen to the new track. Continue browsing through the tracks until you find one that you like. You will create a short audio cut from the track. The cut should be one minute or less. Select a starting point for the cut by clicking the **Set Start** button. Select an ending point by clicking **Set End**. Click **Pause** and then click **Try It!** If you wish to change the cut, repeat the process. When you are satisfied with your cut, click **Keep**.

10. Save the stack as **Play**.

**TIP**

If you do not hear any sound, verify that the CD is turned on and attached to the computer. Make sure the CD is resting properly in the cradle and the speakers are turned on.

**TIP**

The CD from which you have selected the cut must be in the CD drive before you click on the Play button.

# *Creating Controller Buttons for the CD*

The CDPlay NBA not only allows you to use tracks from audio CDs, but provides a controller so you can create your own buttons for controlling play, the track, the amount of a track, pause, resume, and stop. These controls are set using the Options button on the CD Controller panel. (See Figure 12-14.) The available options are described on the next page.

**FIGURE 12-14**
CD Controller Panel (Tracks 1 to 11 Selected)

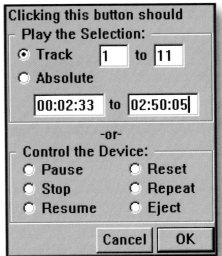

## CD CONTROLLER OPTIONS

| OPTION | RESULT |
| --- | --- |
| Track | Allows you to specify the range of tracks to be played. The tracks are selected by number. To select only one track, enter the same track number in both fields. |
| Absolute | Allows you to specify the exact starting and ending points by time. The time is entered in minutes, seconds, and hundredths of seconds. This option gives you very precise control. |
| Pause | Allows you to specify that when the button is clicked, the CD will pause. |
| Stop | Allows you to specify that when the button is clicked, the CD will stop playing. |
| Resume | Allows you to specify that when the button is clicked, the CD will resume playing from the point that it was stopped. This control is used in conjunction with the Pause or Stop button. |
| Reset | Allows you to create a button that will reset the controller to the beginning of the cut. |
| Repeat | Allows you to repeat the previous selection. |
| Eject | Allows you to create a button to eject a CD. This button can be useful when more than one CD is used in a stack. |

## STEP-BY-STEP ▷ 12.4

1. Add a new card. Add a new button. Name the button **Play**. Choose the button style, color, and text.

2. Position the button on the card and click outside the button.

3. Choose **New Button Actions**.

4. Choose **CDPlay**.

5. Select **Use this NBA**.

6. Click **Options**. Select Track under Play the Selection and enter **1** in the first field and the

number of the last track in the second field, as shown in Figure 12-14.

7. Click **OK**, **Keep**, **OK**, and **Done**. Test the Play button. It will begin with the first track and play the entire CD, unless some action stops the CD.

8. Save the stack as **Play1**. Keep the stack open.

9. Add a new button named **Stop**. Position the button on your card and click outside the button.

## STEP-BY-STEP 12.4 CONTINUED

10. Choose **New Button Actions**. Choose **CDPlay**. Choose **Use this NBA**.

11. Select **Options** from the CD-Audio Controller window. See Figure 12-15 to identify the Options button.

**FIGURE 12-15**
CD-Audio Controller Window

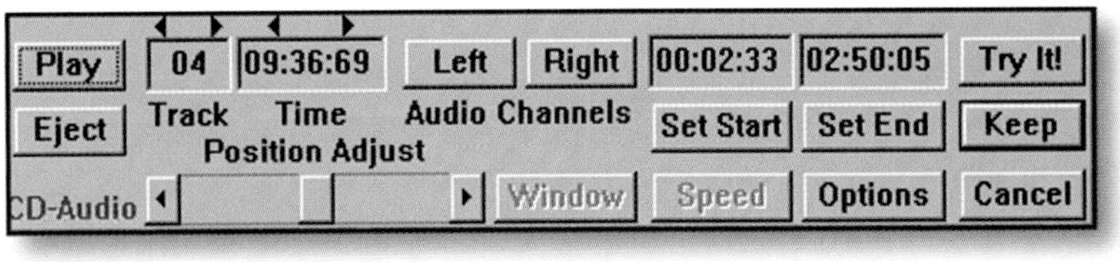


12. Under Control the Device, select **Stop**, as shown in Figure 12-16.

13. Select **OK**, **Keep**, **OK**, and **Done**.

14. Test the **Play** and **Stop** buttons. Notice that each time you stop the CD and then click **Play**, the CD begins playing from Track 1.

15. Save your stack as **Play2**. Keep your stack open.

**FIGURE 12-16**
Stop Control

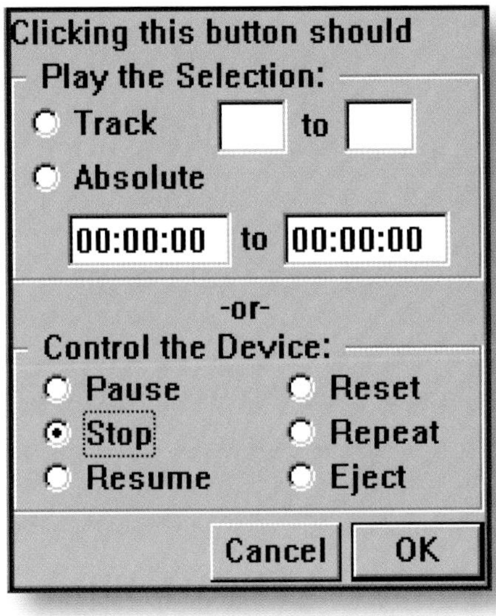


## CHALLENGE ACTIVITY 12.2

SCANS

1. Using the same procedures from the previous activity, create a resume button for your card.

2. Name the button **Resume**.

3. Save the stack as **Play3**. Close your stack.

# HyperStudio Media Library

The HyperStudio Media Library is a wonderful resource located on the HyperStudio CD-ROM. Not only does it have a large collection of graphics, photos, premade cards and predesigned backgrounds, but it also includes a large selection of sounds, music, and sound bites.

Depending on how HyperStudio was installed, the HS Media Library is accessible through the CD-ROM drive on your computer or through your network. Once you locate this resource, your ability to add sounds and graphics to your stacks increases immensely. Using this library will enhance your stacks, make your projects more exciting, and add a dynamic quality to your work. Once a media object is added to the stack from the CD-ROM or network, the image becomes part of the stack. Therefore, the HyperStudio CD-ROM does not need to be in the CD drive each time the stack is used.

## STEP-BY-STEP ⟹ 12.5

**You must have access to the HyperStudio CD-ROM to complete this Step-by-Step.**

1. Create a new stack. Use the default card size.

2. Insert the HyperStudio CD-ROM in your CD-ROM drive if necessary.

3. From the File menu, choose **Import background**.

4. Choose **Disk file**, if necessary.

5. Navigate to the CD drive or network drive. Figure 12-17 shows a sample screen for connecting through a CD drive.

 **TIP**

If you do not have access to a CD-ROM drive in your computer, ask your instructor if you have access through a network.

 **TIP**

Sound, color graphics, and video elements are generally large files. It is advisable to use the default card size to save memory.

**FIGURE 12-17**
CD Drive

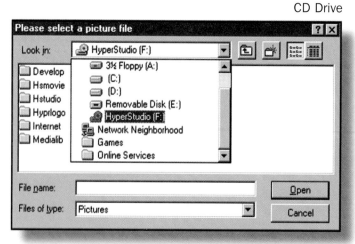

✓ **NOTE:**

This Step-by-Step assumes you are referencing the CD. If you are connecting to the Media Library through a network, your screens may look somewhat different. However, the same basic steps apply. Ask your instructor for help if necessary.

STEP-BY-STEP 12.5 CONTINUED

6. Double click on the **Medialib** folder shown in Figure 12-18.

7. Double click the **Scrnbkgd** folder, then double click on the **Topimage** folder. Click on the **insetblu** file, as shown in Figure 12-19. Click **Open**. Your card should look like Figure 12-20.

8. Add a new card to the stack.

(continued on next page)

**FIGURE 12-18**
Folders in the Medialib Folder

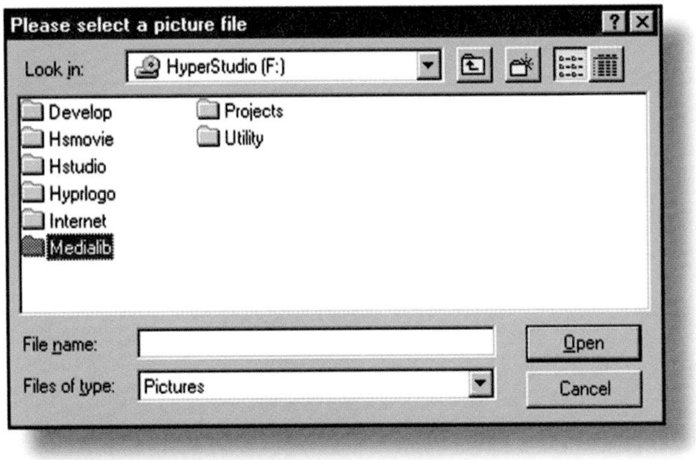

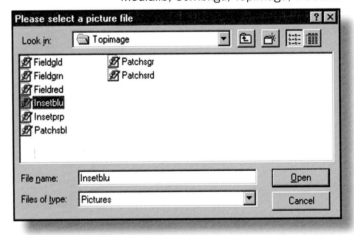

**FIGURE 12-19**
Medialib, Scrnbkgd, Topimage, Insetblu

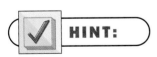

**HINT:**

If you see a window that asks if you wish to have the image resized to fit your screen, select **YES**.

**9.** Import a different background for Card 2 from the Medialib folder. When you return to the Please select a picture file window, the Topimage folder is open. Move up one folder level. Double click on **Spitfire**. Your screen should look like Figure 12-21. Double click **Drstscpe**. The new background for Card 2 will look like Figure 12-22.

**10.** Add a new card.

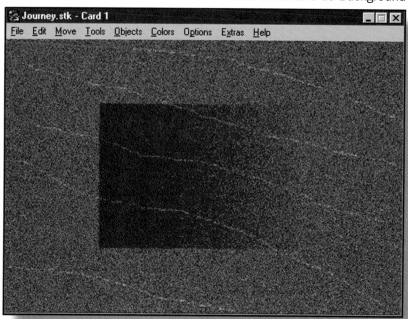

**FIGURE 12-20**
Card 1 Insetblu as Background

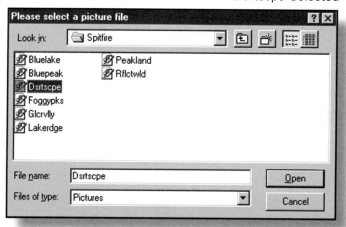

**FIGURE 12-21**
Dsrtscpe Selected

STEP-BY-STEP 12.5 CONTINUED

11. Import a different background for Card 3 from the Medialib folder. Double click **foggypks**. The new background for Card 3 will look like Figure 12-23.

12. Add a new card and import a background. Move up two levels of folders and double click on **Photglry**. Double click on **Objects**. Then double click on **honycmb**. Card 4 should look like Figure 12-24.

(continued on next page)

**FIGURE 12-22**
Card 2 with Background

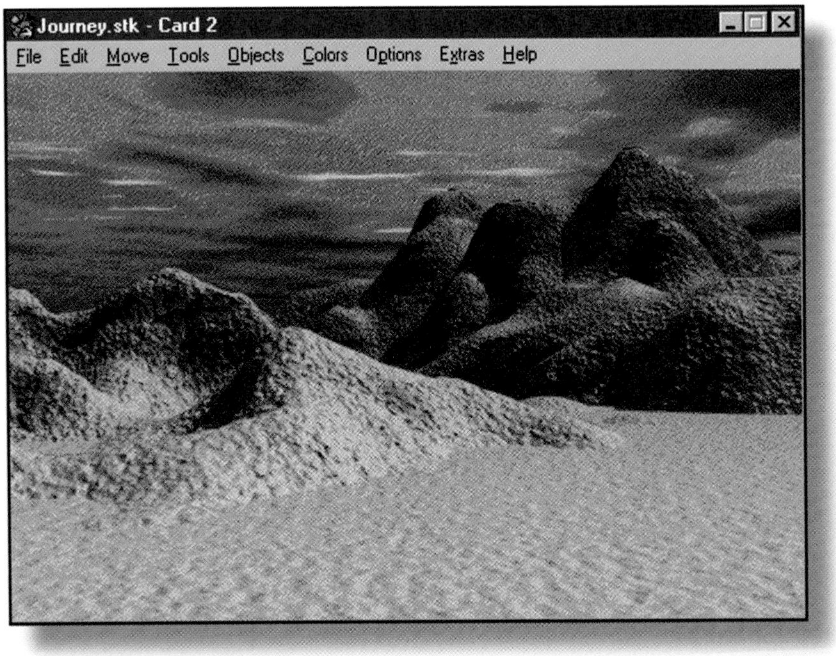

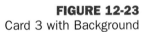

**FIGURE 12-23**
Card 3 with Background

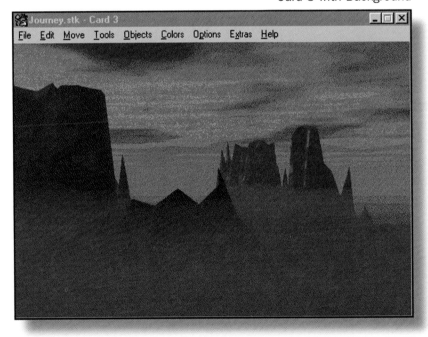

**13.** Add a new card and import a background. Move up one level of folders and double click on **Space**. Double click on **astrsale**. Card 5 should look like Figure 12-25.

**14.** Add a new card and import a background. Move up one level of folders. Double click on **Sealife**. Then double click on **anglfish**. Card 6 should look like Figure 12-26.

**FIGURE 12-24**
Card 4 with Background

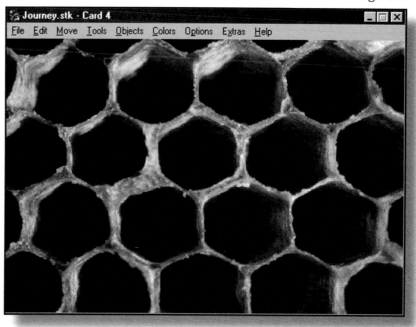

**FIGURE 12-25**
Card 5 with Background

**15.** Save your stack as **Journey**. Keep the stack open.

**FIGURE 12-26**
Card 6 with Background

## HyperStudio Media Library Sounds

The HS Media Library includes a large selection of sounds ranging from musical selections to animal sounds. It includes common and not-so-common sound bites ranging from familiar sounds to special effects. In Step-by-Step 12.1, you added sounds to buttons and graphic objects. These sounds came from the files placed on your hard drive when HyperStudio was installed, such as the elephant's roar. In Step-by-Step 12.2, you created a recording, and in Step-by-Step 12.3, you played music from an audio CD. From these Step-by-Steps, you learned that sound can highlight a point or set a mood. Sound engages an additional sense of the user and adds quality to the stack. Certain types of sound can help the user retain more of the information presented in a stack.

In the next Step-by-Step, you will add sounds found in the HS Media Library.

## Menu Tamer

As you create a stack or presentation, you will use various items from the menubar. For example, you will frequently switch between tools on the tool palette and use the Objects menu to add buttons, graphics, and text fields.

Once a stack has been completed, you may not want the user to have access to the menubar. The Menu Tamer found on the Extras menu can be used to hide and display the menubar. This extra helps to make the finished presentation look more professional.

1. Go to Card 1 of the Journey stack. Card 1 will be the Title card. Create a text object. Select an appropriate font and size for the type. Make the type **bold** and **centered**. Key the following:

**FIGURE 12-27**
Themvers.wav

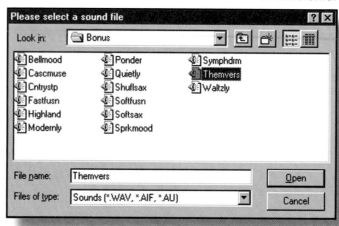

   **Journey**
   **Created by**
   **Your name***
   **Current date**

   *Replace with your first and last names.

2. Add a button to Card 1. Name the button **Start**. Use any type of button you like as long as it is not invisible. Choose a color for the text and button's background that will make it easy to locate and read. Move the button to an appropriate place on the card.

3. Select **Next card** from the Actions window. Use the default transition. Select **Play a sound** from the Actions window.

4. Choose **Disk Library**, if necessary. Move up as many levels as needed to locate the HyperStudio CD-ROM.

5. Double click the **Medialib** folder. Double click **Sndmusic**, then double click **Bonus**. Click on the **themvers.wav** file, as shown in Figure 12-27. Click **Open**.

 **TIP**

When using a stack with sound and color graphics, it is wise not to use up additional memory on transitions.

**6.** Click **OK** in the Tape deck window. Click **Done**. Card 1 should look similar to Figure 12-28.

**7.** Test your button. It should play the short musical cut and move to Card 2.

**HINT:**

Remember to change to Browse mode to test the button.

**FIGURE 12-28**
Completed Card 1

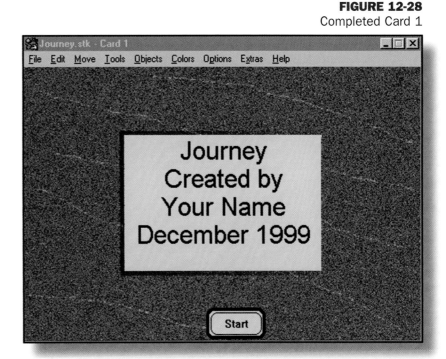

**Journey
Created by
Your Name
December 1999**

Start

**8.** Save your stack. Keep your stack open.

**9.** Add an invisible button to Card 2. Position the button to the left side of the card. Select **Next card** from the Actions window. Use the default transition. Select **Automatic timer**. Adjust the number of seconds to activate after to **5**. Choose **OK** and **Done**.

**10.** Move to Card 1 and press the **Start** button to test the button sequence. You should hear music and move from Card 1 to Card 2, and, after five seconds, to Card 3. The action will stop at Card 3.

**11.** Copy the button from Card 2 and paste it onto Cards 3, 4, and 5. Do not paste the button onto Card 6.

(continued on next page)

**HINT:**

If the sequence described in Step 10 does not occur, correct the problem before continuing.

**HINT:**

Once you have chosen the Automatic timer from the Actions window, it will be difficult to work on the stack or make changes when you are in Browse mode.

**FIGURE 12-29**
Cards in the Journey1 Stack with Painted Text Added

12. Save the stack. On Card 6, add two visible buttons. One button should return the user to the first card. The other button should offer an option of quitting the program.

13. Test the stack. You should hear the music as the cards move from one to the other. The action should stop when Card 6 is reached. Save the stack as **Journey1**.

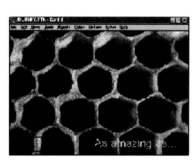

14. Using the **Text** tool, write the following text on each of the cards. See Figure 12-29 for suggested text placement.

   Card 2: **In all the world...**
   Card 3: **There is nothing**
   Card 4: **As amazing as...**
   Card 5: **One individual's**
   Card 6: **Imagination.**

15. Save the stack.

16. Making sure you are not in Browse mode, move to Card 1.

17. From the Extras menu, select **Menu Tamer.**

**18.** Use the default selection **Hide all menu bars**, as shown in Figure 12-30. Click **OK**.

**19.** Test the stack. Notice that the menubar only appears on the first card of the stack.

**20.** Save the stack as **Journey2**. Close your stack.

**FIGURE 12-30**
Menu Tamer

The shortcut to remove the menubar from the card you are on is **Ctrl + M** for Windows and  **+ M** for Macintosh. You can replace the menubars by repeating the keyboard shortcut, or you can return to the card on which the menubar is still displayed and access the Menu Tamer from the Extras menu.

C H A L L E N G E   A C T I V I T Y ⟹ **12.3**

Take some time to explore the sounds and graphics in the HS Media Library. Create a new stack for your exploration.

- ■ Listen to at least ten new sounds.

- ■ Write down the location and a description of the sounds so that you can find them again.

- ■ Locate five screen backgrounds.

- ■ Write down the location and a description of the backgrounds so that you can find them again.

- ■ Locate at least five images.

- ■ Write down the location and a description of the images so that you can find them again.

- ■ Exit the stack without saving it.

# Summary

In this lesson, you learned that:

- Sound is a valuable element in a HyperStudio stack.
- You can use a variety of sounds from the samples.stk.
- You can use sounds to provide feedback in a stack.
- You can attach sounds to graphic objects.
- You can insert a broader variety of sounds from the HyperStudio CD-ROM Disk Library.
- You can play sounds in your stacks from audio CDs using the CDPlay NBA.
- You can create control buttons to control audio CDs.
- There are many pictures, photos, and backgrounds in the Media Library on the HyperStudio CD-ROM.
- You can set up a slide show and use a sound cut in the background.
- You can hide the menubar for stack presentations.

## VOCABULARY

CD-audio controller

CDPlay NBA

Menu Tamer

Narration

Sound bite

## LESSON 12 REVIEW QUESTIONS

### MULTIPLE CHOICE

**Circle the letter to indicate the item that best completes each of the following statements.**

1. Sound can be used to:
   - **A.** present information
   - **B.** provide feedback
   - **C.** set a mood
   - **D.** all of the above

2. Sound can be attached to:
   - **A.** a graphic object
   - **B.** a button
   - **C.** a text field
   - **D.** all of the above

**3.** In order to play a sound, you must be in:
   **A.** Browse mode
   **B.** Selector mode
   **C.** Edit mode
   **D.** all of the above

**4.** When using feedback, it is a good idea:
   **A.** to provide positive feedback
   **B.** to provide negative feedback
   **C.** use annoying sounds
   **D.** none of the above

**5.** You can use sounds:
   **A.** from an audio CD
   **B.** from a CD-ROM
   **C.** from the HyperStudio Media Library
   **D.** all of the above

**6.** When using sounds and graphics, it is important to remember to:
   **A.** conserve memory
   **B.** have a good time
   **C.** be creative
   **D.** all of the above

**7.** The CDPlay NBA will:
   **A.** play a CD
   **B.** provide controls to play a CD
   **C.** provide controls to pause a CD
   **D.** all of the above

**8.** The HyperStudio Media Library contains:
   **A.** sounds
   **B.** graphics
   **C.** photos
   **D.** all of the above

**9.** Which is a HyperStudio NBA?
   **A.** Menu Tamer
   **B.** Quit
   **C.** Storyboard
   **D.** all of the above

**10.** Which is a HyperStudio Extras feature?
   **A.** Menu Tamer
   **B.** RollCredits
   **C.** Quit
   **D.** none of the above

# COMPLETION

**Answer the questions below in the space provided.**

1.  Where is the elephant.wav sound file located?

2.  How do you attach a sound to a graphic object?

3.  What are some guidelines for using sound as a feedback tool in a stack?

4.  What would be some good uses for narration in a stack?

5.  What are some of the uses for the CDPlay feature in a stack?

6.  What are the additional options offered by the Options button on the CDPlay feature?

7.  When using the Menu Tamer, name two ways to undo the action once you have hidden the menubar in the stack:

    **a.**

    **b.**

8.  What is the process for incorporating a sound cut into a stack?

## LESSON 12 PROJECT 12.1

1. Create a two- or three-card stack that asks a question and provides feedback.

2. Use the Animal1 through Animal3 stacks as guidelines.

3. Incorporate sound and graphics into the stack to provide feedback for making choices.

4. Save the stack as **Feedback**.

## LESSON 12 PROJECT 12.2

1. Find or write a short poem.

2. Using the Journey stack as a guideline, create a six-card stack, including a Title card. (You can make the stack larger if you need to.)

3. Use a series of pictures from the HS Media Library to illustrate the poem.

4. Add text for each stanza or line of your poem.

5. From the HS Media Library, choose a sound to play through the stack.

6. Create a slide show of your stack.

7. Save as **Poem**.

## CRITICAL THINKING ACTIVITY

SCANS

1. As a class, in small groups, or individually, list at least three benefits and three detriments of using sound to present information.

2. Write one paragraph comparing a silent presentation or project to a presentation or project that incorporates sound.

# LESSON 13

# WORKING WITH QUICKTIME VIDEO

## OBJECTIVES

**Upon completion of this lesson, you will be able to:**

- Insert a QuickTime video clip into a stack.

- Create buttons to control video.

- Create different types of video controllers.

- Use QuickTime and AVI video tips to create a video insert.

🕐 **Estimated Time: 1 hour**

You must have QuickTime or Media Player installed on your computer to complete this lesson. If you cannot access the CD-ROM for this lesson, use what is available in the HyperStudio Samples stack. You may reuse resources if you do not have access to the HyperStudio Media Library, the CD-ROM that accompanies this book, or another CD-ROM with multimedia resources.

# *Video*

Video is the final multimedia element you will add to your repertoire. When used properly, video is a great way to capture your user's attention. And not only is video exciting to use, but a short video can convey information that would not be as clear or as descriptive using words or animation. For some subjects, animation does not work as well as video. Video is best used to present real-life information, current events, procedures, and simulations. There are times when video will be the best tool to present ideas. Video can transform an idea into an actual experience and make the information more meaningful. We all learn differently. For some, seeing the concept or idea will have a profound and lasting effect.

## QuickTime and AVI Video

Apple Computer created QuickTime, which is a method of using video in digital format on your computer. Most Macintosh computers today have a QuickTime player installed in the system. This means that even if you do not have the QuickTime application to make or edit your own video clips, you can still play clips that are in the QuickTime format. Windows computers can play AVI through Media Player which is installed with Windows. Many Windows computers can also play QuickTime video. The video examples in this text will be QuickTime.

Video clips can be resized to be larger or smaller, the same way that graphics are resized. However, when enlarged, the video will take up more memory and may slow your computer down. This will depend on the configuration of your computer.

Both QuickTime and AVI video files can be played. In Windows, the Media Player plug in that allows you to play AVI files is standard. The QuickTime player, for those who don't have it installed, resides on the HyperStudio CD-ROM and can be installed, if it is not already available to you.

HyperStudio lets you interact with QuickTime and AVI files by making it simple to include this medium in your stacks. The HyperStudio CD-ROM includes some video clips. Using NBAs, you can easily insert the clips in your stack and use objects, text, or buttons to play the video.

 **TIP**

When you are using multimedia elements such as video and audio, there may be variations in performance due to differing computer configurations. Since computers do not have the same components, there may be inconsistencies in the outcome when you are working with multimedia. If you have problems as you work these steps, notify your instructor. Some of the steps may need to be modified to meet the standards of the equipment you are using. When you work with technology, you can always count on variable outcomes. Although this can be frustrating, it can also be a way to learn more in order to overcome the challenges.

## STEP-BY-STEP ⇨ 13.1

1. Open a new stack. Use the default card size.

 **HINT:**

Macintosh users will need to adjust the color setting to 256 colors.

2. Once your settings are adjusted, save the stack as **QTstack**.

3. Add a button on the first card. Name the button **Play Movie**. Use the shadow rectangle button. Use the filmstrip icon, as shown in Figure 13-1.

4. Move the button to the right center of the card.

(continued on next page)

**FIGURE 13-1**
Filmstrip Icon

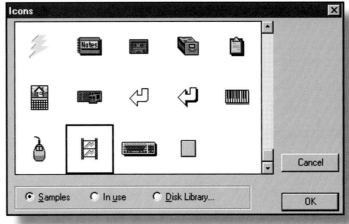

**257**

**5.** From the Actions window, choose **Play a movie or video**, as shown in Figure 13-2.

**6.** Choose **Disk file (QuickTime or AVI movies)**, as shown in Figure 13-3. Click **OK.**

**7.** Select **HSMovies** from the Hstudio folder. Select **Heat**, as shown in Figure 13-4.

**8.** With the video selected, move the video to the left center of the card.

**9.** Click outside the video clip. Click **Try It**. The movie should play, and you should hear the audio and see the video.

**HINT:**

If you do not have both audio and video, ask your instructor to check the connections on your computer and to be sure the correct software is available on your computer.

**FIGURE 13-2**
Play a Movie or Video

**FIGURE 13-3**
Disk File (QuickTime or AVI Movies)

**FIGURE 13-4**
Heat File

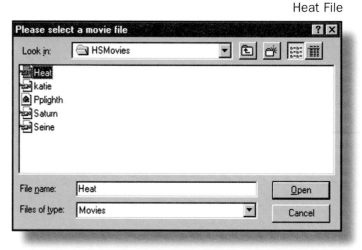

## STEP-BY-STEP 13.1 CONTINUED

**10.** Select **Use movie controller**, as shown in Figure 13-5. This adds a slider to the bottom of the clip. The controller allows the user to start and stop the video.

**11.** Click **OK**, then **Done**. When you return to Card 1, only the Play Movie button will be visible.

**12.** In the Browse mode, press the **Play Movie** button. The video clip will appear as shown in Figure 13-6. You can use the controller to stop and start the clip and to move backward and forward in the clip.

**13.** Save the stack.

**FIGURE 13-5**
Use Movie Controller

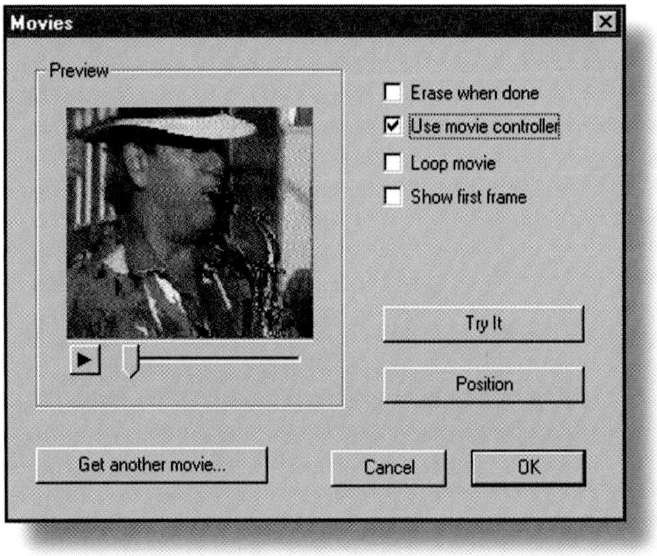

**FIGURE 13-6**
Movie and Button on Card

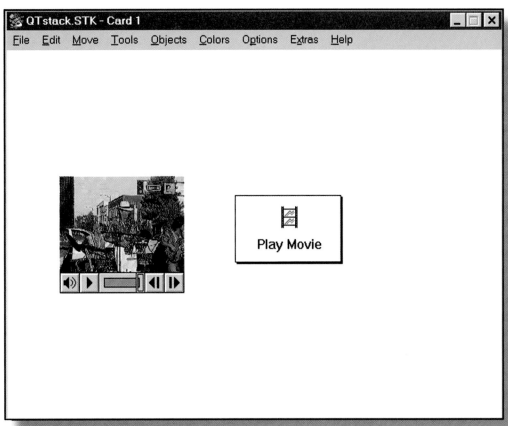

# Video Tips

1. **Less is more.**
   Use short clips of about 20 to 30 seconds or less. Short clips will take up less space on your disk, hard drive, or zip drive. You can use two short clips or divide one clip into two parts to show a longer clip. This may enable you to save each clip on a floppy disk.

2. **Use video with good resolution.**
   Use video that is clear and easy to see, especially if you are following a step-by-step procedure.

3. **Don't oversize the video.**
   Depending on your computer and the version of QuickTime or Media Player installed on your computer, you could end up with a mosaic effect when you drag a picture to enlarge it. Also, resizing a video clip will use more RAM memory. If you use too much RAM memory, the clip will not run properly.

4. **Use relevant video clips.**
   Just as with graphics or text, use video when it is the best medium to convey the message. Don't overuse video so that it detracts from or competes with the information you are presenting.

5. **Using the video controllers.**
   When you insert a video clip into a stack, you have several options about how it will appear and how it can be controlled. The options appear in the table below.

 **TIP**

There are two types of memory on computers. One type is RAM memory. This is the memory that the computer uses to run the programs you are using. The more RAM memory you have, the more complex tasks you can perform. Most of today's computers have a minimum amount of 8 megabytes of RAM. A megabyte is a measurement unit. The other type of memory is storage memory. This generally refers to the amount of information you can store on the computer's hard drive. Most of today's computers hold a gigabyte or more of information on the hard drive. That means you can store many programs and files on the hard drive.

## VIDEO CONTROLLERS

| SELECTION | ACTION |
|---|---|
| **Erase when done** | When selected, this will make the video clip disappear after it has played. |
| **Use movie controller** | When selected, a controller bar will appear under the movie clip that allows you to start, stop, and pause the movie. |
| **Loop movie** | When selected, this will cause the movie to constantly repeat when finished. |
| **Show first frame** | When selected, the first frame of the movie will appear on the card like a graphic image when you arrive at the card. |

## STEP-BY-STEP 13.2

1. Create a five-card stack using the default size. Macintosh users must specify 256 colors.

2. On the first card, the Title card, import the background **solrsstm** from the HSArt folder. See Figure 13-7.

3. Add a button. Name the button **Start**. Use an oval button with a **gray** background and **black** text. Add the planet earth icon, as shown in Figure 13-8.

4. Move the button to the bottom center of the card and resize it as needed.

5. From the Actions window, choose **Next card** (use the default transition) and **Play a sound**. From the files listed, choose **BEAMDOWN.WAV**. Click **OK** and **Done** as needed to complete the button.

(continued on next page)

**FIGURE 13-7**
Solrsstm File

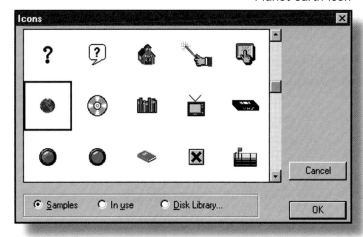

**FIGURE 13-8**
Planet earth icon

---

**INTERNET** The federal government has plans to link schools, government agencies, colleges, and universities to a network that will be much faster than the current Internet. This new network is called the National Research and Education Network (NREN).

**6.** Add a text object and place it along the top center of the card. Resize the object to allow a one-word title. The object should not have a frame or be scrollable. It should have a **black** background with **dark gray** text. Use the font **Artistik**, size **36**, and align **center**. Key **Space** as the title of the stack. The Title card should look like Figure 13-9.

**HINT:**

If you do not have the Artistik font, select another font.

**7.** Click the **Start** button. You should hear the sound and be moved to Card 2. This will be the Main Menu card.

**8.** Save the stack as **Space**. Keep it open.

**9.** Import a background for Card 2. Access the drive with the HyperStudio CD-ROM. From the medialib folder, select **scrnbkgd**, **lairdstd**, and the **grknitmn** file. Card 2 should look like Figure 13-10.

**FIGURE 13-9**
Title Card for Space Stack

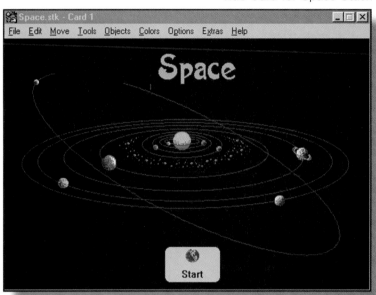

**FIGURE 13-10**
Main Menu Card in Space Stack

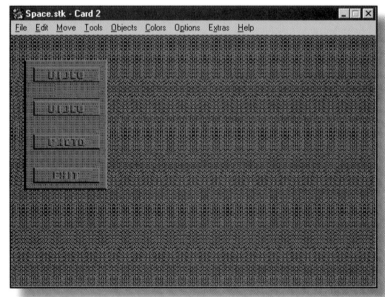

**10.** Save the stack. Keep the stack open.

**11.** Move to Card 3. Import a background. Select **medialib**, **scrnbkgd**, **proclect**, and the file **blsunlgt**. Card 3 should look like Figure 13-11.

**12.** Add a button to Card 3. Name the button **Play Video**. Use the button of your choice. Do not add an icon. Select a background color and a text color that coordinates with the background and is easy to read. Move the button to the bottom center of the screen and resize as needed.

**13.** Click outside the button. From the Actions window, select **Play a movie or video**. Select **Disk file** as the source for the video, and click **OK**.

**14.** From the HStudio folder, select **HSMovies** and the **saturn** file, as shown in Figure 13-12.

**FIGURE 13-11**
Card 3 of Space Stack

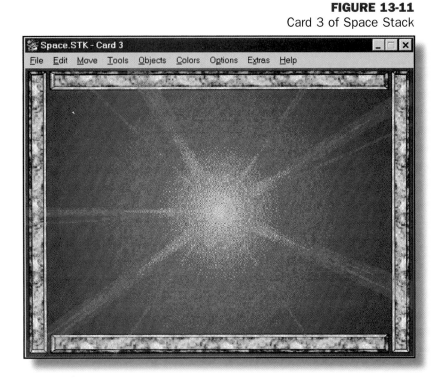

**FIGURE 13-12**
Saturn File

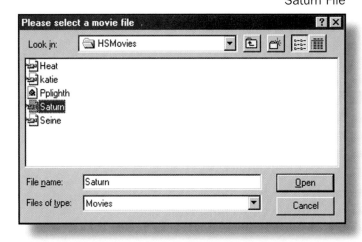

(continued on next page)

**263**

**15.** Place the video in the center of the card. Click outside the video. In the Movies window, select **Show first frame**, as shown in Figure 13-13. The Show first frame option results in the first frame of the video clip being visible whenever you move to the card.

**16.** Click **Try It**. You will notice that the video does not have an audio component.

**17.** Click **OK**. From the Actions window, select **Play a sound**. Select **Disk Library**. Select **korg.wav** from the HSSounds folder, as shown in Figure 13-14.

**FIGURE 13-13**
Show First Frame

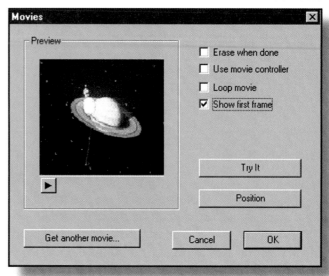

**FIGURE 13-14**
Korg.wav

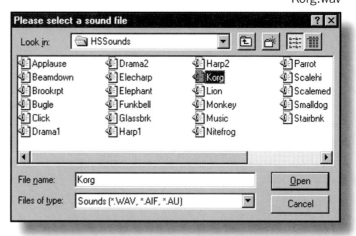

**18.** Test the button. You should see the video of Saturn and hear the korg sound file. Your card should resemble Figure 13-15.

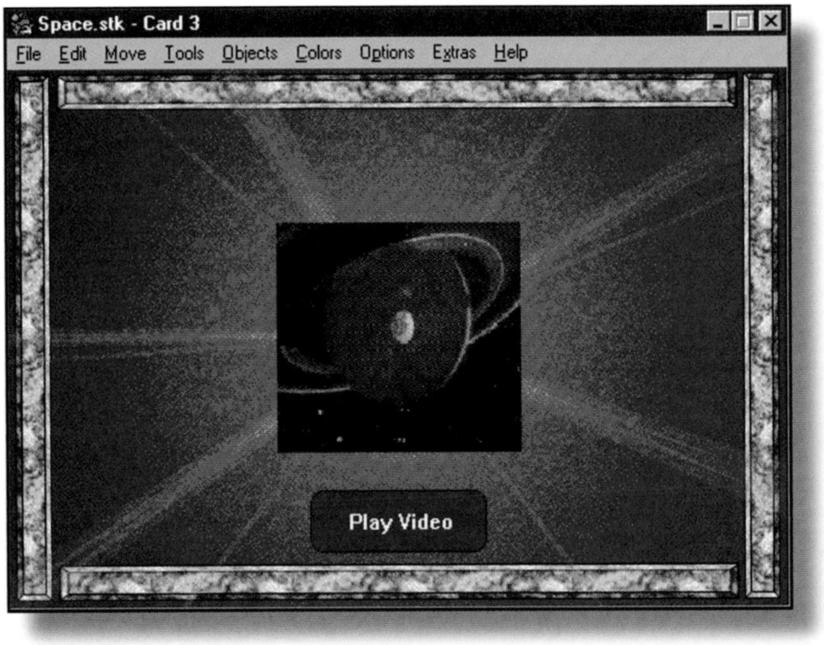

**19.** Return to Card 2. Add a new button. Make the button invisible and size it to fit over the video button template on the Main Menu card. From the Actions window, select **Another card** and use the arrows to locate the card with the video on it, Card 3. Select the **Dissolve** transition and the **Fast** speed. Click **OK** and **Done**.

**20.** Test the button. It should move you to the videocard.

**21.** Move to Card 4. Import a background. Access the drive with the HyperStudio CD-ROM. From the medialib folder, select **clipart**, and the **spacevew** file, as shown in Figure 13-16.

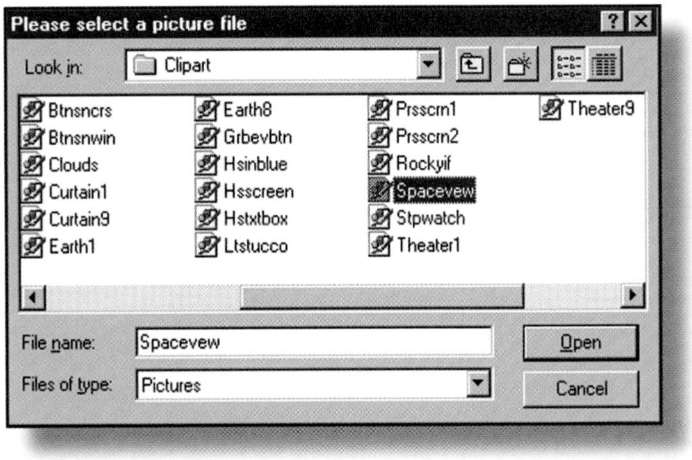

(continued on next page)

**FIGURE 13-15**
Card 3 with Button and Video

**FIGURE 13-16**
Spacevew File

**22.** Save the stack.

**23.** Add clip art from the files on the HyperStudio CD-ROM. From the medialib folder, select **photoglry**, **space**, and **moon**. Select a section of the moon, as shown in Figure 13-17.

**24.** Slide the clip art into the bottom right corner and adjust for size, as in Figure 13-18.

**25.** Add a graphic object from the files on the HyperStudio CD-ROM. From the space folder, select **erthmoon**. Select just the moon and click **OK**. Move the moon to the upper left corner of the card.

**FIGURE 13-17**
Partial Moon

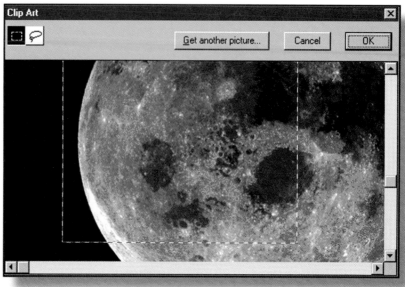

**FIGURE 13-18**
Moon in Corner of Card

 **HINT:**

Since the clip art you added in Step 23 was located in the space folder, HyperStudio automatically returns to that folder. The space folder is located in the photoglry folder, which is in the medialib folder.

**26.** Click outside the graphic. From the Graphic Appearance window, click **Actions** and select **Play a sound**. Select **Disk Library**. From the medialib folder on the CD-ROM drive, select **sndmusic**, **soundfx**, and the **cosmic.wav** file, as shown in Figure 13-19.

**FIGURE 13-19**
Cosmic.wav

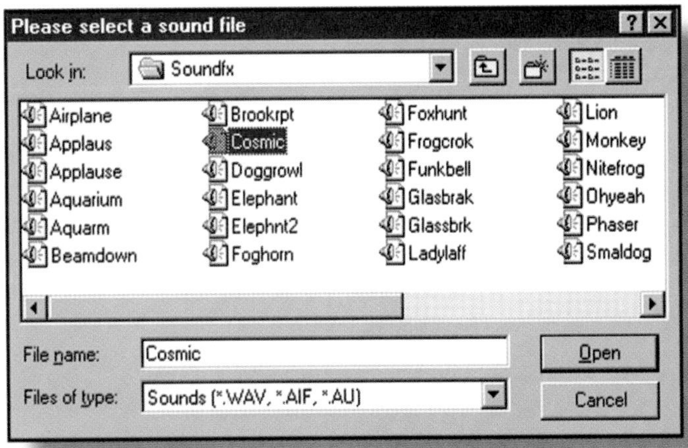

**27.** Play the sound. Click **OK**, **Done**, and **OK**.

**28.** Using the Text paint tool, key **Click Here** on the graphic object.

**FIGURE 13-20**
Earth and Moon

**29.** Select the graphic using the **Square Selector** tool. Choose **Effects** from the Edit menu. Select **Scale and Rotate** and choose **Counter-clockwise** and **90** degrees. The result should look like Figure 13-20.

**30.** Save the stack as **Space1**. Keep the stack open.

## Adding Video to a Text Field

You can insert video into your stack in a variety of ways. You have already played video using a button, but you can also use your imagination to insert video in less predictable ways. For example, you could insert video as an action for an object or text field. You can create a text object to present information and then reinforce the concept with a hidden video. Remember that your goal is to effectively use video to convey your ideas.

**STEP-BY-STEP 13.3**

1. With the Space1 stack open, move to Card 5.

2. Import a background. Access the drive with the HyperStudio CD-ROM. From the medialib folder, select **scrnbkgd**, **studmich**, and the **strsfrmd** file.

3. Insert a text object. Use the default size for the object. The object should have a frame, but not be scrollable. Make the background **black** and the text **dark gray**. Select **Arial** for the font, size **18**, and align **left**.

4. Key:

   **Space has long been the dream and the mystery of the imagination.**

   **To see a picture from space click on this text.**

   The screen should resemble Figure 13-21.

**FIGURE 13-21**
Card 5 Text Object

**5.** Select the text object field with one of the edit tools. Click twice on the field and click **Actions** from the Text Appearance window. Select **Play a movie or video**.

**6.** Select **Disk file** and click **OK**. Access the drive with the HyperStudio CD-ROM. From the medialib folder, select the **mormovie** folder and the **erth3d** file, as shown in Figure 13-22. Leave the object in the center of the text field.

**FIGURE 13-22**
Erth3d File

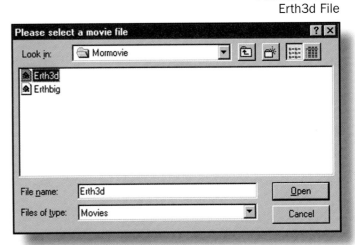

**7.** From the Movies window, select **Erase when done**, as shown in Figure 13-23. Click **OK**, **Done**, and **OK**.

**FIGURE 13-23**
Erase when Done

**8.** Test the field by returning to Browse mode and clicking in the center of the text field. The video of the rotating earth should appear, play, and then disappear.

**9.** Save the stack as **Space2**. Keep the stack open.

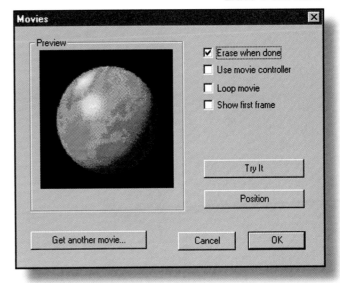

**HINT:**

To change the actions of a text field, select the text field with one of the edit tools and choose Actions from the text field window.

# Completing Navigation/Testing Your Stack

As you create more diverse and imaginative stacks, it is important to remember some basics, such as complete and accurate navigation. Always test and retest your stacks to make sure that all of the buttons and other features work correctly. You might ask someone else to test it for you also. Although you may think the navigation is adequate, someone else using the stack may notice weaknesses in the navigation. Not only should a user be able to easily navigate among the cards, but the navigation plan should allow the user to view the stack in the order you intended, to move in the ways you intended, and to be able to exit when the user wants to.

## STEP-BY-STEP ⟹ 13.4

1. With the Space2 stack open, go to the Title card. Using one of the edit tools, select the **Start** button. Copy the button and paste it onto Card 3, the first movie card.

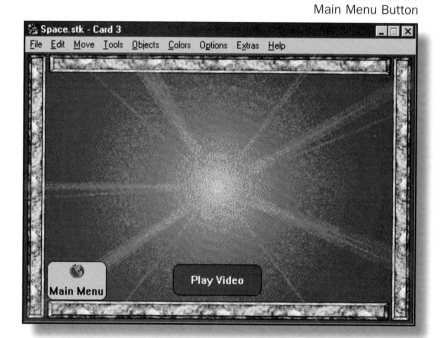

**FIGURE 13-24**
Main Menu Button

2. Double click on the button. Change the name of the button to **Main Menu**. Click the **Actions** button. Deselect **Play a sound** and select **Another card**. Using the arrow, find the Main Menu card. Use the default transition. Your card should resemble Figure 13-24.

3. Test the button. It should return you to the Main Menu card.

4. Copy the Main Menu button to Cards 4 and 5.

5. Save the stack as **Space3**.

6. Go to the Main Menu card. Copy and paste this card for backup. Go to the first Main Menu card.

7. Using the **Square Selector** tool, select the video button. Copy and paste the selection. Move the copied button to cover the audio button, as shown in Figure 13-25.

8. Create an invisible button for the second video button whose action goes to Card 5, the text field card. Use **Dissolve** as the transition and **Fast** as the speed.

9. Copy and paste the invisible video button to create an invisible button for the Photo option. The button action goes to Card 4, the photo card. Use **Dissolve** as the transition and **Fast** as the speed.

10. Save the stack.

11. Create a Quit NBA for the EXIT button.

12. Add a text object. Name the object **Credits**. The background should be **black** and the letters **dark gray**. Make the size of the text object about one line high and about two inches wide. Make the font size **18**. Deselect Draw Frame and Scrollable. Key suitable text for the stack credits, such as:

> **This stack
> was created
> by [Your Name]
> for the [class name]
> on [current date].**

(Look forward to Figure 13-29 to see a sample of the roll credits screen.)

(continued on next page)

 **TIP**

The second Main Menu card is a backup card in case you make a mistake with the background of the card. If you do not need to use this card after you have completed the procedure, you will eliminate it from the stack. If you need to use the backup card, you can delete the first card. Also, since you saved before beginning this part of the process, you can always close the stack, selecting **Don't save**, and reopen the stack.

**FIGURE 13-25**
Two Video Buttons

**13.** On the Main Menu card, add a new button. Make this an invisible button. Name the button **CREDITS** and select **Show Name**, as shown in Figure 13-26. Make the Name color **white** and click **OK**. Move the button below the other buttons.

**14.** Click outside the button. From the Actions window, select **New Button Actions**.

**15.** Select **HideShw2 NBA**. Select **Use this NBA**. In the Hide/Show window, enter the name of the object, **CREDITS**, select **Text object**, and select **Flip (hide/show)**, as shown in Figure 13-27. Click **OK**.

**FIGURE 13-26**
Button Appearance Window

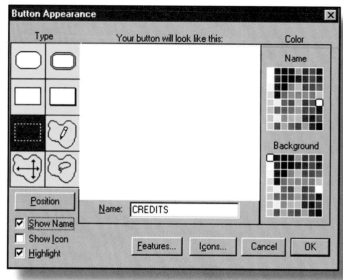

**FIGURE 13-27**
Hide/Show NBA

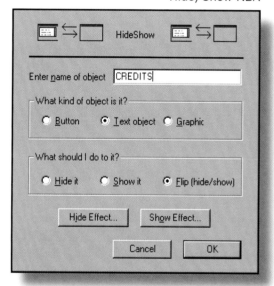

**16.** From the New Button Actions window, select **RollCredits**. Select **Use this NBA**. Key in the name of the text object, **CREDITS**. Use the default settings, as shown in Figure 13-28. Click **OK** twice, then click **Done**.

**17.** Test the button. The text field object should appear and scroll to the end. (See Figure 13-29.)

**18.** Delete the extra Main Menu card.

**19.** Save the stack as **Space4**.

**FIGURE 13-28**
RollCredits NBA

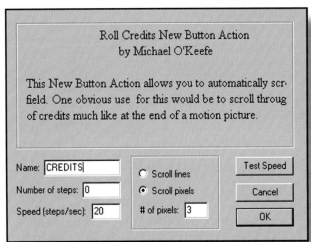

**FIGURE 13-29**
Rolling Credits on Card

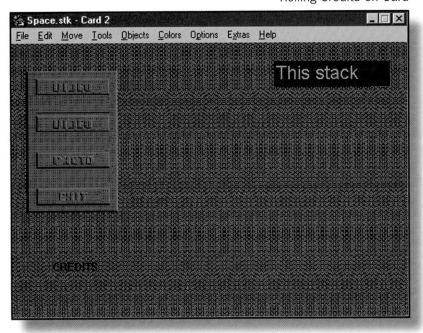

**SCANS**

1. Add another card to the Space3 stack. The card, Card 6, should include:

   ■ an imported background

   ■ a QuickTime or AVI video that is accessed through a button

   ■ a text object explaining the video

   ■ sound to accompany the video if it does not have sound

   ■ a button to return to the Main Menu

2. Update the Main Menu to include navigation to the new card. Save the revised stack as **Space5**.

# Summary

In this lesson, you learned that:

■ Video can be inserted into your HyperStudio stacks.

■ QuickTime and AVI video are digital forms of video.

■ Video is a dynamic multimedia tool.

■ You can use buttons to play video in your stacks.

■ You can choose to use a video controller for your video clip.

■ You can add an audio element to a video clip.

■ You can use objects to play video.

■ You can use text fields to access video.

■ Less can be more when using video.

■ You should not oversize the video.

■ Relevant video clips are a creative way to express ideas.

■ You must test the stack for correct navigation and correct functioning.

## VOCABULARY

AVI

Digital format

QuickTime

Video clips

## LESSON 13 REVIEW QUESTIONS

### TRUE/FALSE

**Circle the T if the statement is true or F if it is false.**

**T  F**  **1.** You can access video through a text field.

**T  F**  **2.** You can access video through clip art.

**T  F**  **3.** A button that controls video can also complete another action.

**T  F**  **4.** You cannot attach a sound to a video clip if it does not already have sound as part of the clip.

**T  F**  **5.** HyperStudio includes several video clips on its CD.

**T  F**  **6.** You can resize a video clip to a larger size.

### COMPLETION

**Answer the questions below in the space provided.**

**1.** Video is accessed by using the _____ menu.

**2.** On the HyperStudio CD-ROM, the _____ folder has additional multimedia resources.

**3.** You can choose to hide a video clip when it is finished playing by choosing _____ from the video controller selections.

**4.** You can have the first clip of a movie appear on a card by choosing _____ from the video controller selections.

**5.** If you resize a video clip into a larger picture, you run the risk of having it play _____ .

## SHORT ANSWER QUESTIONS

**Answer the questions below in the space provided.**

1. What are two reasons for using video in a stack?

   a.

   b.

2. What is QuickTime?

3. Name and explain two video tips:

   a.

   b.

4. What is the procedure for adding video to a stack using a button?

5. What is the procedure for adding video to a stack using a text object?

6. What are the movie controller choices for video?

7. Explain the function of two of the movie controller choices:

   a.

   b.

8. How do you add a video from the HyperStudio CD-ROM?

9. Why is it important to test your stack?

## LESSON 13 PROJECT 13.1

1.  Reexamine the **MyTopic** stack you created in Lesson 5, Project 5.1.

    ■ Look at the storyboard you created for the stack.

    ■ Redesign the storyboard to include new cards for the stack that have graphics, sound, and video.

    ■ Add at least one new card for each of the subtopics.

    ■ Insert the sound, video, and graphics in the stack.

2.  Save the stack as **Proj13**.

## LESSON 13 PROJECT 13.2

1.  Create a storyboard for a five-card stack. Choose your own topic. Include a:

    ■ Title card

    ■ Main Menu card

    ■ three text objects with information about your topic

    ■ at least one video using a button

    ■ at least one video using a text object

    ■ at least one video using a graphic object

    HINT: You may want to review the videos that are available with HyperStudio before selecting a topic for the stack.

2.  Save the stack as **Video**.

## CRITICAL THINKING ACTIVITY

1.  List advantages for using video in a stack. What are some projects that would benefit from this type of interaction?

2.  List possible drawbacks for using video in a stack. When might video be detrimental to a project or presentation? List projects that could be included in this category.

# MORE VIDEO

## OBJECTIVES

**Upon completion of this lesson, you will be able to:**

- Insert live video in a stack.

- Use irregular shapes for video frames.

- Use different button types.

- Play video through graphic objects.

- Print to video.

**⏱ Estimated Time: 1 hour**

To complete portions of this lesson, you need to have access to a live video source such as a camcorder, laser disc, or video player. You will also need a multimedia computer or computer with a digitizing card that allows you to input a video signal. Your instructor can advise you if this equipment is available.

## *Using Live Video*

O̲nce you begin to use multimedia to express yourself, you will only be limited by your imagination. Video is one of the most exciting features of multimedia. With live video, you will add a dynamic level to your projects and presentations.

Imagine creating a science project, videotaping each of the steps and the final experiment, and presenting the video clips in a HyperStudio stack.

Imagine creating a personal autobiography that includes videotaped segments from members of your family. Think how much more effective the live video would be than a written report.

Suppose you could create a multimedia resume that not only listed your qualifications and experience, but included a video clip that personally introduced yourself and your work or experience.

Perhaps you are learning to speak in a different language. You could create a live video that would demonstrate your progress and include it in a stack. You could also create a video tutorial to help others learn language skills.

Many courses now require portfolios to assess your progress. A HyperStudio stack with videotaped segments could demonstrate your progress in the course and be a dynamic way to express what you have learned.

Live video allows you to become the director as you choose what to include and what to edit. When you add live video to your stacks, you have full say in what and how you present the information in your own style. Although HyperStudio does not provide editing capabilities, if you have a special board or card in your computer called a digitizing board, you will be able to shoot live video and play it in your computer. There is software available that will allow you to edit your video sequences on the computer. Ask your instructor if such software is available in your classroom or computer lab. You can also edit the video sequences on a VCR and then input it into the computer after you have digitized the parts you want.

## STEP-BY-STEP 14.1

**To complete this Step-by-Step, you must have access to the files on the HyperStudio CD-ROM.**

**1.** Open the HyperStudio program. Make sure you have access to the files that are on the HyperStudio CD-ROM.

**2.** Select **Sample Projects** from the Main Menu card of HyperStudio.

**3.** Select **Commercial**. Use the **Next** button to move to Project #3, **Portfolio Assessment**. Double click on the opening screen of the project.

**4.** Navigate through the stack.

**5.** Review the stack. Make a list of the technical features that are used, such as:
- video
- live video
- sound
- animation
- types of navigation techniques

**6.** Make a list of some of the creative projects that are used.

**7.** Create a list of four projects that you could create and include in an evaluation portfolio.

# Resizing Video Frames

Depending on your version of AVI or QuickTime video, you will probably see a small frame of video when you import video clips. As you learned in Lesson 13, you can control how the video clip is presented. One of the controls allows you to determine the size of the picture.

As previously stated, when you increase the size of the video picture, you use more of the computer's RAM memory. Depending on the amount of memory in your computer, this may not have any effect at all. However, increasing the size may have some detrimental effects. Two common effects are a distortion of the picture, which is called a mosaic because it looks like a tiled mosaic with the picture broken into small bits. Another common problem is that the video may not play at the correct speed. This can cause the video portion to be out of sync with the audio portion of the clip or the clip to play in a jerky manner. If either problem occurs, you have enlarged the picture too much. Some versions of QuickTime may not allow you to change the picture size.

1. Create a new stack. Use the standard card size.

2. Add a button. Name the button **Play Video**. Use the style, icon, and colors of your choice.

3. From the Actions window, select **Play a movie or video**.

4. From the Video/Movie Source window, select **Video (Make your own movie)**, as shown in Figure 14-1. Click **OK**.

5. HyperStudio will ask you to save your movie even though you haven't made the movie yet. For File name, key the name of your movie, as shown in Figure 14-2. Click **Save**.

6. From the Preview window, select Video Options. (See Figure 14-3.) Click **OK**.

**FIGURE 14-1**
Make Your Own Movie

**FIGURE 14-2**
Movie Save As Window

 **TIP**

When using video in a stack, you must store the actual video clip with the stack or in a place that the computer can access the movie for the stack using the path you originally set up when you created the video. It is a good idea to create a folder for the stack and video clips that you will need.

**FIGURE 14-3**
Preview Window

**7.** From the Video Setup window, shown in Figure 14-4, select **Video Format**.

**8.** The Video Format window will control the size of your video picture. Use the default setting and click **OK**. Figure 14-5 shows one default setting; your defaults may be different.

**9.** Select **Video Source** from the Video Setup window. Refer to Figure 14-4.

**10.** The Video Driver window, shown in Figure 14-6, is used to specify the source of the incoming signal. Make your choices based on the following guidelines:

- Select the appropriate choice from the Connector column. If you are using a cable, select **Cable**. If you are using an RCA cable, select **Composite**. If you are using a special S-Video cable, which is an 8-pin connector, select **S-Video**.

- If you are in the United States, you are using the NTSC signal. Select **NTSC** under Standard.

- Select **Mirror Display**.

- You may adjust the Brightness, Contrast, Color, and Tint according to the color quality of your picture.

When you have made your adjustments, click **OK**.

(continued on next page)

**TIP**

If you have made adjustments that you want to undo, click **Default** to return to the original settings. Then make your new choices.

**FIGURE 14-4**
Video Setup Window

**FIGURE 14-5**
Video Format Window

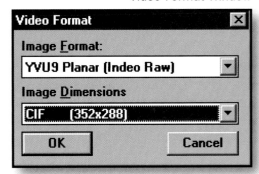

**FIGURE 14-6**
Video Driver Window

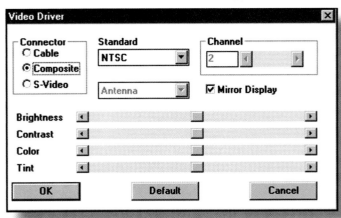

**11.** Set up the video you wish to capture. When you have the camera set up or the laser disc or video player set to the frame you have chosen, press **Record**.

**12.** When you have finished the segment, click the mouse. Select **Try It!** to see the results. If you are not satisfied, reset the camera, laser disk, or video player and record the segment again.

**13.** When you are satisfied with the result, click **OK**. (See Figure 14-7.)

**14.** Your movie should be in the center of your screen with your button beneath it, as shown in Figure 14-8. Save the stack as **Vpract**. Keep the stack open.

**FIGURE 14-7**
Try It and OK in the Preview Window

**FIGURE 14-8**
Card with Movie and Button

 **HINT:**

It is better to make several short movies rather than one long movie. Try to keep your clips 14 to 20 seconds long to preserve enough memory to run your programs. You will be surprised how much you can put into 20 seconds.

# Editing Movies

HyperStudio has limited editing capabilities for video clips that are input through a video source. With the HyperStudio video player, you can select the segments you wish to use and create a file that can be saved and stored for future use in your stacks. There are other editing programs that allow you to practice much more sophisticated editing techniques, such as putting together different video clips from a variety of sources and using transitions, fade outs, and character generation of text over video. These types of techniques are beyond the scope of this text. However, if you are interested, ask your instructor if you have access to a suitable video editing program.

# Creating Video Storyboards

In previous lessons, you learned how to use a storyboard to plan your projects and organize your thoughts. When you plan video projects, a storyboard is a critical tool for developing a precise and effective production. When you use video in a stack, you will probably end up creating two storyboards—one for the overall plan of the stack and another for the video segments you will use.

A video storyboard is a little different from the storyboards you have been working with for your stacks. A video storyboard will have:

- Pictures to represent what will be on the screen. These pictures can be line drawings but should represent the type of picture you will see.

- Information about the sounds that will be played—the script, music, or background sounds. If you are working with a stereo system, you may have a script and music or background sound on another channel.

- The type of video shot that will be used: extreme close-up, close-up, medium shot, long shot, or extreme long shot. An extreme close-up would probably be a part of a person's face. A close-up would be the person's entire face. A medium shot would include about half of a person's body and a little of the background. A long shot would include all of the person's body and more of the background. An extreme long shot would be similar to a wide landscape shot, for example, the shot may show the pyramids and you may not even be able to see the person.

- Any other information such as lighting or props that should be included in the particular shot.

You can draw in the pictures that fit the descriptions. They only have to be detailed enough to represent the shots you will take when you make your video segments. Figure 14-9 shows a sample video storyboard that describes the shots and includes rough drawings.

 **INTERNET** Flames are angry messages sent to people who break the rules on Netiquette. Netiquette is the term that has been coined to describe the rules governing etiquette, or good manners, on the Internet.

**FIGURE 14-9**
Video Storyboard

Card #4 Video Segment

| Scene 1 | Scene 2 | Scene 3 |
|---|---|---|
|  | 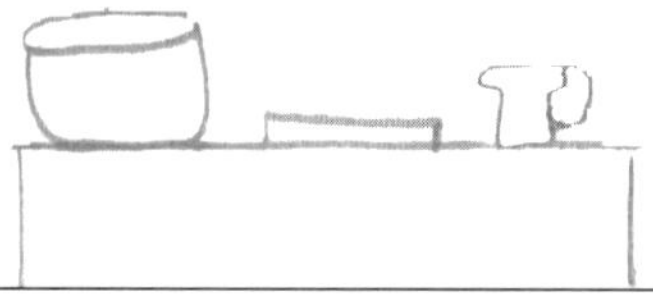 |  |
| Script:<br>"I am going to show you how to bake chocolate chip cookies." | "You will need the following equipment: a cookie sheet, a large bowl, a hand mixer, a measuring cup, a large spoon, and an oven." | "You will need the following ingredients: 1 cup flour, 2 tbs butter, $^{1}/_{2}$ cup sugar, 2 eggs, 1 tsp vanilla, and a bag of chocolate chips." |

| Scene 4 | Scene 5 | Scene 6 |
|---|---|---|
|  |  |  |
| "Mix the ingredients in a bowl." | "Bake at 350 degrees for 8–10 minutes." | "This is the final delicious snack." |

# Using Irregular Shapes

Along with the ability to edit or create a video, HyperStudio allows you to play movies behind graphic objects. The result is that the movie appears to be playing through the object. For example, you could import a picture or draw a picture of a doghouse. Then you could put a video of a dog in the door to the doghouse. It would appear as though the dog were in the doghouse.

Using objects as a frame for your video gives you the opportunity to create interesting settings for the video clips.

**STEP-BY-STEP ⟹ 14.3**

1. With Vpract open, add a new card to the stack.

2. Add clip art. From the disk file, select HSArt and **album**. Use the **Square Selector** tool to select the entire picture. Resize the graphic as needed to fill the screen.

3. Double click on your **Text** tool. Select a font, size **16**, and choose the color **black**. Key **Click Here**, as shown in Figure 14-10.

**FIGURE 14-10**
Click Here

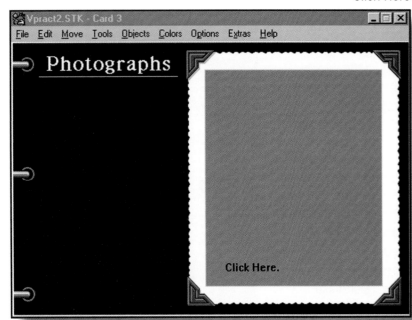

4. Click outside the picture. Use the **Lasso Selector** tool to select the gray area of the photo album, as shown by the red dashes in Figure 14-11.

**FIGURE 14-11**
Gray Area Selected

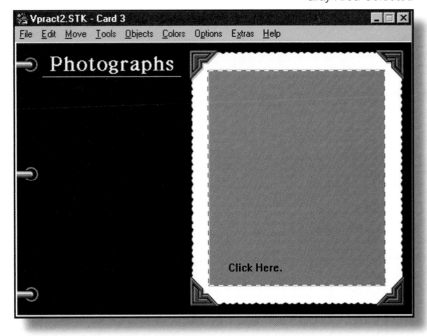

5. From the Objects menu, select **Add a Graphic Object**. You will see a window asking, "Do you want to turn the selected part of the screen into a graphic object?" Select **Yes**.

**FIGURE 14-12**
Movie in Photo Album

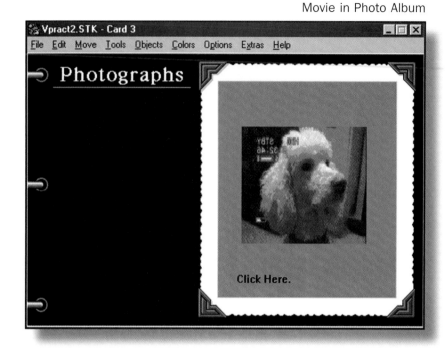

6. In the Graphic Appearance window, click **Actions**. Select **Play a movie or video**. Choose a movie you have created or one from the HyperStudio resources. Move the movie to the center of the gray photo area, as shown in Figure 14-12. Click **OK** and **Done** as needed to complete the process. When you click on the gray area, the movie should play.

7. Save the stack as **Vpract1**. Keep the stack open.

**TIP**

Macintosh users will need to select Play over Objects from the QuickTime Movies window.

## CHALLENGE ACTIVITY ⟹ 14.1

**SCANS**

1. Open Vpract1, if necessary.

2. Using the album as the background for the stack, add at least three new cards.

3. Insert video clips and photos into the stack. (Use at least two videos and two photos.) Add some text to explain or caption the pictures.

4. Create a combined Title and Main Menu page to function as the album cover with navigation to each of the album pages.

5. Save the stack as **Album**.

# *Using Different Button Types*

You have worked with a variety of buttons and button actions in previous lessons. You have learned how to select button actions, button appearances, button options, and New Button Actions. HyperStudio offers more choices and features for you to choose from when you use buttons.

## Object Features

The Object Features window, shown in Figure 14-13, lists various options. Each is described in the following table.

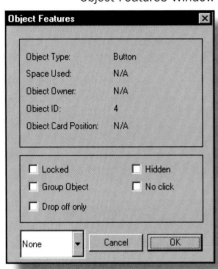

**FIGURE 14-13**
Object Features Window

**Locked**   This is similar to a Read Only text field. When this feature is checked, the button cannot be moved or changed by the user. To edit the button in any way, you would have to unlock the button by deselecting Locked from this window.

**Group Object**   This feature will place the button and all of its actions on all of the cards in a group.

**Drop Off Only**   This selection will prevent the button from interacting with the cursor and the button will only work when a graphic object is dropped on it. This feature is often used when creating games.

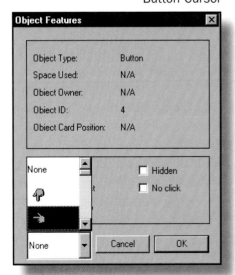

**FIGURE 14-14**
Button Cursor

**Hidden**   The hidden feature will keep the button invisible so that it cannot be clicked or accidentally activated. This feature can be used if you had a button with an automatic timer that needed to be hidden until it was time for it to show or for an action to occur.

**No Click**   This allows the user to activate a button by simply passing the mouse over it.

**Button Cursor**   The default mode of this feature is None. This feature allows you to select a cursor with the hand pointing in a different direction than the usual browser hand. When this feature is used, the hand changes direction when you pass the mouse over the button. Two of the available hand shapes are shown in Figure 14-14.

**287**

## Additional Button Types

You have used the oval, double oval, rectangle, shadow rectangle, and invisible buttons in other lessons. There are still three button types that you have not used: Freehand, Lasso, and Expanding. Each of these allows you to be creative with your button design.

The Freehand button lets you draw your own button shape using a pencil cursor. The Freehand button is selected in Figure 14-15.

The Expanding Area button lets you choose a large area for your button to cover. The Expanding Area button is selected in Figure 14-16.

The Lasso button lets you choose an object on the screen to become the button. The Lasso button is selected in Figure 14-17.

**FIGURE 14-15**
Freehand Area Button

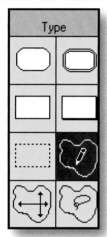

**FIGURE 14-16**
Expanding Area Button

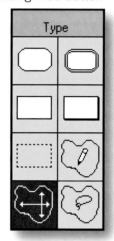

**FIGURE 14-17**
Lasso Area Button

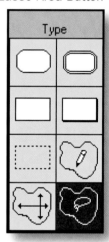

STEP-BY-STEP 14.4

1. Create a new stack. Use the standard card size.

2. Add clip art. From the disk file, select HSArt and **computr2**. Use the **Lasso Selector** tool to select the large computer, keyboard, and monitor. The result of your selection is shown in Figure 14-18.

3. Use the **Lasso Selector** tool to select the blue screen of the monitor.

4. Add a graphic object. Click **Yes** when asked "Do you want to turn the select part of the screen into a graphic object?" Click **OK** without making any selections in the Graphic Appearance window.

5. Add a button. In the Button Appearance window, select the Lasso button as shown in Figure 14-17. Name the button **Click Here**. Use **red** for the text color and select **Show name**.

**6.** Click the Features button and choose the cursor hand pointing down. Click **OK** twice.

**7.** When you see the window, "This button needs a shape, please give it one now," as shown in Figure 14-19, click **OK** .

**8.** Use the **Lasso Selector** tool to select the keyboard. You will see the window, "Your button's shape has been defined," as shown in Figure 14-20. Select **OK**.

**9.** From the Actions window, select **Play a movie or video**. Select **seine.avi** from the HSMovies folder. Click outside the movie area. Click **OK** and **Done**.

(continued on next page)

**FIGURE 14-18**
Clip Art Computer, Keyboard, and Monitor

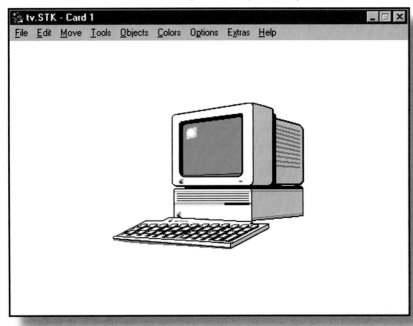

**FIGURE 14-19**
"This button needs a shape, please give it one now" Window

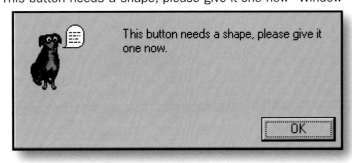

**FIGURE 14-20**
"Your button's shape has been defined" Window

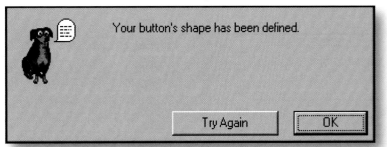

**10.** Move the movie over the computer screen and size it to fit over the blue screen. Click outside the movie. Click **OK** in the Preview window and do not select any of the options. Return to **Browse** mode and try the keyboard button. Your screen should resemble Figure 14-21. The cursor hand should turn upside down when you pass the mouse over the button area.

**FIGURE 14-21**
Movie Playing Through Graphic Object

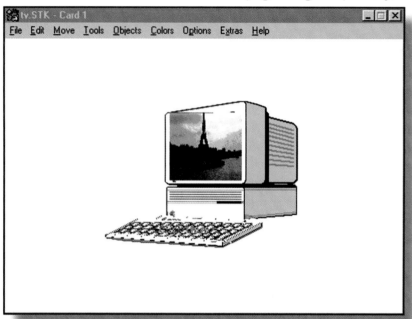

**11.** Save the stack as **TV**. Keep the stack open.

**12.** Add a new card and import a background. Use the **educatn2** file located in the HSArt folder as the background.

**FIGURE 14-22**
School Selected

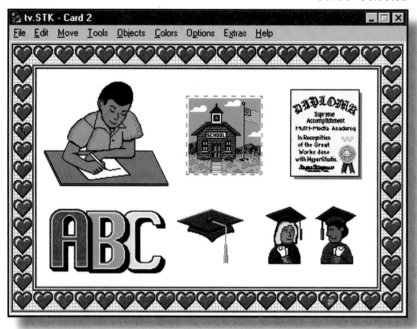

**13.** Use the **Square Selector** tool to select an area around the picture of the school, as shown in Figure 14-2.

**14.** While the area is selected, select **Add a Graphic Object** from the Objects menu. When asked if you want the selected area to be a graphic object, click **Yes**, then **OK**.

**15.** Add a button. Name the button **Click to Play Video**. Choose **red** as the text color. Select the **Expanding Area** button. (See Figure 14-16.) Select **Show Name**. Click **OK**. Your selections should match Figure 14-23.

**16.** When you see the window "This button needs a shape, please give it one now," click **OK**.

**17.** Click and drag the cursor across the area of the blue sky in the school picture from one side to the other. Then release the mouse button. A window will inform you that your button's shape has been defined. Click **OK**.

**18.** From the Actions window, select **Play a movie or video**. Access the files from the HyperStudio CD-ROM. From the **hsmovie** folder, select the **mwriting** file, as shown in Figure 14-24. Click **Open**.

(continued on next page)

**FIGURE 14-23**
Button Appearance Window

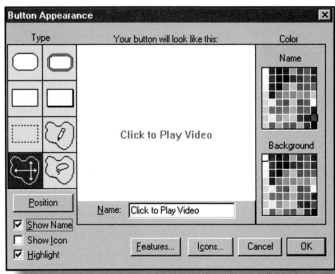

**FIGURE 14-24**
Mwriting File

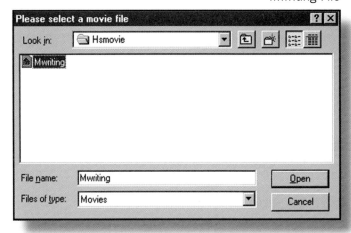

**19.** Size the movie to fit over the school area that you selected before. Choose **Use movie controller**. Click outside the movie area, then click **OK** and **Done**.

**20.** Return to **Browse** mode and try your button. You should be able to click on the schoolhouse picture to play the movie as in Figure 14-25.

**21.** Save the stack as **TV1**. Keep it open.

**FIGURE 14-25**
Movie Playing Over Schoolhouse

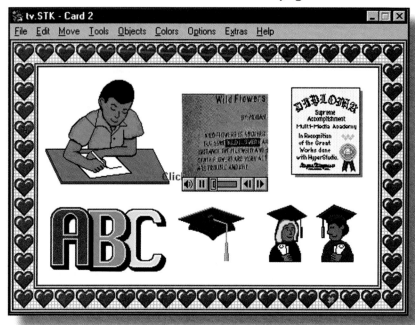

## CHALLENGE ACTIVITY ⇒ 14.2

Add another card to the stack. Use one of the new buttons from this lesson. Insert a video into a graphic object. Add a Title card and Main Menu card for the stack. Add appropriate navigation. Save the stack as **TV2**.

## Print to Video

Print to video is a unique feature that allows you to record your stacks on a video recorder. To use this feature, your computer must have a video-out card to transfer the image from the computer to the recorder.

This feature allows you to show your presentations to people who don't have access to a multimedia computer and HyperStudio. With your presentation recorded on a videotape, you simply put the tape in a VCR and play it for your audience.

**For this next Step-by-Step, you will need to have a video-out connection that is connected to a VCR.**

## STEP-BY-STEP ⟹ 14.5

1. Open stack **TV2**.

2. Make sure the connections are set up to record from your computer.

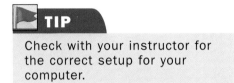

**TIP**

Check with your instructor for the correct setup for your computer.

3. Select **Print to Video** from the File menu.

4. From the Print to Video window, select **Print all cards automatically** and have a **3**-second pause between cards, as shown in Figure 14-26. Click **Start**.

5. Click the mouse to stop.

6. Check the VCR to be sure the recording worked. Close the stack.

**FIGURE 14-26**
Print to Video Window

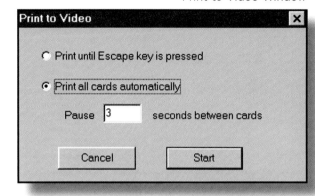

# *Summary*

In this lesson, you learned that:

■ Video is a dynamic multimedia resource to use in your stacks.

■ HyperStudio makes it easy to insert video in your stacks.

■ Video is a novel way to present information.

■ You can use a storyboard to plan and organize your video productions.

■ You can control the source of the video signal and the quality of the picture.

■ You will need to limit the length of your video clips to about 14 to 20 seconds.

■ You can edit your own video to make QuickTime and AVI movies.

■ You can play QuickTime and AVI movies over or through graphic objects.

■ The Lasso button allows you to select a part of the screen as a button.

■ The Expanding Area button allows you to select large parts of the screen as a button.

■ The Freehand Area button allows you to draw your own button shape.

- You can change the direction of the cursor when it floats over a button.

- You can create buttons that do not need to be clicked by the cursor.

- You can print your stacks to a video recorder.

## VOCABULARY

| | |
|---|---|
| Digitize | Mosaic |
| Digitizing board | Video storyboards |

## LESSON 14 REVIEW QUESTIONS

### MULTIPLE CHOICE

**Circle the letter to indicate the item that best completes each of the following statements.**

1. When you enlarge a video picture, you run the risk of taking up too much room:
   A. on the screen
   B. in the hard drive
   C. in the HyperStudio program
   D. none of the above

2. When using live video, you will be:
   A. asked to save the clip before you create it
   B. given choices about how the video clip will appear on the screen
   C. given choices about the video controller
   D. all of the above

3. If you are using a video signal in the United States, you are most likely using:
   A. PAL format
   B. SECAM format
   C. NTSC format
   D. none of the above

4. The Video Driver window allows you to control the:
   A. video source
   B. video connector
   C. size of the video picture
   D. all of the above

5. HyperStudio includes edit tools that:
   A. are very sophisticated
   B. allow you to determine the length of a video clip you are creating
   C. allow you to use transitions in the video
   D. none of the above

6. When you use an irregular shape for viewing video, you are using:
   A. clip art
   B. an object
   C. an NBA
   D. none of the above

7. A group item refers to a:
   A. text field
   B. graphic
   C. button
   D. all of the above

8. A no click button means:
   A. if you click on it, it will deactivate
   B. you don't have to click on it for it to work
   C. if you click on it, something will happen
   D. none of the above

9. To create a button that is the entire screen, you would use:
   A. the Expanding Area button
   B. the Invisible button
   C. the Lasso button
   D. all of the above

## COMPLETION

**SCANS**

**Answer the questions below in the space provided.**

1. What are some of the positive aspects of using live video in a stack?

2. How does the use of live video allow you to become the "ultimate director"?

3. When resizing a video frame, what should you be aware of?

4. Describe the process of inserting a video clip in an irregular object.

5. Name the three buttons presented in this lesson and explain how they function:

   a.

   b.

   c.

6. How can you change the direction of the hand cursor?

7. What is the relationship between video and computer memory?

8. How does multimedia allow you to express yourself in new ways?

## LESSON 14 PROJECT 14.1

This is a group project designed to allow each group member to create a video segment and build it into a HyperStudio stack. The group will either choose a topic or be assigned one. The group should create a storyboard for the entire project, with each group member contributing his or her portion. In planning, make sure the Title card and Main Menu card express the topic of the stack. The plan should include a video segment from each group member.

Work together to create the various video segments that will be needed for the project. Then create the HyperStudio stack or stacks. Group members can either work together to create one large stack or each group member can create a stack for their portion of the presentation. If separate stacks are created, the stacks should be linked to a main stack through the Main Menu card.

Create a folder for your stack, using the topic as the name of the folder. Save the title stack as **grpproj**. (If linked stacks are created, they should be saved as **grpproj1**, **grpproj2**, etc.)

NOTE: If you do not have the equipment to videotape segments, use available video clips for your presentation.

## LESSON 14 PROJECT 14.2

For this project, you will be asked to design an imaginary stack using one of the projects you identified in Step 7 of Step-by-Step 14.1. You will not actually create the stack. This will give you unlimited access to equipment and resources.

■ Write a stack storyboard for the project. Assume that you have all the resources necessary to create live video and record sounds.

■ Create a video storyboard for two video clips that you would shoot and include in the stack.

■ Draw a flow chart of the navigation for the stack.

## CRITICAL THINKING ACTIVITY

List at least three projects that include live video that you could create for your school, your community, or an organization to which you belong. Write a brief description of a video segment you would shoot for one of these projects.

LESSON

15

# ADVANCED VIDEO
# TECHNIQUES

## OBJECTIVES

**Upon completion of this lesson, you will be able to:**

- Access and play a laser disc from your stacks.

- Import QuickTime or AVI files from the Internet.

- Import QuickTime or AVI files from interactive encyclopedias.

- Link stacks.

- Manage disk storage space.

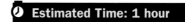

**⏱ Estimated Time: 1 hour**

# *Laser Discs*

You may not have used a laser disc before. Laser discs resemble CD-ROMs except they are much larger. A laser disc can store the same types of multimedia elements that a CD-ROM can. The benefit of a laser disc is that images and information are stored at specific addresses and can be located by random access. An address on a laser disc is a number assigned to the information. The address allows you to move immediately to the frame containing the information.

Unlike a CD-ROM drive, the laser disc player is always external to the computer. You need another monitor to see the information on the laser disc, similar to watching a videotape. You can access information on a laser disc in three ways:

- using a remote control

- using a barcode reader

- linking laser disc information to a HyperStudio stack on your computer

In order to control the laser disc player from your computer, you will need a connector cable that connects your computer's modem port to the laser disc player. Not all laser disc players have this

TIP

HyperStudio supports Pioneer laser disc players. If you have a Sony laser disc player, you will need to contact Sony for a driver to install on your computer. If you have questions about the driver, refer to the troubleshooting section in the HyperStudio reference manual.

connector. Check the manual of your laser disc player. Windows users will use a serial connector cable called a CC12 or CC13. Macintosh users will use a CC04 or RS232 cable.

There are two types of laser discs. They look the same, but they store information differently. The CAV disc holds up to 30 minutes of information per side and can hold a still frame indefinitely. The CLV disc holds up to one hour of information per side but will not hold a still frame. When you rent a movie on laser disc, it is generally in the CLV mode. Many laser discs are intended for educational use, especially when they contain libraries of still photos, which will be on CAV discs.

The laser disc is a good companion for a HyperStudio stack. The laser disc can play longer video segments without using up any of the computer's memory or storage space. Also, you can have several cards relating to one image that you can hold in a still frame on the laser disc player's monitor. The setup for a laser disc is similar to the setup for a VCR and monitor. The only difference is the connection between the CPU and the laser disc player, as shown in Figure 15-1.

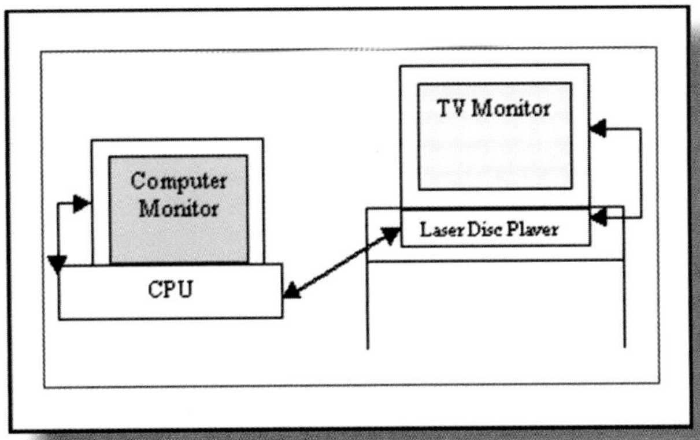

A typical use of laser disc with a HyperStudio stack is to have a card that asks a question or states some information. Then, by clicking on a button, you can see a movie clip or picture to add information or support the information. An example is that you have the text from a Shakespearean soliloquy on the HyperStudio card and when you click the button, the laser disc plays the video of that soliloquy. Or if you were presenting a report about Shakespeare, you could present your information and then show a clip to dramatize the information, as shown in Figure 15-2. But remember, the movie would play on the TV monitor, not the computer screen.

**FIGURE 15-1**
Laser Disc Player Setup with Computer

**FIGURE 15-2**
Shakespearean Report

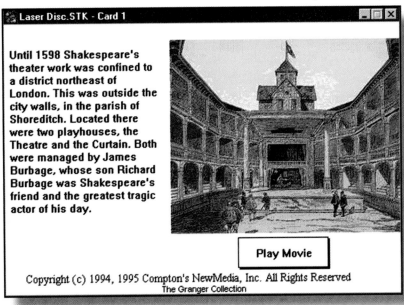

299

Another use could be to define some information. For instance, you describe the hunting habits of the gray wolf on a card. When you click the button on the card, the laser disc plays a portion of a video showing a wolf hunting, as shown in Figure 15-3.

**FIGURE 15-3**
Wolf Stack

# STEP-BY-STEP ⟹ 15.1

**You must have a laser disc player connected to your computer to complete this Step-by-Step.**

1. Create a two-card stack.

2. Go to Card 1. Based on the laser disc selection you have available, select a topic for your card that can have a laser disc component to support the information. Create a card similar to the examples given in Figures 15-2 and 15-3. Do not create the button at this point.

3. Save the stack as **Lsrdsc**.

4. Add a button. Name the button **Play Movie**. Select **Play a movie or video** from the Actions window. Select **Laserdisc player** from the Video/Movie Source window, as shown in Figure 15-4.

**FIGURE 15-4**
Laserdisc Player

5. If you see a prompt similar to the dialog box in Figure 15-5, ask your instructor to check the connections between your computer and the laser disc player.

6. When you are connected to the laser disc player from your computer, you will see the LaserDisc Control window. Check the connections by pressing **Start**, as shown in Figure 15-6.

7. After the disc plays for a while, enough for you to know you can control it, press **Pause**.

8. Using your remote control, display the numbers that are the addresses for the

different frames on the laser disc. Find the clip you would like to use for this card. Write down the clip's beginning and ending numbers. If you are planning to use a still frame or photo, the beginning and ending numbers will be the same.

9. Key the beginning and ending numbers for the clip you want in the **Begin** and **End** fields of the LaserDisc Control window. Click **OK**.

10. Test the button. Save the stack. Leave the stack open.

**FIGURE 15-5**
Unable to Find the LaserDisc Player Dialog Box

**FIGURE 15-6**
LaserDisc Control Window

**You must have a laser disc player attached to your computer to complete this Challenge Activity.**

On Card 2 of the Lsrdsc stack, create another display for interaction with the laser disc player. Use the previous Step-by-Step as your guide. If you

have the ability to use still frames from the laser disc, select three single frames to use. Otherwise select three clips to use. Create three buttons, one for each frame or clip.

Test your buttons and save the stack as **Lsrdsc1**. Close the stack.

# *Importing QuickTime from the Internet*

In Lessons 13 and 14, you learned to use clips from the HyperStudio resource library and to create your own clips for use in stacks. Another way to include video in your stack is to download QuickTime clips from other sources such as the Internet.

To use downloaded video clips, you must be aware of two things. First, the video clip you download will have to be stored somewhere on your computer. If possible, you should place the original clip in the same folder as the stack you plan to use it in. You will not be able to play the video clip on a different computer unless you have the actual video clip along with the stack. If you wish to have the clip as a resource, add it to the Hsmovie folder or to a folder of your own for video resources. Video clips are large files; therefore, you will have to plan carefully to make the best use of available storage space on your hard drive, ZIP disk, or other storage medium.

Second, you must consider the copyright law and the restrictions it places on using the work created by others. "Copyright" is the protection afforded to the author or creator of a work. It states that the work belongs to that author or creator and except in some specific instances, others may not use the work without permission. The law states that no one else can make money from the sale of the work and if others use the work, their use should not deprive the author or creator of monetary remuneration or payment.

The law does allow for fair use of copyrighted material. Fair use allows limited use of the work of another for educational purposes. Therefore, you can use a video clip created by someone else for a class assignment. However, you should not give or sell a stack containing copyrighted material to others.

You should also give proper credit to the creator of the work that you are using. Review the copyright statements included in Figures 15-2 and 15-3. If you are not sure about your right to use another's work, it is best to write to the copyright holder and ask permission.

In addition to supplying the copyright information, it may be wise to include a disclaimer along with the stack credits like the one below when you are copying resources from the Internet or other resources.

"*DISCLAIMER* All images, sounds, and video linked or embedded in this belong to the copyright owners and are presented solely for evaluation or educational purposes granted by the Fair Use Agreement. I do not claim rights to any of this material."

## Internet Basics

When you use the Internet, you are able look for information by using a database called a search engine. *Excite* and *Yahoo* are two popular search engines. To use a search engine, you key in a topic you wish to find such as video clips. You will then see a list of possible places or sites otherwise called URLs where your topic is addressed. When you see the list you can click on one of the places in the list and you will go to that site, just as you would click on a button in HyperStudio to go to another card. From that site you can go back to the original list or you can go to another place that might be mentioned at the site you are exploring. You can see that there is an extraordinary amount of information to be accessed on the Internet. Some of the sites may not have the information you wish to research. You may have to go back and define the topic more clearly. For instance if you keyed sports, you would probably get back a very long list of "hits" or matches on the database. But, if you keyed winter sports, the list would be a bit shorter. If you keyed figure skating, you would have a better chance of getting a list of just the particular information you requested rather than many unneeded resources.

Once you have found a site that is useful, you can set up a Bookmark. A bookmark is a way of tagging an Internet site so that you can return to it without having to search for it again or without even having to key the address of the site. When you want to go to the site, you choose the site from the bookmark list.

Below are some Internet sites that list video resources. If you have access to the Internet, you can search for other sources. Internet sites are accessed by URLs. URL stands for Uniform Resource Locator and acts as the address for the site. When searching for sites, the URLs are displayed in a different color, usually blue. The site may be quickly accessed by double clicking on the URL.

- **EXPERIMENTAL FILMS AND VIDEO CLIPS**
  http://ribblevision.com/

- **MPEG Animation & Movie Lists**
  http://uwalpha.uwinnipeg.ca:8001/mov.html

- **NASA**
  www.nasa.gov/gallery/video/index.html

---

## STEP-BY-STEP ⟹ 15.2

**You will need to be connected to the Internet to complete this Step-by-Step.**

1. Create a folder named **Video_Clips**. You will use this folder to store clips that you download for use with your HyperStudio stack.

**TIP**

If you are using a computer at school or one that is attached to a network, check with your instructor about the best location for your folder.

(continued on next page)

2. Connect to the Internet. Using your Internet browser, go to a Search Engine and key **QuickTime clips**, as shown in Figure 15-7. (The graphics for this lesson are based on the use of the Netscape browser and Excite search engine.)

3. Click **Search** to find QuickTime clips. You will get a list similar to the one in Figure 15-8.

(continued on page 306)

**FIGURE 15-7**
Search Engine

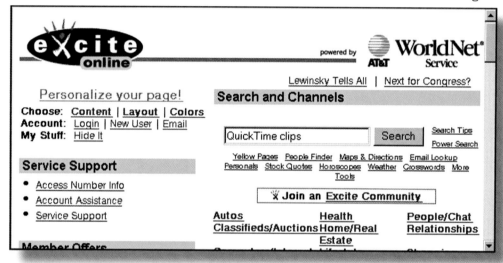

 Many Internet connections from schools and homes are dial-in connections. With a dial-in connection, the Internet tools and programs are located on a host computer; your desktop computer can only display what the host processes.

**FIGURE 15-8**
Internet Search List

Lesson (15) Advanced Video Techniques

**77% Video Links** - Register with Video Links Enter your e-mail address below to be notified of changes and updates at our site. Video Links is independently owned and operated, however, all QuickTime clips, and other related media are the property of their respective creators. http://video-links.com/

**73% Hollywood Online: ...all about movies...** - Hollywood Online is the premier Web site covering both Hollywood and the motion picture industry. Come explore our extensive movie content including video clips, trailers, sound bytes, photos, games, news, event coverage, box office charts, reviews, production notes, credits and much more. http://www.hollywood.com/

**73% Poltergeist: The Legacy** - The official site for MGM's thrilling and suspenseful television series. Every week The Legacy battles the evil spirits and supernatural creeps from the depths of the underworld who fight to take over our world. Join them in their fight for good to triumph over evil.
http://www.thelegacy.com/

**73% Welcome to NTT Software Corporation** - InterSpace lets you communicate in a virtual environment! See, listen, and talk to people from around the globe and create worlds with our authoring tools.
http://www.is.ntts.com/

**72% <title Blue Thunder Movies Over 1800 movie clips and 850 movie post...** - Recent and new movie clips and posters available. Over 1200 movie clips and 600 posters here. http://bluethundermovies.simplenet.com/

**72% Multimedia Help** - AquaPenn®Multimedia Help QuickTime Video The video clips on the AquaPenn web site require that you have QuickTime software installed on your Macintosh or Windows computer.
http://www.aquapenn.net/aquapenn.net/mm_help.html

**72% Welcome to Artbeats: Leader in Digital Stock Footage!** - Digital Film, Backgrounds, Seamless Textures & Stock Video Footage for Prepress, 3D Imaging, Multimedia, Non-Linear and Linear Video Editing & Web Design. http://www.artbeats.com/

**72% MPEG and QuickTime Movie Collection** - If You have MPEG player, you can play following movies The Shareware of NET TOOB Multimedia Player for Windows 3.x and Win95, which supports MPEG-1, AVI, MOV & FLC/FLI, can be gotten from All mpg files were copied from network.
http://uwalpha.uwinnipeg.ca:8001/mov.html

**72% Production** - You will need a QuickTime player to view our video clips. If you don't have one and would like to view these clips, download it! If you're wondering just how long it will take you to download one of our movie clips, check out our download calculator (a great place to bookmark for future reference). http://www.golden-dome.com/Production/clips.html

**72% NOVA Online | Bomb Squad | Robo Clips** - You'll need one of three (free) software plugins— Vivo, RealPlayer, or QuickTime to be able to view the video clips of robots in action below. If you already have the software, choose an appropriate connection speed (Vivo, RealVideo) or the file size (QuickTime, AVI) to view a clip. http://www0.pbs.org/wgbh/nova/robots/clips/

**4.** Double click on the URL for one of the sites listed, and you will be taken to a page similar to the one in Figure 15-9. Explore the site to identify clips. Depending on the site, you may be able to preview the clips. Print the list of available clips for future reference. If you are able to, place a bookmark for the site.

**5.** Go to the following site: http://www.cc.gatech.edu/gvu/animation/Areas/secondary/Movies/runnerFlags.mov

**6.** If you are asked to specify the type of video player you are using, select **QuickTime** or the type of video used on your computer.

**7.** Play the movie, if your browser allows it. Figures 15-10 and 15-11 show two frames of the visualization.

**FIGURE 15-9**
Internet Site Containing QuickTime Video Clips

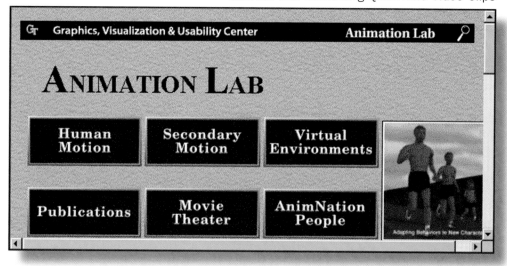

**FIGURE 15-10**
Play the Movie

**FIGURE 15-11**
Runner in Movie

**STEP-BY-STEP 15.2 CONTINUED**

**8.** To save the movie for your stack, Windows users will right click the mouse on the movie and choose **Save Movie**, as shown in Figure 15-12. Save the movie as **Runner** in the Videos Clips folder you created in Step 1.

**9.** Open HyperStudio. Create a new stack using the standard card size.

**10.** Save the stack as **Runner** in the Video_Clips folder.

**11.** Add a button. Name the button **Runner**. Use any button type you like, except the invisible button. Move the button to the bottom of the screen. Select **Play a movie or video** from the Actions window. Select **Disk file** and double click on **runner.mov**.

**12.** From the Movies window, select **Erase when done**, **Use movie controller**, and **Show first frame**, as shown in Figure 15-13. Click **OK** and **Done** as needed to complete the process.

**TIP**

Macintosh users will go to the File menu. Choose Save as. Select the folder where you wish to save the movie on your computer and name the movie.

**FIGURE 15-12**
Save Movie (Windows Users)

(continued on next page)

**FIGURE 15-13**
Movies Window

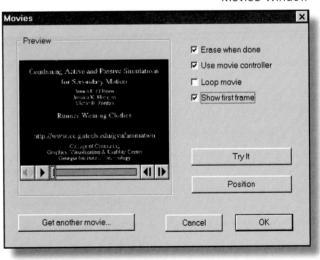

**13.** Create a text object that gives credit to the site where you accessed the animation. The object will not be scrollable or have a frame. Make the text **8** points in the font of your choice. Place the field in the center of the card and resize it as needed. As shown in Figure 15-14, key:

**This video was accessed at The Georgia Institute of Technology Internet site at: http://www.cc.gatech.edu/gvu/animation/ Areas/secondary/Movies/runnerFlags.mov**

**14.** Save the stack. Close the stack.

**FIGURE 15-14**
Credit Text Object

# Playing Two Movies on the Same Card

HyperStudio allows you to show more than one movie on the same card. You can do this by creating a button for each clip or animation. You may set up the movies side by side or have them play in the same position but at different times. HyperStudio will not let them overlap.

## STEP-BY-STEP 15.3

1. Open a new stack. Use the standard card size. Name the stack **Stars** and save it in the same folder with the Runner stack and movie.

2. Go to the Internet and find the movie site: http://deathstar.rutgers.edu/people/bochkay/movies.html

3. Select **Attacking the Empire** from the Other Stuff list.

4. Play the movie and save it to your Video_Clips folder under the name **flight**.

5. Go back to the list and select **Fly Through of Mt Everest**. Play the movie and save it to your Video_Clips folder under the name **everest**.

6. Close your Internet connection.

7. Return to the Stars stack.

8. Add a button. Name the button **Flight**. Use any button type, except the invisible button. Move the button to the bottom left of the screen. Select **Play a movie or video** from the Actions window. Select **Disk file** and double click on **flight** in the Video_Clips folder.

9. In the Movies window, select **Use movie controller** and **Show first frame**. Click the **Position** button and move the video to the left center of the screen. Click **OK** and **Done** as needed to complete the process.

10. Test the button to verify that the video clip plays on the left side of the screen above the Flight button.

**TIP**

If you have trouble accessing this site, ask your instructor to choose another site and change the names of the movies and buttons appropriately.

**TIP**

Unless your instructor directs you otherwise, select movies marked as **QuickTime**.

11. Add a new button to play a movie. Following Steps 8 through 10 above, create an Everest button to play the Everest video clip. Place the button and video on the right side of the card.

12. Along the bottom of the card, add a text box to give credit to the site where you accessed these clips. Key:

    **These resources are from the Internet movie site at: http://deathstar.rutgers.edu/people/bochkay/movies.html.**

13. Save the stack. Keep the stack open.

Add a new card to the Stars stack. Using the same two video clips, create a button for each clip and place the buttons side by side. Do not use the movie controller for these clips. Position the movies in the same location on the card. Save the stack as **Star1**.

Since HyperStudio will not play two videos in the same space, you will find when you test your buttons that each movie will play separately. Compare the results with Card 1 on which both clips play at the same time. Close the stack when you have finished making a comparison of the two cards.

# Loading Resources from Interactive Encyclopedias

When you use resources from an interactive encyclopedia, the same copyright restrictions apply. Some encyclopedias allow you to copy video clips, graphics, and text. Many do not. Most allow you to copy text, but be careful not to plagiarize the text content. Give credit to any sources that you use. Encyclopedias that do not intend for their movies and video clips to be copied will not build in any controls to the program that allow you to make a copy. Respect the wishes of the program designers and do not use other software to copy what is clearly not intended for copying.

If you are taking several clips from the same CD-ROM, you will not have to download them. Simply be sure you have access to the CD and that it is loaded in the drive when you run the stack. It would be a good idea to tell your user the name of the CD that should be in the drive when using the stack. You might present this information on the Main Menu of the stack. The process for importing the movies is the same as with the HyperStudio CD-ROM used in Lesson 13.

# Linking Stacks

HyperStudio button actions allow you to link stacks together, which means you can create a button that will take you to another stack. This is very useful for several reasons. If there are several people working on the same project, it enables everyone to be able to work on their stacks at the same time on different computers. Also, it is a good way to reduce the size of a stack by dividing it into several smaller stacks. This can make it possible to save small stacks on a floppy disk.

If you are working on a group project and planning to link stacks, use storyboards and flow charts to clearly identify the contents of each stack. When linking stacks, you will need a main stack. Sometimes this is a one- or two-card stack that acts as a main menu stack. All of the stacks can easily be linked to this stack using the Another stack feature from the Actions window. Each linked stack must contain a button to return to the main stack. It is a good idea to place all of the linked stacks in the same folder on the hard drive of the computer where you will be showing your stacks. You will need to load all of the stacks to be linked on the same hard drive in order to program the button action.

**STEP·BY·STEP** 15.4

1. Create a three-card stack. Use the standard card size. Save the stack in the Video_Clips folder. Name the stack **GroupMnu**.

2. On the first card, import a background from the HyperStudio CD-ROM. The file to import, **patchsbl**, is located in the medialib folder, scrnbkgd folder, and topimage folder.

3. On Card 2, select the red speckled pattern from the color palette, as shown in Figure 15-15. Use the **Paint Bucket** tool to fill the card.

4. Go to Card 3. Using the **Text** tool, select the **BookwomanSH** or other font, **bold**, and **36** points. Key **Main Menu** in the center of the card, as shown in Figure 15-16.

(continued on next page)

**FIGURE 15-15**
Red Speckled Pattern

**FIGURE 15-16**
Main Menu Painted with Text Tool

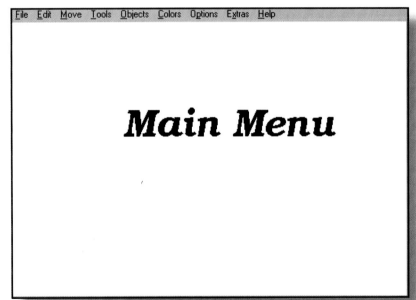

5. Use the **Lasso Selector** tool to select the Main Menu text, as shown in Figure 15-17. Copy the text and paste it on Card 2, over the red speckled pattern.

6. From the Edit menu, select **Effects**, then select **Cookie-cutter**.

7. With the text still selected, copy and paste it on Card 1, as shown in Figure 15-18.

8. Delete Cards 2 and 3.

9. Save the stack.

**FIGURE 15-17**
Text Selected with Lasso Selector Tool

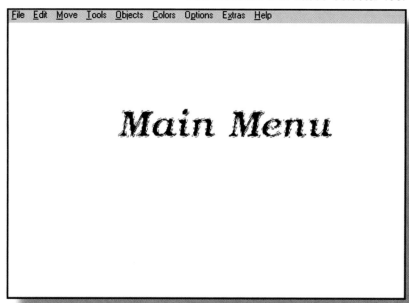

**FIGURE 15-18**
Main Menu Cookie-Cutter Effect on Card 1

10. Add a button to the card. Name the button **Runner**. Place the button in the middle of the card. Select **Another stack** from the Actions window, as shown in Figure 15-19.

11. Locate the Runner stack, select it, and click **Open**.

12. Use the **Iris close** transition and **Fast** speed.

13. Add another button named **Stars**. Place it below the Runner button. Following Steps 10 through 12 above, link the button to the Stars stack.

14. Save the stack. Close the stack.

15. Open the **Runner** stack.

16. Create a button named **Return to menu** to return to the **GroupMnu** stack. Place the button in the upper right corner of the card. Use the **Iris open** transition and **Fast** speed.

17. Save the **Runner** stack.

**FIGURE 15-19**
Another Stack Selected

18. Copy the **Return to menu** button. Open the **Stars** stack. Paste the **Return to menu** button.

19. Save the stack. Close the stack.

20. Test all of your buttons. Close the open stack.

# *Managing Disk Storage Space*

As you work with more multimedia and your stacks become larger and more sophisticated, you will need to consider the limitations of your computer. The computer uses RAM memory and storage space. If you are sharing the computer in a classroom, lab, or communal environment, you may need to find ways to save your work without using up the resources that are shared by the group.

When you have a stack open, you can choose About this stack from the Objects menu to see how much memory and disk space are actually being used by the stack. (See Figure 15-20.) **Current memory used** identifies how much of the total memory available is being used by the stack. When you share backgrounds, you save memory. When you access QuickTime movies, sounds, icons, and New Button Actions, they are only held in memory while they are being used; therefore, they do not occupy the memory unless they are being used.

**Disk space needed** tells you how much storage space you actually need to have on your hard drive to save the stack. **Available memory** lets you know how much memory is available to other operations, such as adding to a stack or accessing another application while the stack is open.

Segmenting your stacks—or breaking them up into smaller stacks—and then linking them is a good way to assure that you will have enough available memory to run the stack. If you are getting messages that you do not have enough memory to run your program or work on your stack, ask your instructor about memory management in your classroom or lab environment.

## STEP-BY-STEP ⟹ 15.5

1. Open the **Star1** stack.

2. From the Objects menu, select **About this stack**. The About Stack window is shown in Figure 15-20.

3. Notice that the amount of memory needed and used for this stack is 5K. On a sheet of paper, write down 5K.

4. Open the **Runner** stack. Write down the number for memory used for this stack. Add it to the first number.

5. Open the **GroupMnu** stack. Notice that the disk space needed and the memory used are larger for this stack. Remember that this stack has a color graphic for a background. The amount of memory used by your computer may vary, but it should be close to the amount shown in Figure 15-21. Write down the number for memory used for this stack.

**FIGURE 15-20**
About Stack Window

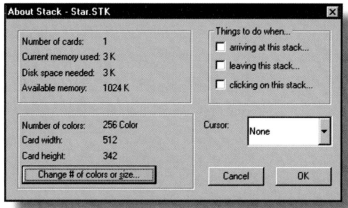

**FIGURE 15-21**
About Stack Window

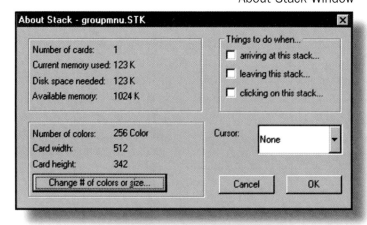

**TIP**

Don't worry if the information about your stacks varies somewhat from the figures presented here. There will be some variation from setting to setting depending on your computer's configuration.

**6.** Open the **Space** stack. Notice that the number for memory used is different than for disk space needed. (See Figure 15-22.) Scroll through the stack and notice the different backgrounds, sounds, and transitions from card to card.

**7.** Close the stack.

**FIGURE 15-22**
About Stack Window

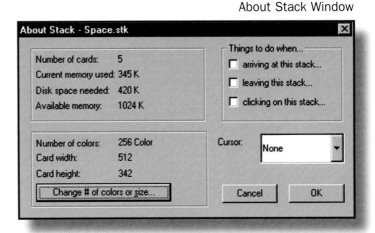

# QTVR

QuickTime Virtual Reality (QTVR) is a software program that allows you to view and or create QuickTime video with a three-dimensional perspective. QTVR movies are similar to a combination of a photo and movie. You can manually control the view you have of the objects in the movie.

There are two types of QTVR, panorama movies and object movies. HyperStudio enables you to include QTVR clips in your stacks, just like QuickTime movies. There are several samples of QTVR on the HyperStudio CD-ROM. They are located in the medialib, QTVR folder. If you have the software and hardware to use QTVR technology, you can create your own movies. Ask your instructor if this technology is available for your class. You will not need QTVR software for the next Step-by-Step.

**STEP-BY-STEP ⟹ 15.6**

SCANS

**1.** Place the HyperStudio CD-ROM in your CD-ROM drive, if necessary.

**2.** Create a two-card stack.

**3.** Make the background of the card black.

**4.** Along the bottom of Card 1, create a text field and key **Click and drag cursor for a panoramic view**. Choose a suitable font and size that allows the sentence to fit on one line.

**5.** Add a button. Name the button **Show Movie**. Move the button to the center of the screen above the text field.

**6.** Choose **Play a movie or video** for the button action.

**7.** Locate the movie in the medialib folder, qtvrmov folder, **Explore** file.

(continued on next page)

**8.** Select **Show first frame**. The completed card should resemble Figure 15-23.

**9.** Test your button. Click the mouse and drag it left and right to view the panoramic effect.

**10.** On Card 2, add a button to play a QTVR object movie. Locate the movie in the medialib folder, qtvrmov folder, **clayman** file.

**11.** Save the stack as **QTVR**. Close the stack.

**FIGURE 15-23**
QTVR Movie

# *Summary*

In this lesson, you learned that:

■ HyperStudio allows you access a laser disc player from a stack.

■ Information is accessed differently on a CD-ROM and laser disc.

■ You need a special cable to connect the laser disc player to a computer.

■ You can use a laser disc to support or dramatize information presented in a stack.

■ The Internet has a wide variety of resources that you can import for your stacks.

■ You can search the Internet for resources.

■ When you load a resource from the Internet, you should save it in a folder with your stack.

■ It is critical to respect copyright information and give credit for resources that you use.

■ HyperStudio allows you to play more than one movie on a card.

■ You can link stacks together in HyperStudio.

■ Linking stacks is a good way to save memory and storage space.

■ Linking stacks allows many people to work on the same project at the same time.

■ It is important to consider disk space management and available RAM.

■ QuickTime movies do not use RAM until they are played.

■ QuickTime Virtual Reality is another form of QuickTime technology.

## VOCABULARY

Barcode reader

Bookmark

CAV

CLV

Copyright

Download

Fair use

Interactive encyclopedia

Internet browser

Laser disc

Linking stacks

QuickTime Virtual Reality (QTVR)

Search engine

Still frames

Uniform Resource Locator (URL)

## LESSON 15 REVIEW QUESTIONS

### TRUE/FALSE

**Circle the T if the statement is true or F if it is false.**

**T  F  1.** There are two types of laser discs.

**T  F  2.** A laser disc operates the same way as a CD-ROM.

**T  F  3.** You cannot play more than one movie on a card.

**T  F  4.** You can easily copy QuickTime movies from an interactive encyclopedia.

**T  F  5.** QuickTime Virtual Reality comes with all QuickTime programs.

**T  F  6.** You only need to backup your stacks occasionally.

# MULTIPLE CHOICE

**Circle the letter to indicate the item that best completes each of the following statements.**

1. You can control a laser disc by:
   A. remote control
   B. bar code reader
   C. computer
   D. all of the above

2. Copyright is:
   A. protection for the author of a work
   B. annoying
   C. the same as plagiarism
   D. none of the above

3. How can you give credit to a resource that you used in a stack?
   A. add a text note with the source information
   B. ask the owner of the resource if you may use it
   C. don't let anyone know that you copied it
   D. none of the above

4. If you have more than one movie on a card:
   A. they must be set up side by side
   B. they can be placed one on top of the other
   C. they will not overlap
   D. all of the above

5. When linking stacks:
   A. remember to have a return button to another stack
   B. you can only have a limited number of stacks
   C. you should not have a main stack
   D. all of the above

6. To get memory information about a stack, you could:
   A. go to the Main Menu card
   B. go to the About this stack from the Objects menu
   C. ask your instructor
   D. all of the above

## COMPLETION

**Answer the questions below in the space provided.**

1. Name some ways to reduce the memory and storage space needed for stacks.

2. What do you need to remember when downloading resources from the Internet?

3. How can you copy a QuickTime movie from the Internet to a HyperStudio stack?

4. Name some reasons for linking stacks.

5. Laser discs come in CAV and CLV types. What is the difference between the two?

6. What is a QTVR movie and how is it different from a QuickTime movie?

## LESSON 15 PROJECT 15.1

1. Divide into small groups and design a research project. As a group, select a topic and design a storyboard for that topic. Each member of the group will have their own subtopic to research. Each subtopic will be created as a separate stack and the stacks will be linked.

   The storyboards must include the basics of a stack, including:
   - a Title card
   - a Main Menu stack that links stacks for each member of the group
   - appropriate navigation

   The stacks will include resources needed to support the topic. In addition to text and graphics, the stacks must include one or more items from the following list:
   - a still from a laser disc
   - a clip from a laser disc
   - a movie clip downloaded from the Internet
   - a movie clip from a CD-ROM (interactive) encyclopedia

2. Create the stacks linking the individual stacks of each member to the Main Menu stack.

3. Save the stacks using appropriate file names.

4. Print the stacks.

## CRITICAL THINKING ACTIVITY

Copyright and ownership of resources are challenging areas to consider. Imagine that you wrote a song and someone used the song in a school project without your permission or giving you credit. How would you feel?

Suppose you spent considerable time researching a topic and writing a paper. You then share this paper with a friend. What if this friend shared the paper with someone else online? Later you discovered that someone else was using pieces of your research and claiming it as their own research. How would you feel?

Divide into small groups and discuss whether the actions described in the previous scenarios are ethical or unethical. Each group should prepare a brief summary of its analysis.

Then think of examples from your own experience about which copyright or ownership questions have arisen. Discuss these situations with the group.

**Insert sounds**

1. Add a button.
2. Select Play Sound from the Button actions window.
3. Locate the sound files you wish to use.
4. Select a sound file or record the sound.
5. Play the sound.
6. Click OK.

**Menu Tamer extra**

1. From the Extras menu, select Menu Tamer.
2. Select Hide all menubars or Show all menubars.

**Insert QuickTime movie**

1. Add a button.
2. Select Play a movie or video from the Actions window.
3. Select the QuickTime or AVI file you wish to use.
4. Place the movie where you want it to show.
5. Select the video options you want to use.
6. Click Try It.
7. Click OK and Done.

**Insert live video**

1. Connect the appropriate cables and equipment to insert video in your computer.
2. Add a button.
3. Select Play a movie or video from the Actions window.
4. Select Video (make your own movie).
5. Select Video Format and OK.
6. Select Video Driver.
7. Choose the appropriate connector and OK.
8. Record the video and play it back with Try It.
9. Name and save the clip.
10. Select OK.
11. Place the movie where you want it to show.
12. Select the video options you want to use.
13. Click Try It.
14. Click OK and Done.

**Play video through graphic objects**

1. Add clip art to a card.
2. Select part of the clip art where you want the video to show.
3. From the Objects menu, select Add a Graphic Object.
4. Make that part of the screen a graphic object by selecting Yes in the window.
5. Select Actions.
6. Select Play movie or video.
7. Choose the movie you wish to play.
8. Place the movie in the selected graphic object area.

| **Access laser disc** | 1. | Make sure your computer is connected to a laser disc player. |
| | 2. | Add a button. |
| | 3. | Select Laserdisc player from the Video/Movie source window. |
| | 4. | Test the connection by pressing Play from the laser disc controller. |
| | 5. | Input the beginning and ending numbers for the clip. |
| | 6. | Choose OK. |
| **Link stacks** | 1. | Add a button. |
| | 2. | Select Another stack in the Actions window. |
| | 3. | Locate the stack on your computer. |
| | 4. | Choose a transition. |
| | 5. | Position the button. |
| | 6. | Add a return or quit button from the new stack. |

## UNIT 5 REVIEW QUESTIONS

### FILL IN THE BLANKS

Complete the following statements by keying or writing the correct answers on a page to be submitted to your instructor. Center *Unit 5 Review Questions* at the top of the page. Number your answers to match the numbers listed here.

1. Sounds can be attached to _____ , _____ , or _____ .

2. You can access additional graphics, sounds, and photos from the _____ folder on the HyperStudio CD-ROM.

3. The _____ NBA allows you to hide the menubar on a card or in a stack.

4. The NBA CD Play will _____ .

5. Most of the video clips you will use in your stack are called _____ videos.

6. Before a stack is finished, you must test it for _____ .

7. Video can be accessed through a _____ , _____ , or _____ .

8. Three button types are _____ , _____ , and _____ .

9. You can add QuickTime movies from _____ , _____ , or the HyperStudio CD-ROM.

10. Connecting stacks using buttons is called _____ .

## WRITTEN QUESTIONS

Key or write your answers to the following questions. Number your answers. Use complete sentences and good grammar.

11. What are some useful ways to use sounds in a stack?

12. Name and explain three video tips.

    a.

    b.

    c.

13. What do you need to do before you finish the stack regarding navigation?

14. What does loop movie mean?

15. What information should be included in a video storyboard?

## UNIT 5 PROJECT

1. Choose a topic for the stack.

2. Create a storyboard and flowchart for the stack.

3. Create the stack.

4. Include at least one each of the following:
   - Title card
   - Main Menu card
   - sound with a button action
   - audio CD sound
   - QuickTime/AVI movie or live video
   - a movie played through a graphic object
   - laser disc access, if available
   - at least two hypertext links.

5. Save the stack as **EP5**.

## UNIT 5 CRITICAL THINKING ACTIVITY

You have been asked to debate the use of sound and video in a stack. Create a list of reasons for and against using sound and video in a presentation.

# ADVANCED TECHNIQUES

# UNIT 6

**Estimated Time for Unit 6: 14 hours**

# ADVANCED GRAPHICS TECHNIQUES

## OBJECTIVES

**Upon completion of this lesson, you will be able to:**

■ Utilize resources from other sources.

■ Utilize resources from CD-ROM encyclopedias.

■ Create layered animations.

■ Draw multiple, filled, and centered objects.

■ Work with filters as effects.

⏱ **Estimated Time: 1.5 hours**

## *Resources from Other Sources*

Y ou have already accessed the Internet, the CD-ROM that accompanies the HyperStudio program, an audio CD, CD-ROM encyclopedias, and a laser disc for resources. The CD-ROM that accompanies this book has additional resources that can be used as you create stacks. There are many available resources you can import into your stacks that will make them more interesting, creative, and interactive.

### Loading Resources from Encyclopedias

When you use resources from an interactive encyclopedia, the same copyright restrictions apply. Some encyclopedias allow you to copy video clips, graphics, and text. Many do not. Most allow you to copy text, but be careful not to plagiarize the text content. Give credit to any sources that you use. Encyclopedias that do not intend for their movies and video clips to be copied will not build in any controls to the program that allow you to make a copy. Respect the wishes of the program designers by not using other software to copy what is clearly not to be used for copying.

If you are taking several clips from the same CD-ROM, you do not have to download them, simply be sure that the CD is loaded in the drive when you run the stack. If your stack will be viewed by others, include the name of the CD in an appropriate location in your stack. For example, you could present this information on the Main Menu card. The process for importing the movies is the same as with the HyperStudio CD-ROM used in Lesson 13.

As discussed in Lesson 15, one of the most important aspects of importing resources from other sources is to observe and respect copyright restrictions and to give appropriate credit to any materials you use in your stacks.

# STEP-BY-STEP ⟹ 16.1

**You must have an encyclopedia or other similar resource available on CD-ROM to complete this Step-by-Step.**

1. Place the encyclopedia CD-ROM into the CD-ROM drive of your computer. (For this activity, we will be referencing *Compton's Interactive Encyclopedia*, 1996 Edition.)

2. Open the **Space4** stack.

3. Add a new card to the stack.

4. Open the encyclopedia CD-ROM.

5. Find information about space or space travel.

6. Copy and paste a paragraph of information from the encyclopedia.

7. Copy and paste a photograph from the encyclopedia.

8. Many of the movies are not available to copy. If you are able to copy a movie, do so and place it in your folder with the stack. Create a button to play the movie.

9. Save the stack as **Space5**. Keep the stack open.

✓ **HINT:**

You will find that most current computer resources have a footer attached that states the copyright information for you. (See Figure 16-1.)

**FIGURE 16-1**
Compton's Copyright Information

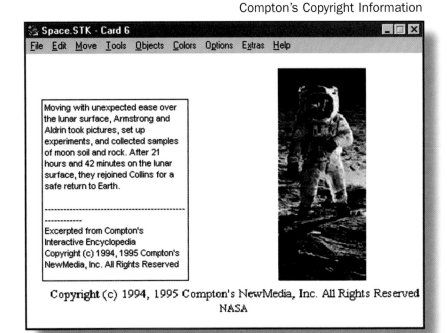

**329**

## CHALLENGE ACTIVITY ⟹ 16.1

Add two cards to the Space5 stack. Use resources from a CD-ROM to prepare the text, graphics, and movies, if possible, for the card. Save the stack as **Space6**. Close the stack.

# Layered Animations

You created several different kinds of animations in previous lessons. There is one more animation that you can create in HyperStudio. It is called a layered animation because it looks as though the animated object is moving behind some of the background, creating a three-dimensional effect. This is done by creating objects that are part of the scenery for the animated objects to move through and around.

## CHALLENGE ACTIVITY ⟹ 16.2

View an example of a layered animation. Make sure the files on the HyperStudio CD-ROM can be accessed. Open HyperStudio. From the Home screen, click **Show Me How**. Then click **HyperStudio Step-by-Step** and **Advanced** **Techniques**. Click the **Next** icon until you locate **WOW**, the first of eleven selections. Click on the **WOW** screen to view the selection. Click on the magic wand icon to view the layered animation. Click **Home** when done.

> **INTERNET**
>
> You connect to the Internet through Internet service providers (ISPs). ISPs allow you to access the Internet and charge a fee for providing the access. There are many ISPs. Among the best known ISPs are Microsoft Network (MSN), America Online, and CompuServe. If one of these service providers is installed on your computer, it can be accessed by double clicking on the appropriate desktop icon or by selecting it from the Programs menu on Windows computers or the Apple menu on Macintosh computers.

## STEP-BY-STEP ⟹ 16.2

1. Create a new stack. Use the standard card size. (Do not use a full-screen card.)

2. Arrange the tool and color palettes alongside your card, as shown in Figure 16-2.

3. Double click on the **Paintbrush** tool and select the brush shape shown in Figure 16-3.

(continued on next page)

**FIGURE 16-2**
Screen with Palettes

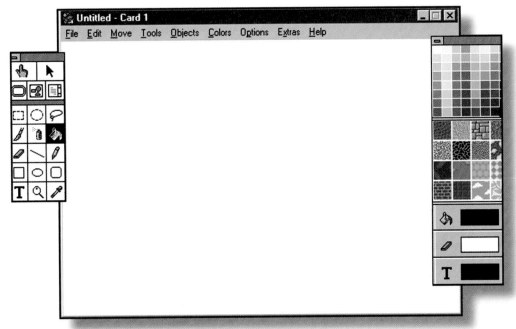

**FIGURE 16-3**
Paintbrush Shape

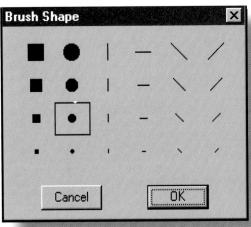

**4.** Using a **medium brown** color, draw seven or eight lines to resemble tree trunks in a forest, as shown in Figure 16-4.

**5.** Select the green pattern in the upper right corner of the pattern palette. Then select the **Spray Can** tool. Your selection will be shown in the color palette, as shown in Figure 16-5.

**6.** Use this tool to create leaves and branches on the trees similar to Figure 16-6.

**FIGURE 16-4**
Tree Trunks

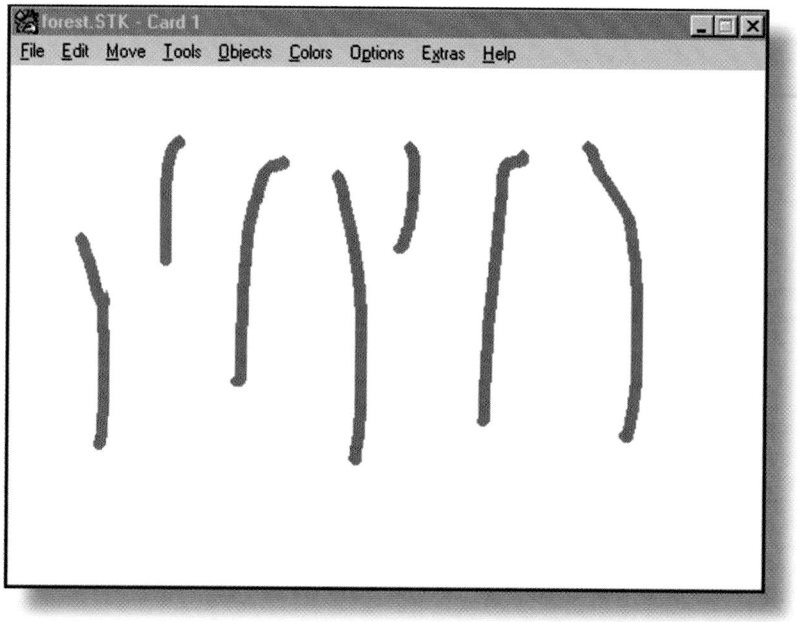

**FIGURE 16-5**
Spray Can Pattern

**FIGURE 16-6**
Leaves on the Trunks

STEP-BY-STEP 16.2 CONTINUED

7. Finish the leaves and branches. Spray paint another green pattern for the grass and bits of other colors to create the ground, as shown in Figure 16-7. Be sure to leave some space around the trees.

8. Add some background color for distance and the sky. Your card should look similar to Figure 16-8.

(continued on next page)

**FIGURE 16-7**
Card with Ground Color

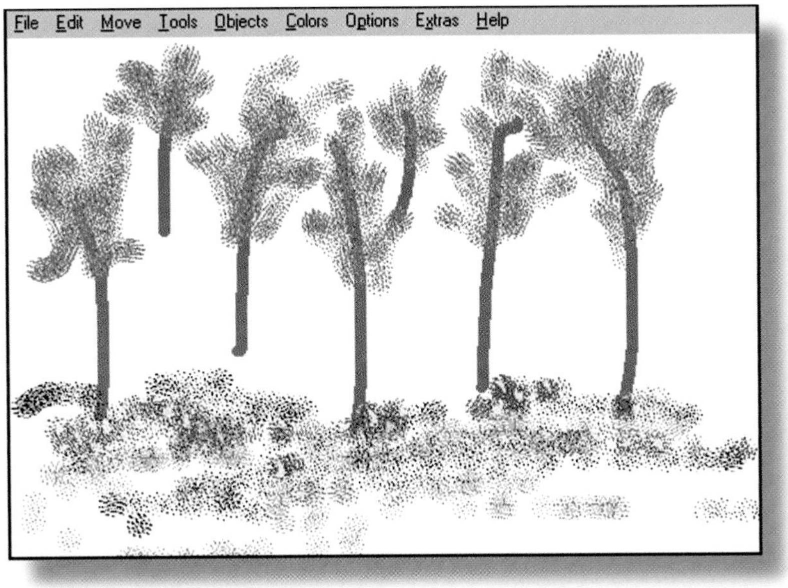


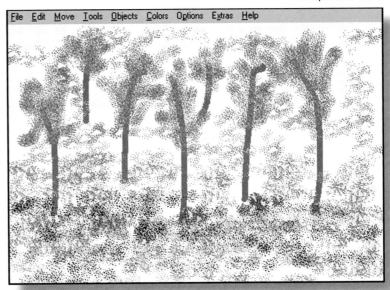

**FIGURE 16-8**
Completed Card

**9.** Create the area for the animation to pass behind by using the **Lasso Selector** tool to select every other tree in a looping movement, as shown in Figure 16-9.

**FIGURE 16-9**
Selected Area

**TIP**

Keep the selected area close to the tree shape.

**10.** With the area selected, choose **Add a Graphic Object** from the Objects menu.

**11.** Click **Yes** if prompted to turn the selected part of the screen into a graphic object.

**12.** From the Graphic Appearance window, click **Actions**. Choose **Play animation**. Go to the **Disk Library**, select **BttrflyB**, and click **Open**.

**FIGURE 16-10**
Path Options Selected

**TIP**

Macintosh users should select Butterfly2.

**13.** Click and drag the butterfly across the screen as though it were flying through the forest. Be sure it crosses the areas that have been selected for it to go behind. Press **Enter** to complete the process.

**14.** From the Path pull-down menu, choose **Path Options**, as shown in Figure 16-10.

**15.** Deselect **Float over**, as shown in Figure 16-11, and click **OK**.

 **TIP**

If Float over is checked, the animation will not float behind the graphic objects.

**16.** Check **Allow clones**, as shown in Figure 16-12. Click **OK**, **Done**, and **OK**.

**17.** Save the stack as **Forest**.

**18.** In the Browse mode, test the animation by clicking on one of the graphic areas. Each time you click on the area, a new butterfly should begin the path. You can have several butterflies on the screen at the same time. That is what the allow clones feature does.

**19.** Keep the stack open.

 **TIP**

If your animation does not float over and behind the picture, verify that the Float over box in the Path Options window is not selected and that you have the Experienced user preference selected from Preferences on the Edit menu. You can change the action by choosing the **Graphic Object** tool or the **Arrow (Edit)** tool, double clicking on the graphic, and choosing Actions.

**FIGURE 16-11**
Deselect Float Over

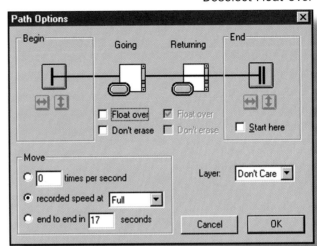

**FIGURE 16-12**
Allow Clones Selected

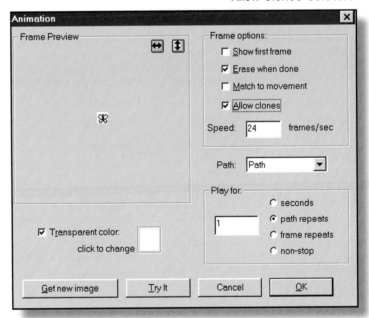

Following the procedure described in Steps 9 through 16 of Step-by-Step 16.2, create a second animation on the bottom of the card in the grassy area. Use **ButtrflyC** for this animation. Test your animations by clicking on the two graphics areas. Your animation should resemble Figure 16-13. Save as **Forest1** and close your stack.

**FIGURE 16-13**
Final Animation

**HINT:**

Animations can move from left to right or right to left across the screen.

# Special Effects Filters

Graphic programs like Adobe Photoshop have special plug-ins that are filters for graphics. These filters allow you to manipulate the graphics to change the color, texture, and many other effects.

HyperStudio offers some plug-ins or add-ons that allow you to create textures and special graphic effects on cards. These effects are included on the Effects menu, as shown in Figure 16-14. They include:

**FIGURE 16-14**
Effects from Effects menu

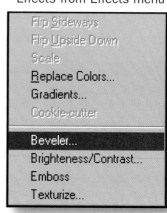

- **Beveler** for a beveled effect around the borders of a card or object.

- **Brightness/Contrast** control to adjust the light and contrast of a card or object.

- **Emboss** effect that creates a raised, or embossed, pattern on the entire card or object.

- **Texturize** effect that allows you to add the look of specific textures to the card or object.

**TIP**

Macintosh users will find these effects on the Edit menu under Effects.

**STEP-BY-STEP ⟹ 16.3**

1. Open a new stack. Use the full-screen card size.

2. From the Edit menu, choose **Effects** and **Beveler**.

3. Select **Flat**. The effect is shown on the left side of the Beveler window in Figure 16-15.

4. Select **Inverse** and deselect **Flat**. The effect is shown on the left side of the Beveler window in Figure 16-16.

5. Do not select Flat or Inverse and view the effect in the Beveler window, as shown in Figure 16-17.

(continued on next page)

**FIGURE 16-15**
Flat Selected from the Beveler Window

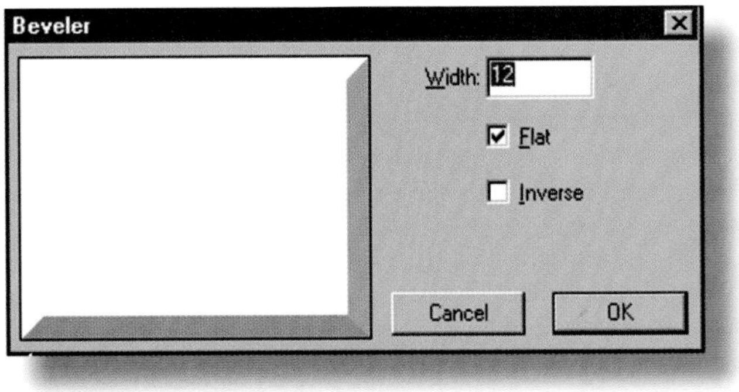

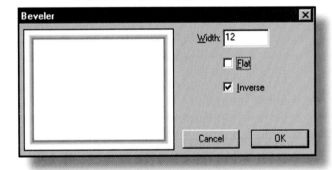

**FIGURE 16-16**
Inverse Selected from the Beveler Window

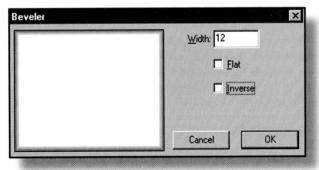

**FIGURE 16-17**
Flat and Inverse Deselected in Beveler Window

**6.** Select both **Flat** and **Inverse** and view the result on the left side of the Beveler window, as shown in Figure 16-18. Choose **Cancel** to close the window.

**7.** Add clip art from the HSArt folder, photos folder, and boyboats file. Use the **Square Selector** tool to select a square from the picture, as shown in Figure 16-19.

**8.** Move the clip art to the upper left section of the card. Leave enough room to place three more squares on the card, as shown in Figure 16-20.

**FIGURE 16-18**
Flat and Inverse Selected in Beveler Window

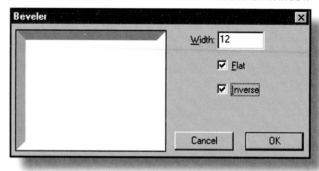

**FIGURE 16-19**
Selected Square from Boyboats Photo

**FIGURE 16-20**
Four Squares of Boyboats Photo

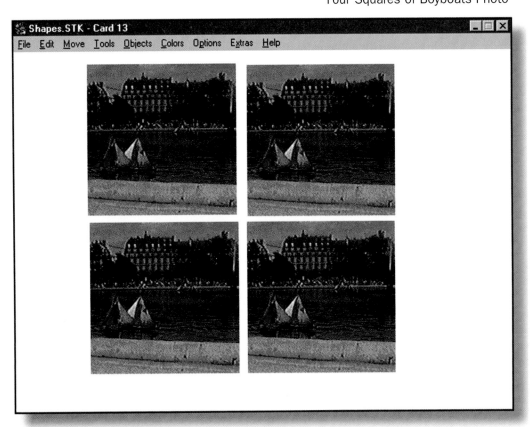

9. Keep the first square selected. (If it is not still selected, reselect it with the **Square Selector** tool.) With the four-headed arrow cursor in the middle of the selection, hold down the **Ctrl** key (Windows) or the **Option** key (Macintosh) and click and drag the mouse to move a copy of the picture below the original. Repeat this process to create the four images shown in Figure 16-20.

10. Select one of the squares. From the Edit menu, select **Effects** and **Beveler**. Select **Flat**, as shown in Figure 16-21. Click **OK**.

**FIGURE 16-21**
Flat Beveler Effect on Boyboats Photo

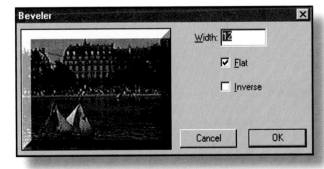

(continued on next page)

**11.** Create a new card.

**12.** From the Edit menu, select **Effects** and **Emboss**. Return to the Effects menu and select **Gradients**. Choose **Vertical** and click **Apply**.

**13.** Use the **Oval Selector** tool to create an oval in the center of the card. With the oval selected, choose **Gradients** from the Effects menu. Select **Circular** and click **Apply**. Click outside the oval to deselect it. The result of the effects you have chosen is shown in Figure 16-23.

**FIGURE 16-22**
Gradients, Vertical

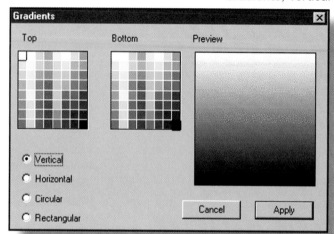

**FIGURE 16-23**
Embossed and Circular Gradient

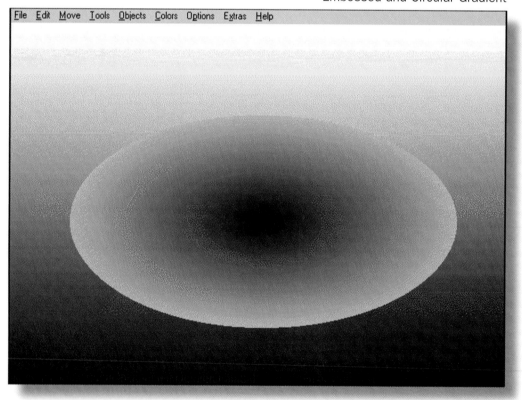

**14.** Save the stack as **Shapes**.

**15.** Return to Card 1. Select one of the photos with the **Square Selector** tool.

**16.** From the Effects menu, select **Emboss**. Your photo should look like Figure 16-24.

**17.** Create a new card. Select **Texturize** from the Effects menu.

**18.** Click on the arrow to see the list of patterns available, as shown in Figure 16-25. Select **Canvas** and click **OK**.

**TIP**

The texture is not a background even though it covers the card. It will leave a hole in the color if you copy or paste any part of it.

**19.** Move to Card 1. Select one of the photos that has not had an effect added. With the **Square Selector** tool choose **Texturize** from the Effects menu. Choose **Raked**, as shown in Figure 16-26. Adjust the **Relief** and **Scale** controls to create a pleasing effect and click **OK**.

**TIP**

Macintosh users should select one of the effects available.

(continued on next page)

**FIGURE 16-24**
Emboss Effect on Boyboats Photo

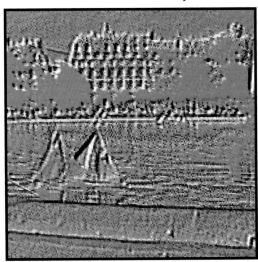

**FIGURE 16-25**
Canvas Effect Selected from Pull-Down List

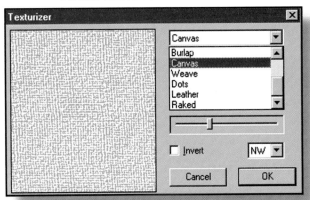

**FIGURE 16-26**
Raked Texture with Relief and Scale Adjusted

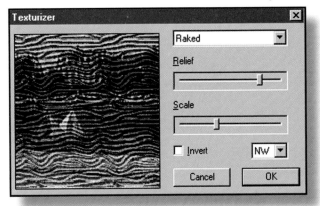

**20.** Go to the card with the canvas texture. Select **Brightness/Contrast** from the Effects menu. Move the slider controls to the left and right to see the different effects. Select an effect similar to Figure 16-27. Click **OK**.

**21.** Return to Card 1. Select the last of the photos with the **Square Selector** tool. Choose **Brightness/Contrast** from the Effects menu. Adjust the controls to achieve an effect similar to Figure 16-28. Click **OK**.

**22.** Save the stack as **Shapes1**. Keep it open.

**FIGURE 16-27**
Brightness and Contrast Effects Window

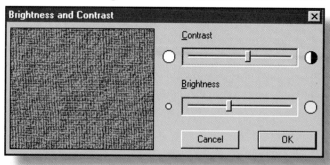

**FIGURE 16-28**
Brightness and Contrast Effects Window

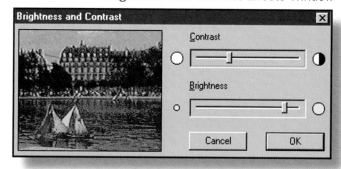

# Draw Options

The Options menu offers additional design choices, as shown in Figure 16-29. These choices are:

■ Draw Filled, which will fill in an object that is drawn with the color chosen.

■ Draw Multiple, which will create multiple images of the shape you are drawing.

■ Draw Centered, which will create multiple but equally centered images of the shape you are drawing.

**FIGURE 16-29**
Options Menu

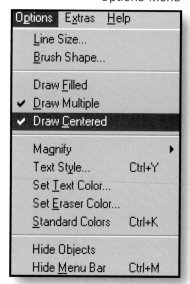

## STEP-BY-STEP 16.4

**1.** With the Shapes1 stack open, add a new card. From the Options menu, select both **Draw Multiple** and **Draw Centered**.

**2.** Using the **Oval** tool, place the cursor in the center of the card and click and drag it out toward the edge, as shown in Figure 16-30.

(continued on next page)

**FIGURE 16-30**
Ovals Using Draw Multiple and Draw Centered

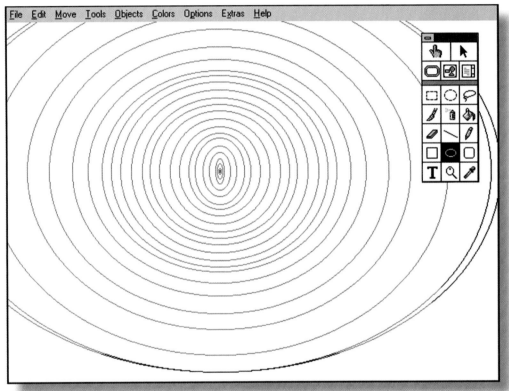

3. Add a new card. Select a **medium brown** color from the color palette. Using the **Rectangle** tool, click and drag the cursor from the center of the card outward, as shown in Figure 16-31.

4. Use the **Paint Bucket** tool to fill in the boxes with different shades of brown, creating perspective similar to Figure 16-32.

**FIGURE 16-31**
Rectangles Using Draw Multiple and Draw Centered

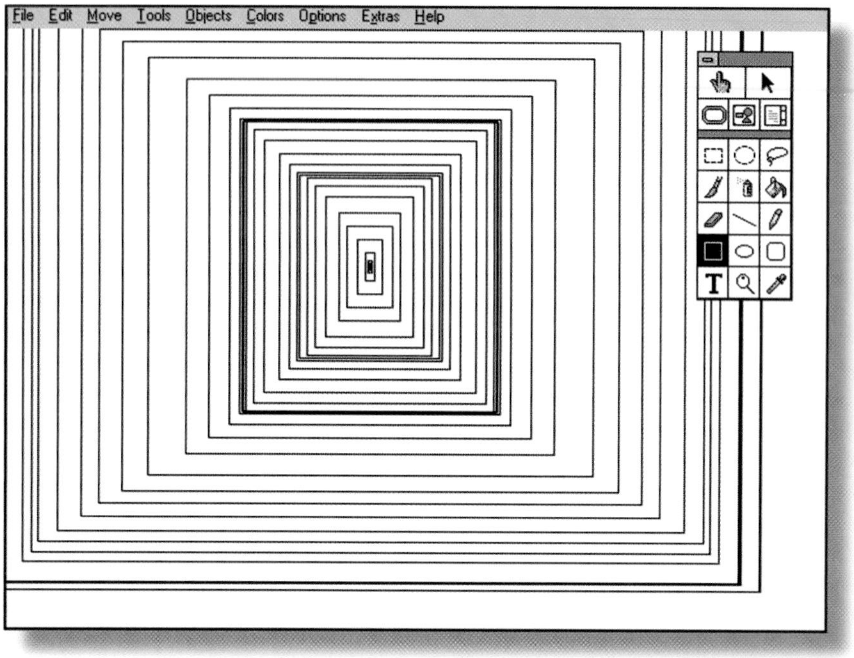

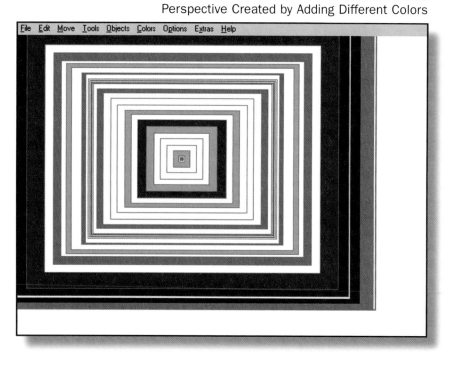

**FIGURE 16-32**
Perspective Created by Adding Different Colors

**5.** Create a new card. From the Options menu, deselect **Draw Centered**. (Only Draw Multiple should be selected.) Using the **Rounded Rectangle** tool, draw several small objects, dragging from left to right, right to left, top to bottom, and bottom to top. Repeat the process with the **Oval** tool. Your card should have shapes that resemble those in Figure 16-33.

**6.** Deselect **Draw Multiple**. Select **Draw Filled**. Select a color of your choice. Draw several circles, rectangles, rounded rectangles, and ovals.

**7.** Save the stack as **Shapes2** and keep it open.

 **TIP**

For unusual shapes, drag the cursor in circles to create spirals. You can change the color of the objects from the color palette.

 **TIP**

Hold down the Shift key while using the Rectangle tool to create a square or the Oval tool to create a circle.

**FIGURE 16-33**
Objects Created Using Draw Multiple

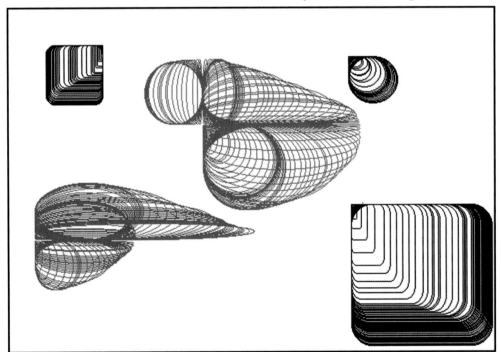

# Using Shapes in Layered Animations

In Step-by-Step 16.2, you created a layered animation by creating a background and adding clip art as the animated object. You can use the various graphic options to create interesting elements for animations. Solid objects and painted objects can be used in the creation of a layered animation.

## STEP-BY-STEP ⟹ 16.5

**1.** Create a new card. Apply gradients in a vertical pattern. Choose a **dark blue** for the bottom and a **light blue** for the top of the card, as shown in Figure 16-34.

**2.** Select **Draw Multiple** from the Options menu. (Deselect **Draw Filled**, if necessary.)

**3.** Using the **Oval** tool and a **dark blue**, draw a spiral shape like a tunnel with an opening at each end, similar to Figure 16-35.

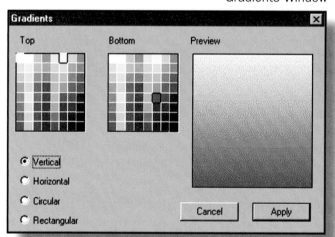

**FIGURE 16-34**
Gradients Window

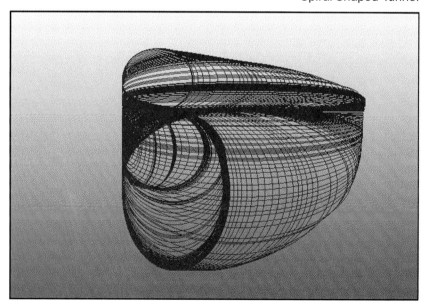

**FIGURE 16-35**
Spiral-Shaped Tunnel

**4.** Using the **Lasso Selector** tool, lasso an area inside the tunnel object, leaving a space at each end of the tunnel unselected, as shown in Figure 16-36.

**5.** Choose **Add a Graphic Object** from the Objects menu to make the selected area a graphic. Click **Yes**.

**6.** From the Actions window, select **Play animation**.

**7.** Select **Disk Library**. From the HSAnim folder, select the **Fish** file, as shown in Figure 16-37. Click **Open**.

**8.** Create a path from one edge of the card, through the tunnel, and out the other end as shown in Figure 16-38.

(continued on next page)

**FIGURE 16-36**
Lasso Selection

**FIGURE 16-37**
Fish File Selected

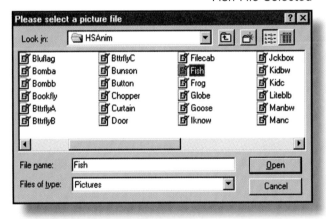

**FIGURE 16-38**
Path Animation

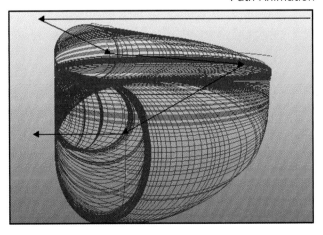

**347**

**9.** From the Path options window, deselect **Float over**. Select **Allow clones** from the Animation window. Click **OK** and **Done** as needed to complete the process.

**10.** In the Browse mode, click inside the tunnel. The fish should appear to enter the tunnel, go behind the tunnel walls, and come out the other end, as shown in Figure 16-39.

**11.** Save the stack as **Shapes3**. Close the stack.

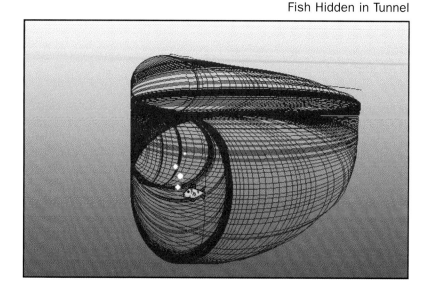

**FIGURE 16-39**
Fish Hidden in Tunnel

# *Summary*

In this lesson, you learned that:

- You can bring resources from other sources, including CD-ROM encyclopedias, into your stacks to make them more interesting and informative.

- You must give copyright credit to resources that you copy for your stacks.

- You can create layered animations using any drawn object for your stacks.

- Layered animations appear to be three-dimensional because the animated object floats over and under selected areas on your card.

- HyperStudio has additional plug-ins for special graphic effects.

- The plug-in effects are located in the Effects menu under the Edit pull-down menu.

- The plug-in effects are: Beveler, Emboss, Texturize, and Brightness/Contrast control.

- The plug-in effects can be used for an entire card or a selected portion of a card or object.

- The Options menu has three options that can be accessed when using the drawing tools. They are Draw Filled, Draw Multiple, and Draw Centered.

- You can use the drawing options separately or combined.

## VOCABULARY

Beveler

Brightness/contrast

Draw centered

Draw filled

Draw multiple

Emboss

Filter

Plug-in

Texturize

## LESSON 16 REVIEW QUESTIONS

### TRUE/FALSE

**Circle the T if the statement is true or F if it is false.**

**T  F**  **1.** You can copy resources from CD-ROM encyclopedias to your stacks.

**T  F**  **2.** Most resources from CD-ROM encyclopedias have copyright information.

**T  F**  **3.** Selecting Inverse only from the Beveler effect will give your screen a frame around all of the edges.

**T  F**  **4.** The Brightness/Contrast controls on the Effects menu can alter the look of the texture on the card or object.

**T  F**  **5.** Choosing Emboss will always alter the entire card.

### MULTIPLE CHOICE

**Circle the letter of the best response for each item.**

**1.** When copying resources from a CD-ROM encyclopedia:
   **A.** some movies won't copy
   **B.** some resources will have copyright information
   **C.** you should include copyright information
   **D.** all of the above

**2.** When selecting an object for a layered animation:
   **A.** use the Lasso Selector tool
   **B.** keep the lasso close to the object
   **C.** leave space between objects
   **D.** all of the above

3. When creating a layered animation:
   **A.** you must select Path Options
   **B.** you must check Float over
   **C.** you can select Allow clones
   **D.** all of the above

4. To frame two sides of a card using the Beveler effect:
   **A.** select Flat
   **B.** select Inverse
   **C.** don't select Flat or Inverse
   **D.** none of the above

5. You can create a layered animation:
   **A.** from an object that you draw
   **B.** from an object that is selected as an object
   **C.** from the HS Animations folder
   **D.** all of the above

## COMPLETION

**Answer the questions below in the space provided.**

1. What is a layered animation? How is it different from an animation?

2. How does a layered animation work?

3. How can you change the shape of the paintbrush?

4. What does the Beveler effect do?

5.  What effect will you get by selecting Draw Multiple from the Options menu? Selecting Draw Filled? Selecting Draw Centered?

## LESSON 16 PROJECT 16.1

1.  Create a two-card stack.

2.  On the first card, create a layered animation using an object you created with the Draw Multiple option.

3.  On the second card, create a layered animation of your choice.

4.  Save the stack as **Projanim**.

## LESSON 16 PROJECT 16.2

1.  Create a stack that displays the four plug-in filter effects you worked with in this lesson. The stack should include a Title card and Main Menu card. A text field should be added to identify the various filters. Choose a photo or clip art graphic and show the different effects you learned in this lesson, including:

    ■  Beveler

    ■  Texturize

    ■  Emboss

    ■  Brightness/Contrast

2.  Save the stack as **Plugins**.

## CRITICAL THINKING ACTIVITY

Describe two or three projects that would make good use of layered animations. Describe or draw a card for one of these projects that includes a layered animation.

## LESSON 17

# MORE ADVANCED TECHNIQUES

## *Crossing Platforms and Using HyperStudio on Computers Without the Program*

The HyperStudio Player makes it easy for you to play your stacks on any computer, even if the computer does not have HyperStudio loaded. The Player is royalty- and copyright-free so that you can load it on any computer to play and show your stacks. The Player does not allow you to make any changes to the stacks; you may simply show them. For Macintosh users, the HyperStudio Player is located in the MyStacks folder, and can be copied to a floppy disk. Windows users will also need to copy the HSPSETUP.EXE file onto a floppy disk in order to run the Player.

The term cross platform refers to the ability of a program to run on either a Macintosh operating system or a Windows operating system. HyperStudio is a cross-platform program, and the stacks you create will run on either a Macintosh or Windows computer. In fact, you can create your stacks using both platforms. For example, if you are using a Macintosh at school and need to complete your stack at home on a Windows computer, you can save your stack to a floppy disk or ZIP disk on the Macintosh computer and reopen the stack on your Windows computer. The only limitations are that the disk must be IBM formatted or formatted to be read on both platforms and the versions of HyperStudio must be the same.

There are some differences between the two programs, however. One of the important factors you must remember is that you must name your files in a way that will be recognized by Windows. Macintosh and Windows. File names must be limited to eight characters. If your stacks are to be used across platforms, include a .stk extension. For instance, project.stk is a valid file name for all platforms.

Another factor to consider is that different computers have different fonts installed. If you know that you will be using or viewing your stack on different computers, it is wise to use basic fonts in text fields, such as Arial and New Times Roman. Your choice of font for painted text will not be affected when viewed on different computers, since it is not treated as text, but as part of the background. However, fonts in text fields and on the buttons may change between computers. For instance, if you create a stack at home and present in class, your screens may look different. If the computer cannot find the font you used, it will insert a default font in place of the unknown font. The fonts that are shared between Macintosh and Windows in HyperStudio are:

- Architect
- Artisan
- Geneva
- Journal
- LightWave
- MarketProduct
- ModernBlck
- PaintStroke
- Schoolboy
- Tiempo
- Wrangler

The NBAs in Windows and Macintosh differ. Macintosh has some NBAs that are not yet featured in the Windows versions of HyperStudio. There are a few other features for Macintosh that are not yet available on the Windows platform, such as playing movies in irregular shapes. The plug-in effects have different names and some of the animation files vary a bit between the two platforms. If you are planning to use both platforms, you will have to check to find the potential sources of problems by testing the stacks carefully on each platform before making a presentation.

Another difference you may find between Macintosh and Windows is a difficulty playing the sounds from one platform in another. When you are planning to create cross-platform stacks, you will need to experiment through trial and error to see which of these sounds to consider or avoid.

# *Magnifying Glass and Eyedropper Tools*

There are two tools on the tool palette that you have not worked with yet. These are the Eyedropper and the Magnifying Glass tools, as shown in Figure 17-1.

---

**INTERNET**

Internet addresses are known as **URLs**. URL stands for **Uniform Resource Locator**. Internet addresses generally begin with **http://**. The letters describe the protocol used to transfer the information, **HyperText Transfer Protocol**. Many published Internet addresses do not include the http:// since it is not technically part of the address. You should, however, add it to the beginning of the address.

---

**FIGURE 17-1**
Eyedropper and
Magnifying Glass Tools

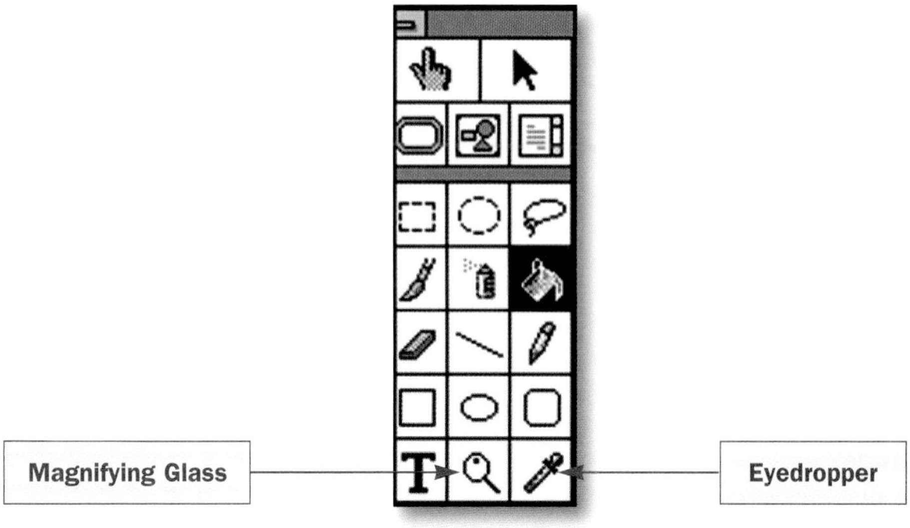

Magnifying Glass

Eyedropper

The Magnifying Glass enlarges an area of the screen. Selecting this tool will change the cursor into a square. Clicking the cursor on an area of the screen enlarges the image and creates a small window showing the entire image. Clicking on the zoomed image again will further enlarge the image.

The Eyedropper tool allows you to grab a color in a background, even if it is not on the color palette, and use it somewhere else on the card. When you select this tool, your cursor turns into an eyedropper. When you place the eyedropper on a color and click, the color becomes the default color and you can use it with any of the paint or drawing tools.

## STEP-BY-STEP ⟹ 17.1

1. Open a new stack. Import the background **Europe**. Make the tool palette visible.

2. Select the **Magnifying Glass** tool, and click the cursor over Italy, as shown in Figure 17-2.

**3.** Click on Italy again, and you will see a closer magnification, as shown in Figure 17-3.

(continued on next page)

**FIGURE 17-2**
First Magnification Size

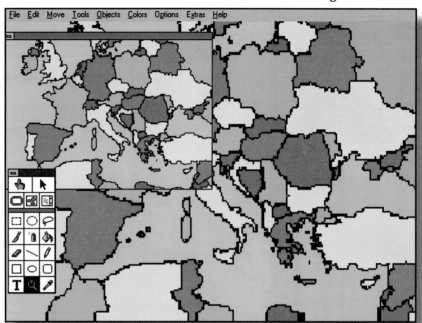

**FIGURE 17-3**
Next Magnification Size

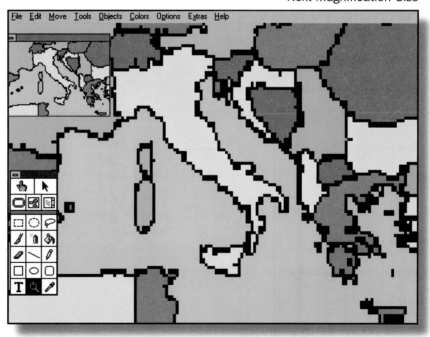

**4.** Click the mouse on Italy again to see the next magnification view, as shown in Figure 17-4.

**5.** Click on Italy again to return to the normal size.

**6.** Click again until you reach the largest magnification.

**7.** Make the color palette visible. Click on the **Eyedropper** tool. Click on the **yellow** color with the eyedropper. Notice the default color in the color palette changes, as shown in Figure 17-5.

**FIGURE 17-4**
Largest Magnification View

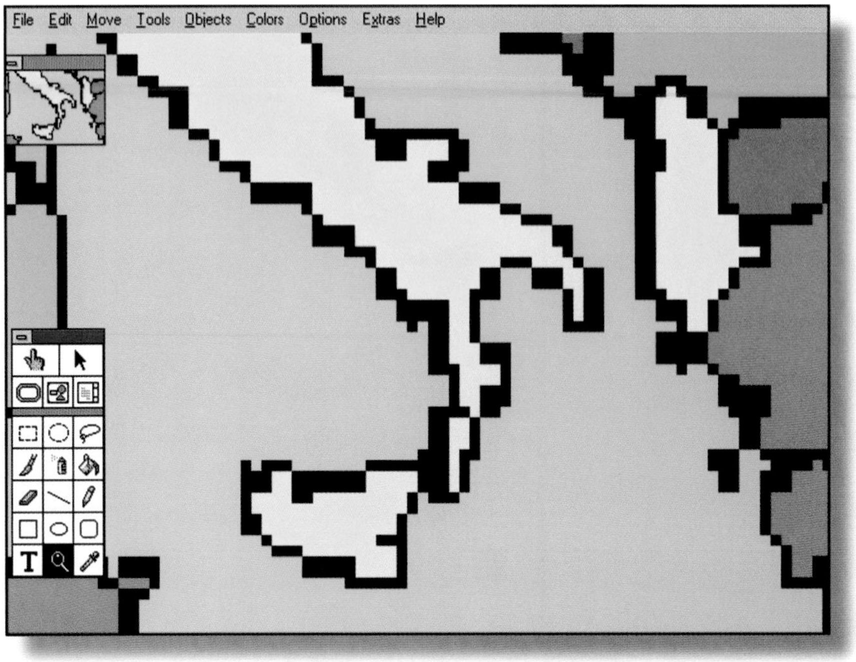

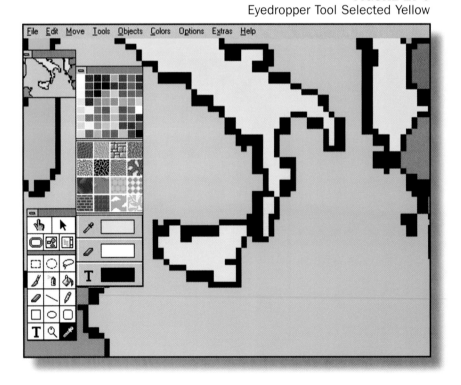

**FIGURE 17-5**
Eyedropper Tool Selected Yellow

**8.** Click on the **Pencil** tool. Click on the **black** edges of the bottom part of the graphic changing it to **yellow**, as shown in Figure 17-6.

**TIP**

If you click two times on the same spot, it will change the color to the color setting of the eraser. Click one more time to change it back to yellow.

**FIGURE 17-6**
Black Border Changed to Yellow

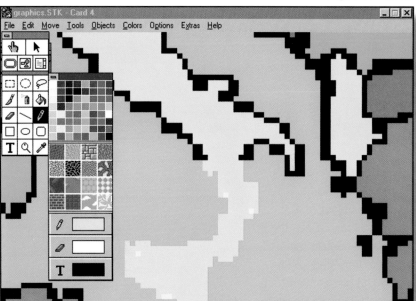

**9.** Press the **Escape** key. The zoomed graphic should return to the normal view, as shown in Figure 17-7.

**TIP**

To return to normal view, use the Escape key or select Magnify 100% from the Option menu.

**10.** Save the stack as **Graphics**. Keep the stack open.

**FIGURE 17-7**
Altered Normal View

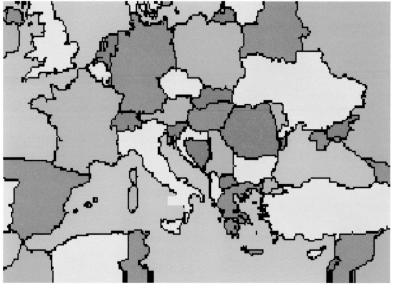

# Bring Closer/Send Farther

In earlier lessons, you learned that there is a hierarchy of the way objects are placed on a card. HyperStudio has the ability to change the hierarchy by bringing an object closer or sending it farther away. This option, found on the Objects menu, allows you to change the order of elements on a card. For instance, if a text object covers a graphic, you can send the text farther back to view the graphic through the text.

1. With the Graphics stack open, select **Add a Graphic Object** from the Objects menu. Open the **Flags** file. Select the **British** flag. Reduce its size and place it near Great Britain, as shown in Figure 17-8.

**FIGURE 17-8**
Flag Graphic

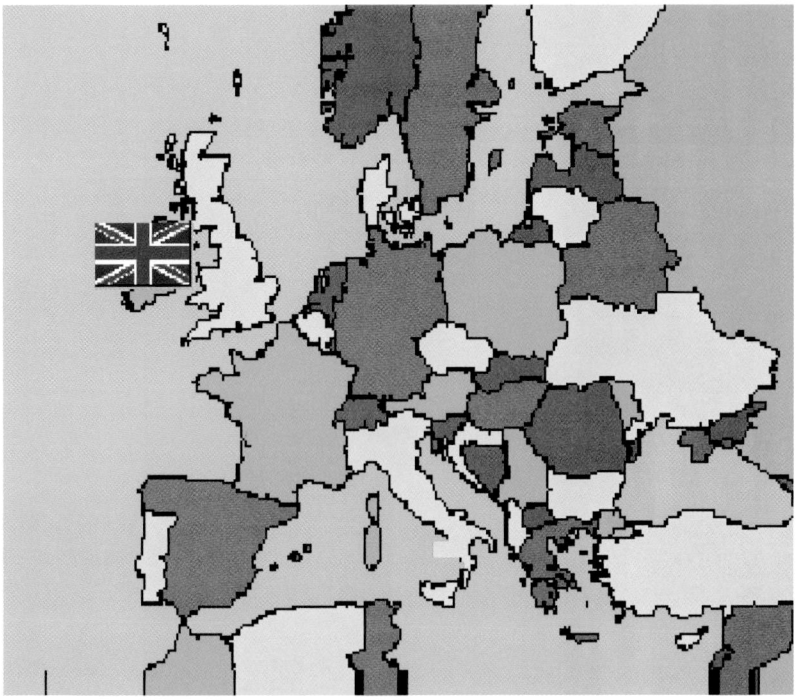

2. Create a new text object. Reduce its size and move it over the flag, as shown in Figure 17-9. The object should have a frame, but should not be scrollable. Make the background **blue**, similar to the blue of the ocean. Select **Architect** font, **center** the text, and select size **12**.

3. Key:

    **You should be able to see the graphic through this text object.**

STEP-BY-STEP 17.2 CONTINUED

4. With the text object selected, choose **Send Farther** from the Objects menu. You should be able to see the graphic through the text field, as shown in Figure 17-10. If necessary, move the text object or the graphic object so that the flag does not overlap the text.

5. Save the stack and keep it open.

**FIGURE 17-9**
Text Object Covering Graphic

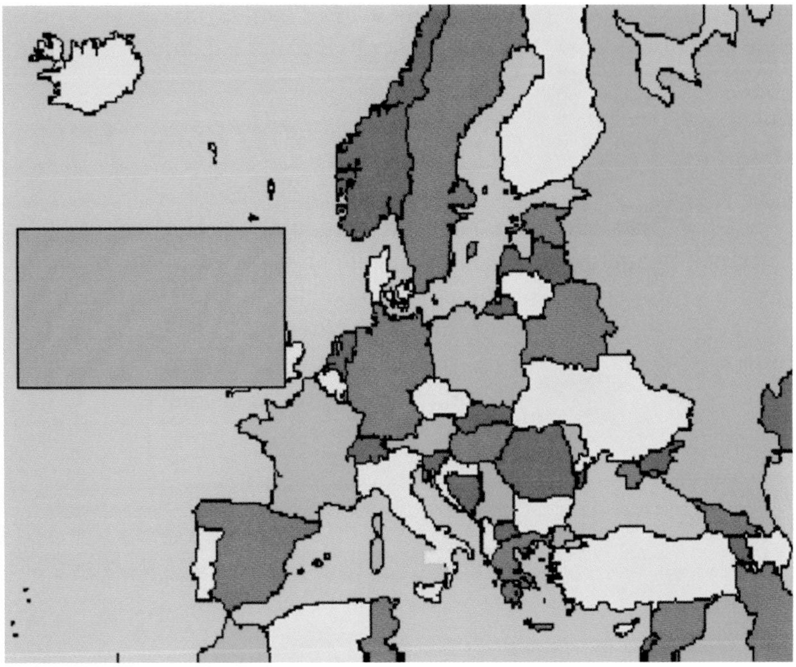

**FIGURE 17-10**
Send Farther Text Object

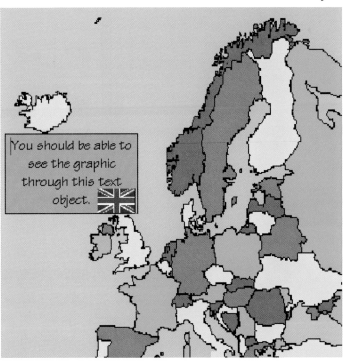

# Marked Cards

Marking a card is a way of locating it through one of the object actions. Marked cards are useful when you are linking stacks. When you link to a stack, HyperStudio automatically opens to the first card in the linked stack. However, using marked cards, you can select a specific card in the linked stack. The button action that will move the user to the marked card is Last marked card.

# Linking Stacks to Other Programs

You can access another application from HyperStudio. Suppose you plan to present some information and then ask the user write an essay or poem about the information in a word processing program. You can set up a button or object action to go to another program, as long as the program is located on the computer's hard drive. When the button or object is selected, it will open the specified application. This type of link is best used when the stack will only be located on one computer so that you can be certain that the linked application is available.

## STEP-BY-STEP 17.3

1. With the Graphics stack open, add a button named **Shapes**. Choose the icon shown in Figure 17-11.

2. Move the button to the lower left corner of the screen.

**FIGURE 17-11**
Icons for Effects Button

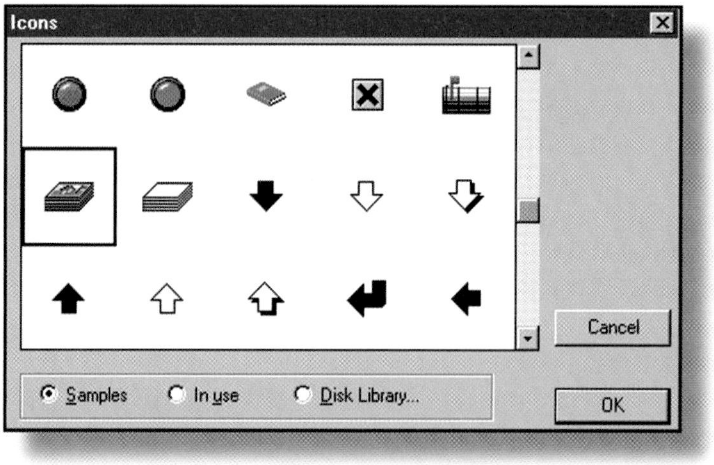

3. Select **Another stack** from the Actions window, as shown in Figure 17-12.

4. Locate the **Shapes3** stack on your computer, as shown in Figure 17-13. Click **Open**. Choose the **Fastest** transition and **Fast** speed. Click **OK** and **Done** as needed to complete the button.

5. Test the button. When asked if you want to save the stack you are leaving, click **Save**. (See Figure 17-14.)

6. You will be on Card 1 of the **Shapes3** stack. Add a button to the card named **Graphics**. Do not include an icon. Position it in the lower right corner of the card. Select the button action of **Another stack**, locate the **Graphics** stack, and click **Open**.

7. Save the stack as **Shapes4**.

8. Test the **Graphics** button. You should see the card shown in Figure 17-15.

**FIGURE 17-12**
Another Stack Selected

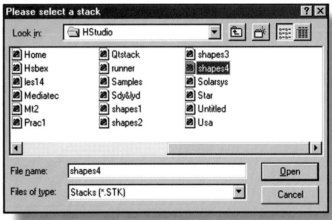

**FIGURE 17-13**
Locate the Shapes4 Stack

(continued on next page)

**FIGURE 17-14**
Save Stack

**9.** Save the stack as **Graphic1** and keep it open.

**FIGURE 17-15**
Graphics Stack

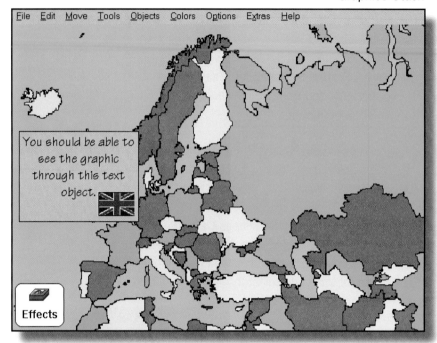

File    Edit    Move    Tools    Objects    Colors    Options    Extras    Help

You should be able to
see the graphic
through this text
object.

Effects

# CHALLENGE ACTIVITY $\Rightarrow$ 17.1

**1.** In the Graphics1 stack, create a new card.

**2.** Load a piece of clip art such as Planets or some other colorful choice.

**3.** Use the **Oval** tool to draw a circle on the card outside of the clip art.

**4.** Dissect the circle with two straight lines making sure the lines go from one side of the circle to the other, like a pie cut in four pieces.

**5.** Use the **Eyedropper** tool to select a color for each section from the clip art.

**6.** When the color is selected in the eyedropper, use the **Paint Bucket** tool to fill one quarter of the circle. When you are finished, you should have four different wedges similar to Figure 17-16.

**7.** Save the stack as **Graphics2**. Close the stack.

**FIGURE 17-16**
Circle with Four Colors from the Colors Used in the Clip Art

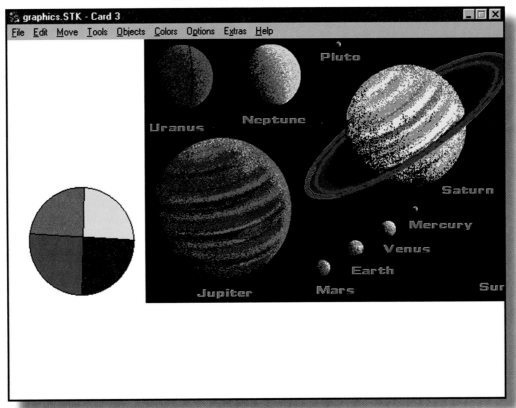

# *Templates*

In Lesson 8, you worked with the Ready Made cards and templates that are provided in HyperStudio. As you may recall, a template is generally a pattern or a "plate" used for duplicating something. Rather than creating a new Main Menu card every time you create a stack, you could use a template that is already patterned with the essential layout components such as buttons, navigation, text fields, spaces for graphics, etc. Then you could adapt the template to the project you are working on at the time. The buttons, text fields, and graphic objects will serve as placeholders. When you use the template in an actual stack, you can modify the placeholders to accommodate the stack you are creating.

In Lesson 16, you learned to use a variety of filters and effects. Now that you have learned how to use most of the HyperStudio tools, you can create some fabulous templates of your own. You can do this by altering one of the backgrounds or templates provided in HyperStudio or by creating templates of your own design.

1. Open a new stack. Use the full screen size, which will vary depending on your computer and monitor configuration.

2. Import a background. Use the **Gazette** file from the HSArt folder.

3. Across the top of the columns add a text field, as shown in Figure 17-17. The object should have no scroll bar or frame. Use a **white** background with **black** text. The text style should be **Arial**, **Bold**, **36**, and **centered**. Key:

   **Headline Goes Here!**

4. Add another text field with no frame or scroll bar. Make the font **Plain**, **12** point, and **left** aligned. Place the field over the first column and resize it, as shown in Figure 17-18.

**FIGURE 17-17**
Headline Text Field

**FIGURE 17-18**
First Column of Text

**TIP**

When you use this as a Main Menu card, the different stories will act as the objects to connect you to the topic card. When you use the template in a stack, you can select the text field, attach Actions, and choose Another card. By selecting the appropriate topic card, you will have created the navigation to that card. You will want to add the navigation after you have created the text that will go into the text field so that it matches the card to which the user will be moving.

**FIGURE 17-19**
Three Text Columns on Template

5. Key **Topic One** for the first news story. Type a few words in the text column. Highlight the title of the story only (Topic One). From the Options menu, select **Text style** and change the font size of the selected text to **18** and alignment to **center**. The remaining text will stay at 12 point and be left aligned.

6. Copy and paste the text field and move the copy to the third column. Paste the field once more, and place the copy over the center column. Reduce the size of the field in the second column to leave space for a graphic, as shown in Figure 17-19.

7. Change the title of each of the copied fields to **Topic Two** and **Topic Three**.

8. Add a graphic object as a placeholder in the middle column. Use any graphic file from your disk as the placeholder graphic. Size it to fit the space.

(continued on next page)

**9.** Create two buttons. Name one button **Previous Page** and assign it the appropriate action. Place the button as shown in Figure 17-20. Copy and paste the first button and name the new button **Next Page**. Edit the button action to assign it the appropriate action.

**10.** Add two more buttons to cover the areas in the headline that say "Extra," as shown in Figure 17-21. Name one of the buttons **Title** and add the action to go to the Title card. Name the other button **Quit** and specify the appropriate action.

**TIP**

You will want to have a Title button in case the previous card in your stack is not the title card. This will depend on your stack structure.

**FIGURE 17-20**
Page with Two Navigation Buttons Added

**FIGURE 17-21**
Quit and Title Buttons

**11.** Save the stack as **Template**.

**12.** Create a new card.

**13.** Use the Beveler effect with **Flat** and **Inverse** deselected.

**14.** Double click on a color on the color palette. From the More Colors! window, select **light purple**, similar to the color shown in Figure 17-22.

**15.** Use the **Paint Bucket** tool to fill the card with color. The card should appear with a beveled border, as shown in Figure 17-23.

(continued on next page)

**FIGURE 17-22**
More Colors Window

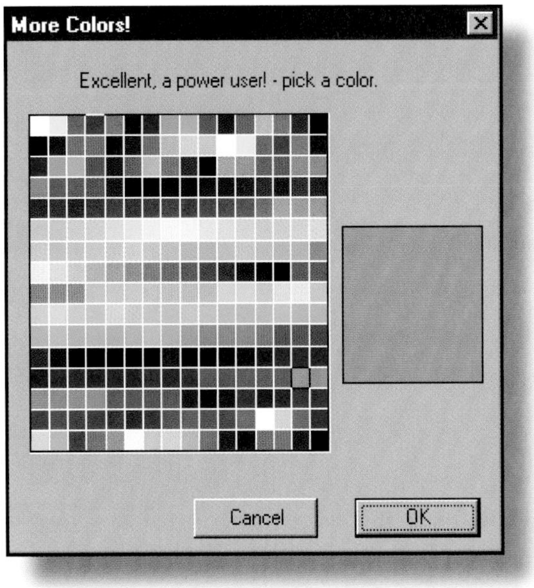

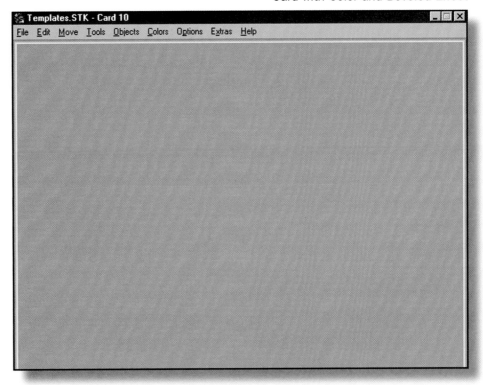

**FIGURE 17-23**
Card with Color and Beveled Effect

**367**

**16.** Choose **Gradients** from the Effects menu. Select **Rectangular**, and choose **light purple** for the outside color and **dark purple** for the Inside color, as shown in Figure 17-24. Click **Apply**.

**17.** Use the **Circle Selector** tool to select a small oval on the card to be used as a button. (If needed, look ahead to Figure 17-29 to view the result of these steps.)

**18.** From the Effects menu, select **Gradients**. Apply a circular gradient keeping the same outside and inside color selections shown in Figure 17-25. Click **Apply**.

**FIGURE 17-24**
Rectangular Gradient Effect

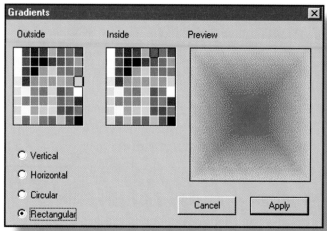

**FIGURE 17-25**
Circular Gradient

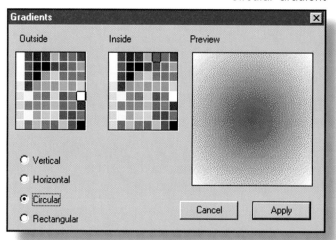

**19.** While the oval is selected, copy and paste it until you have two rows of three buttons each, as shown in Figure 17-26.

**20.** Save your stack.

**21.** Create a text field for the first oval. Align the field to the left of the button and have it cover the left half of the inner square, as shown in Figure 17-27. The field should not be scrollable or have a frame. Use **MarketProduct** font, size **16**, **black** text, **left** alignment. Click the **Feature** button and select **Transparent**. Key: **Topic One** in the text field, as shown in Figure 17-27.

(continued on next page)

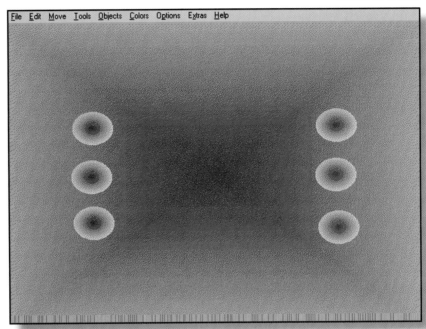

**FIGURE 17-26**
Rows of Ovals

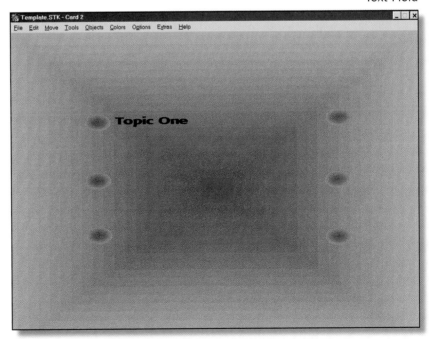

**FIGURE 17-27**
Text Field

**22.** Copy and paste the field until you have two columns of three fields each to match the buttons. The right column should be right aligned, as shown in Figure 17-28. Change the text in the fields as needed.

**FIGURE 17-28**
Two Rows of Text Objects

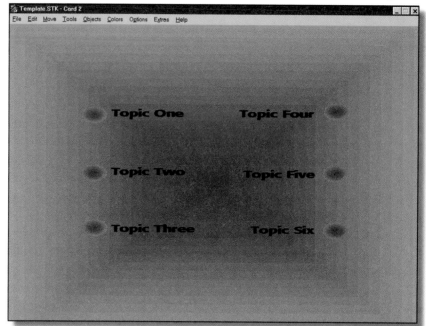

**23.** Add a text field to the top of the card. Make the field nonscrollable, without a frame and transparent. Use **black** text, **MarketProduct** font, size **48**, and **center** alignment. Key **Main Menu** as shown in Figure 17-29.

**FIGURE 17-29**
Main Menu Card

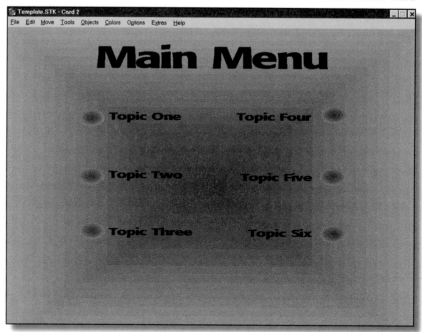

**24.** Add invisible buttons for each of the ovals. You will program the buttons when you use the template in a stack.

**25.** Save the stack as **Templat1**. Close the stack.

**TIP**

When you use a drawn object for a button with an invisible button over it, you cannot delete the drawn object if you do not need all of the buttons, since it will leave a hole in the background.

# *Summary*

In this lesson, you learned that:

- Cross platform refers to using a stack on both Macintosh and Windows operating systems.

- When playing your stacks on a computer that does not have the HyperStudio application, you will need to install a copy of HyperStudio player on that computer.

- HyperStudio player will let you view a stack but not make any changes.

- If you are running a HyperStudio stack on a different computer than the one on which the stack was created, you will need to include any movies, sounds, or other attachments in the folder with your stack.

- When using HyperStudio in a cross platform situation, you may encounter problems with fonts, sounds, or NBAs.

- You can use the Eyedropper tool to match colors.

- You can use the Magnifying Glass tool to zoom in on a portion of the screen.

- You can change the object hierarchy by using the Bring Closer/Send Farther option.

- You can link one stack to another.

- You can link a stack to another program application.

- Templates are patterns that include basic layout and components.

- You can use filters and effects to create dynamic original templates.

## VOCABULARY

Bring closer                                    Send farther

Cross platform                                  Template

Marked cards

## TRUE/FALSE

**Circle the T if the statement is true or F if it is false.**

**T    F    1.** To play a Macintosh HyperStudio stack on a Windows computer that does not have HyperStudio installed, you will need HyperStudio player and an HSPSETUP.EXE stack.

**T    F    2.** To play a Windows HyperStudio stack on a Macintosh computer, you will need HyperStudio player and an HSPSETUP.EXE stack.

**T    F    3.** The Geneva font is a common font between Macintosh and Windows.

**T    F    4.** A template usually has placeholders for objects in its layout.

**T    F    5.** To enlarge an area of a picture, you would use the Eyedropper tool.

**T    F    6.** To match a color on a HyperStudio card, you would use the Magnifying Glass tool.

## MULTIPLE CHOICE

**Circle the letter of the best answer for each statement.**

**1.** If you want a HyperStudio stack to run cross platform, you must:
  **A.** use up to an eight letter name with a .stk at the end
  **B.** include a HSSETUP.EXE file
  **C.** attach any movies or sounds in the stack folder
  **D.** all of the above

**2.** When using HyperStudio stacks between Macintosh and Windows, you may have some problems with:
  **A.** fonts
  **B.** NBAs
  **C.** sounds
  **D.** all of the above

**3.** The Eyedropper tool is:
  **A.** used for magnification
  **B.** used for matching colors
  **C.** another name for zoom
  **D.** all of the above

4. When using the Magnifying Glass tool:
   A. each time you click the mouse the view zooms in more
   B. it is also called zoom
   C. it makes it easier to alter a background or graphic object by the pixel
   D. all of the above

5. With HyperStudio you can choose an action:
   A. to go to another application
   B. to go to another stack
   C. to go to a previous stack
   D. all of the above

6. When creating templates, you can:
   A. create your own background
   B. use a preset background
   C. combine your own background and a preset background
   D. all of the above

## COMPLETION

**Answer the questions below in the space provided.**

1. What is meant by cross platform?

2. What does the Bring closer/Send farther option do?

3. How can you link HyperStudio to another application?

**4.** Why would you link HyperStudio to another application or program?

**5.** What is the purpose of the Eyedropper tool?

**6.** What is the purpose of the Magnifying Glass tool?

## LESSON 17 PROJECT 17.1

Practice marking cards and linking from one stack to another stack in the following activity.

**1.** Open the **Country9** stack.

**2.** On the Main Menu card, create a button to go to stack **USA1**.

**3.** Create a button on the Main Menu card in USA1 stack to return to the Country9 stack.

**4.** Resave both stacks.

**5.** Test the buttons.

## LESSON 17 PROJECT 17.2

1. Create templates to add to your Template stack. Include the following:
   - two Main Menu card templates
   - two Title card templates
   - two topic page templates

2. Include at least three of the following filter effects you practiced in Lesson 16 on the six card templates:
   - Beveler effect
   - Gradients effect
   - Emboss effect
   - Brightness/Contrast control
   - Texturize effect
   - Draw multiple
   - Draw filled
   - Draw centered

3. Include navigation buttons, graphic and text placeholders, and any other details that will make the template useful.

4. Save the stack as **Templat2**.

5. Print the stack.

## CRITICAL THINKING ACTIVITY

List several good reasons for spending time creating templates. Describe or draw a template that could be used for a tutorial or presentation.

# LESSON 18

# TESTING FUNCTIONS

## OBJECTIVES

**Upon completion of this lesson, you will be able to:**

■ Create tests and informational surveys.

■ Use the user's name function.

■ Use the correct and incorrect answer functions.

■ Use the test results function.

■ Create passwords.

**⏱ Estimated Time: 1.5 hours**

## *Creating Tests and Informational Surveys*

As you have probably noticed at this point in the lessons, HyperStudio provides many services and supports an array of project types. A useful tool in HyperStudio is the ability to create a stack that gathers information from the user. This information can assess how well your stack works or how interactive it is. You can also gather opinions or views about the material you have presented. HyperStudio can also be used to test a user's progress in a tutorial situation.

Step-by-Steps 18.1 through 18.3 direct you to create a test stack that will present information and then test a user's ability to provide the correct answer. First you will create a stack that has a set of questions with the answers contained in buttons. Each button, whether correct or incorrect, takes you to the next card. Then you will learn how to record and read the test results.

### Buttons in the Testing Function

Testing function is one of the choices in the Things to Do section of the Actions window. When you are creating buttons to be used in the testing function, HyperStudio presents four choices. The button will:

■ be a correct answer

■ be an incorrect answer

■ ask for the user's name

■ have no testing function

Each button, no matter its testing function, will also take you to another location. In the example you will create, the button action will always take the user to the next card.

## Using the User's Name Function

HyperStudio assumes that more than one user will take the tests that you create. Therefore, it has a button action that allows you to record the user's name. This action will help you apply the test results to the correct individual and allow users to feel that the stack is more personally identified with them.

## STEP-BY-STEP ⟹ 18.1

1. Create a three-card stack, consisting of a Title card, a Directions card, and a question card.

2. On the Title card, insert a background of the United States. Include a transparent text object without a frame. Select a font, style, and size that look attractive on the card. Center the copy. In the text field, insert copy that reads: **How Well Do You Know the United States?** (See Figure 18-1.)

3. Create a folder for the stack. (See Appendix A or B if you need help creating a folder.)

4. Name the folder **Tests**. Save the stack in the Tests folder as **Testing**.

(continued on next page)

**FIGURE 18-1**
Title Card

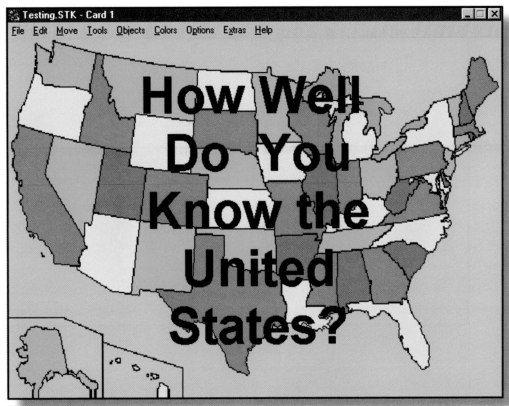

**5.** Add a **Next card** action to the text field of the Title card. Choose the **Fastest** transition and **Fast** speed. Test the action, which will move you to Card 2.

**6.** On Card 2, the Directions card, use a vertical or horizontal gradients effect from **blue** to **white**.

**7.** Add a transparent text object that is nonscrollable and without a frame. Select **dark blue** text, **Arial**, **Plain** font, size **20**, and **left** aligned. Key the following:

Directions

Test your knowledge about the United States.

Read the clues and then press the button that you believe is the correct answer.

To begin, click the button below.

**8.** Highlight **Directions**. From the Options menu, select **Text Style**, and change the alignment to **Center**. When you are finished, your card should resemble Figure 18-2.

**FIGURE 18-2**
Directions Card

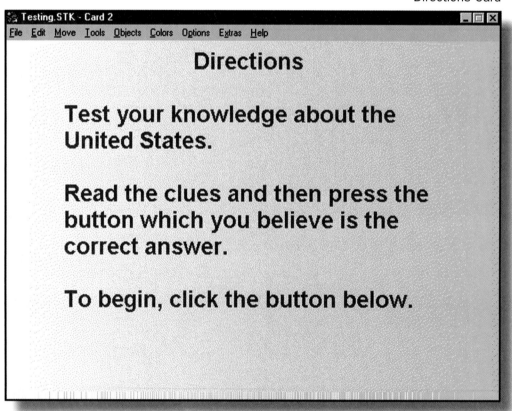

**9.** Add a button. Name the button **Start Here**. Make the button's name **white** and the background **dark blue**. Move the button to the bottom center of the card.

**10.** From the Actions window, select **Next card** and choose a transition. Then, select **Testing functions**, as shown in Figure 18-3.

**11.** Select **ask for the user's name**, as shown in Figure 18-4.

**12.** Test the button. When you click it, you should see the window shown in Figure 18-5.

(continued on next page)

**FIGURE 18-3**
Testing Functions Window

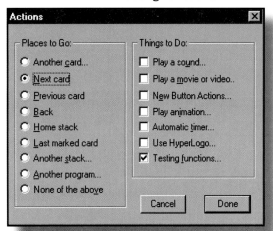

**FIGURE 18-4**
Testing Window with "ask for the user's name" Selected

**FIGURE 18-5**
"Hello, please enter your name" Window

**13.** Key your name and click **OK**. HyperStudio will move you to the next card. Your finished Card 2 should look like Figure 18-6.

**14.** Save the stack. Leave the stack open.

FIGURE 18-6
Directions Card with Start Here Button

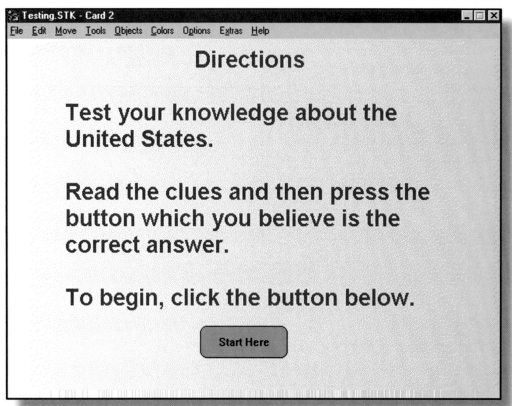

# *Using the Correct and Incorrect Answer Functions*

In order to be able to score the test results, you will need to identify incorrect and correct answers. Typically, buttons are used to supply a series of answers, similar to a multiple-choice question. Each question should have one or more correct answers. If a user chooses a correct answer, HyperStudio will add 1 point to the user's score. An incorrect answer adds 0 to the score.

You will specify the next card action for every testing function button. As soon as the user selects a response, he or she is moved automatically to the next card. The same transition and speed should be specified for each button on a card. You will not include navigation that takes the user back, since you don't want the responses to be changed. Often, sound cues are included with the buttons.

# STEP-BY-STEP ▷ 18.2

1. With the Testing stack open, move to Card 3 to create a question card.

2. Add clip art to the card by using the **Lasso Selector** tool to select the state of Florida from the USA file. While the Florida clip art is selected, choose **Scale** from the Effects menu, and resize the clip art to **150**%. Move it to the upper right side of the card.

3. Add a nonscrollable text object with a frame, dark text color, and a **yellow** background. Use **Arial**, **Plain**, size **20**, and **left** aligned text. Move the text field to the left side of the card

and resize it to fill the entire depth of the card. In the text field, key the following:

**Home of the Everglades, this state is known as the Sunshine State. It is also home to the satellite and missile-launching center of Cape Canaveral.**

**What is the name of this state?**

Your card should resemble Figure 18-7.

(continued on next page)

**FIGURE 18-7**
Florida Question Card with Text and Clip Art

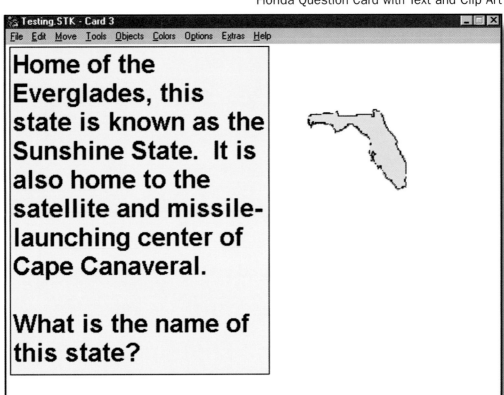

4. Add a button to the card. Name the button **Florida**. Match the button background to the **yellow** text field background. Make the button's name a dark color. Place it below the clip art of the state.

5. From the Actions window, choose **Next card** and select a transition. Then choose **Testing functions**, as shown in Figure 18-8.

6. Select **be a correct answer** from the Testing window, as shown in Figure 18-9. Click **OK**.

7. Copy the button and paste it. Move the new button directly below the first button. Change the new button's name to **California**. Click on the **Actions** button. From the Actions window, select **Testing functions** to deselect it and then select it again. Choose **be an incorrect answer**, and click **OK**.

8. Select **Play a sound** from the Actions window. Use the **Boing** sound. Your Actions window should look like Figure 18-10. Click **Done**.

**FIGURE 18-8**
Next Card and Testing Functions Selected

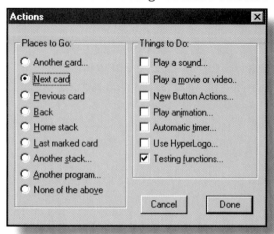

**FIGURE 18-9**
"Be a correct answer" Selected

**FIGURE 18-10**
Play a Sound and Testing Functions Selected

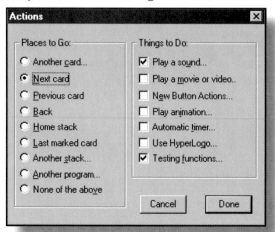

**9.** Copy the California button and paste two more times, moving the new buttons below the existing buttons. Change the names of the new buttons to **Alaska** and **Texas**. Arrange the buttons alphabetically so that they are consistent on each card. Your card should look like Figure 18-11.

**10.** Test your buttons. Each button should move you to Card 4. When you choose the wrong answer, you should hear the Boing sound.

**11.** Return to Card 3, if necessary. Save your stack as **Testing1**. Leave it open.

**12.** Copy and paste the card. Using the **Square Selector** tool, select the clip art and delete it.

Add clip art of the state of Texas from the USA file. Move it to the same location as the state of Florida, making sure it is above the buttons.

**13.** Change the text object background color to red. Delete the existing text and key the following:

**This state was once a part of Mexico. Known as the Lone Star State, it is only second to Alaska in size.**

**What is the name of this state?**

(continued on next page)

**FIGURE 18-11**
Four Buttons on Question Card

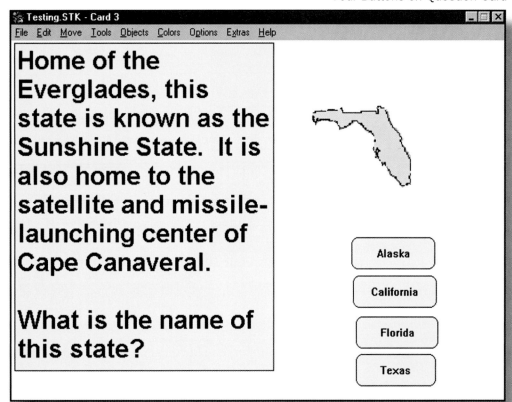

**14.** Using Figure 18-12, change the buttons in the following ways:

- Change the buttons' background color to red.

- Change the testing function to make the Texas button the correct answer and all other buttons the incorrect answers.

- Use the Boing sound only with incorrect answers. Do not play a sound with the correct answer.

**15.** Test all the buttons and make changes, as necessary.

**16.** Save your stack as **Testing2**. Leave the stack open.

**FIGURE 18-12**
Texas Question Card

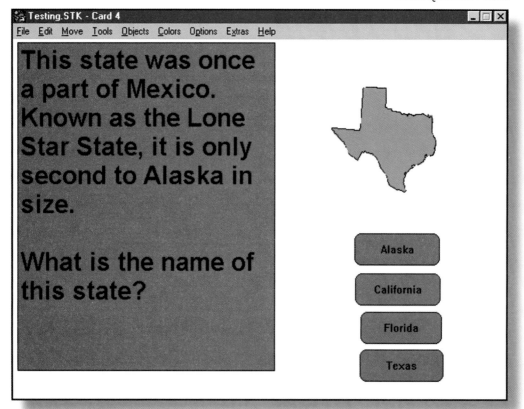

## CHALLENGE ACTIVITY ⟹ 18.1

With the Testing2 stack open, create the last two state cards, Alaska and California.

- Change the clip art to the appropriate state. Scale the state's size, if necessary.

- Adjust the button actions so that the correct answer action is with the correct state name button. Keep the buttons in alphabetical order.

- Use the Boing sound only with incorrect answers.

For Alaska, use green as the background color for the text and buttons. Use the following text:

**The largest of the states, it is known as the Land of the Midnight Sun. It was originally purchased from Russia and later became the 49th state.**

**What is the name of this state?**

For California, use red as the background color for the text and buttons. Use the following text:

**Known as the Golden State, it was colonized by Spain. This state is famous for the Gold Rush, which began in 1848 at Sutter's Mill.**

**What is the name of this state?**

Create a final card to let users know that they have completed the quiz.

Place a Quit button on the final card in the stack. Select your own design for the background of this card. Key:

**You have completed the quiz.**
**Thank you for your time.**

Save the stack as **Testing3**.

**HINT:**

Your last two state cards should look like Figures 18-13 and 18-14.

**FIGURE 18-13**
Alaska Card

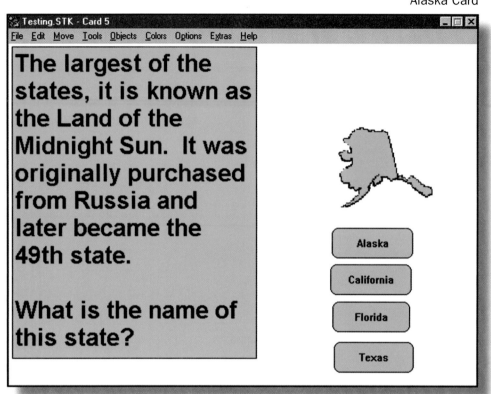

**FIGURE 18-14**
California Card

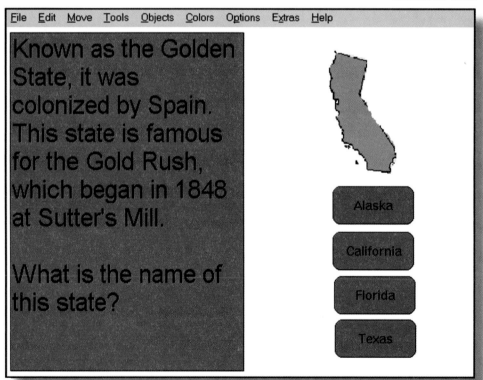

# *Using the Test Results Function*

Once your user has completed the testing stack, you will need a means to read and interpret the test results. When the user leaves the test stack, HyperStudio scans the stack and writes a text file with the results. The user can leave the stack either by quitting HyperStudio, going to another stack, or linking to another program or application. You, therefore, should have a Quit button at the end of each testing stack.

The text file that HyperStudio creates is named *HSTest.txt*. The text file is stored in the same folder as the test stack. This file can be opened by any word processing program, including Windows Notepad and Macintosh Simple Text. The file is cumulative, that is all test results are added to this file until the file is deleted. If you are creating more than one test stack, store each in a different folder. That way, the HSTest.txt file will contain results for one test stack only. The text file will look similar to Figure 18-15.

The text file is read as follows:

**FIGURE 18-15**
Text Test Score

```
Testing2.STK
Marie
01/22/99        16:58:47
3
Alaska
4
Texas
5
Alaska
6
California
SCORE
1
4
-END-
```

- The first line, Testing2.stk, is the name of the stack.

- The next line shows the user's name.

- The third line indicates the date and time of the test.

- The next two lines show a card number and corresponding correct answer button name. Each question card is identified by number and correct answer button.

- After all questions have been identified, the word SCORE indicates that the following lines show scoring statistics.

- Below SCORE is the number of correct responses. In Figure 18-15, only one question was answered correctly.

- The last number indicates the number of items to which the user responded. In Figure 18-15, the user responded to all four questions.

- End marks the end of this user's test.

In the Testing stack you created in Step-by-Step 18.1 and 18.2, there were four card questions and four possible correct responses.

A score of :
4
4
would mean 4 correct responses out of 4 total responses.

A score of
3
4
would mean 3 correct responses out of 4 total responses.

If many users have trouble with the same question, you may need to change the question or replace it with a different question.

## STEP-BY-STEP ⟹ 18.3

**To complete this Step-by-Step, you must know how to open files in a word processing program.**

1. Open the **Testing3** stack, if necessary.

2. Enter a name that is not your own, and take the test.

3. The first time you take the test, answer all the questions correctly. Quit the stack.

4. Open the **Testing3** stack again. Use a different name. This time answer all the questions, but answer one of the questions incorrectly. Quit the stack.

5. To view the text file test results, open any word processing program. Locate and open the **HSTest.txt** file, which HyperStudio automatically saves in the same folder as the test stack. In this case, the file is stored in the Tests folder. Your score should look like Figure 18-16 for the correct answers test and Figure 18-17 for the incorrect answers test.

6. Close the word processing program.

 **HINT:**

If your files are not stored in the HyperStudio application on the hard drive, locate the Test folder where you store your stacks. If you cannot find the text file, run a Find on your hard drive for **HSTest.txt**.

**FIGURE 18-16**
Correct Test Answers

```
Testing2.STK
Don
01/22/99        17:39:34
3
Florida
4
Texas
5
Alaska
6
California
SCORE
4
4
-END-
```

**FIGURE 18-17**
Incorrect Test Answers

```
Testing2.STK
Willie
01/22/99        17:50:02
3
California
4
Texas
5
Alaska
6
California
SCORE
3
4
-END-
```

# Creating Passwords

The Preferences window allows you to specify a password for a stack. Most of the stacks that you create for classroom use will not include password protection. However, a testing stack presents a good opportunity to use a password. Password protection will ensure that no one has the ability to alter your stack. For password protection to work, you must select Lock stack from the Preferences window, as shown in Figure 18-18.

When a stack is locked, the Main Menu is changed so that the user cannot access most of the tools used to create and edit a stack. In order to unlock a stack that is password protected, the user must enter the password in the Stack password field in the Preferences window.

Remember, a locked stack that is password protected can only be unlocked using the password. Do not forget the password you have chosen.

**FIGURE 18-18**
Password Specified and Lock Stack Selected

---

STEP-BY-STEP ⟹ 18.4

1. Create a new stack. Use any card size. Create a new folder for the stack. Name the folder **Tests2**, and name the stack **Survey**.

2. Select **Preferences** from the Edit menu.

3. In the Stack password field, key **Secret**. Select **Lock stack**.

(continued on next page)

---

**INTERNET**

Increasingly, the Internet is being used for commerce. Products and services are bought and sold. Banking and financial transactions are being conducted via the Internet. To safeguard these transactions, many security features have developed to protect the sensitive data. Among the security features are digital encryption, digital signatures, and firewalls.

**4.** Click **OK**. You will notice that your card menu is altered. The menubar will look like Figure 18-19. You will not be able to make changes to the stack.

**5** From the Edit menu, select **Preferences**.

**6.** You will see the screen in Figure 18-20. Notice that the check boxes are gray, which means you cannot change them. Key in your password, **Secret**. The boxes will become available to change. Deselect **Lock stack** to unlock the stack, and click **OK**. The full menubar should be restored.

**7.** Save the stack. Leave the stack open.

**FIGURE 18-19**
Menubar when Locked Stack is Selected

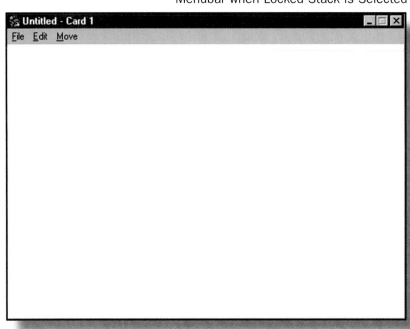

**FIGURE 18-20**
Preferences Window when Stack is Locked

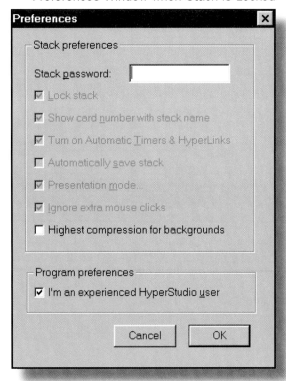

# Data Collection

HyperStudio's testing function is also useful for data collection. You can collect data for general information purposes or for opinions surveys. For instance, you might create a stack to gather data about the opinions of your classmates regarding ethical issues, school issues, or news items of interest to you. When using a stack for a survey or data collection, you probably would not want to ask respondents to enter their names.

In a survey, there may be no wrong answers, although there may be preferred responses. In order to record the button choices that the user makes, you must choose a correct or incorrect answer response. You must decide which answers are preferred and select them as correct answers. You can have more than one correct response for each question in your survey.

Since you want respondents to give you their best responses, you would not want to use sounds to reinforce answers.

In Step-by-Step 18.5, you will prepare a survey stack to determine how people feel about ethical issues and technology.

### STEP-BY-STEP ⟹ 18.5

**SCANS**

1. With the Survey stack open, add two cards. Move to Card 1 and create a Title card. Use the **prchment** background from the HSArt folder or one of your own choice. Add **What is Ethical?** as the title of your stack. Add clip art that represents technology to your Title card. Include a button to move to the next card. Your Title card should resemble Figure 18-21.

(continued on next page)

**FIGURE 18-21**
Survey Title Card

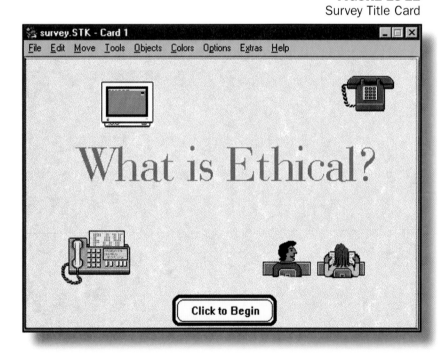

**2.** On Card 2, create a background of your own choice. Add a transparent text object and key the following:

**Directions:**

**On each card you will be asked a question. Please select the answer that you agree with the most. There are no wrong answers. Please complete the three questions. Thank you for taking this survey.**

**3.** Provide a button for the user to move to the next card. Name the button **Start Here** or some other beginning direction. The Directions card should resemble Figure 18-22.

**4.** Create a background for Card 3. Add a graphic object and key:

**A friend has a computer game that you like to play. You ask to copy the game. Your friend says, "No."**

**What should you do?**

**5.** Add a button. Name the button: **Buy the game**. Make the button attractive and have it match your text field. Move the button to the bottom center of the card, as shown in Figure 18-23. Make the

**FIGURE 18-22**
Survey Directions Card

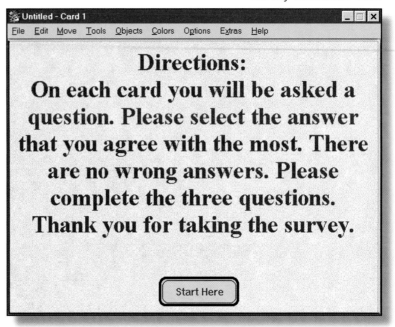

**FIGURE 18-23**
Survey Card 3

button action, **Next card** and **Testing function**. Choose **be a correct answer**.

## STEP-BY-STEP 18.5 CONTINUED

6. Copy the button and paste it twice. Move one button to the left of the Buy the game button and the other button to the right. Name one of the buttons: **Copy it anyway**. Name the other button: **Get a new friend**. Change both of the buttons to be incorrect answers. Your card should resemble Figure 18-23.

7. Copy and paste the card. Change the background, the color of the text object, and the color of the buttons. Key:

   **You receive an insulting and upsetting message on-line. You do not know who sent it.**

   **What should you do?**

8. The three buttons should read:

   **Ignore it**
   **Tell an adult**
   **Send a nasty response**

   Ignore it and send a nasty response are incorrect responses, while tell an adult is a correct response. Your card should resemble Figure 18-24.

**FIGURE 18-24**
Survey Card 4

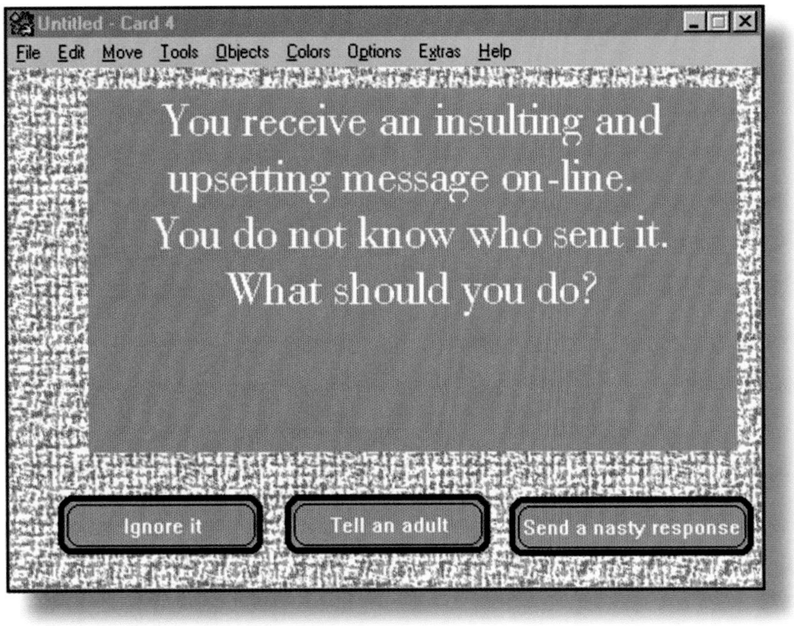


(continued on next page)

**9.** Copy and paste the card. Change the background, the color of the text field, and the color of the buttons. Key:

**You receive an e-mail message that contains embarrassing information about one of your classmates.**

**What should you do?**

**10.** The three buttons should read:

**Ignore it**
**Tell an adult**
**Send it to a friend**

Both ignore it and tell an adult are correct responses. Your card should resemble Figure 18-25.

**11.** Add a card to the stack. Place a Quit button on the card. In the text field, thank the user for taking the survey. Ask the user to press the Quit button. Your card should resemble Figure 18-26.

**FIGURE 18-25**
Survey Card 5

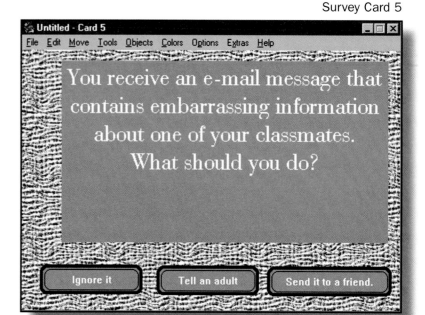

**FIGURE 18-26**
Survey Card 6

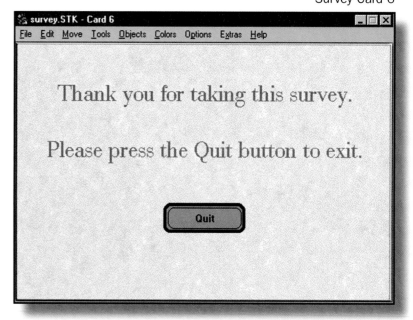

 **TIP**

In a survey, there may be more than one "correct" response. Some surveys would have no correct or incorrect responses. However, to collect the data, you must assign each button a correct or incorrect response function.

**12.** Save the stack as **Survey1**.

**13.** Test all the buttons, making any necessary changes.

**14.** Select **Preferences** from the Edit menu. Key **Secret** in the Stack password field. Select **Lock stack**. Save and close the stack.

**15.** Open the **Survey1** stack from the Tests2 folder. Take the survey, answering all the questions.

**16.** Open the **HSTest.txt** document in a word processing program. Your test results should be similar to Figure 18-27.

**17.** Print the survey test results. Close the word processing application.

**FIGURE 18-27**
Survey Results

```
survey.STK

01/23/99      14:19:39
3
Buy the Game
4
Tell an adult
5
Tell an adult
SCORE
3
3
-END-
```

# *Summary*

In this lesson, you learned that:

◼ You can use HyperStudio stacks to gather information and administer tests.

◼ You can personalize a stack by requesting a user's name with the testing function.

◼ You can attach button actions to score correct or incorrect answers.

◼ You can use a word processing program to view test results from a testing stack.

◼ You can attach other button actions to testing function buttons.

◼ You must leave the test stack for the test results to be compiled.

◼ You can create passwords to control use and editing of a stack.

## VOCABULARY

Data collection

Locking stacks

Passwords

Testing function

Test results function

User's name function

## LESSON 18 REVIEW QUESTIONS

### TRUE/FALSE

**Circle the T if the statement is true or F if it is false.**

**T  F**    **1.** To record the answers to a stack, you must choose be a correct answer.

**T  F**    **2.** Testing function buttons should not have any other actions attached.

**T  F**    **3.** To get the test results from a testing stack, you must exit the stack first.

**T  F**    **4.** You should provide directions for a user in a testing stack.

**T  F**    **5.** You should include the user's name function on a survey stack.

**T  F**    **6.** You must give a sound clue for testing function buttons.

### MULTIPLE CHOICE

**Circle the letter of the item that is the best response for each of the following statements.**

1. Adding a password to a stack:
   **A.** prevents editing
   **B.** does not prevent editing
   **C.** can be done through the Tools menu on the toolbar
   **D.** none of the above

2. The test results are:
   **A.** in the stack folder
   **B.** accessed through a word processing program
   **C.** named HSTest.txt
   **D.** all of the above

3. When choosing the button actions for a testing function button, you can choose:
   A. be a correct answer
   B. be an incorrect answer
   C. ask for the user's name
   D. all of the above

4. To view test results, you must leave the test stack by:
   A. quitting HyperStudio
   B. linking to another stack
   C. linking to another application
   D. all of the above

5. To personalize a stack, you can:
   A. add a password
   B. ask the user's name
   C. add a sound to the answer buttons
   D. none of the above

6. To find out the test results, you must:
   A. leave the stack
   B. open a different stack
   C. ask the user's name
   D. all of the above

## COMPLETION

**Answer the questions below in the space provided.**

1. Name several uses for a test stack.

2. What does the user's name function do?

3. Describe how you add a password to a stack.

4.  Describe how you remove a password from a stack.




5.  Name the four button action options in a testing function.

    a.

    b.

    c.

    d.

6.  Explain the procedure to access the results from your test stack.




7.  Explain what each line means in the following test stack results:

    | Line 1  | Question.Stk      |
    |---------|-------------------|
    | Line 2  | 2/14/98   11:15:45 |
    | Line 3  | 3                 |
    | Line 4  | Atom              |
    | Line 5  | 4                 |
    | Line 6  | Nucleus           |
    | Line 7  | 5                 |
    | Line 8  | Protein           |
    | Line 9  | SCORE             |
    | Line 10 | 2                 |
    | Line 11 | 3                 |

## LESSON 18 PROJECT 18.1

1.  Create a testing stack, using a topic of your choice. Include the following:

    ■ Title card

    ■ directions card that includes a button to record the user's name

    ■ thank you card with Quit button

    ■ at least three question cards containing at least two buttons per card with testing function and next card actions

    ■ appropriate graphics, backgrounds, and navigation

    ■ password protection and a locked stack

2.  Save the stack as **Mytest** in the **Project 18** folder. Print the stack. Take the test at least three times with different names. Print the test results.

## LESSON 18 PROJECT 18.2

1.  Create a survey stack, using a topic of your choice. Include the following:

    ■ Title card

    ■ directions card

    ■ thank you card with Quit button

    ■ at least three survey questions containing at least two buttons per card with testing function and next card actions

    ■ appropriate graphics, backgrounds, and navigation

    ■ password protection and a locked stack

2.  Save the stack as **Info** in the **Project18** folder. Print the stack. Take the survey at least three times. Print the test results. (NOTE: The test results are cumulative. You should see the results from Project 18.1, as well as the results from Project 18.2.)

## CRITICAL THINKING ACTIVITY

Select several topics that would be a good basis for an informational survey. Choose two of the topics and develop a set of ten questions and possible responses for each topic.

Describe the process you would use to create a group survey with each group member completing a different set of questions. Each section must eventually be linked.

# MYSTERY THEATER

**Upon completion of this lesson, you will be able to:**

■ Create actions when arriving at a card.

■ Create actions when leaving a card.

■ Use the Hide/Show NBA to create pop-up effects.

■ Import images from digital cameras.

■ Import images from scanners.

■ Hide card number from stack name.

🕐 **Estimated Time: 2 hours**

## Creating Special Effects

You can use HyperStudio to create games and add interesting effects to your stacks. In this lesson you will practice having images and text appear and disappear from the cards. You will create a Mystery Theater tour to practice this effect.

## Arriving at Card/Leaving Card

The About this Card option on the Objects menu allows you to program certain actions when arriving at or leaving a card. This allows you to hide some parts of the card such as text fields or graphic objects so that when you open the card they are invisible until an action is performed.

# STEP-BY-STEP ⟹ 19.1

1. Create a new stack. Use the standard card size. Use the **Paint Bucket** tool to fill the card with black.

2. Using the **Draw Filled** option, choose a **dark gray** color and draw a rectangle that looks like a door. Repeat this process, drawing a smaller rectangle and filling it with **black**, as shown in Figure 19-1.

(continued on next page)

**FIGURE 19-1**
Door on Card 1

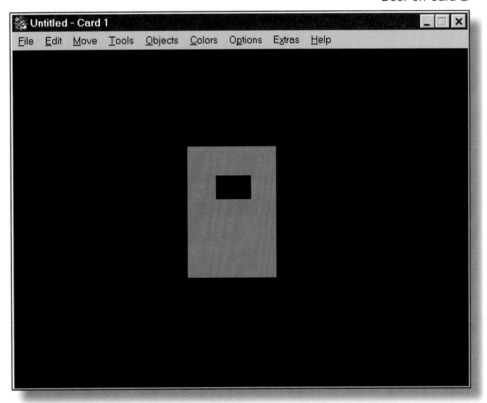

Add a text object for the title. The object should not be scrollable or have a frame. Make the background **black** and the text **gray**. Use the font **Architect**, **bold**, **24**, and **centered**. Key **Mystery Theater**, as shown in Figure 19-2.

3. Create an invisible button that covers the door. Make the button action **Next card**. Use an **Iris close**, **Slow** transition.

4. Add a card. Add clip art from the **Medialib** folder on the HyperStudio CD-ROM. Select

**Clipart**, **thtrcrtn** and the **curtain1** file. Size it to fit the card. Card 2 should look like Figure 19-3.

5. Add a graphic object to Card 2. From the HyperStudio CD-ROM, select **Medialib**, **Clipart**, and the **Rockyif** file. Select the stars part of the card, as shown in Figure 19-4.

(continued on page 404)

 **TIP**

Macintosh users should select the **Rocky interface** file.

**FIGURE 19-2**
Mystery Theater

**FIGURE 19-3**
Theater Curtain

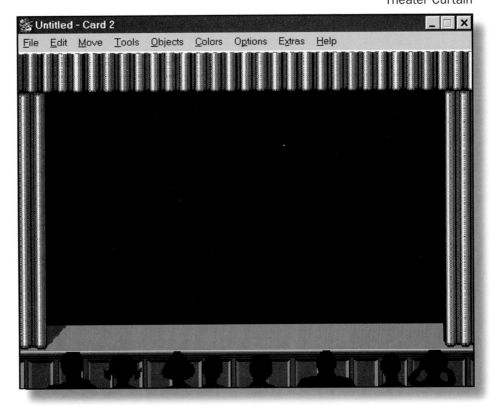

**FIGURE 19-4**
Rockyif Stars

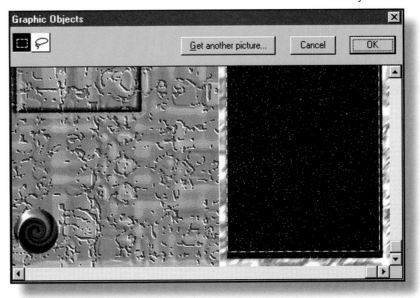

**6.** Stretch the graphic selection to fit in the black space between the curtains and stage, as shown in Figure 19-5.

**7.** Add a text object to Card 2. Place the text object in the center of the card. Name the text field **Welcome**. Make the background transparent and deselect **Draw frame**. Make the text **light gray**. Use the **LightWave** font, **Plain**, size **16**, **centered**. Key:

**Welcome to the Mystery Theater.... Click anywhere to begin the journey...**

Your card should look like Figure 19-6.

**8.** From the Objects menu, select About this Card, as shown in Figure 19-7.

**9.** In the Things to do when section, select **arriving at this card**, as shown in Figure 19-8.

(continued on page 406)

**FIGURE 19-5**
Stars Graphic

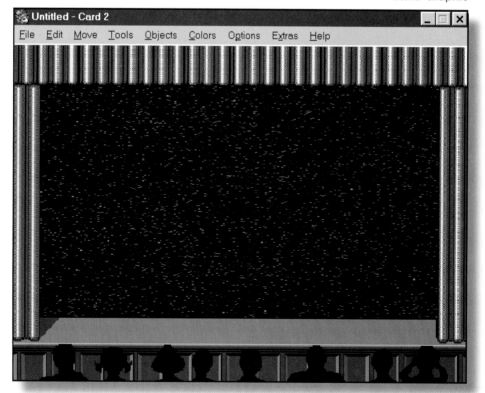

**FIGURE 19-6**
Welcome Text

**FIGURE 19-7**
About this Card

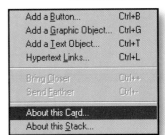

**FIGURE 19-8**
Arriving at This Card

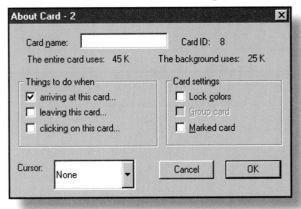

**4 0 5**

**10.** From the Actions window, select **New Button Actions**, as shown in Figure 19-9.

**11.** Select HideShw2 NBA, as shown in Figure 19-10.

**12.** Click **Use this NBA**.

**FIGURE 19-9**
Actions Window

**FIGURE 19-10**
HideShw2 NBA

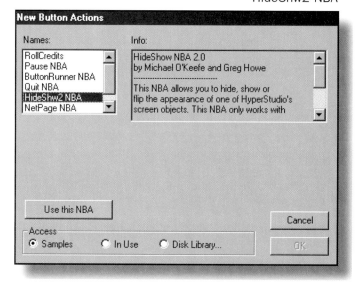

**13.** Key **Welcome** as the name of the object. Select **Text object** and select **Show it**, as shown in Figure 19-11. Click **Show Effect**. Select the **Dissolve Medium** transition and click **OK**.

**14.** Click **OK** twice, then click **Done**. From the About Card - 2 window, select **leaving this card**.

**15.** Select **New Button Actions**. Select **HideShw2 NBA** and click **Use this NBA**. Key **Welcome** as the name of the text object. Select **Text object** and select **Hide it**, as shown in Figure 19-12. Click **Show Effect**.

**16.** Select the **Fastest** transition and **Fast** speed. Click **OK** three times, then click **Done** and **OK**.

**17.** Return to **Browse** mode. Move to Card 1 and try the effects. The text object should be hidden when you open the card and appear while you watch.

**HINT:**

You can return to Browse mode by pressing **Shift + Tab**.

**18.** Edit the text field. Give the text field a **Next card** action. Use the **Iris open** transition effect and **Slow** speed.

(continued on next page)

**FIGURE 19-11**
Show It

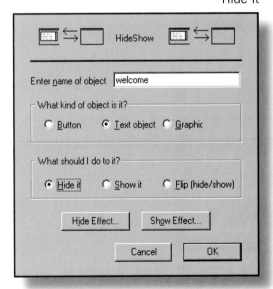

**FIGURE 19-12**
Hide It

**19.** Save the stack as **Mystery**.

**20.** Copy Card 2. Paste the card. Delete the text object on Card 3.

 **HINT:**

To delete the text object, select it with the **Arrow (Edit)** tool or the **Text Object** tool and press the **Delete** key on the keyboard.

**21.** Add a graphic object. From the HyperStudio CD-ROM, navigate to the **photglry** folder, select **people**, and the **Womanlvs** file. Crop a close-up of the face, as shown in Figure 19-13.

**22.** From the corner of the graphic reduce the size until it is about the size shown in Figure 19-14.

**23.** Click outside the graphic object. In the Graphic Appearance window, name the graphic **Woman**.

**24.** From the Objects menu, choose **About this Card**. Deselect and then select **arriving at this card**. Deselect and then select **New Button Actions**. Choose **HideShw2 NBA**. Click **Use this NBA**.

**25.** In the object name field, key **Woman**. Select **Graphic**. Select **Show it**, as shown in Figure 19-15. Click **OK**.

(continued on page 410)

**FIGURE 19-13**
Womanlvs Graphic

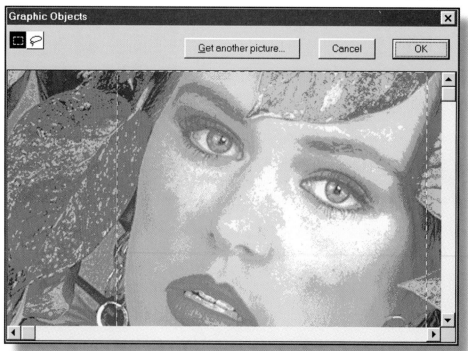

**FIGURE 19-14**
Card 3

**FIGURE 19-15**
Show It

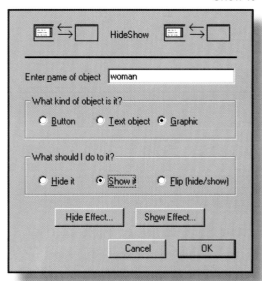

**26.** Return to the About Card - 3 window. Deselect and then select **leaving this card**. Follow the procedure from the steps above to hide the graphic when leaving the card.

**27.** Save the stack.

**28.** With the **Arrow (Edit)** tool or the **Graphic Object** tool selected, double click on the graphic. Click **Actions**. Select **Next card**. Select **Iris Open**, **Slow** for the transition effect.

**29.** Add a card. Use the **Paint Bucket** tool to make the card **black**.

**30.** Add a graphic to the card from the **HSArt** folder, **Dingbat2** file. Use the **Rectangle Selector** tool to capture the snowflake, as shown in Figure 19-16.

**31.** Place the snowflake in the middle of the black card. Name the graphic **flake**.

**32.** Save the stack as **Mystery1** and keep it open.

**FIGURE 19-16**
Dingbat2, Snowflake

## CHALLENGE ACTIVITY 19.1

**1.** Use the HideShow procedure described in Step-by-Step 19.1 to make the snowflake materialize upon arriving at the card.

**2.** Use the HideShow procedure to make the snowflake disappear when leaving the card.

**3.** Give the snowflake graphic the action of **Next card** using the **Iris Close**, **Slow** transition.

**4.** Test the results.

**5.** Save the stack as **Mystery2**. Keep the stack open.

# Creating a Sense of Perspective

Using HyperStudio's many graphics tools, you can create effects and perspectives by the way you arrange your graphic images. To create a perspective of a diminishing horizon, you can arrange graphics in a way that they get smaller and closer together. You will see how this works in Step-by-Step 19.2.

# Pop up Objects/Hide Show NBA

You have practiced using the Hide/Show New Button Action when arriving or leaving a card. You can also use this New Button Action to reveal text and graphics when the user takes action. For instance, the user may click on a certain word in the text to make a graphic appear. This is similar to using a hypertext link. Alternately, the user may click on a graphic object to make a text field appear.

In Step-by-Step 19.2, you will continue to enhance the Mystery Theater tour.

## STEP-BY-STEP ⟹ 19.2

1. Add a card to the **Mystery2** stack. Fill the card with **black**.

2. Add clip art. From the HSArt folder, select the **Dingbat2** file. Use the **Lasso Selector** tool to select the tall column on the left, as shown in Figure 19-17.

(continued on next page)

**FIGURE 19-17**
Selected Column

**411**

**3.** Move the column to the left, about an inch from the left border, as shown in Figure 19-18.

**4.** Use the **Square Selector** tool to select the column. Copy and paste it. Move it to the other side of the card, as shown in Figure 19-19.

**5.** Paste the column two more times. Use the corner arrow to reduce the height of the pasted columns, and place the smaller columns in the position shown in Figure 19-20.

(continued on page 414)

**FIGURE 19-18**
First Column

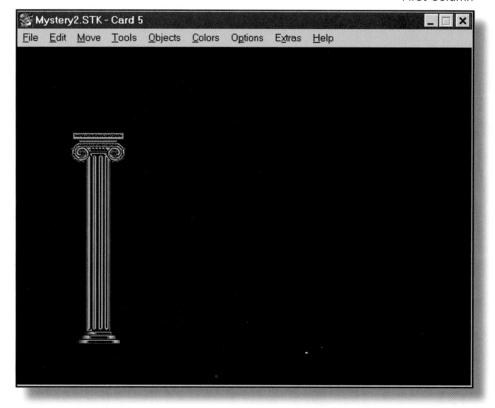

**FIGURE 19-19**
Two Columns

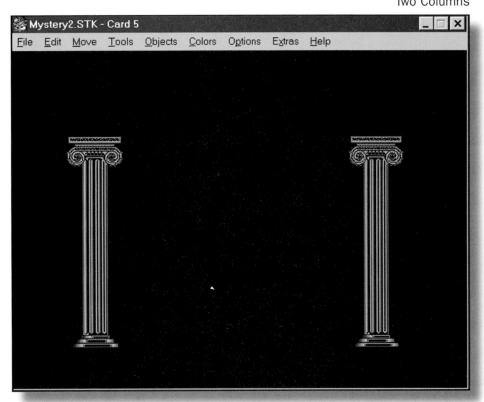

**FIGURE 19-20**
Four Columns

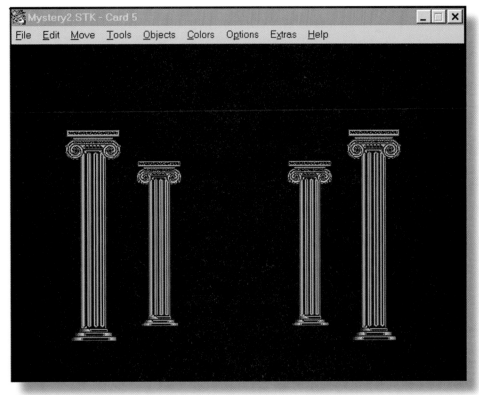

**6.** Using the **Square Selector** tool, select one of the smaller columns. Copy and paste it. Resize and place it so that it matches Figure 19-21. Repeat the process to create the sixth column. Notice the sense of depth created by these three sets of columns.

**7.** Create a small door in the background using **Draw Filled** and the **Rectangle** tool with **medium gray** selected, so that your card resembles Figure 19-22.

**HINT:**

If any white or gray bleeds through, use the **Eraser** tool and **black**. To make a straight erasure, hold down the **Shift** key while erasing.

**8.** Save the stack as **Mystery3**.

**9.** Add an oval button to Card 5. Name the button **Click Here!** Make the button background **black** and the letters **gray**. Place the button on the bottom center of the card. The button action for the button should be **Next card**. Use the **Iris close**, **Slow** transition.

**10.** Select **About this Card** from the Objects menu. Select **arriving at this card**. Select **New Button Actions**. Select **HideShw2 NBA**. Click **Use the NBA**.

**11.** Key **Click Here!** as the name of the button. Select **Button** and **Show it**, as shown in Figure 19-23. Click **Show Effect**. Select **Dissolve**, **Medium** from the Show Item Transitions window, and click **OK**.

**FIGURE 19-21**
Six Columns

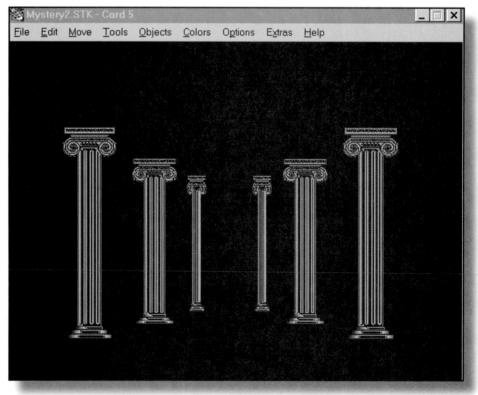

**FIGURE 19-22**
Final Columns with Door

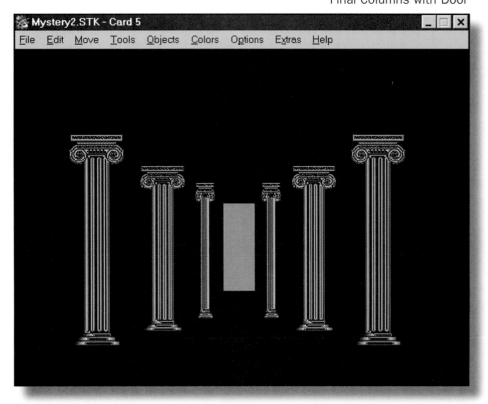

12. Return to the About this Card window. Select leaving this card.

13. Follow the procedure that you have learned to hide the button when leaving the card.

14. Save the stack as **Mystery4**. Keep the stack open.

**FIGURE 19-23**
Show Button Window

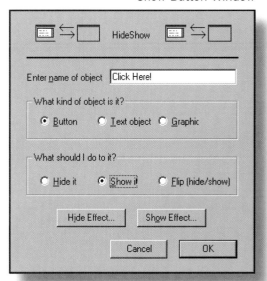

## Digital Cameras/Scanners

You have imported images into HyperStudio from the HyperStudio CD-ROM, from the Internet, and from other CD-ROM resources. In Step-by-Step 19.3, you will be able to use images from a digital camera or from a scanner.

The digital camera is an excellent source for pictures or images to be used in HyperStudio. You can either use pictures you have taken with a digital camera or you may plan a project and take pictures with a digital camera to meet your project's goals.

Once you have taken the picture, you can store it on a floppy disk or on the computer's hard drive. Some digital cameras store the images directly to a floppy disk. If you are using a Windows computer, you must use IBM-formatted disks in the digital camera. If you are using a computer in a classroom or computer lab situation, you must follow your instructor's procedures for storing digital images. Wherever the image is stored, it can be imported into HyperStudio as a graphic object, as clip art, or as a background.

If you have access to a scanner, you can scan pictures from books, calendars, drawings, or any other medium that will lay flat on the scanner bed. Your instructor will explain how to use the scanner that is in your environment.

Once you have accessed the scanner and followed the scanning directions, you can choose to save the scanned image to a disk or folder on the hard drive or you can import the image directly into HyperStudio. A scanned image that is brought directly into HyperStudio can be imported as a background, added as clip art or a graphic object, or simply copied and pasted from the scanner's software into HyperStudio. If you do not want to save the image for any other use, copying and pasting will use less storage space, as the image will only be saved within the HyperStudio stack.

## STEP-BY-STEP ⟹ 19.3

If you do not have access to a digital camera or a scanner, substitute other images that are available to you to complete this Step-by-Step.

1. With the **Mystery4** stack open, add a new card after Card 5.

2. Scan an image or take a digital photo for a background on the new card.

**HINT:**

Large, color images use a lot of RAM memory. If you have limited memory, you should consider using smaller images or black and white line art.

**3.** Import a background for Card 6. Windows users should select **scanner or video** in response to "Where do you want to get your graphic?" Locate the scanned or digital camera image to use as the background. If possible, select or create an image that will add to the mystery theme of the stack, as shown in Figure 19-24. Select an image that works with the other backgrounds in the stack.

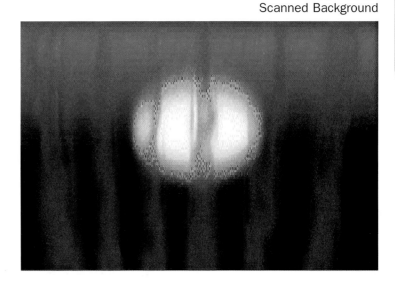

**FIGURE 19-24**
Scanned Background

**4.** Add a graphic object that is either a scanned image or a digital camera image. The object should coordinate with the background. Size the image so that some of the background is still visible, as shown in Figure 19-25, with the snake as the graphic object.

(continued on next page)

**FIGURE 19-25**
Card 6 with a Graphic Object

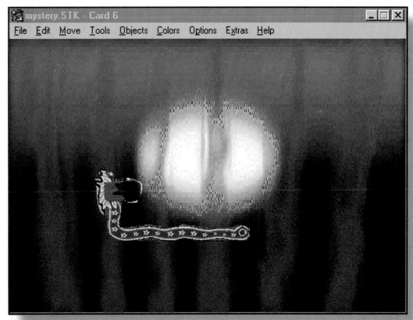

**5.** Click outside the graphic object. Name it **graphic1**.

**6.** Add a text object. Place it along the bottom of the card, or in another suitable location. The text object should not be scrollable and should not have a frame. Make the background transparent and select a text size and color that will be easily read. Key:

**Click on the word Secret to reveal a surprise. Click on the surprise to go to another surprise.**

**7.** Highlight the word **Secret**. Using the Options menu, select **Set Text Color** and make the word a different color, as shown in Figure 19-26.

**8.** With the word Secret still selected, choose **Hypertext Links** from the Objects menu, as shown in Figure 19-27.

**FIGURE 19-26**
Text with Secret in Different Color

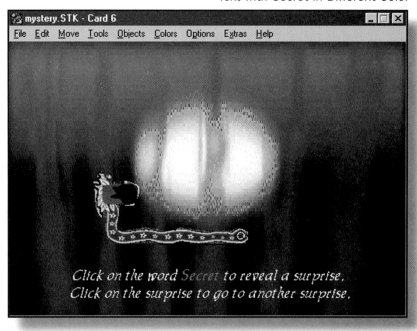

**FIGURE 19-27**
Hypertext Links

9. Choose **Add Link**, as shown in Figure 19-28.

10. Click **Actions**. Select **New Button Actions**. Select **HideShw2 NBA**. Click **Use this NBA**. Key the name of the graphic, **graphic1**. Select **Graphic**. Select **Show it**. Click **OK** twice and **Done** twice.

11. From the Objects menu, select **About this Card**. Select **leaving the card**. Select **New Button Actions**. Select **HideShw2 NBA**. Click **Use this NBA**. Key the name of the graphic, **graphic1**. Select **Graphic**. Select **Hide it**. Click **OK**, **OK**, **Done**, and **OK**.

12. Leave the card and then return to it. The object should be hidden. When you click on **Secret**, the object should appear.

**HINT:**

If the process does not work, go through it again. Check to be sure you have chosen the graphic and that you have spelled the name of the graphic exactly the same way as it is named. Go back and check the spelling of the graphic object if you are not sure. Repeat Steps 4 through 12, making sure to use the same graphic name throughout.

**FIGURE 19-28**
Add Link

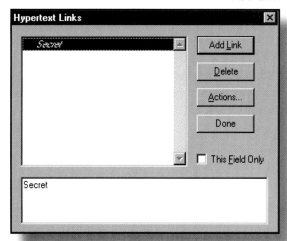

13. Add a **Next card** action to the graphic. Use **Iris close**, **Slow** for the transition.

14. Add a new card. Import a background using a scanned or digital camera image.

15. Add a graphic object from a scanned or digital camera image. You will use the graphic object to show a text object.

(continued on next page)

**16.** Click outside the graphic object. Click **Actions.** From the Actions window, select **New Button Actions**. Select **HideShw2 NBA**. Click **Use this NBA**. Key the name of the text object: **text1**. Select **Text object**. Select **Show it**, as shown in Figure 19-29. Select **OK**, **OK**, **Done**, and **OK**.

**17.** Add a text object. Name it **Text1**. Place it along the bottom of the card, or in another suitable location. The text object should not be scrollable and should not have a frame. Make the background transparent and select a text size and color that will be easily read. Key:

**Congratulations, you have completed the Mystery Theater tour.**

**Click Quit to exit or Begin to start over.**

Your card should resemble Figure 19-30.

**18.** Save the stack as **Mystery5**. Keep the stack open.

**FIGURE 19-29**
Graphic HideShow Window

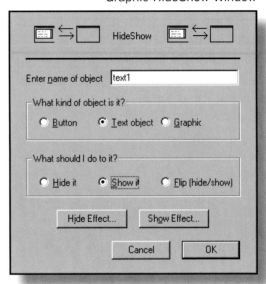

**FIGURE 19-30**
Card 7 with Graphic and Text Object

**CHALLENGE ACTIVITY** ⇒ **19.2**

1. With the Mystery5 stack open, complete the necessary steps to hide the text field when you leave the card.

2. Use Hypertext links to add actions to the words **Quit** and **Begin**. Quit should exit HyperStudio and Begin should take you to the first card in the stack.

3. Save the stack as **Mystery6**. Keep the stack open. Card 7 should resemble Figure 19-31.

**TIP**

It is a good idea to change the colors of the text links before you assign actions to them.

**FIGURE 19-31**
Card 7 with Hypertext Links

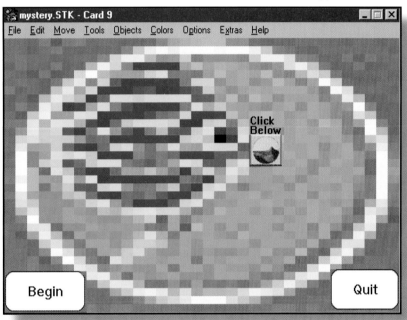

# *Hide Name of Stack and Card*

To create a more professional and clean presentation, you can hide the card number from the stack name displayed in the menubar. Since many stacks do not move in a linear fashion, stack users could be confused by card numbers. Also, when you have clear navigation from card to card, the user has no need to know the card number.

1. With the **Mystery6** stack open, go to the Preferences window. Deselect **Show card number with stack name**, as shown in Figure 19-32.

2. Test the stack. When everything works correctly hide the menubar. Save the stack as **Mystery7**.

**FIGURE 19-32**
Preferences Window

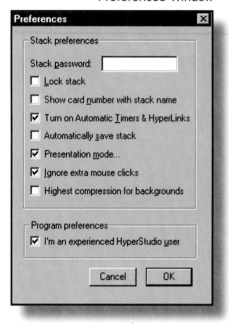

# Summary

In this lesson, you learned that:

■ You can automate actions when arriving at or leaving a card.

■ You can hide or show text objects, buttons, and graphic objects using the Hide/Show New Button Action.

■ You can create a sense of perspective by manipulating sizes and placement of objects.

■ You can use the Hide/Show NBA to create pop-up effects.

■ You can import backgrounds and graphics from digital cameras and scanners.

■ You can hide the card number from the stack name in the title bar.

## VOCABULARY

Digital camera                          Pop-up effect

Perspective                             Scanner

## LESSON 19 REVIEW QUESTIONS

### TRUE/FALSE

**Circle the T if the statement is true or F if it is false.**

T  F    **1.** You cannot use a graphic to show a text object.

T  F    **2.** You can use a word in a text object as a hypertext link.

T  F    **3.** You can use a hypertext link to show a graphic or text object.

T  F    **4.** Showing objects getting smaller and closer together gives an impression of a diminishing horizon.

T  F    **5.** The About this Card window is accessed through the Options menu.

### COMPLETION

**Answer the questions below in the space provided.**

**1.** What is the sequence for hiding a button when leaving a card?

**2.** How can you create perspective on a card using graphics?

**3.** What is the procedure for showing a text object when arriving at a card?

**4.** What is meant by a pop-up effect?

**5.** What is the procedure for importing a background from a scanned image?

**6.** How can you hide the card number from the stack name in the title bar?

## LESSON 19 PROJECT 19.1

**1.** Create a stack of at least six cards. Make your own mystery theater or game using the Hide/Show NBA to create pop-up effects. Include the following:

- a storyboard
- at least four things to do when arriving at this card
- at least four things to do when leaving this card
- at least one graphic that shows a text object
- at least one text object that shows a graphic
- at least one hypertext link that shows a graphic or text object
- one card with some perspective effect
- one card with a scanned picture, if a scanner is available
- one card with an image from a digital camera, if this resource is available

2. Thoroughly test your stack.

3. Print the stack.

4. Save the stack as **Popup**.

## CRITICAL THINKING ACTIVITY

Discuss different ways that you could create a sense of perspective in a stack. What type of graphics work well? For what purposes would perspective be useful?

# INTERNET PUBLISHING WITH HYPERSTUDIO

## OBJECTIVES

**Upon completion of this lesson, you will be able to:**

- Create a stack for the Internet.

- Apply the HyperStudio tips for an online stack.

- Use NetPage NBA to set up e-mail buttons.

- Use NetPage NBA to set up URL buttons.

- Use the Export WebPage extra to prepare stacks to go online.

- Use a web browser.

- Test the execution of the stack for a web browser.

🕐 **Estimated Time: 1 hour**

## *Introduction to the Internet*

You may have some experience with the Internet. For those of you with Internet access while you have been working on this text, you have accessed the Internet to find resources and perhaps to do some research. The Internet is an exceptional place for finding and sharing information and resources. Virtually anyone can put anything on the Internet. That is both a good and a bad thing. Remember, just because something is on the Internet doesn't necessarily make it true.

The Internet is a large communication system that connects computers worldwide. Part of the Internet is a smaller system called the World Wide Web, or WWW. If you are on the World Wide Web, you are on the Internet. But you can be on the Internet and not be on the World Wide Web. Think of the Internet as a map of all of the streets and highways in the entire world. Think of the WWW as selected freeways that are on the street maps.

Your school, your class, or even you personally can place a stack on the Internet to share with other people. HTML code is the language of the Internet. However, you do not need to know HTML code to prepare your stack for viewing on the Internet. HyperStudio includes some New Button Actions and some Extras that will translate the stack into HTML code for you.

To get to the Internet or WWW you will need to have access, like an on-ramp to the information highway. The access is gained through an Internet provider. There are many Internet providers. Some popular ones are America Online, Prodigy, and CompuServe. Your school or school district may have a site on the Internet. This is probably not through one of the larger providers mentioned above. If your school has an Internet site, your instructor may allow you to put your stacks on the school site.

Many businesses and organizations have sites and many people have home pages on the World Wide Web. These sites or home pages are like homes or stores on the map. A home page usually provides information about the person or organization that created the page. Home pages exist to share research, events, news, and opinions. Just like a good HyperStudio stack, a good home page will generally have a theme.

# Creating a Stack for the Internet

In this lesson, you will prepare and create a home page stack to go on the Internet. If you do not have access to the Internet, you can still participate in many of the activities in this lesson; complete the parts that you can. If you do not have Internet access, you will not be able to use the browser, access online information, or upload your stack. However, you can follow the step-by-steps to create a stack for the Internet that could be uploaded at another time when you have Internet access. Ask your instructor if you are not sure about your access to the Internet.

First, you will have to plan your stack. For this Step-by-Step, you will use the storyboard that was created for this lesson. You will see the storyboard when you begin Step-by-Step 20.1.

## Tips for HyperStudio Online Stacks

There are some important tips to keep in mind when creating a stack to go online. Some tips are technical, some improve the look of the stack, and some are for safety. If you are required to sign an acceptable online use agreement, you must also observe the conditions of that agreement.

### TECHNICAL

- Keep the size of the stack small. This will be important for memory considerations. Use a card size of about 535 x 300.

- Use the minimum number of colors since colors consume memory.

- Limit the number of sound files.

- QuickTime movies are not embedded in your stack. You should ask your instructor how to include them in your stack for Internet viewing.

### AESTHETICS/CONTENT

- Remember that the contents of your stack reflect directly on you. Someone seeing your stack on the Internet will not know what you are like, and they will form an impression of you by your content, how well the stack works, and how well it is planned and implemented.

- Use appropriate topics and graphics.

- Do not use foul or indecent language.

- Do not spread gossip or negative information about anyone.

### SAFETY

- Minors should generally not use a last name.

- Do not put your phone number or address on your home page.

- Do not put personal information on the Internet.

**427**

**SCANS**

**You must have Internet access for step one of Step-by-Step 20.1.**

1. Before you create your own stacks, review some of the stacks that others have created for the Internet. If you have access to the Internet, go to one of the following sites to view some very good sample stacks:

   http://www.hyperstudio.com

   http://www.mobot.org/PFG/

http://207.137.159.30/resource/ hsplugin/samples.html

The opening cards of several sample stacks are shown in Figure 20-1.

2. Create a new stack. Make the card size **512** by **342**, as shown in Figure 20-2. This is the closest to the recommended card size for Internet publishing.

**FIGURE 20-1**
Sample Stacks

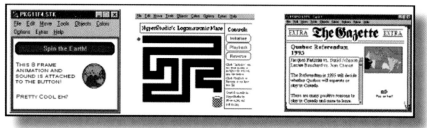

**FIGURE 20-2**
Card Size

**3.** Look at the storyboard/flowchart in Figure 20-3. This will be the blueprint for the stack. Use the first card as a combined Title and Main Menu card. Use a circular gradient progressing from **dark blue** to **light blue** for the card's background. (You may substitute colors of your choice for this activity.)

**FIGURE 20-3**
Web Stack Storyboard/Flowchart

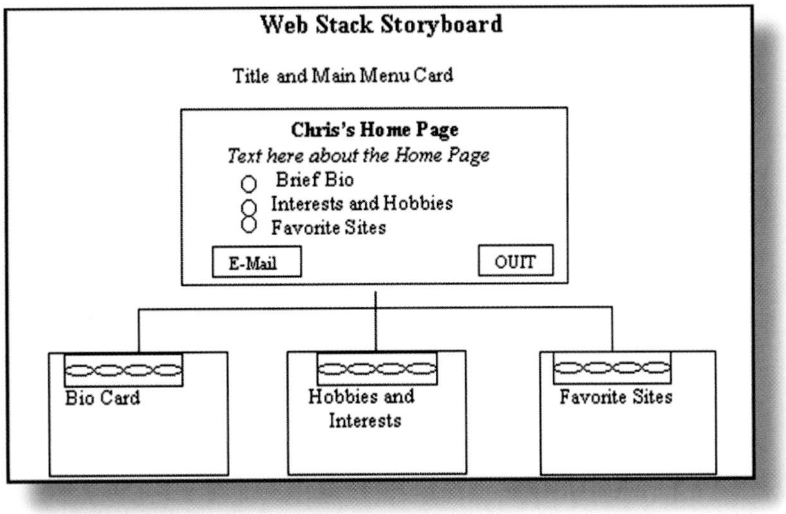

**Web Stack Storyboard**

Title and Main Menu Card

**Chris's Home Page**
*Text here about the Home Page*
○ Brief Bio
○ Interests and Hobbies
○ Favorite Sites

E-Mail                    QUIT

Bio Card          Hobbies and          Favorite Sites
                  Interests

**4.** Add a transparent text object without a frame for your title. Choose a font, a size, and **center** the text. Key:

**(Your first name)'s Home Page**

**5.** Add another transparent text object without a frame. Use the same font in a smaller size and key a few words such as:

**Welcome to my home page. I hope you will enjoy exploring these pages.**

**6.** Add a new card. Use a rectangular gradient for the background. Keep the same color choices as the Title card.

**TIP**

You may have to adjust the font size or font type to make the information fit.

(continued on next page)

**7.** Add a button. Name the button Main Menu. Make the button dark blue with white text. Make the button as small as possible so that the button's name just fits within the button. Position the button as shown in Figure 20-4. Do not assign an action yet.

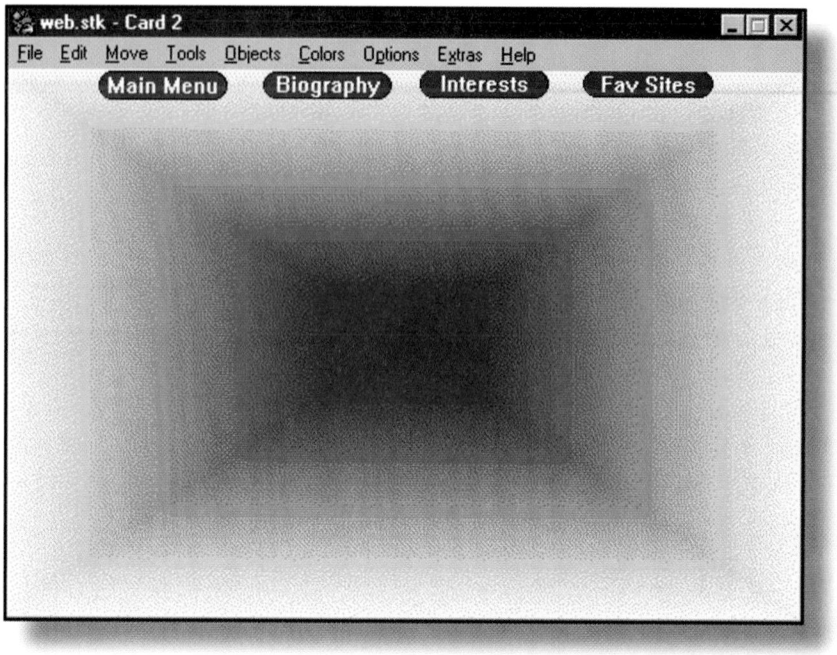

**8.** Copy and paste the button three times. Position them as shown in Figure 20-4. Name the other buttons **Biography**, **Interests**, **Fav Sites**.

**9.** Copy the card and paste it twice.

**10.** Return to Card 1.

**11.** Create a new folder. Name the folder **Net**. Save the stack as **Web** in the Net folder.

**FIGURE 20-4**
Card 2 with Buttons

web.stk - Card 2

File  Edit  Move  Tools  Objects  Colors  Options  Extras  Help

Main Menu    Biography    Interests    Fav Sites

**TIP**

For continuity, the same buttons will appear on each card.

**12.** Create three buttons for each of the topic pages in your stack. Use the shadowed rectangle for the buttons shape. Add two more buttons. Name one **Send Me An E-Mail**. Name the other button **Quit**. Do not attach any actions to these buttons at this time. The page should resemble Figure 20-5.

**FIGURE 20-5**
Finished Title and Main Menu Card

**13.** Attach the appropriate actions to the Topic buttons. You will assign an action to the Send Me An E-mail button later in the lesson. Use the **QuitNBA** for the Quit button.

- Card 2 is the **Biography** card.

- Card 3 is the **Interests** card.

- Card 4 is the **Favorite Sites** card.

**14.** Attach the appropriate actions to each of the buttons on each of the topic cards.

**15.** Save the stack as **Web1**.

(continued on next page)

TIP

For the button name that matches the card you are on, do not include a button action.

**431**

**16.** On the biography card (Card 2), add a scrolling text field on the right half of the card. Choose appropriate text and background colors. Key some information about yourself. Do not include personal information such as your address or phone number. You may add a graphic or photo from any source of your choice on the left side of the card, as shown in Figure 20-6.

**FIGURE 20-6**
Biography Card

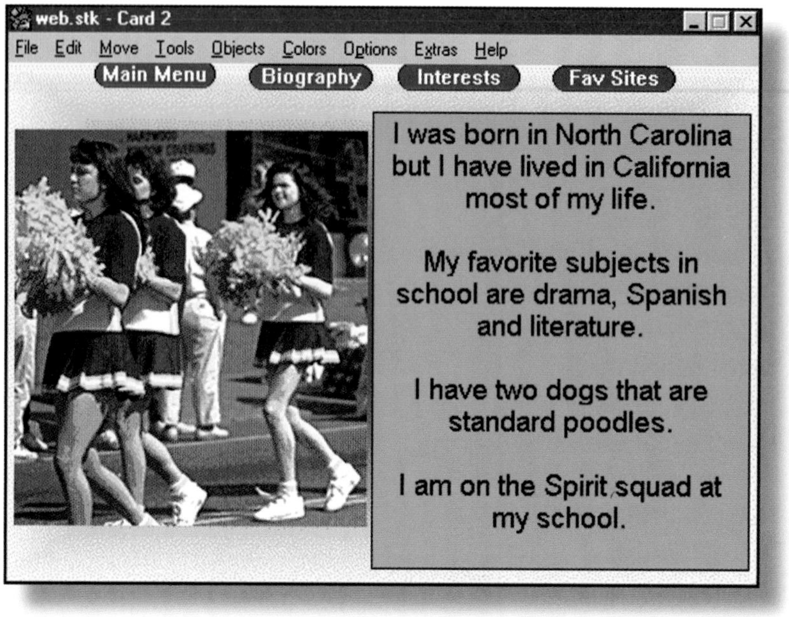

I was born in North Carolina but I have lived in California most of my life.

My favorite subjects in school are drama, Spanish and literature.

I have two dogs that are standard poodles.

I am on the Spirit squad at my school.

**17.** Save the stack as **Web2**. Keep the stack open.

# Using NetPage NBA to Set Up E-Mail Buttons

HyperStudio makes it easy to send e-mail right from your stack. A new button action allows you to send e-mail. If you had a page on the President of the United States, you could include an e-mail button directly to the White House, and your user could send a message to the President. You can also set up a button to let people send e-mail to your e-mail address. If you include your e-mail address on the button, you can get feedback from people about your stack and network with other people who have similar interests.

In Step-by-Step 20.2, you will create a button to send yourself an e-mail message.

**HINT:**

You can only send yourself an e-mail message if you have an e-mail address. Ask your instructor if there is an address you can use if you do not have one.

## STEP-BY-STEP 20.2

**1.** With the Web2 stack open, move to Card 1.

**2.** Using the **Arrow (Edit)** tool, double click the **Send Me An E-Mail** button. Click **Actions**. Select **New Button Actions**. Select **NetPage NBA**, as shown in Figure 20-7.

**3.** Click **Use this NBA**.

**4.** In the window, key **mailto:** and enter your own e-mail address. An example is shown in Figure 20-8.

**5.** Click **OK**, **OK**, and **Done**.

**6.** Test your button.

**7.** Save the stack as **Web3**.

**FIGURE 20-7**
NetPage NBA Selected

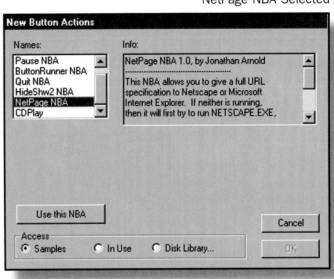

**FIGURE 20-8**
Do URL Window

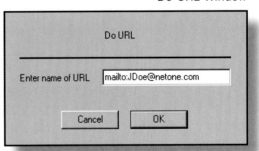

 **HINT:**

You may need to be connected to your Web server for this button to work. If the button does not work, ask your instructor about your Internet access. This feature will not work with America Online, CompuServe or Prodigy Internet providers.

# Setting Up URL Buttons

A URL is the shorthand for a web site address. A URL may look like:

■ www.hyperstudio.com

or may look like

■ http://www.whitehouse.gov

The URL is the location of the site and the way that you can access it. The NetPage NBA you used in Step-by-Step 20.2 can also be used to connect to Internet sites. When you include a web site address or link through the NetPage NBA, you allow those who view your stack to link to a different site on the Internet to get more information or access related sites.

One of the advantages of using links in your stack is that users can access the most up-to-date information available on the link. If you create a stack for a current event topic, users of your stack can access the latest information from the web.

# Using a Web Browser

A Web browser is software that helps you navigate on the Internet. The Internet uses ASCII language. ASCII is a binary code language that is not user-friendly.

The first Web browser to change the way the Internet was accessed was Mosaic. Mosaic is an object-oriented language. That means that you can navigate by using icons or hypertext to move from one link or site to another.

The two most common Web browsers at this time are Netscape Navigator and Microsoft Internet Explorer. The object-oriented Web browsers are the vehicles that help you explore the Internet with ease. You can examine a typical browser page in Figure 20-9.

**FIGURE 20-9**
Netscape Navigator Browser Page

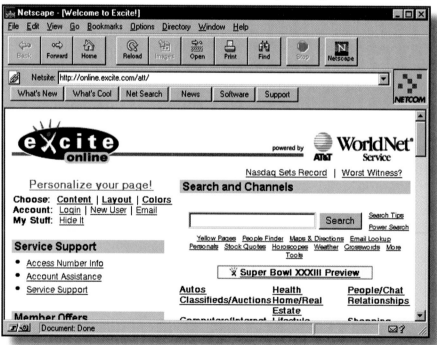

## CHALLENGE ACTIVITY ⟹ 20.1

1. Connect to the Internet.

2. Use your browser to find three sites of interest to you.

3. Write down the URLs of the sites and a brief review of what is on the site.

## STEP-BY-STEP ⟹ 20.3

**Macintosh users must be using System 7.1 or later. Users also must have access to Netscape Navigator or Microsoft Internet Explorer and have Mac TCP installed. The NBA will not work with AOL, Prodigy, or CompuServe.**

**Windows users must have access to Netscape Navigator or Microsoft Internet Explorer. You may need to have the Internet link active before activating it in HyperStudio. You can toggle between applications by using the Alt + Tab keys.**

1. Access the Internet and use a search engine to find a site that is related to one of your interests. For example if your interest is the Winter Olympics, find a site about the event. If your interest is government, find a site about it. If your interest is a particular author, find a site about him or her. Write down the URL or address of the sites on a piece of paper for later use.

2. With the **Web3** stack open, go to the Interests page (Card 3).

3. Add two scrollable text objects with frames. Enter some information about one of your interests in each field. If you like, add a graphic relating to the areas of interest.

(continued on next page)

**HINT:**

Review Lesson 15 for information about using search engines to research a topic. Ask your instructor for help with this if you are a new Internet user.

**4.** Add a button for each site. Do not connect any actions to your buttons at this point. Your card should resemble Figure 20-10.

**5.** Double click on one of the buttons using the **Arrow (Edit)** tool. Click **Actions**, and select **New Button Actions**. Select **NetPage NBA**. Click **Use this NBA**. In the Do URL window, key the address of the URL such as: http://www.slc2002.org/. See Figure 20-11. Click **OK**, **OK**, and **Done**.

**FIGURE 20-10**
Card 3, Interests

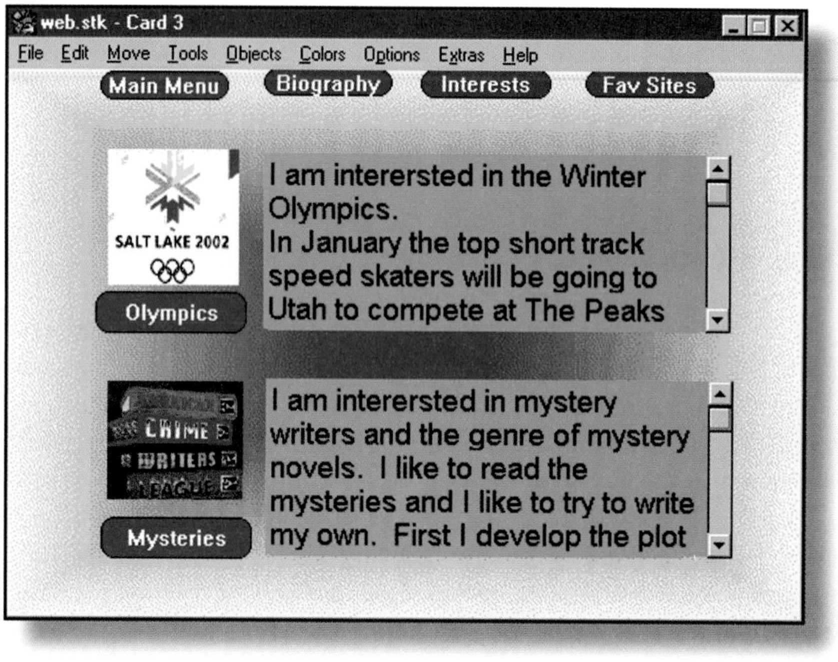

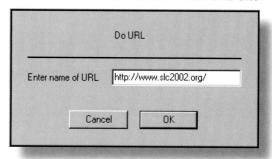

HINT:

You can copy the URL address from the site and paste it in the Do URL window.

**6.** Repeat Step 5 for the second button.

**7.** Test both buttons.

**8.** Save the stack as **Web4**. Keep the stack open.

**FIGURE 20-11**
Do URL Window with URL Site

HINT:

You will need to be connected to the Internet for the buttons to work.

## CHALLENGE ACTIVITY ⟩ 20.2

**1.** Go to the Favorite Sites page (Card 4) in the **Web4** stack.

**2.** Create buttons and provide the URL addresses for at least four web sites.

**3.** Decide on a layout for the buttons and a short explanation of the links.

**4.** Save the stack as **Web5**. Keep the stack open.

# *Using Export WebPage Extra*

The Export WebPage extra is a HyperStudio tool that prepares stacks to go online by adding an accompanying HTML stack. The HTML stack is posted to the web and can be viewed with a web browser. This extra will also allow you to create special multimedia effects for web pages by placing a HyperStudio stack within the Web page. The sites you viewed in Step-by-Step 20.1 were created using this extra.

## STEP-BY-STEP ⟩ 20.4

**1.** With the Web5 stack open, resave the stack as **web.stk**. If you get a message that asks if you want to replace an existing stack, choose **Yes**.

**2.** From Extras menu, select **Export WebPage**, as shown in Figure 20-12.

(continued on next page)

**TIP**

You will need to save the stack with the .stk extension to place the stack on the Web.

**FIGURE 20-12**
Export WebPage Extra

3. When you see the **"Would you like to create a Web page that displays this stack?"** select **Yes**, as shown in Figure 20-13.

4. In the Save Web page named window, key the file name **web.stk.html**, as shown in Figure 20-14. Click **Save**.

5. You should see the window shown in Figure 20-15. Close the stack.

**FIGURE 20-13**
"Would you like to create a Web page that displays this stack?" Window

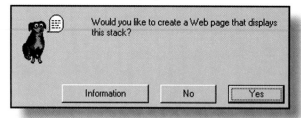

**FIGURE 20-14**
Save web page as

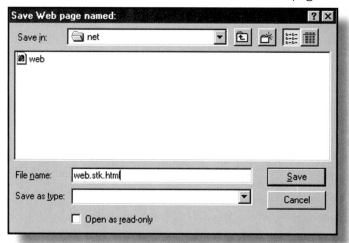

**FIGURE 20-15**
HTML Stack

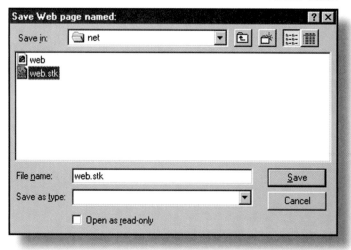

# *Testing the Execution of a Stack*

Like all stacks that you create, you should test them before you allow others to view them. To test the execution of a stack that you have saved to the Web, you will use your Web browser, not HyperStudio.

In Step-by-Step 20.5, you will use your Web browser to view the web stack. The steps are written for Netscape Navigator. If you are using a different browser, ask your instructor for directions if you experience any difficulties.

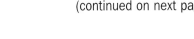

1. Open your browser.

2. Select **Open Page** from the File menu.

3. Click **Choose File**. Locate your HyperStudio web stack. Select it, as shown in Figure 20-16. Click **Open**.

4. If you see a window that warns of a security hazard, read it and click **Continue**. (See Figure 20-17.)

(continued on next page)

**FIGURE 20-16**
Locate and Select Your Stack

**FIGURE 20-17**
Warning Window

**HINT:**

If you have trouble seeing your stack on the Internet, you may have to load a HyperStudio plug-in. To get the latest plug-ins from HyperStudio go to the HyperStudio web site at www.hyperstudio.com, download, and install the plug-in.

**5.** Click **Open**.

**6.** When you see the window in Figure 20-18, double click on the puzzle piece or graphic to open it.

**7.** This icon should launch the Web stack. Try the stack.

**8.** Move to Card 1. Click the **Send Me An E-Mail** button and fill in the information, as shown in Figure 20-19. Use an e-mail address assigned by your instructor.

**9.** Click **Send**.

**10.** Close the stack, exit the browser, and disconnect from your Internet provider.

**FIGURE 20-18**
Web Icon to Launch the Stack

**FIGURE 20-19**
Send an E-Mail Message

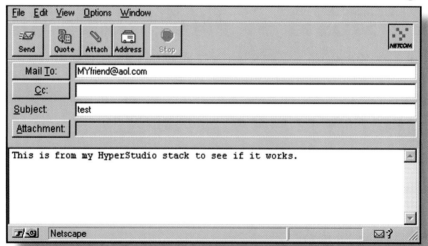

# *Summary*

In this lesson, you learned that:

■ The Internet is a world wide communication system.

■ The World Wide Web is part of the Internet.

■ You need an Internet provider to access the Internet.

■ There are home pages and sites for businesses, organizations, and individuals on the Internet.

■ Your stacks will reflect you personally.

■ You should not use foul or indecent language in your stacks.

■ Your topics should be appropriate.

■ You should not spread gossip or malicious information.

■ You should not post personal information.

■ You should keep your stack size small.

■ You should use a minimum number of colors in stacks that will be viewed online.

■ You should minimize the number of sound files that are used in stacks to be viewed online.

■ You can use the NetPage NBA to include e-mail links.

■ You can use the NetPage NBA to include URL links.

■ You can use Export WebPage extra to create an HTML stack for viewing on the Internet.

■ A browser is object-oriented software for navigating on the Internet and World Wide Web.

■ You can test the execution of a stack using your browser software.

## VOCABULARY

| | |
|---|---|
| Browser | Internet |
| E-mail | Internet provider |
| Export WebPage extra | NetPage NBA |
| Home page | Web site |
| HTML code | World Wide Web |

## TRUE/FALSE

**Circle the T if the statement is true or F if it is false.**

**T  F**   **1.** The Internet is the same as the World Wide Web.

**T  F**   **2.** An Internet provider provides access to the Internet.

**T  F**   **3.** An Internet provider provides access to the World Wide Web.

**T  F**   **4.** A full screen size is not recommended for an online stack.

**T  F**   **5.** A URL is a web site address.

**T  F**   **6.** To set up an e-mail button you must key "mailto: at the beginning of the Do URL window.

## MULTIPLE CHOICE

**Circle the letter of the best answer for each statement.**

**1.**   Object-oriented refers to:
   **A.** icons
   **B.** text
   **C.** text and icons
   **D.** none of the above

**2.**   To access the Internet you will need:
   **A.** an Internet provider
   **B.** a Web browser
   **C.** a computer
   **D.** all of the above

**3.**   When creating a stack to be viewed online:
   **A.** keep the stack size small
   **B.** limit the number of colors
   **C.** test the stack navigation
   **D.** all of the above

**4.**   The first step to creating an online stack is:
   **A.** plan the stack using a storyboard
   **B.** get an online provider
   **C.** make your stack small
   **D.** all of the above

5. To set up a button to go to a URL site:
   A. use NetPage NBA
   B. use Export WebPage extra
   C. use HTML
   D. all of the above

6. A common Web browser is:
   A. Mosaic
   B. Netscape Navigator
   C. Microsoft Internet Explorer
   D. all of the above

7. A browser is:
   A. an Internet provider
   B. object-oriented software
   C. ASCII
   D. all of the above

## COMPLETION

**Answer the questions below in the space provided.**

1. Name three tips to consider when creating an Internet stack.

   a.

   b.

   c.

2. What is a home page?

3. What is an Internet provider?

**4.** What is a Web browser?

**5.** What is the function of the Export WebPage extra?

**6.** What are the functions of the NetPage NBA?

## LESSON 20 PROJECT 20.1

Create a storyboard for a stack about your school, your class, or an area of study. The stack will be designed for viewing on the Internet. As you plan the stack, include:

■ 4 to 8 cards

■ general navigation buttons to the different cards in the stack

■ button links to sites on the Internet

■ at least one link to send an e-mail

## LESSON 20 PROJECT 20.2

Create the stack from the storyboard in Project 20.1. Save the stack as INET. Print the stack. Execute the Export WebPage extra to create an HTML stack. Test the stack on your browser.

## LESSON 20 PROJECT 20.3

In small groups, select a topic for a stack. Design a Main Menu for the group project. Each student in the group will have his or her own topic and must design a one or two page stack. Use a storyboard or organizational chart to plan what each portion each student will contribute. Then create your stack, allowing each group member to participate in the stack creation.

Test your stack and make any refinements needed. Decide on a group name for your project. Use this name to save the stack. Prepare the stack for the Internet. Print the stack.

## CRITICAL THINKING ACTIVITY

List some general items that you think should be included in any online stack. List some of the topics and areas that you think should not be included in an online stack. Be prepared to discuss your lists in class or in a group.

# *Review of Procedures*

**Layered animations**

1. Use the Lasso Selector tool to select a pattern of objects on a card.
2. While the objects are selected, choose Add a Graphic Object from the Objects menu. Click Yes.
3. Choose Actions.
4. Choose Play animation.
5. Locate and select the animated object you wish to use.
6. Drag the object in a path over the card. Press Enter when done.
7. Choose Path and Path options.
8. Select Float over in the Path Options window. Click OK.
9. If you want multiple animations of the same object, select Allow clones.
10. Test the path by choosing Try It.
11. Click OK and Done, as necessary.

**Draw multiple, centered, or filled**

1. From the Options menu, select one or more of the drawing effects. Selected effects appear with a checkmark beside them on the Options menu.
2. Click on the option once again to deselect it.

**Filter effects**

1. Use one of the selector tools to select the area of the clip art to which you want to add the effects.
2. From the Edit menu, select Effects.
3. Choose the effect you want to apply.
4. Make appropriate selections for the effect.

**Bring closer/Send farther**

1. Select the object.
2. While the object is selected, choose Bring Closer or Send Farther from the Objects menu.

**Marked cards**

1. Move to the card that you wish to mark.
2. From the Objects menu, select About this Card.
3. Select Marked card.
4. Select OK.

**Creating test buttons**

1. Add a new button.
2. Select Testing functions from Actions window.
3. Select one of the four choices in the Testing window.

**Passwords**

1. From the Edit menu, select Preferences.
2. Key a password in the Stack password field.
3. Select Lock stack.
4. Click OK.

| **Hide/Show NBA for arriving or leaving a card** | 1. Name the graphic, button, or text field that you wish to hide or show. |
| | 2. From the Objects menu, select About this Card. |
| | 3. Select arriving at this card or leaving this card. |
| | 4. Choose New Button Actions. |
| | 5. Select HideShw2 NBA. |
| | 6. Click Use this NBA. |
| | 7. Key the name of the button, graphic, or text object. |
| | 8. Select the type of object. |
| | 9. Select the action. |
| | 10. Select Show effect. |
| | 11. Choose a transition. |
| | 12. Select OK and Done, as needed. |

| **Hide card number on stack** | 1. From the Edit menu, select Preferences. |
| | 2. Deselect Show card number with stack name. |

| **NetPage NBA for E-mail** | 1. Add a button. |
| | 2. Select New Button Actions from the Actions window. |
| | 3. Select NetPage NBA. |
| | 4. Select Use this NBA. |
| | 5. Key "mailto:_____@_____. |
| | 6. Click OK and Done, as needed. |

| **NetPage NBA for URL** | 1. Add a button. |
| | 2. Select New Button Actions from the Actions window. |
| | 3. Select NetPage NBA. |
| | 4. Select Use this NBA. |
| | 5. Key the Internet address in the window. |
| | 6. Click OK and Done, as needed. |

| **WebPage Extra** | 1. Create a folder for your stack. |
| | 2. Save the stack in the folder, using an appropriate file name. Include the extension .STK after the name. |
| | 3. From the Extras menu, select Export WebPage. |
| | 4. Respond Yes to "Would you like to create a Web page that displays this stack?" |
| | 5. Locate your stack folder. |
| | 6. Key the name of your stack including ".Stk.html" at the end of the name. |
| | 7. Close the stack. |
| | 8. Open the browser and locate the stack. |
| | 9. Test the stack in the browser. |

### FILL IN THE BLANKS

**Complete the following statements by keying or writing the correct answers on a page to be submitted to your instructor. Center** *Unit 6 Review Questions* **at the top of the page. Number your answers to match the numbers listed here.**

1.  When an animation appears to float over and behind objects on a card, it is called a(n) _____ .

2.  Plug-in effects are _____ .

3.  When using the Beveler effect, two options you can choose are _____ and _____ or a combination of the two.

4.  The Magnifying Glass tool is used to view a(n) _____ version of the card.

5.  The Eyedropper tool is used to select and match _____ .

6.  A card with a predesigned plate or pattern that would save and use to duplicate is called a(n) _____ .

7.  When creating tests or surveys you can choose the following options: _____ , _____ , _____ , or _____ .

8.  Locking a stack so that no one else can change it is called using a(n) _____ .

9.  Two popular Web browsers are _____ and _____ .

10. An Internet site address is called a _____ .

### WRITTEN QUESTIONS

**Key or write your answers to the following questions. Number your answers. Use complete sentences and good grammar.**

11. What is copyright and how does it apply to resources in a stack?

12. What does cross platform mean? How does it apply in HyperStudio?

13. Why would you mark a card in a stack?

14. What two actions can you perform using the NetPage NBA?

15. What service does a Web browser perform?

## UNIT 6 APPLICATIONS

### UNIT 6 PROJECT

1. Choose a topic for a stack that would lend itself to a survey or test to be placed on the Internet.

2. Create a storyboard and flow chart.

3. Use graphics to present information and then ask for user responses.

4. Create the stack.

5. Include at least one each of the following in the stack:
   - layered animation
   - an object drawn multiple, centered, or filled
   - filter effect
   - testing function buttons
   - HideShw2 NBA for arriving or leaving a card

6. Hide the card numbers for the stack.

7. Create either a NetPage e-mail or URL button.

8. Include a WebPage extra to place the stack on the Internet.

9. Save the stack as **EP6**.

### UNIT 6 CRITICAL THINKING ACTIVITY

List reasons that stack creators may want to publish stacks on the Internet. List the possible advantages and disadvantages of making stacks available via the Internet.

# CAPSTONE SIMULATION

🕐 **Estimated Time: 2 hours**

## GOALS

**To complete this simulation, you will:**

- Create a storyboard.

- Create a flowchart.

- Create a presentation stack.

- Demonstrate and implement a variety of HyperStudio procedures within the stack.

- Present the stack.

- Evaluate the stack.

# Getting Started

Your school is considering the purchase of HyperStudio for all of its computer labs. You have been asked to create a presentation for the Purchasing Committee that will demonstrate HyperStudio's range of performance capabilities.

The committee has no knowledge of the techniques or multimedia possibilities available in HyperStudio, but it has decided to purchase some type of multimedia-authoring tool. Your stack must demonstrate the possibilities available with HyperStudio, including a demonstration of many of HyperStudio's features. Your stack should demonstrate and explain each of the features you select.

# Planning the Stack

Create a storyboard and a flow chart for your stack. Use the list of elements in the Stack Contents section as you develop the storyboard. List on the storyboard the file name you will use for your stack, **CapXXX**, where XXX are your initials.

# *Stack Contents*

The stack must include the following:

- Title card
- Main Menu card
- Credits card
- Topics cards
- Example cards
- appropriate navigation, sounds, graphics, and text
- accurate information
- credits for resources from outside sources
- Four graphic and/or clip art objects
- Two different transitions
- Two different uses of sound
- One Ready Made or original template
- Eight of the topics below and at least two features for each topic except for tests, Internet, and video.

To demonstrate HyperStudio's features, choose from the list below. Each feature will be one of the topic cards for your stack and will have related cards attached that explain and demonstrate two choices from each topic. For instance, text would be one topic. You would demonstrate how to use two of the text features. Graphics would be another topic.

## Text (Choose 2)

Text paint tool
Transparent text fields
Cookie-Cutter effect
Shadow text

## Options, Effects, and Extras (Choose 2)

Draw centered
Draw multiple
Draw filled
Beveler
Texturize
Emboss
Box Maker
Menu Tamer

## Graphic Effects (Choose 2)
Scale and Rotate
Gradients effect
Flip Upside Down
Flip Sideways
Replace Colors

## Navigation (Choose 2)
Text field action
Hidden button
Graphic action
Hypertext links

## NBAS (Choose 2)
HideShw2 NBA (graphic or text)
RollCredits NBA
Quit NBA
ButtonRunner NBA

## Animations (Choose 2)
Path animation
Animate objects animation
Frame animation
Slide show animation
Layered animation

## Video (Choose 1)
Play QuickTime or AVI movie
Play live video
Play original QuickTime of AVI movie clip
Access laser disc player from stack
Play video through graphic objects

## Tests (Choose 1)
Quiz (including correct and incorrect test responses)
Survey (information gathering test)

## Importing resources (Choose 1)
Import video
Import sound
Import graphics
Import photo from digital camera
Import scanned image

## Internet (Choose 1)
NetPage URL
NetPage E-mail
Export WebPage

# Creating and Testing Your Stack

Use your storyboard and flow chart to create the stack you have planned. Remember to save your stack often. As you are creating complex cards, remember to create duplicate cards at appropriate points. Also, remember to use shortcuts like copying and pasting when possible.

Test your stack as you complete various parts. For example, test the navigation to and from the Main Menu card as soon as it is completed. This allows you to make corrections and changes as you go. When your stack is completed, test all elements a final time, making sure all parts of your stack work as planned.

# Evaluating Your Stack

Using the Stack Self-Evaluation Checklist, evaluate your stack. Correct all items marked as poor. Decide if you need to change any elements marked as OK.

# Printing Your Stack

Print all the cards of your stack, using two or four cards to a page to save paper. Review the printouts as a final check on the quality of your stack. Submit the presentation, printout, and Stack Self-Evaluation Checklist to your instructor.

# Letting Others Evaluate Your Stack

Make your presentation available to at least two other learners or friends. Give them a copy of the Stack Evaluation Checklist. Ask them to view the presentation and complete the checklist using the back of the checklist for any specific comments.

Based on the feedback you receive, revise your stack. Be sure to test your stack again after you have completed the revisions.

## STACK SELF-EVALUATION CHECKLIST

| CRITERIA | EXCELLENT | OK | POOR |
|---|---|---|---|

**Overall**

| | | | |
|---|---|---|---|
| There is a Title card. | _____ | _____ | _____ |
| Title card defines topic. | _____ | _____ | _____ |
| There is a Main Menu card. | _____ | _____ | _____ |
| Main Menu card is clear. | _____ | _____ | _____ |
| Theme of the stack is clearly represented. | _____ | _____ | _____ |
| Stack is organized well. | _____ | _____ | _____ |
| Stack flows well from card to card and topic to topic. | _____ | _____ | _____ |

**Graphics**

| | | | |
|---|---|---|---|
| The graphics set the tone of the stack. | _____ | _____ | _____ |
| Graphics are appropriate and add to the content of stack. | _____ | _____ | _____ |
| Graphics are easy to see. | _____ | _____ | _____ |

**Text**

| | | | |
|---|---|---|---|
| Text is easy to read. | _____ | _____ | _____ |
| Text is spelled correctly. | _____ | _____ | _____ |
| Text is grammatically correct. | _____ | _____ | _____ |
| Text explains the content well. | _____ | _____ | _____ |

**Navigation**

| | | | |
|---|---|---|---|
| The navigation scheme is user-friendly. | _____ | _____ | _____ |
| Buttons are consistent in style and placement. | _____ | _____ | _____ |
| User can easily exit the presentation at appropriate points. | _____ | _____ | _____ |
| It is easy to move around the stack. | _____ | _____ | _____ |
| You can return to the Main Menu from appropriate cards. | _____ | _____ | _____ |
| Overall navigation is functional and clear. | _____ | _____ | _____ |
| All buttons actions operate correctly. | _____ | _____ | _____ |

**Sound**

| | | | |
|---|---|---|---|
| Sounds are appropriate. | _____ | _____ | _____ |
| Sounds help to convey message of the stack or card. | _____ | _____ | _____ |

**Video**

| | | | |
|---|---|---|---|
| Video is appropriate. | _____ | _____ | _____ |
| The video helps to convey the message of stack or card. | _____ | _____ | _____ |

**Interactivity**

| | | | |
|---|---|---|---|
| The stack is interactive. | _____ | _____ | _____ |
| The stack encourages the user to participate. | _____ | _____ | _____ |

**Content**

| | | | |
|---|---|---|---|
| Credits are included. | _____ | _____ | _____ |
| Information is correct. | _____ | _____ | _____ |

# STACK EVALUATION CHECKLIST

| CRITERIA | EXCELLENT | OK | POOR |
|---|---|---|---|
| **Overall** | | | |
| There is a Title card. | _____ | _____ | _____ |
| Title card defines topic. | _____ | _____ | _____ |
| There is a Main Menu card. | _____ | _____ | _____ |
| Main Menu card is clear. | _____ | _____ | _____ |
| Theme of the stack is clearly represented. | _____ | _____ | _____ |
| Stack is organized well. | _____ | _____ | _____ |
| Stack flows well from card to card and topic to topic. | _____ | _____ | _____ |
| **Graphics** | | | |
| The graphics set the tone of the stack. | _____ | _____ | _____ |
| Graphics are appropriate and add to the content of stack. | _____ | _____ | _____ |
| Graphics are easy to see. | _____ | _____ | _____ |
| **Text** | | | |
| Text is easy to read. | _____ | _____ | _____ |
| Text is spelled correctly. | _____ | _____ | _____ |
| Text is grammatically correct. | _____ | _____ | _____ |
| Text explains the content well. | _____ | _____ | _____ |
| **Navigation** | | | |
| The navigation scheme is user-friendly. | _____ | _____ | _____ |
| Buttons are consistent in style and placement. | _____ | _____ | _____ |
| User can easily exit the presentation at appropriate points. | _____ | _____ | _____ |
| It is easy to move around the stack. | _____ | _____ | _____ |
| You can return to the Main Menu from appropriate cards. | _____ | _____ | _____ |
| Overall navigation is functional and clear. | _____ | _____ | _____ |
| All buttons actions operate correctly. | _____ | _____ | _____ |
| **Sound** | | | |
| Sounds are appropriate. | _____ | _____ | _____ |
| Sounds help to convey message of the stack or card. | _____ | _____ | _____ |
| **Video** | | | |
| Video is appropriate. | _____ | _____ | _____ |
| The video helps to convey the message of stack or card. | _____ | _____ | _____ |
| **Interactivity** | | | |
| The stack is interactive. | _____ | _____ | _____ |
| The stack encourages the user to participate. | _____ | _____ | _____ |
| **Content** | | | |
| Credits are included. | _____ | _____ | _____ |
| Information is correct. | _____ | _____ | _____ |

# Introduction to Windows 95 and Later

Microsoft Windows, a graphical user interface (GUI) software, is an operating system based on the metaphor of the computer as a desktop. The opening screen is your working area with access to the tools you use regularly and the programs installed on your computer. Graphical user interface software allows the user to interact with the computer by using pictures (icons) and buttons that allow you to give commands to the computer without having to memorize key functions or learn a new computer language. It is intended to be intuitive so that a new user can look at the screen and by clicking on words or pictures, figure out how to navigate around the environment.

Benefits of the Windows operating system include:

- **Universal Interface Design.** All of the programs that run in Windows have similar features allowing you to accomplish tasks in similar ways. For instance, most programs have a menubar, and on the menubar, are some consistent menu choices such as File. From the File menu, the user can generally open files, save files, or quit the program.

- **Multitasking.** Windows allows you to run more than one application at a time and allows you to have more than one document open at a time. You can move between programs or documents without having to open and close them each time you move between them. This improves time management.

- **Plug and Play.** Windows has drivers that allow you to easily install software by automatically placing it in the necessary folders and areas of the computer system.

- **File names.** Windows 95 and later have overcome the DOS-based file naming limit of eight characters plus a three-character extension. In Windows 95 and later, file names may have up to 255 characters.

# Common Features of Windows Programs

Most Windows programs share a common look and feel. When you open a Windows program, you will see:

**Title bar**  Contains the name of the open file and the minimize, maximize/restore, and close buttons. The minimize button hides the file from view and places a reference to it on the task bar. (The task bar is described below with the Windows desktop.) The maximize/restore button toggles between a full-screen view of the file and a reduced view. The close button closes the program and all open files. You will be prompted to save your work before closing the program. If you close a program without saving the work you have done, you will lose the work.

**Menubar**  Contains the main menu for the program. The main menu items will vary from program to program. However, common elements include File and Help. The menus for each of the main menu items are accessed by clicking on the item's name. From the list of items on the menu, you make your selection by double clicking on it.

The HyperStudio window is shown in Figure A-1. The common parts of the window are identified.

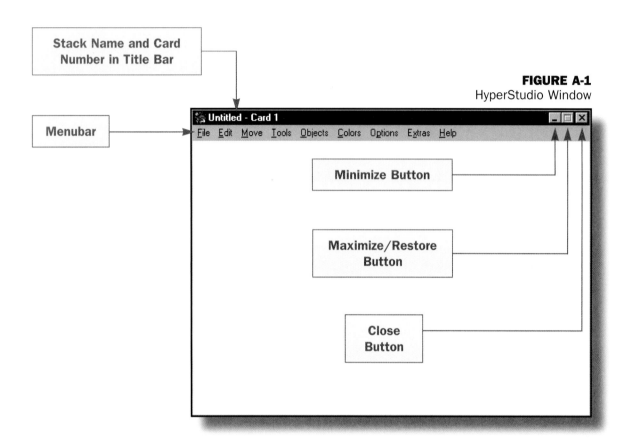

**FIGURE A-1**
HyperStudio Window

# *The Mouse*

The Windows mouse allows you to select and highlight information, click on icons and text, scroll windows, drag items, and access menu commands.

The Windows mouse has two or three buttons on it. The left button is used to select and highlight objects and text. The right button allows you to access menus for commands. If there is a center button it acts as a double click. The actions that can be performed with a mouse are:

| | |
|---|---|
| Click | Press down and quickly release the mouse button. This is the most common mouse action. |
| Double click | Click twice in rapid succession. You will use a double click to open files. |
| Click and drag | Hold down the left mouse button and drag the mouse. You will use this technique to create path animations. |
| Right click | Click the right mouse button. This action is rarely used in HyperStudio. |

# *The Desktop*

All Windows applications can be accessed from the desktop. The desktop serves as the launch pad for all work you will do within the Windows environment. The desktop consists of the working area, which contains various icons. These icons vary from computer to computer. At a minimum, there should be icons labeled My Computer, My Briefcase, and Recycle Bin. If you are connected to a network, you will see the Network Neighborhood icon. If the computer includes a Web browser, you will see an icon for it.

Depending on the way computer programs, such as HyperStudio, have been installed, you may see shortcut icons for various programs. Shortcut icons are a convenient way to launch commonly used programs. They are most useful when they are limited to a small number and are kept organized. If a HyperStudio icon appears on the desktop, you may launch (open) the program by double clicking on the icon. The process for creating shortcut icons is described on page 463.

## The Taskbar

The other main element on the desktop is the taskbar. The taskbar is generally located at the bottom of the screen in the default mode; however, it can be moved to the top or sides of the desktop. The taskbar contains the Start button, a button for each open application, various icons, and a clock.

The Start button accesses the Start Menu and is described below. The icons on the right side of the taskbar vary from computer to computer. These icons represent various utility programs that are launched when Windows is started. These programs generally function without any action on your part. If you need to change any of the settings for these programs, simply double click on the icon. In Figure A-2, for example, the left icon is the volume control for the computer's speakers. The last item on the taskbar is a clock that indicates the current time. In Windows, the time is usually set when the computer is installed. It will maintain the correct time even when the computer is shut down.

**FIGURE A-2**
Windows Taskbar

When you open an application, a button for it will appear on the taskbar, as shown in Figure A-2. From the taskbar, you can easily switch between open applications by clicking on the application's button.

## The Start Button

The Start button opens the Start menu, shown in Figure A-3, from which you can choose:

Programs     Allows you to launch all programs currently installed on your computer.

Documents     Allows you to open recently used documents without first opening the program. When you double click on a specific document, the associated program is launched and the document is automatically opened.

Settings     Gives access to the control panels, printer, and taskbar to customize their operation.

| | | |
|---|---|---|
| Find | Launches Windows' Find utility, which helps you search for a document, folder, or application. | |

Help — Takes you to Windows' Help menu.

Run — Allows you to install new programs.

Shut Down — Allows you to shut down or restart your computer.

Windows provides an assortment of accessories that are automatically installed with the program. They are accessed by clicking on the Programs option on the Start menu and then clicking on Accessories. The commonly used accessories include:

| | |
|---|---|
| Calculator | Makes available a full functioning calculator from which results can be copied and pasted into other programs. |
| Character Map | Allows you to insert symbols and characters not found on the keyboard. |
| Fax | Allows you to send and receive fax messages with appropriate software. |
| Notepad | Allows you to key text into a simple, but limited, word processing program. |
| Paint | Allows you to create simple graphics for use in other applications. |
| System Tools | Includes utility programs for maintaining the system. |
| Tips, Tours and Wizards | Helps you learn to use Windows efficiently. |
| WordPad | Allows you to key text and create simple word processing documents. WordPad can handle larger documents than Notepad and has more formatting options. |

## My Computer

The My Computer icon on the desktop offers the user the ability to access any of the computer drives and peripherals to locate and manage files anywhere on your computer. The My Computer window is shown in Figure A-4.

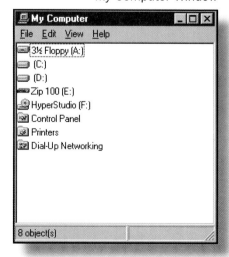

# Control Panel

The control panel can be accessed from the My Computer window and from the Start Menu. The control panel lets you manage tasks concerning the maintenance, appearance, and operation of your computer. The control panel window in Figure A-5 displays the various items with small icons. The items in the control panel are described below.

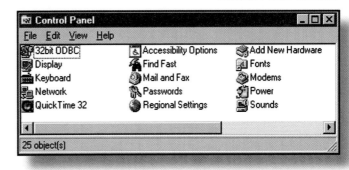

| | |
|---|---|
| 32bit ODBC | Stores information about how to connect to a program installed on your computer. |
| Display | Lets you make adjustments to the way the desktop and screen appear including screen savers and wall paper, which is the background appearance of the desktop. |
| Keyboard | Allows you to adjust the keyboard, including a choice of languages. |
| Network | Sets your computer up for networking. |
| QuickTime | Displays the QuickTime Video control panel. |
| Accessibility Options | Allows for setting up the computer for ease of operation for persons with disabilities. |
| Find Fast | Aids fast retrieval of folders, files, and programs. |
| Mail and Fax | Lets you send and receive fax and e-mail with appropriate hardware installed. |
| Passwords | Allows you to set up and change passwords. Do not change these settings if you are working in a classroom or computer lab situation. |
| Regional Settings | Allows you to set up your computer for a number of different regions or countries. |
| Add New Hardware | Allows you to add new hardware and helps it to run correctly. |
| Fonts | Allows you to add or remove fonts. |
| Modems | Helps to configure modem used with computer. |
| Power | Allows Windows to manage power on the computer. |
| Sounds | Provides a listing of sounds built into the Windows system. |

# Windows Explorer

Windows Explorer allows you to quickly and easily locate and manage files on your computer. It is accessed from the Programs menu. The Explorer window, shown in Figure A-6, has two frames. The left frame is the All Folders view, which displays the drives and folders located on the drives. The right frame shows the files within the folder chosen in the All Folders frame.

## Recycle Bin

The Recycle Bin is located on the desktop. It functions like a trash can in an office. When you wish to delete a file, you drag it to the Recycle Bin or send it there by choosing Delete from the menu. When there are items in the Recycle Bin, it appears to have paper in it. To view the items in the Recycle Bin, double click on it. An item in the Recycle Bin cannot be opened. However, you can move it from the Recycle Bin to your desktop for viewing.

When the Recycle Bin is open, you can pull down the menu to empty it. Once the Recycle Bin has been emptied, the files that were deleted cannot be recovered. Place files in the Recycle Bin only when they are no longer needed.

# *File Management and Naming Files*

File management activities include formatting disks, creating folders, renaming files and folders, copying and pasting files, and moving files and folders. Each of these items is described below.

| | |
|---|---|
| Formatting Disks | From the My Computer window, select the drive with the floppy disk icon (generally, the A drive). From the File menu, select Format. Follow the instructions to complete the formatting. NOTE: Formatting a disk erases any data currently stored on the disk. You will not be able to recover the data once it has been deleted. |

| | |
|---|---|
| Creating Folders | Select the drive and location where you would like the new folder. From the File menu, select New, then Folder. A new folder will appear with the name New Folder. Key a name for the folder to replace the words "New Folder." |
| Renaming Folders and Files | Select the text under or beside the folder or file you wish to rename. Right click and select Rename. Key the new name. |
| Copy and Pasting Folders and Files | To copy a folder or file either right click the mouse and select copy then right click in the new location and select paste or hold down the Ctrl key while you drag the folder or file to a new location. |
| Moving Folders and Files | To move a folder either right click and choose move or hold down the Shift key while you drag the folder or file to the new location. |

# *Shortcuts*

Shortcuts are desktop icons for the applications you use most often. You can create shortcuts so that you can access the applications directly from your desktop. To create shortcuts:

1. Click the Start button, click Programs, and click Windows Explorer.

2. Locate the program file you wish to place on the desktop and select it. Program files include an .exe extension at the end of the file name.

3. Right click and select Create Shortcut.

4. Drag the icon that appears to the desktop.

You can rename a shortcut by highlighting the text under the icon and keying the new name. To delete a shortcut, select it, and while it is highlighted, press Delete.

# Introduction to Macintosh OS8

Macintosh OS8, a graphical user interface (GUI) software, is an operating system based on the metaphor of the computer as a desktop. The opening screen is your working area with access to the tools you use regularly and the programs installed on your computer. Graphical user interface software allows the user to interact with the computer by using pictures (icons) and buttons that allow you to give commands to the computer without having to memorize key functions or learn a new computer language. It is intended to be intuitive so that a new user can look at the screen and by clicking on words or pictures, figure out how navigate around the environment.

The Macintosh operating system features:

■ **Universal Interface Design.** All of the programs that run in Macintosh OS8 will have similar features allowing you to accomplish tasks in similar ways. For instance, most programs have a menubar. The menubar contains some consistent menu choices such as File. From the File menu, the user can generally open files, save files, or quit the program.

■ **Multitasking.** Macintosh OS8 allows you to run more than one application at a time and have more than one document open at a time. You can move between programs or documents without having to open and close them each time you move between them. This improves time management.

■ **Plug and Play.** Macintosh has drivers that allow you to easily install software by automatically placing it in the necessary folders and areas of the computer system.

# The Macintosh Window

## The Menubar

The menubar is found along the top of the Desktop window. (See Figure B-1.) The items available on the menubar are the Apple menu, File menu, Edit menu, View menu, Special menu, and Help menu. In the right corner of the menubar is the Finder icon that allows you to switch between applications or return to the desktop. When you are using an application, the Finder icon changes to the icon identified with the program that you are using. When you change applications, the icon will change.

## Apple Menu

The Apple menu allows you to locate applications and tools that you use frequently. You can add and delete items from this window through the Control Panel. Items generally displayed in the default menu include:

| | |
|---|---|
| About this computer | Provides basic operating system and memory information. |
| Apple DVD Player | Opens the Control Panel for a DVD to play. |
| Apple System Profiler | Provides system overview of memory, serial number, processor information etc. |
| Apple Video Player | Opens the Control Panel for a video CD to play. |
| Apple CD-Audio Player | Opens the Control Panel for an audio CD to play. |
| Automated Tasks | Sets up Applescripts that perform tasks such as file sharing. |
| Calculator | Opens a calculator program. |
| Chooser | Lets you choose the printer you wish to use. Also provides access to AppleTalk, which is networking software built into Macintosh computers. |
| Connect to... | Allows you to connect to the Internet if you have valid preferences set up. |
| Control Panel | Accesses many tools for managing your computer, its appearance, and its operation. See below for more information. |
| Find File | Helps to search for a file or document or application. |
| Graphing Calculator | Lets you calculate graphs. |
| Key Caps | Allows you to key accents and special characters. |
| Note Pad | Accesses a program that lets you make notes for yourself no matter which program you are in. |

| Recent Applications | Provides a list of recent applications you have opened. |
| Recent Documents | Provides a list of recent documents that you have opened. |
| Scrapbook | Lets you save pictures or text to paste in other places. |
| Simple Sound | Lets you choose the alert sounds your computer uses. |
| Stickies | Creates notes similar to Post-It notes on your screen. |

## File Menu

The File menu includes options for creating folders and files, managing files, getting information about folders and files, and finding files.

## Edit Menu

The Edit menu allows you to undo your last action, copy, cut, and paste.

## View Menu

The View menu is used to change the way icons are displayed on your desktop.

## Label Menu

The Label menu allows you to create a color coding system for your folders and files.

## Special Menu

The Special menu provides the following options:

| Clean Up Window | Rearranges the items on your desktop. |
| Empty Trash | Deletes from the hard drive or the desktop the folders and files you have placed in the trash can since the last time it was emptied. |
| Eject Disk | Ejects floppy disks from the drive. |
| Erase Disk | Removes all the information from the disk. Use this item with caution. |
| Sleep Mode | Puts your computer in a power saving mode. |
| Restart | Restarts the computer. NOTE: Any work that has not been saved will be lost. |
| Shut Down | Turns off the computer. NOTE: Any work that has not been saved will be lost. |

# *Application's Title Bar*

When you have an application open, three options are available in the title bar of the application's window (see Figure B-2):

1. To close a window, click in the small box on the left side of the title bar.

2. To hide the document and leave only the title bar on screen, click the outside box on the right side of the title bar.

3. To increase and decrease the size of the document window, click the inside box on the right side of the title bar.

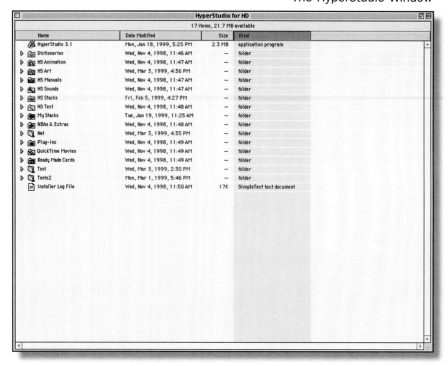

| Name | Date Modified | Size | Kind |
|---|---|---|---|
| HyperStudio 3.1 | Mon, Jan 18, 1999, 5:25 PM | 2.3 MB | application program |
| ▷ Dictionaries | Wed, Nov 4, 1998, 11:46 AM | — | folder |
| ▷ HS Animation | Wed, Nov 4, 1998, 11:47 AM | — | folder |
| ▷ HS Art | Wed, Mar 3, 1999, 4:36 PM | — | folder |
| ▷ HS Manuals | Wed, Nov 4, 1998, 11:47 AM | — | folder |
| ▷ HS Sounds | Wed, Nov 4, 1998, 11:47 AM | — | folder |
| ▷ HS Stacks | Fri, Feb 5, 1999, 4:27 PM | — | folder |
| ▷ HS Text | Wed, Nov 4, 1998, 11:48 AM | — | folder |
| ▷ My Stacks | Tue, Jan 19, 1999, 11:25 AM | — | folder |
| ▷ NBAs & Extras | Wed, Nov 4, 1998, 11:48 AM | — | folder |
| ▷ Net | Wed, Mar 3, 1999, 4:35 PM | — | folder |
| ▷ Plug-ins | Wed, Nov 4, 1998, 11:49 AM | — | folder |
| ▷ QuickTime Movies | Wed, Nov 4, 1998, 11:49 AM | — | folder |
| ▷ Ready Made Cards | Wed, Nov 4, 1998, 11:49 AM | — | folder |
| ▷ Test | Wed, Mar 3, 1999, 2:30 PM | — | folder |
| ▷ Tests2 | Mon, Mar 1, 1999, 5:46 PM | — | folder |
| Installer Log File | Wed, Nov 4, 1998, 11:50 AM | 17K | SimpleText text document |

# The Mouse

The Macintosh mouse allows you to select and highlight information, click and double click on icons and text, scroll windows, drag items, and access menu commands. The mouse has one button. The actions that can be performed with a mouse are:

Click   Press down and quickly release the mouse button. This is the most common mouse action.

Double click   Click twice in rapid succession. You will use a double click to open files.

Click and drag   Hold down the mouse button and drag the mouse. You will use this technique to create path animations.

You can select more than one item at a time by holding the Shift key while you select items.

# The Desktop

## Hard Drive

The hard drive is the storage unit that holds all of the files you want to save on your computer as well as the operating system and system files. You can access any files or applications from the hard drive. The hard drive appears on the desktop, generally in the upper right hand part of the screen. Double clicking on the hard drive icon will open the window. You can name your hard drive by selecting the name under the icon and keying in a different name. However, you should not change the name of the hard drive of school or computer lab computers.

## Launcher

Some Macintosh computers come with a special program called the Launcher. The launcher is a desktop program that gives you easy access to programs on your computer. You can access the Launcher from the Control Panel.

## Apple Extras

This folder is on the hard drive and includes programs to compliment the computer's operation. It includes AppleScript and QuickDraw GX. This folder is generally installed when the operating system software is installed.

## Alias

An alias is a file that points to another item such as a program. To create an alias, select the folder for which you want to create an alias and then select **Make Alias** from the **File** menu. This will set up a placeholder connected to the actual application.

## Trash Can

This icon is similar to a waste paper basket in an office. It is located on the desktop. When you want to delete a file, folder, or application, drag its icon to the Trash Can. When there are items in the trash, the Trash Can appears to be fuller than when it is empty. You can double click on the Trash Can icon to view its contents. An item in the trash cannot be opened, but it can be removed from the trash can by dragging it onto the desktop.

When the Trash Can is emptied, by selecting Empty Trash from the Special menu, the items are erased and generally cannot be recovered. It is wise to review the list of items in the Trash Can before emptying it.

## Control Panel

The Control Panel is accessed from the Apple menu. It lets you manage tasks concerning the maintenance, appearance and operation of your computer. The options available include:

| | |
|---|---|
| Appearance | Lets you make adjustments to the way the desktop and screen appear including screen savers and wall paper, which is the background appearance of the desktop. |
| Apple Menu Options | Provides access to add or delete menu items. |
| AppleTalk | Provides access to setup AppleTalk preferences. |
| Color Sync | Lets you setup color preferences. |
| Configuration Manager | Allows you to configure your computer to send and receive fax and e-mail with appropriate hardware. |
| Date and Time | Lets you set date and time preferences. |
| Desktop Pictures | Lets you manage and choose the appearance of the desktop background. |
| Extensions Manager | Allows you to manage files that are saved and used from installed programs. |
| File Sharing | Manages shared files on a network. |

| | |
|---|---|
| Keyboard | Allows you to make adjustments to the keyboard including a choice of languages. |
| Launcher | Accesses program for easy access of applications. |
| Map | Accesses a world map with longitude and latitude coordinates. |
| Memory | Opens window containing memory information. |
| Modem | Helps to configure modem used with computer. |
| Monitors and Sound | Sets monitor and sound preferences. |
| Mouse | Controls mouse preferences. |
| Numbers | Allows for number formatting. |
| PPP | Sets up configuration to run information over a network or Internet. |
| QuickTime | Accesses QuickTime video control panel. |
| StartUp Disk | Sets up information for computer startup. |
| TCP/IP | Sets up configuration to run information over a network or Internet. |
| Web Sharing | Allows you to create your own web server to share files on an intranet or internet system. You must be connected to a TCP/IP network. |

# File Management and Naming Files

| | |
|---|---|
| Formatting Disks | Select the floppy disk drive. Select Format from the File menu. Follow the instructions to complete the formatting. NOTE: Formatting a disk erases any data currently stored on the disk. You will not be able to recover the data once it has been deleted. |
| Creating Folders | Select the hard drive and location where you would like the new folder. Select New Folder from the File menu. |
| Renaming Folders and Files | Select the text under or beside the folder you wish to rename. Key the new name. |
| Copy and Pasting Folders and Files | To copy a folder or file, select it, select Copy from the Edit menu. Move to the destination location, select Paste from the Edit menu. |
| Moving Folders and Files | To move a folder, highlight the folder and use the mouse to drag the folder or file to the new location. |

# *Menus*

## File Menu

| | |
|---|---|
| **New Stack** | Creates a new stack. |
| **Open Stack** | Opens an existing stack. |
| **Save Stack** | Saves a named stack. |
| **Save Stack As** | Saves and names a new stack. |
| **Import Background** | Loads a picture as a background. |
| **Export Screen** | Saves a screen as a file. |
| **Add Clip Art** | Lets user add clip art pictures. |
| **Print** | Lets user print a card or stack. |
| **Page Setup** | Lets user set up the print orientation. |
| **Print to Video** | Lets user record a stack on a VCR. |
| **Exit** | Quit HyperStudio. |

# Edit Menu

| | |
|---|---|
| **Undo** | Allows user to Undo the last action. |
| **Cut** | Removes selected item. |
| **Copy** | Allows user to copy selected item. |
| **Paste** | Allows user to place cut or copied item. |
| **Clear** | Allows user to remove selected item. |
| **New Card** | Places a new card in the stack immediately after the current card. |
| **Ready Made Cards** | Allows user to place an existing card template in the stack. |
| **Delete Card** | Removes a card from the stack. (When an object is selected, this menu item indicates the type of item that will be deleted.) |
| **Cut Card** | Removes current card from the stack but holds it to be pasted. (When an object is selected, this menu item indicates the type of item that will be cut.) |
| **Copy Card** | Copies the current card. (When an object is selected, this menu item indicates the type of item that will be copied.) |
| **Edit this Object** | Allows you to edit selected object. |
| **Effects** | Provides a variety of graphical effects for selected clip art. |
| **Erase Background** | Removes the background of a card. |
| **Preferences** | Allows user to set program preferences for program management. |

# Move Menu

| | | |
|---|---|---|
| **Back** | Moves user to previous location. | |
| **Home** | Moves user to the HyperStudio Home card. | |
| **First Card** | Moves user to first card in stack. | |
| **Previous Card** | Moves user to the card in front of current card. | |
| **Next Card** | Moves user to the card after the current card. | |
| **Last Card** | Moves user to the last card in the stack. | |
| **Jump to Card** | Allows user to decide which card to go to. | |
| **Find Text** | Allows user to locate a specific text name or block. | |

# Tool Palette

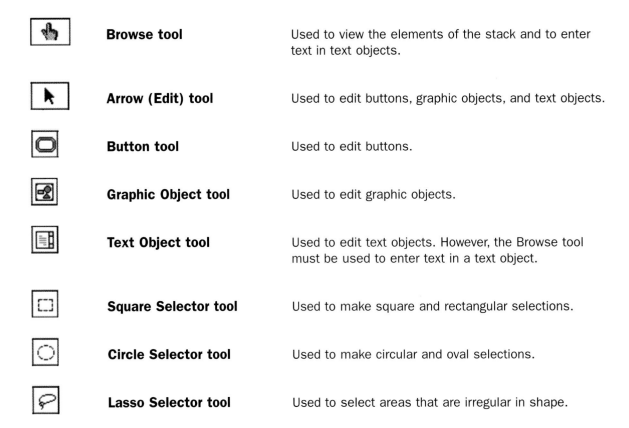

| | Browse tool | Used to view the elements of the stack and to enter text in text objects. |
| | Arrow (Edit) tool | Used to edit buttons, graphic objects, and text objects. |
| | Button tool | Used to edit buttons. |
| | Graphic Object tool | Used to edit graphic objects. |
| | Text Object tool | Used to edit text objects. However, the Browse tool must be used to enter text in a text object. |
| | Square Selector tool | Used to make square and rectangular selections. |
| | Circle Selector tool | Used to make circular and oval selections. |
| | Lasso Selector tool | Used to select areas that are irregular in shape. |

| | | |
|---|---|---|
| **Paintbrush tool** | Used to paint colors using brush strokes on cards. |
| **Spray Can tool** | Used to paint colors using a spray effect on cards. |
| **Paint Bucket tool** | Used to fill areas of the card with solid colors. |
| **Eraser tool** | Used to erase the entire background or selected areas of cards. |
| **Line tool** | Used to draw lines on cards. |
| **Pencil tool** | Used to draw on cards similar to pencil strokes. |
| **Rectangle tool** | Used to create square and rectangular objects. The tool can be used to create the outline of the object or be filled with a color. |
| **Oval tool** | Used to create circular and oval objects. The tool can be used to create the outline of the object or be filled with a color. |
| **Rounded Rectangle tool** | Used to create rounded square and rectangular objects. The tool can be used to create the outline of the object or be filled with a color. |
| **Text tool** | Used to paint text on cards. Once painted text is completed, it cannot be edited or changed without erasing it. |
| **Magnifying Glass tool** | Used to zoom in on an area of the card. |
| **Eyedropper tool** | Used to select a color on the card to be used with one of the drawing tools. |

# Objects Menu

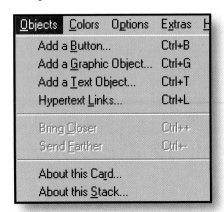

| | |
|---|---|
| **Add a Button** | Lets user add a button to a card. |
| **Add a Graphic Object** | Lets user add a graphic object to a card. |
| **Add a Text Object** | Lets user add a text object to a card. |
| **Hypertext Links** | Lets user create a hypertext link for selected text. |
| **Bring Closer** | Allows selected item to move closer in hierarchy. |
| **Send Farther** | Allows selected item to move back in hierarchy. |
| **About this Card** | Opens window with information about current card. |
| **About this Stack** | Opens window with information about the stack. |

# Colors Menu

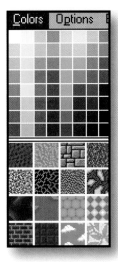

**Color Palette**      Double click on a color swatch to access a larger palette.

**Patterns Palette**   Access to patterns that can be painted on cards.

# Options Menu

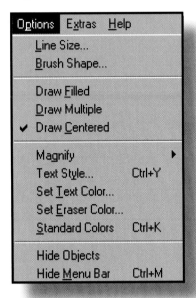

| | |
|---|---|
| **Line Size** | Opens window to select width of line tool. |
| **Brush Shape** | Opens window to select shape of paintbrush. |
| **Draw Filled** | Allows objects drawn to be filled with selected color. |
| **Draw Multiple** | Creates exact multiples of shape as shape is being drawn. |
| **Draw Centered** | Creates multiple objects that are equally centered. |
| **Magnify** | Opens window to enlarge selected area. |
| **Text Style** | Opens window to define selected text attributes. |
| **Set Text Color** | Opens window to change selected text color. |
| **Set Eraser Color** | Opens window to define color that Eraser will paint. |
| **Hide Objects** | Hides graphic objects on the card. |
| **Hide Menu Bar** | Allows user to hide the menubar for a stack. |

# Extras Menu

| | |
|---|---|
| **Extra Manager** | Allows user to add or delete Extras from the menu. |
| **Check Spelling** | Allows user to spell check the text on cards in stack. |
| **Box Maker** | Allows user to draw three-dimensional boxes. |
| **Export WebPage** | Converts a stack into HTML code for Internet viewing. |
| **Menu Tamer** | Allows user to hide menubar in a stack. |
| **StoryBoard** | Shows miniature representation of the cards in a stack. Can move or delete cards from this window. |
| **Title Card** | Makes current card the first card in the stack. |

# Help Menu

**Contents**              Accesses HyperStudio's help information.

**About HyperStudio**     Window with scrolling information about HyperStudio.

# HyperStudio Tools & Tips

 ## Browse Tool

Used for stack navigation, keying information in text objects, and activating objects such as buttons.

**Shortcut:** Shift + Tab to go between Browse tool and Arrow (Edit) tool.

 ## Arrow (Edit) Tool

Used to edit or move graphic objects, buttons, or text objects. With object selected, double click to edit object.

 ## Button Tool

Used to edit or move buttons.

**Shortcut:** Double click on a selected button to go to Button Appearance window.

**Options:** Move a button in a straight line by holding Shift during the movement.

## Graphic Object Tool

Used to edit or move graphic objects.

**Shortcut:** Double click on a selected button to go to Graphic Appearance window.

## Text Object Tool

Used to modify or move an existing text object.

**Shortcut:** Double click on a selected object to go to Text Appearance window.

## Square Selector Tool

Used to capture or select a square or rectangular area or object for editing, deleting, or moving.

**Shortcut:** Double click to select the entire background for changing the color, or deleting or moving a background. Shift + Tab returns to Browse mode.

**Options:** Resize selection proportionally by clicking and dragging in the corner.

## Circle Selector Tool

Used to capture or select a circular or oval area or object for editing, deleting, or moving.

**Options:** Holding Shift while selecting an area will produce a symmetric circle selection.

## Lasso Selector Tool

Used to capture or select an irregularly shaped object or area for editing, deleting, or moving.

## Paintbrush Tool

Used for freehand painting of shapes or backgrounds. Can be modified for color selection and brush shape.

**Shortcut:** Double click on Paintbrush icon to change brush shape. Brush shape can also be changed from the Options menu.

**Options:** Hold Shift while painting for straight lines.

## Spray Can Tool

Produces a stream of spray paint in the color or pattern chosen. Used for backgrounds, blending, and painting. Can produce a light dusting or concentrated color.

**Options:** Choose color from color palette. Hold Shift while painting for a straight line.

## Paint Bucket Tool

Used to fill shapes with selected color or patterns.

## Eraser Tool

Used to erase backgrounds, clip art, or paint objects. Will erase the background of the paint object as well.

**Shortcut:** Can be used to color a card or area by erasing in a chosen color. Double click to change the color used by the tool.

**Options:** Hold Shift while erasing to erase in a straight line.

## Line Tool

Used to draw lines in chosen color or pattern. Can be used for freehand drawing.

**Shortcut:** Double click tool to select the thickness of the line. Line thickness can also be changed from the Options menu.

**Options:** Can be used with draw centered or draw multiple. Hold Shift key while drawing line to maintain a straight line.

## Pencil Tool

Used to draw freehand shapes with chosen color, pattern, and line thickness.

**Shortcut:** Double click on tool to access magnification zoom.

**Options:** Hold Shift while drawing for straight lines.

## Rectangle Tool

Used to draw square or rectangular shapes in chosen color.

**Shortcut:** Double click changes the tool to a filled shape.

**Options:** Can be used with Draw Filled, Draw Multiple or Draw Centered. Holding Shift while drawing will produce square shapes.

## Oval Tool

Used to draw round or oval shapes in chosen color.

**Shortcut:** Double click changes the tool to a filled shape.

**Options:** Can be used with Draw Filled, Draw Multiple or Draw Centered. Holding Shift while drawing will produce symmetric circles.

## Rounded Rectangle Tool

Used to draw rounded rectangular shapes in chosen color.

**Shortcut:** Double click changes the tool to a filled shape.

**Options:** Can be used with Draw Filled, Draw Multiple or Draw Centered. Holding Shift while drawing will produce rounded squares.

## Text Tool

Used to paint text in chosen color, font, and font size. Will remain on the card as a painted object.

**Shortcut:** Double click tool to choose text style.

**Options:** Text modification can be selected from the Options window.

## Magnifying Glass Tool

Used to zoom in on portions of a screen. Can be used to refine painted objects.

## Eyedropper Tool

Used to match colors. When clicked on a color will match the color for the chosen tool.

## STACK NAMES FOR HYPERSTUDIO TUTORIAL

| LESSON # | STEP BY STEPS | CHALLENGES | END OF LESSON PROJECTS |
|---|---|---|---|
| **Lesson 2** | Prac1 | | Proj2 |
| **Lesson 3** | USA<br>Prac2<br>Prac3 | | Prj3-1<br>Prj3-2 |
| **Lesson 5** | USA1<br>Personal<br>Person1 | | Safety1<br>MyTopic1 |
| **Lesson 6** | Country<br>Country1<br>Country2<br>Country3<br>Country4<br>Country5<br>Country6 | | MyTopic2<br>Safety2 |
| **Lesson 7** | Country7<br>Country8<br>Country9<br>Border<br>Border1<br>Border2<br>Border3<br>Border4<br>Border5 | Chaleng7 | Safety3<br>Graphic1 |
| **Lesson 8** | Bckgrnd<br>Family1<br>Family2<br>Family3<br>Effects<br>Animat | Family4<br>Effects1 | Effects2<br>Animat1 |

(continued on next page)

| LESSON # | STEP BY STEPS | CHALLENGES | END OF LESSON PROJECTS |
|---|---|---|---|
| **Lesson 9** | Animat2<br>Animat3<br>Animat4<br>Animat5<br>Animat7 | Animat6 | Proj91<br>Mouse |
| **Lesson 10** | Mouse1<br>Mouse2<br>Mouse3<br>Mouse4<br>Mouse5 | Present<br>Mouse6 | Safety4<br>MyTopic3 |
| **Lesson11** | PC<br>PC1<br>PC2<br>Box<br>Box1<br>Box2 | Presidnt<br>Graphic2<br>Graphic3 | Timeline<br>Show |
| **Lesson 12** | Animals<br>Animal1<br>Animal2<br>Play<br>Play1<br>Play2<br>Play3<br>Journey<br>Journey1<br>Journey2 | Animal3 | Feedback<br>Poem |
| **Lesson 13** | QTstack<br>Space<br>Space1<br>Space2<br>Space3<br>Space4 | Space5 | Proj13<br>Video |
| **Lesson 14** | Vpract<br>Vpract1<br>TV<br>TV1 | Album<br>TV2 | grpproj |
| **Lesson 15** | Lsrdsc<br>Runner<br>Stars<br>GroupMnu<br>QTVR | Lsrdsc1<br>Star1 | (learners<br>select<br>appropriate<br>file names) |

| LESSON # | STEP BY STEPS | CHALLENGES | END OF LESSON PROJECTS |
|---|---|---|---|
| **Lesson 16** | Space4<br>Space5<br>Forest<br>Shapes<br>Shapes1<br>Shapes2<br>Shapes3 | Space6<br>Forest1 | Projanim<br>Plugins |
| **Lesson 17** | Graphics<br>Shapes4<br>Graphic1<br>Template<br>Templat1 | | Templat2 |
| **Lesson 18** | Testing<br>Testing1<br>Testing2<br>Survey<br>Survey1 | Testing3 | Mytest<br>Info |
| **Lesson 19** | Mystery<br>Mystery1<br>Mystery3<br>Mystery4<br>Mystery5<br>Mystery7 | Mystery2<br>Mystery6 | Popup |
| **Lesson 20** | Web<br>Web1<br>Web2<br>Web3<br>Web4<br>web.stk | Web5 | INET<br>(groups select<br>appropriate<br>file names) |

# SKILLS MASTERY CHECKLIST

|  | SKILL | ✓ | DATE |
|---|---|---|---|
| **Lesson 1** | Open and close HyperStudio | _____ | _____ |
| **Lesson 2** | Open stack | _____ | _____ |
|  | Create stack | _____ | _____ |
|  | Name stack | _____ | _____ |
|  | Save stack | _____ | _____ |
| **Lesson 3** | Create a background | _____ | _____ |
|  | Use paint tools | _____ | _____ |
|  | Create borders | _____ | _____ |
|  | Create objects | _____ | _____ |
|  | Create new cards | _____ | _____ |
| **Lesson 4** | Create a storyboard | _____ | _____ |
|  | Create an organizational chart/flow chart | _____ | _____ |
| **Lesson 5** | Utilize objects menu | _____ | _____ |
|  | Copy |  |  |
|  | Paste | _____ | _____ |
|  | Cut |  |  |
|  | Insert text object | _____ | _____ |
|  | Format text object | _____ | _____ |
|  | Create buttons | _____ | _____ |
|  | Create buttons with icons | _____ | _____ |
|  | Develop a four-card stack | _____ | _____ |
| **Lesson 6** | Edit buttons | _____ | _____ |
|  | Edit text objects | _____ | _____ |
|  | Create button transitions | _____ | _____ |
| **Lesson 7** | Insert graphics | _____ | _____ |
|  | Insert clip art | _____ | _____ |
|  | Size graphics | _____ | _____ |
|  | Edit graphics | _____ | _____ |
|  | Change card size | _____ | _____ |
|  | Use icons | _____ | _____ |
| **Lesson 8** | Use Ready Made cards | _____ | _____ |
|  | Copy backgrounds | _____ | _____ |
|  | Share backgrounds | _____ | _____ |
|  | Extras menu | _____ | _____ |

(continued on next page)

| | SKILL | ✓ | DATE |
|---|---|---|---|
| **Lesson 8 (cont'd)** | Special effects with graphics | _____ | _____ |
| | Spell check | _____ | _____ |
| | Storyboard Extra | _____ | _____ |
| | Title card Extra | _____ | _____ |
| | Cookie-cutter effect | _____ | _____ |
| | Gradients | _____ | _____ |
| | Scale and rotate | _____ | _____ |
| | Print | _____ | _____ |
| **Lesson 9** | Hide/Show NBA | _____ | _____ |
| | Path animations | _____ | _____ |
| | Animate graphics | _____ | _____ |
| | ButtonRunner NBA | _____ | _____ |
| **Lesson 10** | Frame animations | _____ | _____ |
| | Save screen captures | _____ | _____ |
| | Shadow text | _____ | _____ |
| | Roll credits | _____ | _____ |
| **Lesson 11** | Hypertext links | _____ | _____ |
| | Time lines | _____ | _____ |
| | Box Maker | _____ | _____ |
| | Slide Show animation | _____ | _____ |
| **Lesson 12** | Insert sounds | _____ | _____ |
| | Insert narrations | _____ | _____ |
| | Insert buttons to control audio CDs | _____ | _____ |
| | Access graphics and sounds from HyperStudio CD-ROM | _____ | _____ |
| | Menu Tamer | _____ | _____ |
| **Lesson 13** | Insert QuickTime or AVI video | _____ | _____ |
| | Create buttons to control video | _____ | _____ |
| | Use different video controllers | _____ | _____ |
| **Lesson 14** | Insert QuickTime or AVI video | _____ | _____ |
| | Using different button types | _____ | _____ |
| | Play video through graphic objects | _____ | _____ |
| | Print to video | _____ | _____ |
| **Lesson 15** | Play laser disc from a stack | _____ | _____ |
| | Import QuickTime from the Internet | _____ | _____ |
| | Import QuickTime from an interactive encyclopedia | _____ | _____ |
| | Manage disk storage space | _____ | _____ |
| **Lesson 16** | Access resources from other sources | _____ | _____ |
| | Layered animations | _____ | _____ |
| | Draw multiple | _____ | _____ |

| SKILL | ✓ | DATE |
|---|---|---|
| Draw filled | _____ | _____ |
| Draw centered | | |
| Use filters as effects | _____ | _____ |

**Lesson 17**

| SKILL | ✓ | DATE |
|---|---|---|
| Work with cross-platform stacks | _____ | _____ |
| Use the Eyedropper tool | _____ | _____ |
| Use the Magnifying Glass tool | _____ | _____ |
| Bring closer/send farther | _____ | _____ |
| Marked cards | _____ | _____ |
| Linked stacks | _____ | _____ |

**Lesson 18**

| SKILL | ✓ | DATE |
|---|---|---|
| Create tests | _____ | _____ |
| User's name function | _____ | _____ |
| Correct answer function | _____ | _____ |
| Incorrect answer function | _____ | _____ |
| Read test results | _____ | _____ |
| Passwords | _____ | _____ |

**Lesson 19**

| SKILL | ✓ | DATE |
|---|---|---|
| Hide/show graphics | _____ | _____ |
| Hide/show text | _____ | _____ |
| Hide/show hypertext link | _____ | _____ |
| Create actions when arriving at a card | _____ | _____ |
| Create actions when leaving a card | _____ | _____ |
| Import images from digital cameras | _____ | _____ |
| Import images from scanners | _____ | _____ |
| Hide card number | _____ | _____ |

**Lesson 20**

| SKILL | ✓ | DATE |
|---|---|---|
| Create a stack for the Internet | _____ | _____ |
| Apply HyperStudio Internet tips | _____ | _____ |
| Use NetPage NBA for e-mail | _____ | _____ |
| Use NetPage NBA for URL | _____ | _____ |
| Use Export WebPage extra | _____ | _____ |
| Test execution of stack on a Web browser | _____ | _____ |

# GLOSSARY

## A

**Alignment (Lesson 5)** The placement of objects or text and page.

**Animations (Lesson 9)** Giving movement or action to something that would otherwise be static.

**Arrow (Edit) tool (Lesson 2)** The tool used to edit buttons, graphic objects, and text objects.

**Authoring tools (Lesson 1)** Software programs that allow users to create such things as presentations.

**AVI (Lesson 13)** A digital video format that can be used to view video on a computer.

## B

**Backgrounds (Lesson 3)** The bottom layer of HyperStudio cards.

**Barcode reader (Lesson 15)** A device used to access information on a laser disc.

**Beveler (Lesson 16)** An effect that creates a flat or inverse edge on the card.

**Bitmaps (Lesson 7)** The file format used to store graphic images supplied on the HyperStudio CD-ROM.

**Bookmark (Lesson 15)** A way of tagging an Internet site so that you can return to it in the future without searching for it or keying the address of the site.

**Borders (Lesson 3)** The areas surrounding a card or object.

**Box Maker (Lesson 11)** A HyperStudio tool on the Extra menu for creating three-dimensional boxes.

**Brightness/Contrast (Lesson 16)** An effect that allows you to control the brightness and contrast of objects.

**Bring closer (Lesson 17)** Brings the selected object up a level in the hierarchy.

**Browse (Lesson 6)** The HyperStudio mode that users must be in to get the button actions to work.

**Browser (Lesson 20)** An Internet tool that allows you to access Web sites and perform searches.

**Browse tool (Lesson 2)** A tool that puts you in Browse mode and allows you to navigate using buttons and object. Must be in this mode to enter text in a text object. Represented by the hand icon on the tool palette.

**ButtonRunner NBA (Lesson 9)** A new button action that allocates control of several buttons or actions on a card to one button.

**Buttons (Lesson 1)** Navigation tools for controlling actions on a card or in a stack.

**Button tool (Lesson 2)** An editing tool that allows you to change the appearance or action of buttons.

# C

**Cards (Lesson 1)**  The screens that make up a stack in HyperStudio.

**CAV (Lesson 15)**  A designation for laser discs defined by the way information is stored. CAV allows still frames and holds 30 minutes per side.

**CD-audio controller (Lesson 12)**  A HyperStudio palette to control an audio CD.

**CDPlay NBA (Lesson 12)**  A new button action used to attach sounds from outside sources such as audio CDs.

**Circle Selector tool (Lesson 2)**  A tool used to select oval and round objects and shapes.

**Clip art (Lesson 7)**  Objects that are added using the Add clip art item from the File menu. Clip art becomes a permanent part of the background.

**CLV (Lesson 15)**  A designation for laser discs defined by the way information is stored. CLV allows 60 minutes per side with no still frame.

**Color palette (Lesson 3)**  The colors available to be used in HyperStudio.

**Component cards (Lesson 4)**  Cards that contain additional information about a topic or subtopic.

**Copied background (Lesson 8)**  A background which is duplicated to a card or group of cards.

**Copy (Lesson 5)**  Command on Edit menu for duplicating an object button or text. Maintains all attributes.

**Copyright (Lesson 15)**  Legal ownership of a work that protects an author's rights to that work.

**CPU (Lesson 11)**  Central processing unit of a computer.

**Cross platform (Lesson 17)**  The ability to use a stack on both a Macintosh and Windows computer.

**Cut (Lesson 5)**  Command on Edit menu that removes an object or text and allows it to be pasted or placed in another place.

# D

**Data collection (Lesson 18)**  The process of accumulating the results of the testing functions.

**Default settings (Lesson 6)**  The settings that are built into a program, but can be changed.

**Delete card (Lesson 3)**  Command on Edit menu to remove a card from a stack.

**Digital camera (Lesson 19)**  Camera that captures images in a digital format.

**Digital format (Lesson 13)**  Format required to play video or audio on a computer.

**Digitize (Lesson 14)**  Process of transforming a signal so that it can be utilized by a computer.

**Digitizing board (Lesson 14)**  A special board or card in a computer that allows video to be shot, edited, and played.

**Download (Lesson 15)**  Process of transferring information from a remote location usually to a computer's hard drive.

**Draw centered (Lesson 16)**  Graphic option used to create multiple but equally centered images of the shape you are drawing.

**Draw filled (Lesson 16)**  Graphic option used to fill an object with a specified color as it is being drawn.

**Draw multiple (Lesson 16)** Graphic option used to create multiple images of the shape being drawn.

**Drawing tools (Lesson 2)** Tools used to draw shapes and objects on cards.

## E

**Edit tools (Lesson 2)** Tools used to change, move, and manipulate existing objects.

**E-mail (Lesson 20)** Mail that is sent by electronic means. To send e-mail through HyperStudio, you must have an Internet service provider.

**Emboss (Lesson 16)** Filter that creates a raised pattern on the entire card or selected object.

**Eraser tool (Lesson 2)** A tool that removes paint objects or covers an area with a color.

**Export WebPage extra (Lesson 20)** A tool that prepares a stack to go online by adding an accompanying HTML stack.

**Extension (Lesson 20)** A file naming convention that places a period and three characters at the end of the file name, as in .stk.

**Eyedropper tool (Lesson 2)** A tool used to select a color on a card to be used as a fill color.

## F

**Fair use (Lesson 15)** Part of the copyright law that allows limited use of another's work for such purposes as educational use.

**File formats (Lesson 7)** Usually identifies the application with which the file is associated or the type of file such as text or graphics.

**File name (Lesson 2)** The name given to a stack when it is saved to identify it on the disk.

**Filter (Lesson 16)** Plug-ins that allow you to manipulate graphics.

**Flow chart (Lesson 4)** A planning tool for mapping the navigation and flow of a stack.

**Font (Lesson 5)** A style of type; the set of characters of a particular style and size.

**Frame animations (Lesson 10)** A type of animation that is based on the movement from one card to another.

## G

**Gradients (Lesson 8)** Variations of hues of colors in a pattern.

**Graphic objects (Lesson 7)** Objects that float over the background and can be assigned actions.

**Graphic object tool (Lesson 2)** The tool used to edit graphic objects.

## H

**Hide/Show animations (Lesson 9)** A new button action that allows you to create a button that will make an object appear and disappear.

**Home page (Lesson 20)** The first page or primary document of a Web site; it is similar to a Title page of a stack.

**HTML code (Lesson 20)** Stands for HyperText Markup Language. Code used to prepare documents for the Internet.

**Hypermedia (Lesson 4)** Use of multimedia elements in a program.

**Hypertext (Lesson 1)** A term referring to a word or phrase that has an action attached to it.

**Hypertext links (Lesson 11)** A text animation that links a word or phrase to another location.

# I

**Icons (Lesson 1)** A picture usually with some action attached to it. Often represents a button or program.

**Import background (Lesson 3)** Adding objects as the bottom layer of a card.

**Interactive encyclopedia (Lesson 15)** An encyclopedia contained on a CD-ROM that has hypertext links and other forms of interactivity.

**Internet browser (Lesson 15)** The tool used to navigate around sites on the Internet.

**Interface (Lesson 5)** The look, design, and integrated elements of a computer program or HyperStudio stack.

**Internet (Lesson 20)** A system of communication that allows users to communicate using computers and modems.

**Internet provider (Lesson 20)** The service that provides access to the Internet for a fee.

# L

**Laser disc (Lesson 15)** A digital storage unit for graphics, text, video, sound, animations, or any combination of these elements.

**Lasso Selector tool (Lesson 2)** A HyperStudio tool used for selecting an object of an irregular shape.

**Linking stacks (Lesson 15)** The process of associating stacks through a button action in a stack that takes the user to another stack.

**Locking stacks (Lesson 18)** The process of limiting access to the stack by making most of the menus and tools unavailable.

# M

**Magnifying Glass tool (Lesson 2)** The tool used to enlarge the view of a portion of a card.

**Main Menu card (Lesson 4)** A common element of stack that serves to direct users through the stack.

**Marked cards (Lesson 17)** A method of identifying a card that can be accessed through the Last marked card button action.

**Menu Tamer (Lesson 12)** An extra tool that allows you to hide or show the menubar on a card or stack.

**Metaphor (Lesson 4)** A symbol that represents one thing being used to represent another.

**Mosaic (Lesson 14)** An effect that makes a graphic or picture look tiled. Usually caused by enlarging an object or picture.

**Multimedia (Lesson 1)** A combination of elements often on a computer that includes a combination of elements, such as audio, text, graphics, photos, video, or animation.

# N

**Narration (Lesson 12)**   A voice commentary that can be included in a stack.

**Navigation (Lesson 2)**   The means of moving around and through a computer program, HyperStudio stack, or the Internet.

**New Button Actions (NBAs) (Lesson 9)** A series of button actions that allow the author to create sophisticated actions for buttons, graphic objects, or text objects.

**NetPage NBA (Lesson 20)**   A new button action that allows you to send and receive e-mail or connect to a URL.

**New card (Lesson 3)**   A command on the Edit menu that places a new card in the stack immediately after the current card.

**Nonlinear buttons (Lesson 6)**   Any button that does not take you to the next card in the stack.

# O

**Object-oriented programming (Lesson 1)**   Programming using icons, graphics, and simple text commands rather than cryptic programming languages.

**Organizational chart (Lesson 4)** A planning tool for mapping navigation for a stack.

**Oval tool (Lesson 2)**   A tool used to draw ovals and circles.

# P

**Paintbrush tool (Lesson 2)**   A tool for drawing colors and shapes on a card.

**Paint Bucket tool (Lesson 2)**   A tool used to fill an area or the entire card with a selected color.

**Passwords (Lesson 18)**   A combination of characters that may be used to protect stacks from unwanted changes by users.

**Paste (Lesson 5)**   Command on the Edit menu that places the contents of the clipboard that have been cut or copied into a new location.

**Path animations (Lesson 9)**   The movement of an object across the screen in an automated action.

**Patterns (Lesson 3)**   Section of the color palette that has various fill patterns.

**Pencil tool (Lesson 2)**   A tool that allows the user to draw on the card similar to writing with a pencil.

**Perspective (Lesson 19)**   A way to create a sense of depth or dimension.

**Pixel (Lesson 7)**   The smallest unit of measurement on a computer monitor. The size on the card is defined in pixels.

**Plug-in (Lesson 16)**   Add-ons to a program that allow additional functions to be performed.

**Pop-up effect (Lesson 19)**   An effect in which a graphic or text object appears to pop-up when a button or hypertext link is selected.

**Preanimated images (Lesson 9)** A group of HyperStudio objects that have built in animation and can be used to create path animations.

**Preferences (Lesson 7)**   Options that the user can select to customize the way HyperStudio functions.

**Printing (Lesson 3)**   Having the cards in a stack print on a laser or inkjet printer. Either 1, 2, or 4 cards can be printed on a page.

**Protocol (Lesson 6)**  A set of conventions or rules governing how things are done.

# Q

**Quick Time (Lesson 13)**  A digital video format that can be used to view video on a computer.

**Quick Time movie (Lesson 5)**  A digital format for video that allows video to be played in stacks.

**QuickTime Virtual Reality (QTVR) (Lesson 15)**  A software program that allows you to create QuickTime video in three-dimensional perspective.

# R

**Ready Made cards (Lesson 8)**  A group of background templates provided by HyperStudio.

**Rectangle tool (Lesson 2)**  A tool used to draw rectangles and squares.

**RollCredits NBA (Lesson 10)**  A new button action that creates a scrolling text field.

**Rotate (Lesson 8)**  Changing the angle of a picture.

**Rounded Rectangle tool (Lesson 2)**  A tool used to create rounded rectangles and squares.

# S

**Save (Lesson 2)**  The File command used to save an existing file with the same name.

**Save as (Lesson 2)**  The File command used to save and name a new file or save an existing file with the same name.

**Scale (Lesson 8)**  Found on the Edit menu and used to proportionally change the size of a picture.

**Scanner (Lesson 19)**  A piece of equipment that digitizes a picture or text for use in a computer.

**Screen captures (Lesson 10)**  Pictures of the contents of the screen that may be used to create slide show animations.

**Scroll lines (Lesson 10)**  An option to make scrolling text fields scroll one line at a time.

**Search engine (Lesson 15)**  An Internet database used to locate Web sites and information.

**Selector tools (Lesson 2)**  Three tools from the tool palette that allow the user to designate a specific area.

**Send farther (Lesson 17)**  Moves selected object down one level in the hierarchy.

**Shared background (Lesson 8)**  When a card actually uses the same background as another card.

**Shadowed text (Lesson 10)**  A special effect for text that makes it appear three-dimensional.

**Slide show animation (Lesson 11)**  An effect that automates the movement of a series of cards to make them appear to be a slide show.

**Sound bite (Lesson 12)**  A sound file.

**Sound files (Lesson 7)**  Files that contain digital sounds.

**Spray Can tool (Lesson 2)** A paint tool that has the effect of spraying a color or pattern over an area.

**Square Selector tool (Lesson 2)** A tool used to select square and rectangular objects and shapes.

**Stacks (Lesson 1)** The name given to a card or series of cards that are saved together as a project or file in HyperStudio.

**Stationary graphics (Lesson 9)** Objects that have no animation and are saved in HyperStudio as .bmp files.

**Still frames (Lesson 15)** An individual image on a laser disc, similar to a slide.

**Storyboard (Lesson 4)** An organizing and planning tool for a stack or video production.

**Subtopic cards (Lesson 4)** The informational cards that are connected to a topic card.

### T

**Templates (Lesson 8)** A master plate or pattern that is used for duplication.

**Testing function (Lesson 18)** Button action that allows you to create and score tests and surveys.

**Testing results function (Lesson 18)** A text file that shows the results of the testing function.

**Text fields (Lesson 6)** An object used to insert text on a card. The text in the object can be changed and edited like a word processing document.

**Text Object tool (Lesson 2)** A tool used to edit text fields.

**Text tool (Lesson 2)** A tool used to paint text on a card. Text created with this tool cannot be changed once Enter is pressed.

**Texturize (Lesson 16)** A filter effect that creates various textures on cards or parts of cards.

**Time line (Lesson 11)** A progression of events displayed graphically. The events are often measured by time.

**Title card (Lesson 4)** The first card in a stack that introduces the stack.

**Tool palette (Lesson 2)** The array of tools used to edit, draw, and paint on cards.

**Transitions (Lesson 6)** An effect that accompanies the movement from card to card and some actions.

### U

**Uniform Resource Locator (URL) (Lesson 15)** A location or address of a site on the Internet.

**User-friendly (Lesson 5)** Easily understood and accessible.

**User's name function (Lesson 18)** One of the testing functions that prompts users to enter their names.

### V

**Video clips (Lesson 13)** Short sections of video footage.

**Video storyboards (Lesson 14)** A software application that is used for letters, memos, and other text-based messages.

## W

**Web site (Lesson 20)**   A location or URL on the World Wide Web.

**Word processing (Lesson 5)**   A software application used to enter and format text.

**World Wide Web (Lesson 20)**   A part of the Internet; accessed through a Web browser.

# INDEX

## KEYBOARD SHORTCUTS—MACINTOSH

To use shortcuts press and hold the  key while striking the other key.

| KEY | EFFECT | KEY | EFFECT |
|---|---|---|---|
|  + A | Add clip art |  + V | Paste |
|  + B | Add a button |  + X | Cut |
|  + C | Copy |  + Y | Text style |
|  + E | Export screen |  + Z | Undo |
|  + F | Find text |  + 1 | First card |
|  + Shift + F | Find next occurrence |  + 9 | Last card |
|  + G | Add a graphic |  + - | Back |
|  + H | Home |  + > | Next card |
|  + I | Import background |  + < | Previous card |
|  + J | Jump to card |  + ; | Preferences |
|  + K | Standard colors |  + F4 | Quit HyperStudio |
|  + L | Hypertext link |  + + | Bring object forward 1 level |
|  + M | Hide/show menubar | Ctrl + - | Send object back 1 level |
|  + N | New card | Shift +  + + | Bring to front |
|  + O | Open stack | Shift +  + - | Send to back |
|  + P | Print | Clear | Deletes selection |
|  + Q | Quit | Shift + Tab | Browse mode |
|  + R | Record | Shift + Ctrl + Tab | Selector tool |
|  + S | Save | Option + Drag | Copy selection |
|  + T | Add text object | Option +  | View buttons |

*Using HyperStudio®: A Complete Tutorial for Windows® and Macintosh®* by Ana Weston Solomon
Quick Reference ©2000 by South-Western Educational Publishing

## KEYBOARD SHORTCUTS—WINDOWS

To use shortcuts, press and hold the Ctrl key while striking the other key.

| KEY | EFFECT | KEY | EFFECT |
| --- | --- | --- | --- |
| Ctrl + A | Add clip art | Ctrl + T | Add text object |
| Ctrl + B | Add a button | Ctrl + V | Paste |
| Ctrl + C | Copy | Ctrl + X | Cut |
| Ctrl + E | Export screen | Ctrl + Y | Text style |
| Ctrl + F | Find text | Ctrl + Z | Undo |
| Ctrl + Shift + F | Find next occurrence | Ctrl + 1 | First card |
| Ctrl + G | Add a graphic | Ctrl + 9 | Last card |
| Ctrl + H | Home | Ctrl + − | Back |
| Ctrl + I | Import background | Ctrl + > | Next card |
| Ctrl + J | Jump to card | Ctrl + < | Previous card |
| Ctrl + K | Standard colors | Ctrl + ; | Preferences |
| Ctrl + L | Hypertext link | Alt+F4 | Quit HyperStudio |
| Ctrl + M | Hide/show menubar | Ctrl + + | Bring object forward |
| Ctrl + N | New card | Ctrl + - | Send object back |
| Ctrl + O | Open stack | Shift+Ctrl + + | Bring to front |
| Ctrl + P | Print | Shift+Ctrl + - | Send to back |
| Ctrl + R | Record | Shift+Tab | Browse mode |
| Ctrl + S | Save | Shift+Ctrl | View buttons |

*Using HyperStudio®: A Complete Tutorial for Windows® and Macintosh®* by Ana Weston Solomon
Quick Reference ©2000 by South-Western Educational Publishing